PSYCHOLOGISM

For most of this century, Western philosophy has been resolutely antinaturalist, and until recently the sharp distinction between the empirical sciences and philosophy seemed almost self-evident: the questions of why they should be separate, and of how they came to be separate, were never asked. These questions are at the heart of Martin Kusch's groundbreaking study.

Antinaturalism rose to dominance in the debate on psychologism among German academic philosophers at the turn of the century. Psychologism, according to received opinion, was decisively refuted by Frege and Husserl. Kusch therefore examines their arguments and, crucially, relates them to the context that shaped that debate and gave those arguments their persuasive force. Drawing on perspectives pioneered by the sociology of scientific knowledge, he reconstructs the dynamics of the psychologism debate; he uncovers its causes and weighs the factors that determined its outcome. What emerges is the fascinating picture of a struggle, between 'pure' philosophy and the newly emerging experimental psychology, for academic status, social influence and institutional power. The triumph of antinaturalism, far from being the only logical conclusion, was dependent on historical contingency.

Introducing forms of analysis new to the history of philosophy, *Psychologism* will make fascinating reading for lecturers and students of philosophy, psychology, sociology and cognitive science; it will also stimulate renewed debate on the prospects of antinaturalism at the close of this century.

Martin Kusch is Lecturer at the Science Studies Unit of the University of Edinburgh. He is the author of *Language as Calculus vs. Language as Universal Medium* (1989), and *Foucault's Strata and Fields* (1991).

PHILOSOPHICAL ISSUES IN SCIENCE
Edited by W.H. Newton-Smith
Balliol College, Oxford

THE RATIONAL AND THE SOCIAL
James Robert Brown

THE NATURE OF DISEASE
Lawrie Reznek

THE PHILOSOPHICAL DEFENCE OF PSYCHIATRY
Lawrie Reznek

*INFERENCE TO THE BEST EXPLANATION
Peter Lipton

*TIME, SPACE AND PHILOSOPHY
Christopher Ray

MATHEMATICS AND THE IMAGE OF REASON
Mary Tiles

METAPHYSICS OF CONSCIOUSNESS
William Seager

*THE LABORATORY OF THE MIND
James Robert Brown

*COLOUR VISION
Evan Thompson

* Also available in paperback

PSYCHOLOGISM

A case study in the sociology of philosophical knowledge

Martin Kusch

London and New York

First published 1995
by Routledge
11 New Fetter Lane, London EC4P 4EE

Simultaneously published in the USA and Canada
by Routledge
29 West 35th Street, New York, NY 10001

Typeset in Baskerville by
Ponting–Green Publishing Services, Chesham, Bucks
Printed and bound in Great Britain by
TJ Press (Padstow) Ltd, Padstow, Cornwall

British Library Cataloguing in Publication Data
A catalogue record for this book is available from
the British Library.

Library of Congress Cataloging in Publication Data
Kusch, Martin.
Psychologism: a case study in the sociology of
philosophical knowledge/Martin Kusch.
p.   cm. – (Philosophical issues in science)
Includes bibliographical references and index.
1. Psychologism.   2. Phenomenological psychology.
3. Frege, Gottlob, 1848–1925.   4. Husserl, Edmund,
1859–1938.   I. Title.   II. Series.
BF41.K87   1994
190'.9'034–dc20   94–43123
CIP

ISBN 0–415–12554–5 (hbk)
ISBN 0–415–12555–3 (pbk)

Philosophy will clip an Angel's wings.
(John Keats)

CONTENTS

Foreword *by David Bloor*   xi
Acknowledgements   xv
Note on appendices   xviii

1 PSYCHOLOGISM: AN INTRODUCTION   1
    Introduction   1
    'The same old story'   2
    Psychologism: Definitions and accusations   4
    The curse of Frege's and Husserl's antipsychologism   6
    Phenomenology and the schism in twentieth-century
       philosophy   12
    Psychologism and sociologism   14

2 TOWARDS A SOCIOLOGY OF PHILOSOPHICAL
    KNOWLEDGE   17
    Introduction   17
    Philosophical versus nonphilosophical histories of
       philosophy   17
    The sociology of philosophical knowledge   23

3 PSYCHOLOGISM REFUTED?   30
    Introduction   30
    Frege's criticism of psychological logic   30
       Frege's arguments in the Grundlagen *(1884)*   30
       Frege's arguments in the Grundgesetze *(1893)*   33
       Frege's review of Husserl's Philosophie der Arithmetik
          (1894)   38
    Husserl's criticism of psychologism in the *Prolegomena* of
       the *Logische Untersuchungen* (1900)   41
       Part I: Logic as practical-normative discipline
          *(*Kunstlehre*)*   41

Part II: The refutation of psychologism   43
Part III: An outline of pure logic   58
Frege's and Husserl's criticisms compared   60

4 THE CRITICISM OF HUSSERL'S ARGUMENTS
  AGAINST PSYCHOLOGISM IN GERMAN
  PHILOSOPHY, 1901–20   63
Introduction   63
Objections to Husserl's main theses   63
  Normative antipsychologism, and logic as a normative
    discipline (H2 and H3)   64
  The distinction between real and ideal laws (H4)   67
  The psychological interpretation of logical principles (H5)   73
  Fallacies as counterexamples to psychological interpretations
    of logical laws (H7)   74
  Scepticism, relativism and anthropologism (H8.1
    and H8.2)   75
  The independence theory of truth (H8.3 and H9.2)   77
  Self-evidence (H8.3 and H9.3)   82
  Thought economics (H10)   87
Further accusations and comments   88
Criticisms and accusations: A summary   92

5 VARIETIES OF 'PSYCHOLOGISM' 1866–1930   95
Introduction   95
Accused and accusers   96
The temporal limits of the debate   98
'Psychologism' before Husserl   101
'Psychologism' after Husserl   107

6 ROLE HYBRIDISATION: THE RISE OF THE NEW
  PSYCHOLOGY   122
Introduction   122
The rise of the new psychology in numerical terms   123
Key figures of the new psychology   127
  Wundt   128
  Brentano   137
  Stumpf   141
  Ebbinghaus   143
  Müller   144
  Külpe   146
  A science of one's own?   148
An obligatory crossing point   150

CONTENTS

7 ROLE PURIFICATION: THE REACTION OF 'PURE
   PHILOSOPHY' AGAINST THE NEW PSYCHOLOGY   160
   Introduction   160
   The cleansing strategies of pure philosophy   161
   Dilthey: Descriptive versus explanatory psychology   162
   The neo-Kantians   169
   Husserl's phenomenology   178
   Pure philosophy and the new psychology   188
   Power politics?   190
   The petition and its background   190
   Wundt's intervention   193
   Marbe's headcount   197
   The Lamprecht–Simmel controversy   200
   Experimental psychology and psychologism   202
   Why Husserl – and not Frege?   203

8 WINNER TAKES ALL: *LEBENSPHILOSOPHIE* AND
   THE TRIUMPH OF PHENOMENOLOGY   211
   Introduction   211
   War and peace   212
   'The genius of war': Pure philosophy goes to war   213
   *'Between the clergyman and the medical doctor': Psychology
      goes to war*   219
   The triumph of phenomenology: Philosophy and
      psychology in the Weimar Republic   224
   The Weimar mentality   225
   From Lebensphilosophie *to phenomenology*   227
   How psychology ceased to be a threat   259

   Summary and conclusions   272
   Notes   279
   Bibliography   289
   Index   317

FOREWORD

How do things stand today between the department of philosophy and the department of psychology? I mean: how do we think of their relative positions on the map of knowledge? Naturally, opinions will vary, and developments in cognitive science have disrupted some of the old certainties, but until recently the answer would have seemed clear to many philosophers – and to some minds the old certainties remain. Philosophy, it would be said, deals with knowledge, with what makes something into knowledge rather than mere belief. Psychology, by contrast, deals with the processes and conditions of coming to know. These are quite different and disjoint concerns. Psychology deals with causes, philosophy with reasons. Philosophy concerns truth; psychology cannot rise above belief and taking-for-true. Well rehearsed lines of this sort tripped off the tongues of bright philosophy students. They would quickly pick up the manner and tone of their tutors in expressing these truths. I don't think it unfair to say that philosophers have culti-vated a certain complacency in this regard and, perhaps unwitting-ly, conveyed to their students a disdain for those who believed they could illuminate knowledge by studying rats in mazes, or learning curves for lists of nonsense syllables or the documentation of a child's growing skills. If the aim was conceptual analysis, only a minimum of factual knowledge of this kind was needed. During the heyday of Oxford ordinary-language philosophy, students would occasionally expose their naivety by asking why the likes of Austin or Ryle didn't study the use of language *empirically*, rather than from the armchair. Such enquiries were not welcome, though I doubt if they ever received a fully satisfactory answer.

The picture was never a simple one and has become progressively more complicated. Philosophers of science always took pride in knowing their science, but they still had to conjure up a boundary of a similar sort to fend off the accusation, and perhaps even the inner fear, that they were just playing at being scientists. Some philosophers have always been interested in psychology, though it has been rare for them to construct their philosophy on, rather than apply it to, psychology. Those few who have adopted this bold scientistic and psychologistic line are probably the ones most conscious of the attitude of mind I have been describing. They will feel it most keenly, because they will provoke it most intensely.

What sustains the sniffiness about goings-on in the psychology department? If the argument of Dr Kusch's fascinating and scholarly book is taken seriously, as it should be, we can begin to see this phenomenon in a new light. We shall not take the arguments and distinctions between reasons and causes, or between knowledge and belief, wholly at their face value. Instead we shall ask: why do we draw these distinctions in precisely the way we do? Are they really so self-evident? Could the wide measure of consensus about the application of these concepts perhaps itself constitute a problem needing explanation? Dr Kusch's book will sensitise us to the role played in all this by institutional arrangements and by the simple fact that decisions at the institutional level have led to the creation of departments with the labels 'philosophy' and 'psychology' respectively. Rather than assuming that these institutional arrangements reflect an underlying conceptual geography, we will appreciate the forces working in the opposite direction, leading us to mould our concepts on the pattern of our institutional structures. Dr Kusch is not, however, offering direct comment on the present state of affairs, but taking us back to the time and place in which those institutional patterns, or the influential models for them, were themselves being created. He is looking at the emergence of experimental psychology within German departments of philosophy, and the processes attending its birth as a separate discipline. There is no compelling reason why that process had to have the outcome it did. There is nothing uniquely rational or logical about it. A simple thought experiment will serve to make the point. Couldn't we imagine the present occupants of what are called 'philosophy departments' distributed among departments of history, economics, law, psychology, sociology and, perhaps in a few cases, physics, mathematics and biology? Is it obvious that this would be a net loss rather than a net gain? Why should there be a department that gathers together activities and material that really consist of one phase of many different lines of enquiry? After all, even some philosophers have advocated versions of this scenario, with their talk of the underlabourer conception, or the gradual replacement of philosophical by scientific questions. All of this is ground that we can see traversed in the story told by Dr Kusch.

If philosophy had an 'essence', one plausible candidate would be 'self-awareness'. It is one of the many oddities of the academic scene that the 'discipline' that might be expected to cultivate a maximum of self-awareness in fact shows so little of this commodity. I don't mean that thoughts about the precarious character of the autonomy of philosophy never enter the heads of individual philosophers – that charge would certainly be untrue. I mean that so little serious academic work is devoted to cultivating a genuine historical aware-ness of the conditions of philosophical enquiry. While the history of the natural and biological sciences has reached an impressive pitch of subtlety and sophistication, until recently the history of philosophy has lagged behind. There are welcome signs of a growing concern with this problem, but it is still true that the history of philosophy has nothing to match the collective and sustained achievements in the history of science. In general, its historio-graphical assumptions are those of the history of science thirty years ago. Dr Kusch is one of a number of scholars taking steps towards altering this situation by modelling his analysis on the approach adopted implicitly and explicitly by many historians of science, particularly sociological historians of science. We have here a marvellously detailed account of how the status of the new activity of experimental psychology was negotiated by the interested parties – a negotiation shot through with competing interests and opposing strategies.

As Dr Kusch rightly emphasises, his sociological analysis does not neglect the *arguments* used by the participants. Quite the contrary: analysis of the arguments is integral to the whole enterprise. The very point at issue for him, as a sociologist of philosophical knowledge, is why the plethora of different arguments emerged in the way it did, assumed the pattern it did and resolved itself in the way it did. He wants to know what gave these arguments their differential rational force, what, for instance, determined the range of factors taken into consideration, the comparisons that were felt to be apt and the consequences that were taken to follow. Thus we hear of the great cultural mission of philosophy contrasted with the more technical interest of experimental results, but also of the intellectual discipline of psychological analysis contrasted with the endless debate and pretentious claims of the multitude of philosophical schools. Dr Kusch carries the story from the turn of the century through the First World War into the turbulence of the Weimar period with its antiscientific, irrationalist *Lebensphilosophie*. Readers who follow the argument will find themselves drawn into a fascinating sequence of connected episodes. We are dealing throughout with a culture where philosophical argumentation was perhaps more serious, more passionate, more intense and scholarly, and reaching a more educated public, than at any other place or time before or since. What are today little more than petty snobberies were in those days full-blooded confrontations over the nature of *Bildung*, full of resonances for citizenship and the nature of social democracy itself. The participants in those controversies were forging the parameters of today's taken-for-granted academic world – and more besides.

David Bloor

ACKNOWLEDGEMENTS

A number of friends, colleagues, students and institutions have seen me through this project. I began working on the research reported here in the spring of 1991 when enjoying the hospitality of the Husserl Archives of the Catholic University in Leuven (Belgium). My stay in Leuven was funded by the Academy of Finland.

I first tested the basic ideas of this book on three 'old' Finnish friends: on Riitta Korhonen in a shabby pub in Leuven, on Jouko Aho in a traffic jam in Holland, and on Heini-Eliisa Hakosalo in an expensive long-distance phone call to Finland. After I had passed these three hurdles, I knew that I was on the right track. These three friends have helped me in many other ways also during later stages of writing this book.

I taught the academic year 1991–2 at the University of Toronto. I am deeply grateful to Calvin Normore for arranging this visit. I collected most of the source material at the wonderful Robarts Library. The staff of the interlibrary loan office, Shamim Allani, Jane Clark, Jane Lynch and Barbara McDowell, provided a level of service and support that I shall never forget. I struck gold in Toronto also as far as my colleagues and students were concerned. I wish to thank especially Bryan Boddy, Jim Brown, Jackie Brunning, Jack Canfield, York Gunther, Ian Hacking, Dominick Jenkins, Bernie Katz, Dennis Klimchuk, Calvin Normore, Arthur Ripstein, Don Robinson and Niko Scharer for discussions, criticism and encouragement. Two further Canadian philosophers, Edwin Mares and Stuart Shanker, have been important email correspondents at early stages of my project.

During the autumn of 1992 I was back in Finland, in the history department of the University of Oulu. While my salary was again kindly provided by the Academy of Finland, the history department absorbed my horrendous photocopying and interlibrary loan bills. The support of Juha Manninen and Erkki Urpilainen was unfailing all through these months. I am also grateful to Eila Kortet and Leena Moisala for photocopying assistance, and to Paula Viander for library help. As far as discussions of my project were concerned, I profited most from encounters with Jouko Aho and Jarmo Pulkkinen. Ian Morris-Wilson helped with the grammar of the early chapters. Alla Räisänen, Henri Urpilainen, Jouko Jokisalo and Maija Kallinen provided moral support.

Since the beginning of 1993 I have worked in the Science Studies Unit of the University of Edinburgh. My interest in the sociology of knowledge grew out of my earlier work on Foucault. I would never have joined the sociologists, however, had it not been for Harry Collins's influence. Collins and I have been working together on another book since 1991, and his help and advice have been important many times. Here in Edinburgh I wish to thank especially Celia and David Bloor, Carole Tansley, Claude Charpentier, Mike Barfoot, John Henry and John Holmwood. David Bloor has commented on parts of the manuscript, has supported me in every possible way, and has contributed a foreword. Celia Bloor and Carole Tansley have corrected the grammar and style of my text; Celia Bloor has also made many brutal comments on the structure of my overall argument, while Carole Tansley has done miracles to my knowledge of poetry, operas, movies, Shakey, and Scottish single malts. Claude Charpentier, Mike Barfoot, John Henry and John Holmwood too have made useful suggestions.

I also wish to thank my friends in Leverkusen (Germany), Auckland and Helsinki. My mother, Erna Kusch, has kept me updated on new philosophical and historical titles published in German, and she has been important in many other ways as well. While I taught at the University of Auckland during the summer of 1993, Peter Kraus, Robert Nola, Martin Tweedale and Julian Young discussed the sociology of knowledge with me for long hours, and they also provided delicious food and unforgettable hospitality. In Helsinki, I am indebted to Eija Törmänen for company, room and board, to Ilkka Niiniluoto for converting me to relativism, to Simo and Kyösti Knuuttila for many discussions on scholastic philosophy late into the night, followed by bed and breakfast, and to Marja-Liisa Kakkuri-Knuuttila, Riitta Korhonen and Tuija Pulkkinen for intellectual stimulation and true friendship over these years.

ACKNOWLEDGEMENTS

Finally, thanks are due to Michael Leiser for his excellent copy-editing, and to Bill Newton-Smith and Adrian Driscoll for risking the publication of a book that many philosophers will reject, thinking '*relativistica sunt, non leguntur!*', and most sociologists ignore, believing '*philosophica sunt, non leguntur!*'.

* * *

I dedicate this book to Jaakko Hintikka. Although his influence on the present book is small, I feel that I have learnt more from him than from any other living philosopher. Hintikka has also been a never failing source of encouragement.

* * *

I would like to think of the present book as the first volume of a trilogy on German-language philosophy of the late nineteenth and early twentieth centuries. The second volume would deal with pessimism and the third with the tradition of dialogical thinking. Just as this first volume blurs borders between philosophy and sociology, the second would do so for the divide between philosophy and art, and the third for the division between philosophy and theology.

NOTE ON APPENDICES

Four appendices to this book are available on the Internet:

Appendix 1: Four earlier approaches to the sociology of philosophy

Appendix 2: Some modern evaluations of Frege's and Husserl's arguments

Appendix 3: The doctrinal background to the new psychology

Appendix 4: Further polemical exchanges over the petition of 1913

These appendices can be accessed directly through the World Wide Web at:

http://www.routledge.com/rcenters/philres/psy_main.html

or via Gopher at gopher.thomson.com. The appendices are in the Routledge Philosophy Resources gopher directory, which can be found by following either *Publishers (Routledge)* or *Resource Centers (Philosophy)* in the main directory.

1

PSYCHOLOGISM: AN INTRODUCTION

INTRODUCTION

For most of this century, Western philosophy has been hostile to the idea that central epistemological, logical or metaphysical questions could be answered by the natural or social sciences. Even the most diverse philosophical schools can be found to agree at least on this issue. Ordinary-language philosophers, logicians, phenomenologists and deconstructionists may well be worlds apart when judged by their various methods, concepts and aspirations, but they all share the belief that naturalism is an unacceptable position.

Perhaps we owe it to the fact that some directions in philosophy (cognitive science, evolutionary epistemology, neurophilosophy) have recently opted out of the long-standing consensus on the irrelevance of science for philosophy that we are now beginning to realise that antinaturalism is not forced upon the philosopher by the order of things or the dictate of reason. As the century draws to a close, naturalism seems again the viable option it was one hundred years ago, and thus it does not seem too pretentious to suggest that our century will perhaps one day be called 'the century of the rise and fall of antinaturalism'. Although the time is not yet ripe for writing the history of the decline of antinaturalism, the moment where it is well worth studying its triumphant rise from the 1880s onwards has certainly arrived.

In this book I shall present a sociological reconstruction of one key aspect of this history. This central episode is the debate over psychologism in late nineteenth- and early twentieth-century German academic philosophy. It was in this controversy – stretching from the 1880s to the 1920s – that many antinaturalistic arguments and sentiments were first systematically developed.

I shall study the psychologism dispute from perspectives suggested by the sociology of scientific knowledge. I am interested in understanding the dynamics of philosophical controversies and the causes of their emergence and termination. No one who is insensitive to the sociological variables of philosophical knowledge has any chance of coming to grips with these fascinating issues. In Chapter 2 I shall explain why this is so. But before that I need to say more on why the psychologism debate is a central episode in the more recent history of philosophy.

'THE SAME OLD STORY'

The most natural starting point for justifying a book-length study of the German controversy over psychologism is a reminder of the standard narrative of the key events in German philosophy between Hegel's death and the turn of the century.[1]

After Hegel's death in 1831, idealistic philosophy in Germany quickly fell into disrepute, and philosophy lost its dominant position in the intellectual field to the natural sciences. Philosophy had to adjust to the changed conditions by remodelling itself. This meant that many philosophers adopted a 'naturalistic' or 'positivistic' attitude, i.e. the viewpoint that the ideal of knowledge and the justification of the empirical sciences holds for philosophy as well. (Others, from Feuerbach to Marx and Engels, went further, and developed materialistic philosophies.) This naturalistic stance implied that philosophers sought to solve philosophical problems, e.g. epistemological, logical and ethical questions, by means of empirical research. Kant's transcendental philosophy was reinterpreted along the way: the study of the Kantian a priori sources of human cognition was now taken to be an enquiry into what is psychologically or physiologically prior to whatever humans obtain as material knowledge, and thus a topic for the physiologists (like von Helmholtz) or the psychologists (like Wundt). This philosophical naturalism reached its peak in the attempt to treat logic in a psychological way. The way for such a treatment was paved by British empiricism (Locke, Hume and Mill). Mill wrote of logic that it is

> not a Science distinct from, and co-ordinate with Psychology. So far as it is a science at all, it is a part, or branch, of Psychology; differing from it, on the one hand as the part

differs from the whole, and on the other, as an Art differs from a Science. Its theoretical grounds are wholly borrowed from Psychology, and include as much of that science as is required to justify its rules of art.

(Mill 1979: 359)

German logicians, like Erdmann, Lipps and Sigwart, followed Mill's lead. For them logic was but 'the physics of thought' (Lipps 1880: 530),[2] and they conceived of logical laws as empirical generalisations of the way humans reason. What is more, Mill and his followers gave a psychological interpretation of mathematics as well. Numbers were ideas or presentations of sorts (*Vorstellungen*), and the existence of ideal, abstract Platonic entities was denied.

But all this was a 'confusion' (Brockhaus 1991: 495), a 'colossal blunder' (McCarthy 1990: 34). Fortunately, along came Husserl and Frege who eventually straightened things out. Thus the era of naturalism in philosophy ended around 1900 when Husserl launched his attack on this naturalism in philosophy. Husserl showed that 'psychologism' (i.e. the attempt to make psychology the foundation of philosophy and the sciences) is a self-refuting doctrine. Husserl himself had been turned against naturalism by the criticism that Frege had levelled against his earlier 'psychologistic' views; and therefore Frege's refutation of 'psychologism' is entitled to historical priority. While Frege was initially ignored by his fellow 'Continental' mathematicians and logicians, his critique of psychologism was later taken up by Russell, Moore, Wittgenstein and the whole line of analytical philosophers from Carnap and Popper right up to Sellars. These thinkers exorcised psychologism from an increasing number of subdomains of philosophy, and thus finalised philosophy's escape from the traps of psychology.

Whatever the superficialities and distortions of this narrative, it should be clear enough that 'The same old story' supports the claim that a study of the controversy over psychologism should be required reading for any student of modern philosophy. After all, if the story is true, then the refutation of psychologism is not only 'one major breaking-point in the history of philosophy' (Brockhaus 1991: 506) and the defining event of all of twentieth-century philosophy (McCarthy 1990), but also 'a salutary tale for those who believe that there is no progress in philosophy': 'Nowadays only a few cranks officially subscribe to that view . . . There is progress in philosophy after all!' (Musgrave 1972: 593, 606).

PSYCHOLOGISM: DEFINITIONS
AND ACCUSATIONS

Most philosophers accept 'The same old story' as presenting the true account of our recent philosophical past. In other words, they hold that psychologism has been decisively refuted by Frege and Husserl. Given this widespread view, it comes as something of a surprise – at least to the 'stranger' to philosophy – that for many philosophers the cancer of psychologism is still alive, and that there is not even agreement on its symptoms or its nature. Indeed, several authors have complained that psychologism is 'a far from clear notion' (Skorupski 1989: 164), 'an exceedingly hazy doctrine' (Scarre 1989: 111), 'systematically obscure' (Notturno 1985: 9), or 'more an epithet than a philosophical position' (Richards 1980: 19). They suggest that it is often far from clear just what the accusation of psychologism amounts to, or that it seems almost impossible to avoid the charge: 'although you believe you have taken every precaution, your worst enemy inevitably points it out' (Richards 1980: 19). One writer has even gone so far as to submit that a study of this strange phenomenon 'would provide an interesting chapter in the sociology of philosophy' (Notturno 1985: 10)!

Although I cannot here write a history of the definitions of psychologism, nor a history of the accusations of psychologism from Frege's and Husserl's days to the present, it is perhaps worth our while briefly to vindicate these disillusioned comments by listing a number of definitions of psychologism from the last fifty years, and by providing a table of accusers and accused:

> Reason, wherever it happens to be realised, is purely and simply reason. To deny this is to commit psychologism.
>
> (Wild 1940: 20–1)

> To be guilty of [psychologism] is to suppose that the term 'means' in such sentences as '"A" means B' stands for a psychological fact involving the symbol 'A' and the item B, whether the psychological fact be analysed in terms of *Schau*, acquaintance or just plain experience.
>
> (Sellars 1949: 430)

> The [logical] relations are objective, not subjective, in this sense: whether one of these relations does or does not hold in a concrete case is not dependent upon whether or what any person may happen to imagine, think, believe, or know

4

about these sentences . . . A discrepancy of this kind, where the problems themselves are of an objective nature but the descriptions by which the author intends to give a general characterisation of the problems are framed in subjectivist, psychological terms (like 'thinking'), is often called psychologism.

(Carnap 1950: 39–40)

[Psychologism is] the doctrine that the empirical sciences are reducible to sense-perceptions.

(Popper 1968: 93)

While psychology may be defined as the theory of mind, psychologism is the theory of a 'healthy', 'normal', 'clear', 'ideal', 'empty', 'purged', 'unbiased', 'objective', 'rational', or 'scientific' mind.

(Lakatos 1978: 208)

[Psychologism is] the thesis that an account of the meaning of words must be given in terms of the mental processes which they arouse in speaker or hearer or which are involved in acquiring a grasp of their sense (or the stronger thesis that these mental processes are what we are referring to when we use the words).

(Dummett 1978: 88)

Let psychologism be the doctrine that whether behaviour is intelligent behaviour depends on the character of the internal information processing that produces it.

(Block 1981: 5)

[Psychologism is] the attempt to analyse characteristically social phenomena in psychological terms.

(Bloor 1983: 6)

Psychologism is the doctrine that psychology provides at least part of the explanatory basis for the constitutive understanding of the mental.

(Cussins 1987: 126–7)

Epistemological Psychologism: The best way for the knowledge process to produce Truth requires that all producers share the same attitude toward the process, namely, they should all intend to produce Truth.

(Fuller 1988: 23)

5

My purpose in listing these definitions is not to evaluate them or to improve upon them. Rather, this list of definitions – which could easily be continued for some time – is meant to convince the reader that there is indeed no consensus among philosophers as to what psychologism amounts to. We must also note the obvious point that the wide variety of characteristics suggested, as well as their vagueness, makes it an easy feat to identify psychologism or psychologistic tendencies in each and every philosophical system. Indeed, almost all major philosophers have at some point or other been accused of psychologism, often after having laid the very same charge at others; Dummett, McDowell, Popper and Sellars are cases in point.[3] However, to write the history of these charges and countercharges for more recent times is not my purpose here. Nevertheless, in order to document the claim that almost all major modern philosophers have been charged with psychologism, at least a table of the main heretics and inquisitors is called for (Figure 1).

It hardly needs a separate argument to make plausible the idea that the strange phenomenon of a whole philosophical community being on the constant lookout for psychologistic tendencies is worthy of some closer sociological attention. The phenomenon at least calls for a closer look at 'The same old story'.

THE CURSE OF FREGE'S AND HUSSERL'S ANTIPSYCHOLOGISM

Unfortunately, things are even more complicated than I have just suggested. 'The same old story' is no longer the only account of the impact of Frege's and Husserl's antipsychologism. During the 1980s a rival story has emerged that sees Frege's antipsychologistic programme in particular as a 'curse' rather than a blessing. Indeed, much of the recent work in analytical philosophy can be understood as a 'revolt against Frege'.[4] If this story is true, then a study of psychologism is called for in order to understand just what went wrong in turn-of-the-century German philosophy; i.e. the controversy over psychologism merits attention not so much as a marvel of philosophical reasoning but rather as an episode which could be said to have taken philosophy (and psychology) down the wrong track.

To provide a rough outline of the recently emerging rival of 'The same old story' is no easy task: the new story is still being written and developed by many different authors. Thus the novel narrative

Accused	Accusers (inter alia)
Aristotle	Sellars (1949: 429)
Armstrong	Kitcher (1979: 243)
Ayer	Wild (1940: 38)
Bergson	Wild (1940: 38)
Berkeley	Wild (1940: 38)
Betti	Gadamer (1975: 483)
Bloor	Fuller (1988: 19)
Boole	Musgrave (1972)
Carnap	Popper (1968: 26), Pandit (1971: 89)
Chomsky	Katz (1981: 189)
Dilthey	Brugger (1988: 308)
Dummett	McDowell (1977: 179)
Frege	Kitcher (1979: 243), Currie (1987: 56)
Geach	McKinsey (1983: 1–2)
Goodman	Sober (1978: 167)
Hume	Wild (1940: 38)
Husserl	Sellars (1949: 429), Dummett (1981: 56)
Kant	Sellars (1949: 429), Fuller (1988: 23)
Locke	Wild (1940: 38)
McDowell	Green (1986: 499)
McTaggart	Wild (1940: 38)
Mill	Nordquest (1979)
Neurath	Popper (1968: 26)
Nietzsche	Habermas (1973: 235), Janssen (1989: 1676)
Plato	Sellars (1949: 429)
Popper	Pandit (1971: 89), Willard (1984: 200)
Quine	Chisholm (1966: 82)
Russell	Sellars (1949: 429)
Sellars	Willard (1984: 193)
Sophists	Wild (1940: 20)
Spengler	Brugger (1988: 308)
Wittgenstein	Wild (1940: 38), Willard (1984: 193)

Figure 1

cannot yet be presented coherently, and assembling its various ingredients calls for some extensive quoting and name dropping.

What then is this new rival to 'The same old story'?

To begin with, Frege has been taken to task for marshalling arguments against his psychologistic opponents that are simply invalid. For instance, a recent detailed study of Frege's anti-psychologistic argument evaluates it as full of 'blunders', and as 'a galaxy of conceptual confusions' (Baker and Hacker 1989: 81, 101). Other authors question Frege's view on the proper relation between philosophy and psychology. To quote Michael Dummett's still fairly sympathetic assessment:

> Where both [Frege and Husserl] failed was in demarcating logical notions too strictly from psychological ones . . . These failings have left philosophy open to a renewed incursion from psychology, under the banner of 'cognitive science'. The strategies of defence employed by Husserl and Frege will no longer serve: the invaders can be repelled only by correcting the failings of the positive theories of those two pioneers.
>
> (Dummett 1991: 287)

Frege's and Husserl's antipsychologism is also often seen to have led to a rather unhealthy division in institutional terms. Essentially it is due to these two thinkers that psychology at its very time of emancipation from philosophy was in fact sent into 'exile': 'while the psychologists were leaving, philosophers were slamming the door behind them' (Sober 1978: 165). Philosophers and psychologists today 'behave like the men and women in an orthodox synagogue. Each group knows about the other, but it is proper form that each should ignore the other' (Macnamara (1986: 1). Students of both psychology and philosophy have 'the frustrating experience of being discouraged from being psychological in their philosophy tutorials and philosophical in their psychology tutorials' (Cussins 1987: 154).[5]

Moreover, Frege's stricture on psychology as well as his conception of the latter, has, according to some authors, led astray a good part of twentieth-century philosophy of science. For example, Isaac Levi speaks of 'the curse of Frege' (1980: 428) in the philosophy of science. Because Frege assumed that the laws of logic are context-independent and totally remote from human thought, he and his followers in the philosophy of science never paid much attention to, and treated as a trivial matter, 'the overarching norms which link the objective norms of logic with prescriptions about how agents ought to think' (1980: 425). Elliot Sober makes the related point that Frege's legacy is to blame for the lack of a logic of discovery. Since Frege assumed, with his psychologistic colleagues, that the psychological differs enormously from person to person (Sober 1978: 169), he and his followers denied all invariances in human psychology. But, Sober goes on to show, this view has become anachronistic: psychological studies show that humans have but a limited number of discovery procedures; that is, far from being idiosyncratic, discovery procedures are invariant in the human species (1978: 174).

In recent years, even the central bastion of Fregean antipsychologism, logic, has come under attack. Some writers confine their neopsychologistic onslaught to inductive logic or the psychology of logic, while others go further and argue for psychologism in the case of deductive logic itself.

In the case of inductive logic, Gilbert Harman (1973) argues that 'the valid principles of inference are those principles with which the mind works'. Harman himself calls this position 'a kind of psychologism' (1973: 18). The standard antipsychologistic reply to such a psychologistic project of treating principles of logic as descriptive of human thinking is that psychologism makes it impossible to account for invalid reasoning. Harman defends himself by pointing out that 'the relevant rules concern the working of the mind when nothing goes wrong: how it works ideally' (1973: 19).

Psychologists studying human logical and mathematical reasoning often retain a good degree of respect for Frege's antipsychologism in logic and mathematics even when they find him guilty of having impeded research on human reasoning. For instance, John Macnamara's (1986) psychological study of logic goes to great lengths to argue that the psychology of logic is compatible even with the Platonist view according to which logical structures are ideal, abstract entities outside space and time (1986: x, 1–20). In fact, for Macnamara the psychological study of logic is largely neutral in ontological matters and seeks merely to study 'how logical intuition is grounded in properties of the mind' (1986: x). Macnamara's theory is modelled on Chomsky's distinction between 'competence' and 'performance'. Whenever a logic (formulated by the logician) is true to human logical intuitions, then this logic amounts to 'a competence theory for the corresponding area of cognitive psychology'. This correspondence between a logical system and human reasoning in a given area can also be expressed by saying that 'to each ideal logic (true to intuition) there corresponds a mental logic' (1986: 22). Errors in reasoning are due to performance factors (1986: 22).

However much Macnamara stresses that his work is not an instance of psychologism, others have either accused the psychology of logic of psychologism, or else have accepted this characterisation without many qualms. Pascal Engel writes that psychologists of logic, while not committed to psychologism in its turn-of-the-century form, are nevertheless 'committed to a different form of psychologism, when they hypothesise that logical laws have a "psychological reality"' (1991: 296). And a recent contribution to the psychology of mathematics (Hurford 1986) holds that 'a study of natural language can illumine mathematics and logic' (1986: 9) and claims that numbers were 'invented by the first people to use numerals' (1986: 12). Small surprise that the same book also contains a spirited defence of Mill against Frege (1986: 133–41).

The recent cognitive-*cum*-evolutionary turn has also left its mark on the philosophy of deductive logic itself. For instance, Susan Haack (1978) finds Frege's arguments against psychologism 'less conclusive . . . than is nowadays fashionable to suppose'; indeed she regards 'at least some form of psychologism more plausible' (1978: 238). Haack distinguishes between three positions *vis-à-vis* the relation between psychology and logic. According to 'strong psychologism' logic is descriptive of how humans in fact think; according to 'weak psychologism' logic is prescriptive of how we should think, and according to 'antipsychologism' logic has nothing to do with mental processes at all (1978: 238). Haack adopts weak psychologism, a position that is frequently attributed to Peirce.[6] Haack's main argument for weak psychologism and against Fregean antipsychologism is the familiar objection to Fregean 'thoughts' (*Gedanken*): it is unclear how we can ever come to grasp these mysterious, ideal entities (Haack 1978: 240–1). As Haack herself points out, the adoption of weak psychologism might completely redraw traditional Fregean borderlines between logic and psychology: 'what, exactly, distinguishes logical from psychological study of reasoning? (It can't be . . . that psychology, unlike logic, is never normative, nor even that it is never normative with respect to truth; consider, for instance, psychological studies of the conditions of reliable/illusory perception)' (1978: 242).

A similar position is endorsed by Brian Ellis (Ellis 1979, 1990). Ellis fully accepts one key sentence of the turn-of-the-century, allegedly deeply psychologistic logician Theodor Lipps: 'Logic is the physics of thought, or it is nothing' (Ellis 1979: 46). For Ellis, the laws of logic are indeed the laws of human thought. They are not empirical generalisations, however, but rather refer to ideally rational belief systems, just like the laws of physics refer to models of idealised entities under idealised circumstances (1979: v). But this qualification notwithstanding, 'logic is a branch of psychology' (1979: 43). Ellis claims that such a conception of logic is inevitable if we want a scientific view of the human being (1979: vi). Like Haack, Ellis is little impressed with the traditional arguments against psychologism: 'I know of no good arguments against it' (1979: 43).

Much of the recent 'anti-antipsychologism' in philosophy goes back of course to Quine's project of a naturalised epistemology, originally presented under the title 'Epistemology Naturalized: Or, the Case for Psychologism' (Willard 1984: 161; Quine ([1969] 1985). In a nutshell, Quine argued that the foundationalist programme of Frege, Carnap and their followers has failed and that therefore epistemology 'simply falls into place as a chapter of psychology and hence of natural science. It studies a natural phenomenon, viz. a physical subject' ([1969] 1985: 24). To the traditional charge against psychologism in epistemology, i.e. that basing epistemology upon psychology is circular in so far as psychology too must be studied by epistemology, Quine's reply is straightforward: 'such scruples against circularity have little point once we have stopped dreaming of deducing science from observations' ([1969] 1985: 19).

I cannot leave the revisionist story of psychologism without quoting passages from two authors, Patricia Churchland and Peter Slezak. Their attitude towards the Frege-inspired armchair philosophy is the most hostile attitude of all those authors who regard antipsychologism as a curse rather than a blessing. For Slezak, the trend towards a naturalisation of philosophy must imply

> in the *practice*, as distinct from the pronouncements, . . . the demise of the philosopher as dilettante and supernumerary commentator . . . If the discipline of AI can be seen in terms of the philosopher's armchair drawn up to the computer console – in Dennett's nice image, then the imperative to don a lab coat is hardly less relevant and compelling.
>
> (Slezak 1989: 138)

And Slezak must already be comfortably dressed in his lab coat, as philosophers who engage in armchair analytical philosophy appear to him 'like the anatomist Vesalius who, while ushering in modern anatomy from its medieval origins, is nevertheless unable to rid himself of galenic principles, in spite of his own contrary evidence (though this is rather too flattering, since Vesalius, after all, succeeded)' (1989: 141).

And to Patricia Churchland the Gettier problem, sense data and

11

the notion of a priori knowledge are no more than 'old curiosities'. Moreover, 'formal semantics now looks like a thoroughly misbegotten project . . . Surely there is something bizarre about the idea that a theory of meaning that has nothing whatever to do with human psychology or neurophysiology can explain the meaningfulness of language' (1987: 545). The 'grand old paradigm' of armchair analytical philosophy is becoming 'enfeebled' and slowly loses its adherents; 'by contrast, there is considerable promise in a naturalistic approach, which draws upon what is available in psychology and neuroscience to inform our research' (1987: 546).

PHENOMENOLOGY AND THE SCHISM IN TWENTIETH-CENTURY PHILOSOPHY

Up to this point I have tried to provide reasons why analytical philosophers as well as psychologists should be interested in a study of the controversy over psychologism in turn-of-the-century German philosophy. To make the case for phenomenologists and other Continental traditions is a lot easier, not least because 'Continental thought' is much more open to accepting historical and even sociological studies into the pantheon of philosophy.

The standard German encyclopaedias of philosophy typically tell 'The same old story' in pretty much the same way as do English and American ones. Whereas Anglo-American writers speak of both Frege and Husserl as the refuters of psychologism, however – usually stressing Frege's priority – German writers often fail to mention Frege at all and instead refer to Husserl and Heidegger as the key figures in overcoming psychologism.[7] This fact already calls for some explanation, of course. Indeed, it hardly needs stressing that a study of the German psychologism debate should be of interest for all those who seek to understand and overcome the 'schism' in Western philosophy, i.e. the 'gap' between analytical philosophy and 'Continental thought'.[8] After all, contributors to that reconciliatory genre usually search for the common ground of the two traditions by returning to Frege and Husserl and to their shared antipsychologism. Unfortunately, in so doing, most scholars have concentrated on trying to determine the extent of the influence of Frege's criticism on Husserl's development. As one recent observer suggested:

Historians of each tradition seem to regard the demonstration of the antipsychologistic priority of its founder as something of a vested interest . . . So on the one hand, we find the portrait of Frege as the clear-minded and dispassionate surgeon who cut through the impenetrable fog of Husserl's rhetoric to locate the cancer of psychologism lurking in the very bowels of phenomenology. But phenomenologists, on the other hand, tend to dismiss this view, insisting instead that . . . Husserl . . . had taken the antipsychologistic cure prior to Frege's critique and of his own accord.

(Notturno 1985: 21–2)

With scholars' attention fixed on this priority dispute, the much more intriguing question as to why Frege was ignored in the antipsychologistic crusade in Germany has never seriously been taken up and thus at least one central feature of the schism has never been addressed.

Even aside from the issue of the relation between Frege and Husserl, it is not difficult to argue that a study of the German psychologism debate must be of interest to the 'Continental philosopher'.

First, accusing other philosophers of psychologism is also popular among key figures in the Continental tradition. Thus, for instance, Gadamer regards as 'psychologistic' any theory of text interpretation for which understanding a text means the recapturing of the writer's intentions and experiences while writing (1975: 483). And Habermas accuses of psychologism those interest theorists of knowledge for whom the interests in question are personal motives such as greed or hatred rather than class interests or transcendental interests (1973: 235). Again one might ask how the same invective 'psychologism' could have become so inflated as to cover such disparate philosophical sins.

Second, it is well known to any student of Husserl that the *Logische Untersuchungen*, published in two parts in 1900 and 1901, constituted Husserl's 'breakthrough' in more than one sense. The *Prolegomena* to this work, which contain Husserl's attack on psychologism, made Husserl famous in German philosophical circles almost overnight. A history of philosophy called it, in 1951, 'the most influential' philosophical work of the twentieth century (Ueberweg and Oesterreich 1951: 512). This raises the question of how this criticism could be so influential. Given 'The same old story', it seems surprising, to say the least, that a philosophical community thoroughly trapped in psychologism should even have bothered to take note of a book by a little-known *Privatdozent,* a book, moreover, which allegedly undermined all of its research.

Third, the criticism of psychologism was also a turning point in Husserl's own development, at least if we believe his own statements in the two forewords to the *Prolegomena.* After all, in the foreword to the first edition Husserl tells us that his new start in logic and epistemology became possible only by disentangling himself from his own earlier psychologism ([1900] 1975: 7), and in the foreword to the second edition he calls the *Logische Untersuchungen* 'a breakthrough' towards his later transcendental phenomenology ([1900] 1975: 8).

Fourth, as we shall see below in great detail, the reception of Husserl's arguments against psychologism was both massive and many-faceted. While only very few authors ignored these arguments, some saw them as a mere restatement of earlier criticisms, some embraced them with admiration, some went to great pains to point out flaws in Husserl's antipsychologism, and many accused Husserl of the very psychologism he claimed to have refuted. Strangely enough, historians of the phenomenological movement have never made a serious attempt to document this reception.

Fifth and finally, there is also something to be gained from a closer scrutiny of the reception of the *Logische Untersuchungen* for understanding Husserl's own subsequent development. Husserl scholars have written many important and erudite studies on Husserl's progression from the *Logische Untersuchungen* to his later transcendental phenomenology. With very few exceptions, these studies decline to look for influences of other philosophers at the time. And even these exceptions confine themselves to either other contemporaneous phenomenologists (i.e. the Munich School) or some of the neo-Kantians (Kern 1964, Schuhmann 1973). But this perspective is too narrow. In order to explain Husserl's shift towards transcendental philosophy, and his ever new attempts to explain his transcendental and eidetic 'reductions', one needs to situate him in the witchhunt for psychologistic tendencies that characterises German philosophy in the first two decades of this century.

PSYCHOLOGISM AND SOCIOLOGISM

My reconstruction of the psychologism debate in Germany is a case study in the sociology of philosophical knowledge. The latter is in turn modelled upon recent work in the sociology of scientific knowledge (SSK). Given this leaning towards SSK, I would imagine that not much argument is needed in order to arouse the interest of scholars of the SSK community in the present endeavour.

However, SSK can also be provided with more direct reasons for being interested in psychologism in general, and the German debate in particular.

To begin with, psychologism is of course a central form of abuse in sociology as well. Recall that Bloor characterises psychologism as 'the attempt to analyse characteristically social phenomena in psychological terms'. In the same passage, he calls such attempts a 'disease', and in a footnote he credits Durkheim with 'the classic denunciation of psychologism', referring his reader to Durkheim's statement that 'the determining cause of a social fact should be sought among the social facts preceding it and not among the states of the individual consciousness' (Bloor 1983: 6, 187). Alas, even in the sociology of scientific knowledge one cannot avoid being charged with psychologism by rejecting it oneself in the strongest terms. Thus Bloor too has been accused of psychologism. Steven Fuller has claimed that a sociology is 'antipsychologistic' only if its 'account of social interaction does not require that social agents have any private mental contents, such as particular desires or beliefs, distinct from their publicly defined role-expectations'. As Fuller sees it, the Edinburgh School (Bloor, Barnes, Shapin, MacKenzie) does not fulfil this criterion and thus 'must be counted as amenable to psychologism'. This is because Bloor's programme 'postulates that social agents have relatively well-defined "interests" which they try to promote by manipulating the course of certain legitimating institutions, such as science' (Fuller 1988: 19–20).

It is also worth recalling that the German psychologism debate strongly influenced the controversy of the late 1920s and early 1930s over the sociology of knowledge. For instance, one of the few people who openly accepted the label 'psychologism' for their own position, Wilhelm Jerusalem, was also one of the early advocates of the sociology of knowledge. Furthermore, various participants in this controversy gave frequent assurances of their antipsychologism. And some writers went further and argued that Mannheim's sociology of knowledge was guilty of psychologism (Lewalter [1930] 1982: 563), that 'sociologism' was the successor disease to psychologism (Spranger [1930] 1982: 635) or that Husserl's arguments against psychologism could be turned, *mutatis mutandis*, against Mannheim's 'sociologism' (Grünwald [1934] 1982: 748–55).

Finally, anyone who studies the German debate over psychologism is sure to be impressed with the parallels between the 'pure' philosophers' hostility towards (experimental) psychology in turn-of-the-century Germany, on the one hand, and the anxiety of many 'pure' philosophers of science about SSK in our own times, on the other hand. Just as back then pure philosophers attacked (experimental) psychology as opening the floodgates to total relativism, scepticism and irrationalism, many philosophers of science today characterise SSK as self-refuting, incoherent, antiscientific and, again, irrational. Surprisingly enough, the parallel fates of SSK and naturalistic, 'psychologistic' philosophy have not (yet) received much attention.

2

TOWARDS A SOCIOLOGY OF PHILOSOPHICAL KNOWLEDGE

INTRODUCTION

Anglo-American philosophers' hostility towards psychology might have abated somewhat in recent years, but their dislike for sociological studies of either the natural sciences or philosophical knowledge has largely remained unchanged. In studying the psychologism debate from sociological perspectives I shall therefore make few friends among mainstream philosophers. In the hope of softening resistance at least marginally, I shall now explain what I mean by 'the sociology of philosophical knowledge', and defend it against some standard criticisms.

PHILOSOPHICAL VERSUS NONPHILOSOPHICAL HISTORIES OF PHILOSOPHY

The sociology of philosophical knowledge represents *one* way in which the history of philosophy can be written. Most Anglo-American philosophers, however, who have pondered the question '*How* and *why* should we study the history of philosophy?', have been dismissive of sociological reconstructions. What I regard as the prevailing Anglo-American way of looking at the history of philosophy comes out perhaps most clearly in the historiographical texts of three eminent historians of ancient and medieval philosophy: Michael Frede (1987, 1988), Jorge Gracia (1992), and Calvin Normore (1990). Central to the standard picture of the history of philosophy in the Anglo-American tradition are two distinctions: the distinction between systematic philosophy and the history of philosophy, and the difference between philosophical and nonphilosophical histories of philosophy.

All three authors hold that, even though knowing the history of philosophy might on occasion be useful and important for the systematic philosopher, the history of philosophy is not essential for philosophy proper (Frede 1987: xxvi; Normore 1990: 225; Gracia 1992: 118). For Gracia, philosophers develop a 'view of the world, or any of its parts, that seeks to be accurate, consistent, and comprehensive' (1992: 56), whereas the historian of philosophy provides accounts of past philosophical ideas. Such accounts inevitably involve philosophical evaluations and interpretations, and thus the history of philosophy is dependent upon systematic philosophy. Yet the dependence relation holds only in one direction: 'the philosophical enterprise as such is not concerned with giving an account of the past and does not need to rely on it to go about its business.' Philosophers or historians who claim otherwise, Gracia suggests, mistakenly equate the historicity of the practice of philosophy with the nonhistoricity of its content (1992: 118).

However, Gracia goes on to stress that, even though the history of philosophy is not an essential part of systematic philosophy, it is nevertheless *useful* for engaging in the latter. He mentions a large variety of ways in which such usefulness might be argued for, but in the end he favours the idea[1] that the study of the history of philosophy 'liberates us from the shackles of cultural provincialism. By revealing to us the way philosophers thought in the past and how they came to do so, it makes us aware of the limitations of our intellectual cultural heritage' (1992: 170).

Frede and Normore, by and large, follow the same view. Normore stresses additionally that the study of the history of philosophy becomes important for systematic philosophy only when the latter encounters 'a crisis of confidence', and that the importance of the history of philosophy to philosophy depends on the severity of such crises (1990: 226). Frede alleges that the history of philosophy increases in importance for systematic philosophy to the extent that it can show that present-day philosophical thought is indebted to, or determined by, philosophical failures of the past (1987: xxvi).

As concerns the distinction between different ways of studying the history of philosophy, the three authors agree that the history of philosophy (as a series of ideas, arguments and theories) can be studied from different perspectives. These perspectives divide into philosophical and nonphilosophical ones. Nonphilosophical ways of studying the history of philosophy supply 'explanations of the occurrence of ideas in terms that are of no interest to the philosopher *qua* philosopher; the accounts are based on considerations that are not intrinsic to the nature of the philosophical ideas themselves' (Gracia 1992: 224). Gracia's list of such nonphilosophical approaches includes, among others, 'the sociological approach'. Gracia remarks that it merits no closer attention 'because it is not widespread'. A sociological study would account for past ideas in terms of social phenomena: 'Thus Voltaire's scepticism might be explained in terms of his French origin and Hume's empiricism might be traced to sociological phenomena prevalent in British society at the time he lived' (1992: 225).

Frede and Normore concur with this view. As Normore sees it, a sociological view of the history of philosophy would involve the assumption that the history of philosophy is 'deeply irrational' and that 'the whole apparatus of reasons for and against a theory is almost entirely just an ideological smoke screen' (1990: 222). Frede suggests that once we give up the idea that philosophers adopt views 'for purely philosophical reasons', we implicitly commit ourselves to contending that the whole enterprise of philosophy is 'misguided' (1987: xix). To be sure, Frede allows for the possibility that the social environment of a philosopher often makes it quite difficult for her to think of certain matters other than as she does and that the school to which a philosopher belongs might make it almost impossible for her to develop views that deviate from her teachers' ideas (1987: xvii). Yet even when such social factors are playing a role, Frede maintains, the philosophical historian of philosophy will not give up her focus on reasons. In so doing she will rely on the assumptions that even mere rationalisations (of social or religious interests) might turn out to be perfectly good reasons, and that even such rationalisations will 'influence the history of philosophy not as rationalisations but as reasons' (1987: xix). Moreover, Frede contends that the ideas of the key figures of the history of philosophy can be explained without recourse to nonphilosophical factors (1987: xvii).

Frede also puts the same idea slightly differently by distinguishing between the 'narrower' and the 'wider' contexts of philosophical ideas. The narrower context is the context of philosophical reasons and arguments, whereas the wider context includes the culture and society in which philosophical reasoning is situated. Exclusive attention to the narrower context is justified in so far as philosophy has its own standards of rational appraisal and enjoys varying degrees of autonomy from the rest of culture. Accordingly, Frede proposes that a philosophical study of the history of philosophy will be an 'internal history', not an 'external history'; a philosophical history of philosophy will not allow 'factors other than philosophical considerations' into its account of the philosophical past (1988: 671).

Frede's, Gracia's and Normore's historiographical proposals are highly representative of analytical philosophers' attitudes *vis-à-vis* the history of philosophy. Despite my own background in the analytical tradition, I wish to set myself apart from its views on the history of philosophy and sociological reconstructions. To begin with, I would like to present three considerations which suggest that the thesis of the nonessentiality of the history of philosophy for systematic philosophy is misleading.

First, note that our three authors' conception of the relation between systematic philosophy and its history is indeed character-istic of just one branch of modern philosophy, i.e. analytical philosophy. The idea that systematic philosophy is – in principle – independent of the history of philosophy goes back to the early days of analytical philosophy, the days of the early Wittgenstein and the Vienna Circle. Wittgenstein's famous dictum, 'What is history to do with me? Mine is the first and only world' (1961: 82e), clearly expresses this view, and so do of course the attempts of logical empiricism to model philosophy upon science. Other traditions in philosophy, for instance those often summarised under the un-happy title of 'Continental thought', have a rather different con-ception of philosophy. Continental figures like Adorno, Benjamin, Heidegger, Foucault, Derrida, Deleuze and Lyotard are undoubt-edly regarded as philosophers of sorts within their respective schools of thought, and, what is more, they would certainly be surprised to learn that, just because most of their writings deal with authors of the past, their work is of no immediate relevance to systematic philosophy. Of course, different philosophical schools of thought are entitled to conceive of their relation to the philo-sophical past in different ways. Thus one cannot deny analytical philosophy the right to regard the past of philosophy as non-essential for its present work simply because this view does not sit well with Continental thought. However, at least Gracia cannot easily invoke this kind of defence. After all, he explicitly states that his book is meant to bridge the gap between the two main traditions in contemporary philosophy (1992: 1–38).

Second, the standard view spelled out by Frede, Gracia and

Normore is unsatisfactory even if we do not measure it against the conceptions of other traditions in philosophy. This much becomes obvious as soon as we start to scrutinise, for instance, Gracia's attempt to argue for the nonessentiality thesis. Roughly his claim is that (systematic) philosophy is after truths about 'the world, or any of its parts', whereas the historian of philosophy is after true accounts of past philosophical ideas. But this distinction is spurious. Why should we assume that the philosopher is concerned with the world only in a nontemporal, synchronic fashion? Isn't the past of the world an essential part of the world? Indeed, given Gracia's all-encompassing definition of the philosopher's task, it is hard to see how any knowledge could fall outside systematic philosophy.

Third, the claim that the history of philosophy is not essential to philosophy proper rules out consideration of a number of issues that, I believe, undeniably are genuine systematic philosophical questions. For instance: how does philosophical knowledge develop over time? Is there progress in the history of philosophy? Why do philosophers disagree? What is the dynamic of theory change in philosophy? What are the conditions on which philosophical theories are accepted or rejected? How do social factors influence the development of philosophical knowledge? What is the relation between philosophy and social institutions or classes? If these questions are philosophical ones, then at least with respect to them the history of philosophy is essential to philosophy.

Thus, I find unsatisfactory the received view of the relation between systematic philosophy and the history of philosophy. But I also regard as ill-founded the notion of a fundamental opposition between philosophical and nonphilosophical, and especially sociological, approaches to the history of philosophy.

The opposition between philosophical and nonphilosophical histories of philosophy rests on the assumption that we are able to make a clear distinction between philosophical reasons and nonphilosophical causes, or between things that interest the 'philosopher *qua* philosopher' and those factors that do not. Unfortunately, none of our authors explains how such lines can be drawn. One only needs to remind oneself of the enormous divergence of interests among philosophers of different traditions to realise that the notion of 'interests of the philosopher *qua* philosopher' is a red herring. Indeed, Gracia's very 'definition' of philosophical reasons (as interesting the philosopher *qua* philosopher) certainly does not

21

rule out social or psychological factors as, say, Adorno's or Derrida's 'interests' make clear enough.

There is also something questionable about Frede's claims that the most important philosophers in the Western tradition can be 'explained' solely from within a narrow philosophical framework, and that 'the historian of philosophy will . . . go on the assumption that philosophical views are usually set forth for philosophical reasons' (1987: xvi). The first claim obviously begs the question in that it presupposes a notion of explanation that already rules out factors other than philosophical reasons. It also relies on the notion, well known from philosophers' hostile reactions to the sociology of scientific knowledge, that sociological perspectives are only to be allowed where a purely internal explanation in terms of 'rational choices' fails. The second suggestion is a prescription rather than a description of what historians do. At least those historians (of philosophy and science) who are influenced by what has sometimes been called a 'hermeneutics of suspicion' (Ricoeur 1970: 32), i.e. the ethos of Marx, Freud and Nietzsche, for instance, will work on the opposite assumption, to wit, the hypothesis that philosophical views usually *are not* set forth for philosophical reasons *alone*.

It is worth noting in addition that Frede, Gracia and Normore mistakenly assume that any sociological approach will always reduce reasons to social causes, e.g. to class interests. But that fear seems exaggerated. At least the kind of sociological approach that I favour in this book seeks to *situate* rather than *reduce* philosophical argument. For instance, in my study of Frege's and Husserl's arguments against psychologism I by no means seek to reduce their arguments to their class position or their positions in the profession. Instead, having reconstructed their arguments, I seek to explain how their arguments became important at a specific point in time, why certain people took up their arguments, how they sought – or neglected to seek – support for their viewpoints, or why Frege's arguments were for a long time ignored. I also focus on the work that went into making or keeping pockets of philosophical argument 'autonomous' or 'nonautonomous' with respect to psychology, and include a study of argumentative strategies used by various sides in the dispute.

A study of these factors is external to philosophy, or nonphilosophical history of philosophy, only if we model the philosopher on the *natural scientist*, who is indeed seldom expected to reflect much on the social character and context of her scientific work. That this image of the philosopher informs Frede's, Gracia's and Normore's writings is again plain at this point. After all, Frede's reference to the autonomy of philosophy is indebted to the idea, popular among scientists and philosophers of science alike, that science is, or has become, autonomous (with respect to society at large), and Normore's suggestion that sociological and historical considerations become important for systematic philosophers only at times of 'crisis' reminds one of Kuhn's distinction between normal science and science in search of a new paradigm. In passing, let us also note that Normore's claim is of course at odds with his further idea that philosophical views may on occasion be ideological and that such ideological views need to be undermined by a 'patient historical tracing of their causal histories' (1990: 219).

However, we recognise that the sociological perspective is anything but nonphilosophical, indeed that it is at the very heart of philosophical questions, if we remember a different ideal of the philosopher, an ideal that arose with Kant and German idealism and that has found supporters in thinkers as different as, say, Marx, Nietzsche, Adorno and Foucault. According to this notion, an essential ingredient of the philosophical enterprise is the questioning of the conditions of its own possibility. I shall not argue for this ideal here; but it is uncontroversial, I believe, to contend that *if* philosophers value this model of the philosopher at all, then the sociological – or, if one prefers, 'genealogical' – study of philosophy must loom large within philosophy itself. From this perspective, the alleged autonomy of philosophical standards cannot be taken for granted but must be questioned as to how it is achieved, what forms of knowledge it is thought to exclude, and why it is accorded any special value in the first place.

To sum up: a sociological study of philosophy does not have to be external to philosophy. It is *potentially* made of the very stuff of which the central philosophical questions are made. The sociology of philosophical knowledge is an eminently philosophical project.

THE SOCIOLOGY OF PHILOSOPHICAL KNOWLEDGE

Philosophical knowledge can of course be studied from different sociological perspectives.[2] The key concept of the approach employed in this study is the notion of *controversy*. The idea that the history of knowledge should focus on controversies over knowledge claims has been much stressed in more recent science studies: the study of controversies enables us to recognise the conventional status of beliefs and practices that, after the closure of the controversy, appear to be self-evident; it allows us to study 'science in the making'; it is called for by the very nature of science and technology as a continuation of war by the same and other means; it offers us a methodological advantage in that it reveals the interpretative flexibility of scientific data; it allows one to identify social interests and the internal and external dynamics of science; and it enables one to pass beyond the sterile opposition of internal and external factors.[3]

My sociology of philosophical knowledge (SPK) takes its main methodological ideas from three key figures in the social studies of science: David Bloor, Harry Collins and Bruno Latour.

From David Bloor's classic *Knowledge and Social Imagery* ([1976] 1991), SPK adopts the two key requirements of 'the strong programme in the sociology of science', i.e. 'impartiality' and 'methodological symmetry'. The first requirement demands that the sociologist of knowledge should 'be impartial with respect to truth and falsity, rationality or irrationality, success or failure' and seek to explain both sides of these dichotomies. The second urges that the explanations provided be 'symmetrical' ([1976] 1991: 7), i.e. the acceptance of beliefs, theories or points of view should never be explained in terms of what it is rational, true or progressive to believe. Instead, the sociologist of scientific or philosophical knowledge must seek social explanations both for views that, as *we* see it, are rational, true and progressive, and for those that are not.

It is also worth emphasising that aligning SPK in some central respects with Bloor's work does not commit us to the view, often unfairly attributed to Bloor, according to which the strong programme in the sociology of knowledge reduces knowledge to social interests or 'an ideological smoke screen' (Normore 1990: 222). First of all, be it noted that for Bloor not all relevant interests are interests of class, church or state. Bloor explicitly allows for 'narrow professional interests':

> Once a theory has been invented and found to have some application there will spring up an interest in its preservation and extension. Its survival means the continued recognition of the achievements of those responsible for its development

... Again, it is routine for scientists to try to expand the scope of their special methods and this frequently gives rise to border clashes and demarcation disputes within the profession.

(Bloor 1983: 157)

Second, Bloor also stresses that scientific language games cannot be reduced to social factors. Instead, he merely urges that, when confronted with either changes in language games or competing usages of key terms, we should 'look for rival groups and track down the causes of the rivalry' (1983: 49). Moreover, Bloor points out that a language game can serve more than one purpose, and speaks of the 'superposition of language games' (1983: 111). Put differently, a scientific or philosophical language game on some esoteric topic, say the precise relation between logic and psychology, can also, at the same time, be a language game about whether or not experimental psychologists should be granted professorial chairs in philosophy departments. But obviously, to say this is not to say that the technical content is irrelevant or a mere smoke screen:

> The final form in which a language-game is actually played can only be understood if one knows all of the factors that underlie each move. If we just look at technical problems confronting a thinker we will not understand why this rather than that is counted as a solution. If we just look at the social circumstances (conceived in a broad and superficial way), we will not discern their connection with the rest of thought.
>
> (1983: 110)

Harry Collins's sociological research programme, variously called the 'radical programme' (1981b) or the 'empirical programme of relativism' (1981a), also emphasises that, from the perspective of the sociology of knowledge, knowledge cannot be explained by reference to 'TRASP', i.e. by reference to what is true, rational, successful and progressive (1981b: 217). In other words, a socio-logical study of knowledge must leave behind 'the natural attitude' of knowledge evaluation. Collins's work, as well as the work of his collaborators (Pinch and Bijker 1984) is interesting for our present purposes because it suggests a useful tripartite format for the study of controversies (Collins 1981a, 1983, 1985; Pinch and Bijker 1984).

The first stage of a controversy study is a demonstration of the 'interpretative flexibility' of given data. As Collins is mainly

25

concerned with experimentation in the natural sciences, he focuses foremost on the interpretative flexibility of experimental outcomes. For the purposes of a sociological study of philosophical knowledge, the relevant data are not so much experimental results but arguments, ideas, concepts and theories. The sociologist of philosophical knowledge thus seeks to document how different authors interpret the disputed terms in a wide variety of ways, how they draw different conclusions from the same premisses, and how they fail to agree on a given issue despite all attempts to provide a 'rational and true' solution.

The second stage is 'concerned with the way that the limitless debates made possible by the unlimited interpretative flexibility of data are closed down' (Collins 1983: 95). Here the focus is on 'mechanisms of closure', that is tactics and strategies that scientists employ in order to force their opponents into agreement. Even though Collins and his collaborators have done little in terms of providing classifications and taxonomies of such closure mechanisms, they have drawn attention especially to two of them, 'rhetorical closure' and 'closure by redefinition of problem' (Pinch and Bijker 1984: 424–8). The first refers to a tactic whereby one seeks to weaken resistance to one's own view by presenting arguments that – albeit not conclusive for the specialist on the forefront of research – are easy to understand and of persuasive appeal for a wider scientific and nonscientific audience. The latter tactic, closure by redefinition of the problem, amounts to changing the terms of the debate; thus, for instance, a controversy over the usefulness of robot butchers might be changed by shifting attention from the considerable waste they produce to the issue of reducing the temperature of abattoirs. Whereas automated butchers seem undesirable from the first viewpoint, they might come to be seen as highly desirable from the second. In the context of philosophical debates we will find the same mechanisms at work, but we shall ultimately want a more fine-grained picture of such tactics.

The third and final step of a controversy study, according to Collins's scheme, is to relate closures and closure mechanisms to the wider social and political context. This too must of course figure centrally in any enquiry into a philosophical controversy, although it will often turn out that this third dimension will be difficult to separate clearly from the second.

Ignoring undeniable differences between Collins and what one might call 'the network school' (Callon, Latour, Law, Rip) in the social studies of science, I shall here follow the latter mainly for the purposes of fleshing out Collins's tripartite format for the study of controversies.

The natural entrance into the network model is the concept of *interest*. In their conception of how the notion of interest is to figure in social studies of knowledge, the 'networkers' differ not only from earlier studies in the Edinburgh tradition of David Bloor ([1976] 1991) and Barry Barnes (1974), studies that allegedly took the category of class interests as unproblematic and given (e.g. MacKenzie 1981), but also from the ethnomethodological critics (Woolgar 1981, Yearley 1982) of the Edinburgh approach, who suggested confining the study of interests to how scientists use that notion themselves. Instead, the networkers propose to study how scientists try to build 'networks', that is to say, try to 'enrol' others by seeking to manipulate, transform and create interests (Callon and Law 1982: 611; Latour 1983: 144). For this purpose, the networkers have developed an elaborate vocabulary. For instance, they speak of 'enrolment' as the construction of networks, and of 'translation' as an umbrella term for different methods of enrol-ment. Translation, in turn, can either take the simple form of 'interéssement', i.e. interesting someone in what one is doing, or the more complicated form of 'problematisation'; in the latter case the network builder attempts to create support for her own project by presenting it as a necessary step towards reaching the goals of other parties (Callon et al. 1986: xvi–xvii; Latour 1987: 108–32). This part of network analysis, especially the detailed elaboration of different enrolment and translation tactics in Latour (1987), amounts to a highly illuminating exercise in the rhetoric of science, and it is of course easily adaptable to the study of philosophical controversies as well. Moreover, this 'new rhetoric' combines easily with more traditional rhetorical perspectives.

Latour has also developed the idea that controversies can be looked upon as struggles over the 'modality' of statements. Thus one and the same statement can have the modality of (1) wild speculation, (2) plausible suggestion, (3) reporting the findings of others, (4) fact-stating and (5) being-taken-for-granted (Latour and Woolgar 1986: 76–82; Latour 1987: 44):

1 Perhaps someone may one day say that psychologism is an incoherent view.
2 It seems reasonable to suppose that psychologism is an in-coherent view.

3 Husserl has claimed that psychologism is an incoherent view.
4 Psychologism is an incoherent view.
5 Chomsky has committed the psychologistic fallacy.

After a statement has reached level (5), it has become 'blackboxed', i.e. the reasoning and arguing in and through which it has become established is typically no longer remembered, and the statement can function – without being itself argued for – in support of further, other claims. Obviously, attending to the modalities of the key claims of a scientific or philosophical controversy provides an excellent means of following the step-by-step evolution of a scientific or philosophical fact.

A summary of the central ingredients of SPK can naturally start from this last-mentioned idea. In order to demonstrate that a sociological reconstruction of philosophical knowledge is possible and fruitful, SPK should not make its task too easy by focusing on statements with very weak modalities. A harder case for SPK is to take a 'philosophical fact' and show in its case how, as Latour and Woolgar once put it, 'a hard fact can be sociologically deconstructed' (1986: 107). Naturally, talk of 'hard facts' in philosophy is to be taken with a grain of salt: statements in philosophy are hardly ever as stable and unquestioned as some statements in the natural sciences. Nevertheless, there certainly are statements in philosophy that fulfil the criteria of

a) being widely accepted, i.e. being incorporated into the standard textbooks,
b) being such that they cannot be ignored or bypassed whenever one works in the respective field, and which
c) can be used without further argument to support new statements.

Statements in philosophy that fulfil these criteria we might call 'philosophical facts', but not much hinges on terminology here.

Given this initial identification of a philosophical fact (Stage 1), the next step in the SPK model is a return to the historical record, i.e. a return to the period in which the selected fact initially had a much weaker modality but was eventually pushed up the ladder of modalities (Stage 2). Subsequently, SPK goes on to demonstrate the interpretative flexibility of (a) the initial low-modality statement, (b) the arguments presented for and against it and (c) the key concepts (*inter alia* key invectives) (Stage 3). After that, the struggle over the modality of the selected statement needs to be mapped. At this stage of the SPK model, one needs to identify interests that inform different interpretative strategies, and to depict these various interpretative strategies as so many strategies of enrolment (Stage 4). And finally, it remains to be explained why the chosen statement rather than its rivals acquired the modality of a fact, that is to say, why and how the advocates of the statement under scrutiny managed to gain the upper hand (Stage 5).

3

PSYCHOLOGISM REFUTED?

INTRODUCTION

One of philosophers' deepest worries with respect to the sociology of knowledge is that sociological studies of science or philosophy ignore the 'technical content' of the controversies under investigation. In order to reduce this anxiety, I shall explain, in this and the following chapter, the arguments for and against psychologism in some detail – and without invoking a single sociological category! In this chapter I shall provide a summary of Frege's and Husserl's case against psychologism.

FREGE'S CRITICISM OF PSYCHOLOGICAL LOGIC

In Frege's case, I shall concentrate on three texts, *Grundlagen der Arithmetik* ([1884] 1934), *Grundgesetze der Arithmetik* (1893) and Frege's 1894 review of Husserl's *Philosophie der Arithmetik* (Husserl 1891b).

Frege's arguments in the *Grundlagen* (1884)

For my present purposes it suffices to take up two lines of reasoning from Frege's *Grundlagen der Arithmetik*: first, his case for a sharp distinction between mathematics-*cum*-logic and psychology, and, second, his criticism of John Stuart Mill's philosophy of mathematics.

The former train of thought is meant to show that

F1 Mathematics and logic are not parts of psychology, and their objects and laws are not defined, illuminated, proven true, or explained by psychological observations or psychological laws.

As Frege sees it, to introduce psychological considerations into the realms of mathematics and logic impedes progress in these latter disciplines. Indeed, as Frege tries to show, the co-operation between mathematics and philosophy has not been fruitful precisely because psychological points of view have intruded into philosophy in general and into logic in particular (xvii).

One central consideration which Frege cites in support of F1 is the following (38):

F2 Whereas mathematics is the most exact of all sciences, psychology is imprecise and vague. Thus it is implausible to assume that mathematics could possibly be based upon, or be a part of, psychology.

Frege does not deny that it might be interesting to study the fuzzy psychological processes, i.e. the changes of ideas (presentations, *Vorstellungen*), that occur when humans calculate. But he stresses that such an investigation can contribute nothing to the precise and exact justification of arithmetical truths. Describing how an idea originates must not be mistaken for defining the content of that idea, nor be confused with proving that content true. The truth of a judgement has nothing to do with whether or not that judgement is thought to be true (xviii).

Moreover, Frege insists that we have to distinguish sharply between our ideas of numbers and these numbers themselves. This is because

F3 Numbers are objective and ideal entities, whereas ideas are subjective and idiosyncratic, psychological entities.

It is precisely because numbers are objective that they are not objects of psychology. Indeed, they are as little objects of psychology as are oceans (34). Furthermore, if numbers were ideas, we would have to allow that numbers change historically, just as ideas do. New kinds of ideas would yield new mathematical truths, and – as the ideas of different individuals are never identical – each individual would have her own, private numbers (37–8).

In order to defend the notion of a strict dividing line between psychology on the one hand, and mathematics and logic on the other, Frege also rejects psychological or physiological interpretations of the Kantian distinctions between the a priori and the a posteriori, and between the analytic and the synthetic:

F4 The distinction between a priori and a posteriori, analytic and synthetic judgements does not refer to differences in the ways in which human consciousness arrives at judgements. Instead, the distinctions refer to different ways in which judgements are justified or proven true.

For instance, arithmetical truths are analytic and a priori because they can be justified without invoking matters of fact (3).

Frege also distinguishes between two meanings of the word 'idea' and stipulates that

F5 The notion of idea should only be used for subjective, psychological ideas, not for objects and concepts.

In other words, 'idea' should be used for the subjective, sensual and picture-like images in an individual's consciousness, images that are governed by psychological laws of association. Frege rejects as confusing a second use of the term 'idea', a use according to which ideas are objective, essentially nonsensual and identical for all minds. Frege suggests that Kant's use of the concept 'idea' blurred the distinction between these two different meanings and that conflating the two uses has led to idealistic and psychologistic tendencies in philosophy and logic (37).

Turning now to Frege's criticism of Mill, Frege argues contra Mill that

F6 Mathematical truths are not empirical and numbers are not properties of aggregates of objects.

First, Mill holds that mathematical definitions of numbers are also empirical claims about matters of fact. Frege rejects this view in pointing out that it would be impossible to say which physical matters of fact are referred to by the definitions of the numbers 0 or 777,864. Moreover, Frege holds, someone who calculates does not thereby have any kind of physical knowledge (9–11).

Second, mathematical truths cannot be based on induction either, as it is unclear just what would be the general inductive law from which all mathematical sentences follow (10).

Third, though it may well be true that we need to have some empirical knowledge in order to learn mathematics, this empirical knowledge contributes nothing to the justification of mathematical truths. Furthermore, Mill systematically mistakes applications of arithmetical sentences for these sentences themselves (12).

Fourth, Mill claims that numbers are properties of aggregates of objects. For any aggregate there exists a characteristic manner in which the aggregate can be sorted into parts, and this characteristic manner is the number of the respective aggregate. But this idea not only fails to account for the numbers 0 and 1, it also overlooks that aggregates can be carved up in many different manners. For instance, a pack of cards can be sorted, *inter alia*, into 52 cards or into two piles of red and black cards (29–30).

Finally, in treating numbers as properties like colour, Mill overlooks that numbers can be predicated of all kinds of different entities, visible and invisible, concrete and abstract (31).

Frege's arguments in the *Grundgesetze* (1893)

Frege's attack on psychological logic in the 'Foreword' of the *Grundgesetze* (1893: xiv–xxv) can be divided into two main parts. The first part (xiv–xvii) accuses psychological logic of reducing truth to taking-to-be-true (*Fürwahrhalten*); the second part (xviii–xxv) seeks to show, more generally, that psychological logic errs in equating the realm of the nonreal with the realm of the subjective.

The argument of the first part unfolds in six steps:

F7 The word 'law' is ambiguous: sometimes it is used to express what is the case or what is true (= descriptive law, law_d), sometimes it is used to express what ought to be done or what ought to be the case (= prescriptive law, law_p).

Thus, for example, laws of physics or geometry state physical or geometrical truths, whereas, say, moral laws are prescriptions (xv).

F8 Every descriptive law can be apprehended or reformulated as a prescription to think in accordance with it. Thus every descriptive law yields a prescriptive law, i.e. a 'law of thought' (*Denkgesetz*).

Frege's way of putting F8 allows for different ways in which $laws_p$ may be dependent upon $laws_d$. Some prescriptive laws might simply have the form 'Accept the truth that X', where X stands for a law_d. Other prescriptions might formulate ways in which the truths stated by $laws_d$ can be reached (If you want to calculate correctly the sum of 3,456 and 463, you should use the following method . . .). Be this as it may, Frege's main point here is that whereas *all* $laws_p$ might appropriately be called 'laws of thought' in so far as they legislate

33

how one ought to think, *only one* species of laws$_d$ should properly be labelled 'laws of thought'. This species is the set of psychological laws$_d$ (xv).

F9 Logical laws$_d$ can be apprehended and reformulated as laws$_p$ and thus as 'laws of thought'. Indeed, logical laws$_p$ deserve this title more than the laws$_p$ of any other discipline. This is because logical laws$_p$ legislate for all thinking: logical laws$_p$ are not topic-specific.

The important point to note here is that Frege does not claim that all logical laws are normative. Contrary to a widespread misreading of Frege, the opposition between psychological laws and logical laws is not, for Frege, the is–ought opposition.[1] Frege writes that 'every law that states what is can be apprehended as prescribing that one ought to think in accordance with it . . . This holds of geometrical and physical laws no less than logical laws' (xv). Thus logical laws are primarily laws$_d$ even though, like other laws$_d$, they too can be reformulated or apprehended as laws$_p$.

F10 Psychological logicians take 'laws of thought' either as laws$_p$ derived from psychological laws$_d$ or then as psychological laws$_d$. This view is mistaken.

As Frege sees it, psychological logicians fail to recognise that there are genuine logical laws$_d$. They start from psychological laws$_d$ which state regularities of human thought. Subsequently, psychological logicians either mistake these psychological laws$_d$ for genuine logical laws$_d$, or else confuse psychological laws$_p$ with logical laws$_p$. It is the ambiguity of the notion 'law of thought', the fact that it is used both for logical laws$_p$ and for psychological laws$_{d\&p}$, which invites this confusion (xv).

In order to make more precise in which respect logical laws$_d$ differ from those psychological laws$_d$ upon which psychological logicians base their allegedly *logical* prescriptions, Frege introduces the distinction between 'true' and 'being-taken-to-be-true'.

First, Frege points out that a psychological law$_p$ merely tells us to conform to current thinking habits; it does not evaluate these thinking habits as to their truth or falsehood. In order to be able to evaluate these thinking habits, one needs a measure which is independent of them. But such a measure cannot be provided by psychological logicians since the only laws$_d$ which they regard as relevant for logic are precisely those laws$_d$ which describe these thinking habits.

Second, these psychological laws$_d$ are laws of taking-to-be-true: they describe under which conditions humans accept the truth of judgements or the validity of inferences; they do not determine under which conditions judgements are true or inferences valid.

Thus, third, psychological logicians conflate truth with being-taken-to-be-true. For instance, Benno Erdmann, Frege's example of a psychological logician, equates truth with general agreement in individuals' judgements. In this way, truth becomes ultimately dependent on what individuals take to be true. But this equation of truth with agreement overlooks the fact that truth is independent of whether or not it is accepted by one, many, all or none. In other words, laws of being true are independent of all psychological laws (xv–xvi): 'If being true is thus independent of being acknowledged by somebody or other, then the laws of truth are not psychological laws: they are boundary stones set in an eternal foundation, which our thought can overflow but never displace' (xvi).

Moreover:

F11 If logical laws were psychological laws$_d$ or psychological laws$_p$, they would be indexed to species, e.g. the human species. Yet logical laws$_d$ are not indexed to species.

Frege raises three main objections against Erdmann's view according to which logical laws have mere 'hypothetical necessity', i.e. according to which the validity of the laws of thought must be restricted to human thought as known up to the present. First, Frege holds that if we were ever to encounter another species that denied, say, the Law of Non-Contradiction, we would not conclude that this species had a different logic; instead we would assume that all members of that species were insane. Second, any conception of logic that rules out the question as to whether we or the other species are right, must be mistaken. And psychological logic, in so far as it reduces truth to being-taken-to-be-true, rules out precisely this query. Third, Erdmann's view makes truth a relative notion. Truth becomes indexed to species and times; what is true for us need not be true for another species, and what is true for the human species up to now might be false for the human species in a future century. But this assumption is completely wrong: truth cannot be relativised to times and species (xvi–xvii).

F12 Logic cannot answer the question as to why we take the most basic logical laws$_d$ to be true.

Frege denies that logic itself can provide an explanation or justification for why we accept, or should accept, logical laws$_d$. Logical laws$_p$ can be justified by referring to logical laws$_d$, and most logical laws$_d$ can be justified by deriving them from more basic logical laws$_d$. But this logical justification must come to an end once we reach the most basic logical laws$_d$. To argue that our nature or constitution forces us to abide by the laws of logic is no longer a *logical* justification, indeed it is to argue from psychological or biological premisses (xvii).

The second part of Frege's critique of psychological logic in general, and Erdmann's views in particular, raises the opposition between truth and taking-to-be-true to the more general level of the opposition between the acceptance and the denial of a realm of objective and nonreal entities. Frege accuses Erdmann of equating the realm of the nonreal with the realm of the psychological and subjective.

F13 It is wrong to assume that real objects and events in space and time exhaust the category of the objective, i.e. of the non-psychological.

Frege's example of objective, nonpsychological entities are numbers. We must not conceptualise numbers as ideas of sorts since, unlike ideas, numbers are identical for all subjects. Just as the moon is independent of how it figures in the ideas of different subjects, so numbers too are independent of how they are represented by us (xviii).

F14 To deny that numbers and concepts are members of a third realm of objective, nonreal entities leads inevitably to idealism and solipsism.

Frege argues for this thesis as follows. First, he points out that a denial of the third realm forces us to treat concepts as ideas. Second, he accuses psychological logicians of seeking to avoid this reduction of concepts to ideas by equivocating on the notion of idea. Sometimes they write as if ideas were something utterly subjective, as if ideas were something that belongs solely to the inner life of the individual. On other occasions, they suggest that ideas are somehow objective and independent of individual minds.

36

Third, this conflation of the objective with the subjective realm affects even the category of real objects and events (in space and time). Since psychological logicians go to great lengths to dissolve the objective-ideal into the subjective-psychological realm, they easily slip into the further mistake of applying the same strategy to real objects and events as well. These too are thus dissolved. The resulting standpoint is idealism: the only entities that exist are ideas. What is worse, this idealism is subjective idealism, or solipsism. Since ideas are bound to subjects, and since there is no identity between the ideas of different subjects, each and every subject lives within her own, unique and incomparable world. And thus, fourth, communication as well as arbitration become impossible. The resulting solipsistic viewpoint has no use for logic as 'the referee in the conflict of opinions'; everyone has an equal right to pronounce her ideas true. There is no longer any standard against which ideas can be measured (xix).

F15 Erdmann's logic exemplifies the dilemmas of psychological logic.

To begin with, Erdmann calls both hallucinated objects and numbers 'objects of an ideal nature'. This already shows that he has no clear notion of the distinction between the second realm of ideas and the third realm of abstract entities. Moreover, Erdmann calls subjects and predicates of judgements 'ideas'. Indeed, for this psychological logician, 'idea' is the '*genus summum*'. No surprise therefore, that Erdmann fails to distinguish between ideas and their content. But, Frege contends, all this is confused. If Erdmann's view were correct, and ideas were all there is, we could not call anything green, as ideas have no colours. Nor could we claim that anything is ever independent of us, since all we could speak about are our ideas (xx–xxi).

As Frege sees it, the tendency of psychological logicians to throw out the category of the real together with the category of the ideal is painfully clear in Erdmann's case. Nevertheless, Erdmann makes one unsuccessful effort to hold on to reality. He claims that when we predicate reality of something, the subject of such a judgement is a 'transcendent' object which is independent of its being presented by an idea. Thus it appears as if Erdmann were a realist after all. But this appearance is deceptive. First of all, Erdmann fails to explain how the present account of predicating reality fits with his general view of judgements, according to which both subject and predicate are always ideas. Second, his talk of transcendence cannot save him from idealism and solipsism, since for him even the transcendent object falls under the *genus summum* of idea. Third and finally, Erdmann's account of the transcendent object leads to a *regressus in infinitum*. For Erdmann, no transcendent object can be present to the mind as such; a transcendent object can be present to the mind only in and through an idea. Thus the transcendent object of one given idea, say I_1, must again be presented to the mind in a further idea, I_2, and the transcendent object of I_2 is accessible only in and through yet another idea I_3; and so on *ad infinitum* (xx–xxiii).

F16 The only way to avoid all these difficulties, and thus the only way to escape from the subjective (psychological) realm, is to understand that coming to know is an activity which grasps rather than creates the objects known.

In other words, in coming to know ideal and real objects and events, we 'grasp' these objects and events. This choice of terminology is meant to get across, once and for all, that *what* we come to know is independent of us. After all, when we literally grasp a physical object, say a pencil, this object is independent both of the act of grasping and of the actor of the grasping (xxiv).

Frege concludes his criticism of psychological logicians by suggesting that their psychological approach makes them miss important logical distinctions, such as those between objects, concepts of the first order (like reality) and concepts of the second order (like existence), or the distinction between 'features' (*Merkmale*) of a concept and 'properties' (*Eigenschaften*) of concepts and objects (xxv). (As Frege explains in *Grundlagen der Arithmetik* (1884: §53), properties of objects are features of the concepts under which these objects fall, and properties of first-order concepts are features of second-order concepts under which these first-order concepts fall. Numbers and 'existence' are second-order concepts.)

Frege's review of Husserl's *Philosophie der Arithmetik* (1894)

Frege's criticism of Husserl's psychological treatment of numbers has three parts. Frege begins by identifying Husserl's psychological premises. Subsequently Frege criticises these premises by pointing to their unacceptable consequences. And finally he shows that Husserl's psychological treatment of numbers is affected by these consequences.

F17 Husserl's premisses are those of the psychological logician.

Husserl's psychological premisses overlap with those of Erdmann. For Husserl, meanings of words, concepts and objects are all but different kinds of ideas. Concept-ideas are less complete and definite than object-ideas (Frege 1894: 316). Moreover, Husserl gives a psychological account of the genesis of (more general) concepts from objects and (less general) concepts: we obtain general concepts by restricting our attention to just some of the properties of objects(-ideas) and concepts(-ideas) (317).

This brings us to Frege's analysis of the unacceptable consequences of Husserl's premisses:

F18 Husserl's psychological premisses erase the divide between the subjective and the objective, make definitions impossible, and hinder an understanding of sameness (*Gleichheit*).

First, as Frege sees it, the conflation of concepts and objects with ideas erases the divide between the subjective and the objective. Furthermore, like Erdmann, Husserl equivocates on the notion of idea: in some places in his book, concepts and objects are understood as subjective, in other places they are taken to be objective. To avoid this conflation, Frege reminds his reader, one always needs to distinguish sharply between ideas as subjective, and concepts, objects, and thoughts as objective, real or ideal entities (318).

Second, the conflation of the meanings of words with ideas leads to the mistaken view that definitions are either circular or false. Say we want to define a string of words, W_1, in terms of another string of words, W_2. The psychological logician will then assume that the meaning of W_1 is one idea, I_1, and that the meaning of W_2 is another idea, I_2. But given this starting point, the psychological logician is faced with a dilemma. If $I_1 = I_2$, then she will say that the definition is circular. Yet if $I_1 \neq I_2$, then she will claim that the definition is false. And thus psychological logicians will feel forced to deny that key concepts, like the concept of number, can be defined at all. What is worse, psychological logicians must even do without a proper understanding of sameness or identity. Since they treat all ideas as numerically distinct, they can never be justified in claiming that two ideas are identical. The only remedy for all these difficulties, Frege suggests, is to accept two insights: a) at least in mathematics extensional definitions are sufficient and b) both sense and reference are objective and distinct from ideas (320).

Third, Husserl's reduction of objects and concepts to ideas leads him to overlook the distinction between concepts of different order, and to neglect the difference between features and properties of concepts (324).

F19 Husserl's psychological premises and their unacceptable consequences are reflected in an unconvincing analysis of the number concept.

Interestingly enough, in his criticism of Husserl's psychological explanation of the genesis of the number concept, Frege does not confine himself to contrasting Husserl's theory with his own account of numbers. He also points out that the psychological processes which Husserl's theory assumes are spurious. For instance, Frege denies that we can combine any arbitrary contents into one idea without relating these contents to one another. He also rejects Husserl's claim that we can abstract from all differences between two contents and still retain their numerical distinctness (316, 323). Again, Frege sees Husserl's mistaken claims as arising from the substitution of ideas for objects and concepts. As ideas are sufficiently elusive and idiosyncratic entities, Husserl is misled into believing that there are no limits as to how they can be restructured and manipulated (317).

Furthermore, Husserl also fails to explain the numbers 0 and 1 or even large numbers in a satisfactory way. Husserl attempts to clarify the concept of number by means of the concept of multitude. But 0 and 1 are not multitudes. And thus Husserl is forced to say that '0' and '1' are 'negative answers' to the question 'How many?' just like 'never' is a negative answer to the question 'When?' Frege rejects this parallel by pointing out that 'never' *denies* that there is an answer to the question 'When?', whereas '0' and '1' are genuine answers to the question 'How many?' (327–8).

As concerns large numbers, Husserl must explain how large multitudes and large numbers can be ideas at all. This is a problem for Husserl because he assumes that numbers are human ideas of sorts, and that human representational capacities are limited. Husserl seeks to solve this difficulty by introducing new kinds of ideas, i.e. 'symbolic ideas'. These are ideas bound to, and dependent on, a sign system. Frege deems this whole notion obscure and suggests that advocating it comes close to adopting the formalist view according to which numbers change when their symbols change (330).

Frege ends by pointing out that amidst all of Husserl's confusions there are some elements which provide some reason for hope. For example, Husserl indirectly concedes that numbers are predicates of concepts, and occasionally he seems to acknowledge that numbers are nonactual, objective entities (324, 331).

HUSSERL'S CRITICISM OF PSYCHOLOGISM IN THE *PROLEGOMENA* OF THE *LOGISCHE UNTERSUCHUNGEN* (1900)

Husserl's criticism of psychologism in the *Prolegomena* of the *Logische Untersuchungen* was the focal point of the German debate on psychologism between 1900 and 1920. Thus I had better give a fairly detailed account of that critique here.

The *Prolegomena* fall roughly into three parts. The first part (chs 1 and 2) defines the sense in which logic is a 'practical-normative discipline' (*Kunstlehre*). The second part (chs 3–10) argues that the theoretical foundations of the logical practical-normative discipline are neither psychological nor biological. And the third part (ch. 11) provides an overview of the true foundations of logic as a practical-normative discipline. These foundations lie in 'pure logic', i.e. a new a priori and purely demonstrative science ([1900] 1975: §3).

Part I: Logic as practical-normative discipline (*Kunstlehre*)

Husserl makes two central claims with respect to the idea of logic as a practical-normative discipline. The first claim can be summarised as follows:

H1 In one of its two main senses, logic can be seen as a practical-normative discipline *vis-à-vis* the sciences. It evaluates methods of scientific justification, and asks: a) under what (empirical) conditions can valid methods be successfully implemented; b) how are sciences to be built up and demarcated from one another; and c) how can scientists avoid making mistakes.

Husserl claims that scientists are unable to justify the ultimate premises and methods of their fields (§4). A theory of science (*Wissenschaftslehre*) is needed to fill this lacuna. This theory of science is a kind of logic. It studies and justifies the methodological procedures regularly employed in science (§§5–6). At the heart of these procedures is a set of topic-neutral methods of justification, i.e. a set of rules of inference (§§7–9). Moreover, in order for a body of knowledge to qualify as scientific, the justifications figuring within it must be systematically interrelated. Thus the theory of science must also study sciences as systematic, structured unities of interrelated justifications (§10). Finally, this logic is a normative discipline. It *evaluates* scientific methods, using as its yardstick the goal or idea of science. This goal is to arrive at the truth (§11).

H2　Every normative discipline D_n, is based upon non-normative, theoretical sentences which in turn belong to one or several different, non-normative, theoretical disciplines. Some of these sentences (and thus sciences) will be essential to D_n, others will be inessential.

Husserl suggests the following interrelations between evaluative attitudes, the value predicates 'good' and 'bad', and normative judgements (i.e. judgements of the form '*a* ought to be *b*', '*a* ought not to be *b*', '*a* must be *b*', '*a* need not be *b*'). First, every normative judgement presupposes an evaluative attitude which divides the entities of a given domain into good and bad ones. Thus the normative judgement 'A promise ought to be kept' presupposes the evaluative, moral attitude which divides human actions into (morally) good and (morally) bad ones. Kept promises are good, broken ones are bad (§14).

Second, a normative judgement expresses necessary and/or sufficient conditions for the possession of a value predicate. To continue with the same example, the normative judgement 'A promise ought to be kept' gives a necessary condition for the goodness of a promise; this condition, obviously, is that the promise be kept (§14).

Third, Husserl suggests that a normative discipline consists of four kinds of elements: 1) a domain of objects; 2) a pair (or scale) of value predicates in terms of which these objects are evaluated as good or bad (or evaluated as better or worse); 3) a set of normative judgements that are based upon value judgements with respect to (1); and 4) a single 'basic norm'. This basic norm is the normative (ought-)sentence which demands of the objects of the given domain that they possess the constitutive traits of the positive value predicate to the highest possible degree. Husserl thinks that the Kantian categorical imperative is an example of such a basic norm. This is because the categorical imperative demands of all acts that they be good in one specific sense: their maxims must be acceptable as general laws (§14).

Fourth, having thus demarcated the notion of a normative discipline, Husserl can go on to define a *practical*-normative discipline. In this case, the basic norm demands the realisation of a general practical aim (§15).

Fifth, normative disciplines are based upon theoretical sentences and disciplines. In short, Husserl reasons as follows. Given a normative sentence of the form

a)   An α ought to be β

and given furthermore that

b) γ is the constitutive content of the predicate 'good' (as defined by the basic norm)

Husserl proposes that the acceptability of (a) depends on the truth of the nonnormative sentence (c):

c)   Only an α which is β has the attribute γ.

Thus, for example, the justification of

a')   A promise (= α) ought to be kept (= β)

depends both upon the basic norm (b')

b')   The furthering of trust among human beings (= γ) is good

and upon the nonnormative sentence (c')

c')   A promise (= α) which is kept (= β) furthers trust among human beings (= γ) (§16).

Finally, as concerns the opposition between 'essential' and 'inessential' theoretical foundations of a normative discipline, Husserl makes the following suggestion. Essential theoretical foundations of a normative discipline are those without which the latter would be impossible. Inessential foundations merely enlarge the normative discipline's domain or allow for finer distinctions and evaluations (§16).

Part II: The refutation of psychologism

The second part of Husserl's *Prolegomena* contains his attack on psychologism in logic. The argument can be divided into several steps.

H3 Proponents of psychologism (i.e. advocates of the view that the essential foundations of logic as a practical-normative discipline are provided by psychology) have no difficulties defending their views against normative antipsychologism (i.e. the view that logic is normative whereas psychology is descriptive and theoretical).

Husserl begins his argument by staging a dialogue between a proponent of psychologism – a 'psychologicist' for short – and an advocate of one special brand of antipsychologism. This brand of antipsychologism, i.e. normative antipsychologism, holds that psychology and logic are divided by the is–ought distinction (§17). The upshot of the debate is that normative antipsychologism is an insufficient response to psychologism.

The psychologicist opens the discussion by pointing out that the theoretical foundations of logic as a normative discipline must be taken from psychology. This is because normative logic evaluates and regiments psychological activities like thinking, judging and inferring (§18). The normative antipsychologicist puts forward two counterarguments. First, he urges that, whereas psychological laws are concerned with how humans *in fact* think and are causal in nature, logical laws prescribe how humans ought to think (§19). Second, the antipsychologicist holds that to base logic on psychology is circular. Psychology itself is possible as a science only if the rules of logic are valid (§19).

Both challenges can be met by the psychologicist. In response to the is–ought distinction the psychologicist points out that thought *as it ought* to occur is but a special case of thought *as it in fact* occurs. Moreover, logical laws are causal, too. Logic is concerned with the conditions under which human reasoners experience judgements as self-evident. And the occurrence of self-evidence is causally dependent upon other psychological events. Finally, the psychologicist also has a twofold rebuttal to the circularity charge. On the one hand, the psychologicist claims that the attack of the antipsychologicist is self-defeating. If it is circular to base normative logic on psychology because the latter presupposes the former, then it is also circular to base normative logic on pure logic. If every science presupposes normative logic, then pure logic must presuppose normative logic, too. On the other hand, the psychologicist distinguishes between two different ways in which psychology might be thought to presuppose laws of logic. Psychology can either take the laws of logic as premisses and axioms of its own theories, or it can rely on laws of logic merely as rules of method *in accordance with which* psychology must proceed. If psychology did the former, the grounding of logic in psychology would be circular. In fact, however, psychology only presupposes laws of logic in the second, weaker, sense and thus taking the theoretical foundations for logic from psychology does not involve any circle in demonstration (§19).

To his own satisfaction Husserl has thus shown that earlier normative antipsychologism is insufficient. Subsequently, he introduces what he takes to be better arguments against, and a better alternative to, psychologism.

H4   Psychologism has three main empiricist consequences. All three can be refuted.

H4.1 *First consequence*: If logical rules were based upon psychological laws, then all logical rules would have to be as vague as the underlying psychological laws. *Refutation*: Not all logical rules are vague. And therefore not all logical rules are based upon psychological laws.

Husserl suggests that all psychological laws are vague. For instance, the laws of the association of ideas are as inexact as meteorological laws. And thus, if logical laws were based upon psychological laws, they should be lacking in precision too. However, anyone familiar with logic knows that at least some logical rules are not vague. Indeed, the logical principles and the laws of syllogistics are absolutely exact. And therefore, the psychologistic interpretation of logic must be false (§21).

H4.2 *Second consequence*: If laws of logic were psychological laws, then they could not be known a priori. They would be more or less probable rather than valid, and justified only by reference to experience. *Refutation*: Laws of logic are a priori, they are justified by apodictic self-evidence, and valid rather than probable. And therefore laws of logic are not psychological.

Whereas H4.1 attended to the difference in precision between psychological and logical laws, H4.2 focuses on the different ways in which we come to know and justify laws of nature and laws of logic. As Husserl sees it, laws of nature are inductive, more or less probable generalisations and known a posteriori, whereas laws of logic are self-evident, valid and known a priori (§21).

In the same context, Husserl also attacks the idea according to which laws of logic *describe* correct human thinking, i.e. *describe* a human thinking unimpeded and unpolluted by irrational, disturbing psychological factors. First, Husserl claims that, in this interpretation of logic, laws of logic would again be causal and therefore probable rather than certain. Second, he points out that the psychologicist has to show how the borderline between correct and incorrect thinking can be drawn in purely psychological terms. And third, he notes that psychologistic logic has failed to prove that there are indeed two qualitatively different kinds of thinking: one kind of thinking that can be explained in terms of logical laws alone, and another kind of thinking that needs to be explained as the outcome of the interplay between laws of logic *and* interfering irrational factors (§22).

Moreover, Husserl charges the psychologicist with neglecting the crucial divide between mental acts in which logical laws figure as contents and these logical laws themselves. Mental acts in which logical laws figure as contents have indeed causes and effects. But these causes and effects must not be transferred to the contents of those acts, i.e. to the logical laws. In other words, psychologistic logicians make the mistake of transferring a property of a mental act to the content or object of that act (§22).

And finally, the psychologicist also overlooks the fact that the laws describing the physical processes and operations within an entity cannot include those laws to which that entity conforms *by virtue of* its specific physical processes and operations. Thus, even though a calculator *conforms* to mathematical laws, this conformity has to be explained by physical rather than by mathematical (or logical) laws. *Mutatis mutandis*, logical laws are not descriptions of those mental processes by virtue of which humans conform to logical laws (§22).

H4.3 *Third consequence*: If logical laws were psychological laws, they would refer to psychological entities. *Refutation*: Logical laws do not refer to psychological entities. And therefore logical laws are not psychological laws.

As Husserl sees it, if the psychologistic interpretation of logic were correct, then logical laws would – at least implicitly – carry existential commitments with respect to psychological entities. Yet logical laws, like *modus ponens*, show no such existential commitments. Husserl claims that all laws of nature imply the existence of matters of fact, although he allows for the possibility that the most abstract laws of mechanics, optics and astronomy do so only indirectly (§23).

Husserl concludes his refutation of the three consequences of psychologistic logic by considering a different brand of psychologism. According to this version of psychologism, logical laws are psychological laws because we arrive at them by reflecting on our individual mental experiences. And the results of this reflection are immediately and apodictically self-evident. Husserl's reply is twofold. On the one hand, he argues that the proposal is a *non sequitur*. Even if we came to know logical laws by reflecting on our experiences, it would not follow that these laws were therefore themselves psychological, or that our experiences were causal antecedents of these laws. On the other hand, this as well as other versions of psychologism all overlook the fact that truths are eternal. It is precisely because truths are eternal that logical laws cannot be laws about states of affairs (be they mental or physical). Husserl attempts to prove this claim by showing that the opposite assumption leads to paradoxes.

Take a logical law like (*):

*) For every truth α, its contradictory opposite $\neg \alpha$ is no truth.

And then assume (a) to (d).

a) Laws about states of affairs are laws about the coming to be and passing away of states of affairs.
b) (*) is a truth.
c) (*) is a law about truths.
d) Laws about truths are laws about states of affairs.

Two paradoxical conclusions follow:

e) Laws about truths are laws about the coming to be and passing away of truths.
f) Laws about truths are laws about the coming to be and passing away of laws about truths (§24).

H5 Psychological interpretations of logical principles distort these principles.

In order to establish H5, Husserl criticises eight psychologistic reformulations of the Principle of Non-Contradiction (PNC) by Spencer, Mill, Meinong, Heymans, Höfler, Sigwart and Lange. For instance, Spencer is quoted as saying that 'the appearance of any positive mode of consciousness cannot appear without excluding a correlative negative mode; and . . . the negative mode cannot occur without excluding the correlative positive mode.' Husserl claims that Spencer's sentence is tautological since positive and negative modes already form a pair of contradictory opposites. But PNC is no tautology (§26).

H6 All empiricism is scepticism and thus absurd.

Husserl argues for H6 *en passant*, in an appendix to his criticism of psychological interpretations of PNC. Husserl criticises both 'extreme empiricism' and Hume's empiricism. Extreme empiricism denies immediate knowledge of logical principles. Hume's empiricism allows that logic and mathematics are a priori but denies that judgements of fact can be rationally justified. Husserl claims that extreme empiricism leads to scepticism because it cannot justify logical principles. In its attempt to justify logical principles, extreme empiricism is faced with a dilemma. Either it makes use of the very logical principles it seeks to justify and thus argues in a circle or it invokes ever more principles of justification and ends up in an infinite regress. Husserl also denies extreme empiricism the option of grounding logic in the habits of everyday life. Such habits would have to be unearthed by psychology. Yet psychology itself uses logical principles. And thus the justification would again be circular.

Hume's empiricism fares no better, according to Husserl. If judgements of fact cannot be rationally justified but only psychologically explained, then the same applies to Hume's own theory as well. Hume's scepticism cannot itself be justified, it can only be psychologically explained (§§25–6, appendix).

H7 The laws of syllogistics cannot be given a psychological interpretation.

Husserl argues that the laws of syllogistics cannot be psychological laws. First, if the laws of syllogistics were laws of thought, then we would never commit fallacies. But obviously humans do commit fallacies. Second, a psychological interpretation of syllogistics cannot explain *why* some inferences are valid and others invalid. Here Husserl turns against the main champion of a psychologistic interpretation of syllogistics, G. Heymans. Heymans proposes that valid inferences can be identified by specifying the 'appropriate [psychological] conditions' under which humans do not commit fallacies. To this Husserl responds by pointing out that the 'appropriate conditions' are either trivial ('be alert') or elusive: it is

48

impossible to specify the necessary and sufficient psychological conditions for the act of inferring correctly.

According to Husserl's counterproposal, the true content of rules of inference is best expressed in terms of ideal incompatibilities. For instance, it holds universally that two sentences of the form 'all m are x' and 'no p is m' are not true unless a sentence of the form 'some x are not p' is also true (§31).

H8 Psychologism in all its variants implies, or is, a form of relativism, namely anthropologism. Relativism is an absurd (*widersinnig*) doctrine.

H8 brings us to the heart of Husserl's 'refutation' of psychologism. His long argument for H8 can be divided into several steps. First comes a criticism of two forms of relativism, Protagorean relativism and 'species relativism'. Protagorean relativism treats the individual human being as *the* measure of truth; species relativism replaces the human individual with biological species. Anthropologism is one form of species relativism. Subsequently, Husserl reduces psychologism to anthropologism, and he singles out Erdmann and Sigwart as the main culprits.

H8.1 Protagorean relativism is an absurd doctrine.

Husserl marshals three arguments against Protagorean relativism. To begin with, he stresses that its advocates will refute themselves as soon as they try to convince others of the truth of Protagorean relativism. Moreover, Husserl maintains that the Principle of Non-Contradiction is part of the meaning of truth; thus it runs counter to the very meaning of truth to claim that one and the same sentence could be true for one person and false for another. And finally Husserl suggests that – on pains of inconsistency – the judgement 'truth is relative' cannot again be merely relatively true. However, Husserl is well aware that none of these arguments is strong enough to convince the Protagorean relativist. Husserl's explanation of why his arguments will not reach the Protagorean relativist is psychological: the latter lacks 'the normal disposition' needed for appreciating the force of the case levelled against her (§35).

H8.2 Species relativism (and thus anthropologism) is an absurd doctrine.

Husserl presents six arguments against the doctrine that truth varies with different species.

First, if truth varies with different species then one and the same judgement could be true for one species and false for another. But this contradicts the meaning of truth. The Principle of Non-Contradiction is part of the meaning of truth, and thus one and the same judgement cannot be both true and false.

Second, the species relativist cannot escape the force of the first argument by suggesting that she or else the members of another, nonhuman species, have an altogether different notion of truth. Either they have the same notion, and then their notion of truth must also be analytically linked to the Principle of Non-Contradiction, or they have a totally different notion, and then what they call 'truth' is not truth at all (§36).

Third, to make truth relative to the constitution of a species makes truth temporally and spatially determined. But this conflicts with the notion of truth. Truths are eternal (§36).

Fourth, species relativism permits the absurd possibility that the constitution of a species implies the nonexistence of that very species. Species relativism must allow that it could be the case that, given the constitution of some species, say S_1, it is true for S_1 that S_1 does not exist. How can the species relativist then say that S_1 exists at all?

Fifth, species relativism must also allow that the constitution of a species is the cause of its own existence. On the premises accepted by the species relativist, the constitution of S_1 may make it true for S_1 that S_1 exists. Thus the judgement 'S_1 exists' is true only because S_1 happens to have a constitution which generates belief in the existence of S_1 (§36).

And sixth, if truth were relative then so would be the existence of the world. This is because the world is the correlate of the ideal system of all factual truths. If truth were relative then there would be no such ideal system and thus no one unique world. Moreover, if all species lacked the constitution needed for believing in a world, there would be no world at all (§36).

H8.3 All forms of psychologism are relativistic.

Husserl claims that Mill, Bain, Wundt, Sigwart, Erdmann and Lipps all advocate versions of psychologism that collapse into species relativism (§38). He goes on to discuss the views of Erdmann and Sigwart in detail.

In Sigwart's case Husserl takes up and rejects five key theses (§39):

1 It is fictitious to assume that a judgement could be true even if no intellect were ever thinking this judgement. *Critique*: It is part of the meaning of the law of gravity that it is true for all times (even prior to its discovery), regardless of whether it happens to be thought by anyone or not. If a certain truth, say, the truth that *p*, is not grasped by anyone, then the truth that *p* remains in the realm of pure ideas. It then remains an *ideal possibility* that this truth is grasped by some thinking beings.

2 A judgement is objectively necessarily true if and only if I can be certain that I shall regard it as true in all circumstances (or, as Husserl expands: if all other human beings do likewise). *Critique*: Factual agreement among individuals of the same species does not amount to, or capture, the ideality of objectively necessary truths like the logical laws.

3 'A logical ground (*Grund*) we do not know is strictly speaking a contradiction in terms.' *Critique*: This contradicts our usage of the notion of *discovery* as when we say that we discover the axioms from which mathematical theorems follow.

4 'All logical necessity presupposes an *existing* thinking being whose nature it is to think in this way.' Moreover, there is no essential difference between assertive and apodictic judgements: every assertion that we utter with full consciousness strikes us as necessary in some sense. *Critique*: Sigwart conflates subjective psychological necessity (perceived coercion) with apodictic necessity. The latter 'constitutes itself' in our grasping of a logical law. He also conflates the apodictic consciousness of necessity with its correlate, the apodictically necessary law.

5 Leibniz's distinction between *vérités de raison et celles de fait* is not clear. *Vérités de raison* are necessary only for those beings that understand the vocabulary in which these truths of reason are expressed. *Critique*: Sigwart conflates psychological with logical necessity, i.e. the necessity of believing the *vérités de raison* with the necessity of the *vérités de raison* themselves (§39).

In Erdmann's case Husserl goes to even greater lengths in order to unmask what he regards as fatal flaws and inconsistencies. The central issue for Husserl is Erdmann's claim that logical laws are merely hypothetically necessary, i.e. that logical laws are necessary only for members of the human species up until the present. Erdmann is not shaken by the objection that we cannot imagine what a radically different logic would be like. On the contrary,

Erdmann holds that our inability to conceive of a radically different logic vindicates his claim that logic is relative to the human species. He also suggests that we would be justified to regard our logic as absolute only if the following condition could be met: we would have to be certain that, as far as logic is concerned, human thought is invariant and without alternatives. But this condition, Erdmann maintains, is not, as a matter of fact, fulfilled. And last but not least, Erdmann claims that objective truth is nothing but certainty for all (§40).

Husserl's list of objections to this theory is long. First, Husserl points out that Erdmann's reasoning seems to rely on the following inference:

a) If logic were relative to the human species, then a different logic would be inconceivable for humans.

b) A different logic is inconceivable for humans.

Therefore:

c) Logic is relative to the human species.

Obviously, this argument is an instance of the fallacy of affirming the consequent. Thus Husserl suggests that Erdmann should say merely that *(a) explains (b)*.

Second, even on this more charitable interpretation, Erdmann's position is not acceptable since (a) is false: it is possible that a member of a given species might deny the very laws of thought which are part of that species' constitution.

Third, on Erdmann's view, the laws of logic are 'laws of thought' which express the nature of human thought. But then the laws of thought would again have empirical, real content. And this is false.

Fourth, Erdmann conflates two kinds of modality, i.e. psychological modalities and logical modalities. While the sentence

a) It is logically possible that the logical laws are not true

is self-refuting, the sentence

b) It is psychologically possible that a human being denies the logical laws

is not self-refuting. On Erdmann's premisses the distinction between (a) and (b) is lost in so far as the obvious truth (b) is denied.

Fifth, if logical laws were, as Erdmann assumes, real, natural, psychological laws, then we should, *pace* Erdmann, be able to imagine alternative logics. After all, we can always imagine alternatives to empirical laws.

Sixth, Erdmann believes that our thinking could change so radically that our present logical laws would no longer be valid. This belief is absurd. Only psychological, empirical laws are variable and have exceptions, but logical laws are invariant and without exception. Erdmann's theory allows for a future race of logical *Übermenschen* with a partially or completely new logic. But these *Übermenschen* could only be counted as mad by the standards of us 'logically ordinary folks'. Moreover, Husserl contends, it is hard to see why Erdmann could not apply his logical racism straightaway, i.e. why he is not ready to speak of the different logics of different existing races.

Seventh, the proponent of anthropologism cannot defend her relativistic stance by pointing out that our evidence for the uniqueness of logic is, inevitably, our apodictic self-evidence. If we give up the belief in apodictic self-evidence, never mind whether it is qualified as 'ours' or not, we end up in absolute scepticism and then all of Erdmann's theory goes by the board as well.

And finally, Erdmann is also mistaken in reducing truth to the agreement of all. To begin with, on this construal of truth, we would never be able to know whether a given assertion was true; after all, we can never ask each and everyone for her opinion. Moreover, the consensus theory leads to an infinite regress. On Erdmann's view, a given judgement, say *p*, would be an objective truth if and only if *p* were valid for all. But to know whether *p* was valid in this way, we would again need universal agreement on this second-level question. And so on ad infinitum. Rather than searching for the opinion of all, Husserl opines, we should accept that truth is not found in the views of all, but rather in the views of the few.

H9   Psychologism is based upon three *prejudices*. All three can be refuted.

H9.1 *First prejudice*: Prescriptions meant to regulate psychological events must be psychologically grounded. *Refutation*: This overlooks an important distinction between (a) laws that *can be used for setting* norms on how to acquire knowledge and (b) laws that *are* norms on how to acquire knowledge.

The distinction Husserl emphasises between (a) and (b) can

perhaps be made clearer by way of an example. A case of an (a)-law would be *modus ponens,*

a) if p and $p \rightarrow q$, then q

whereas an example of a (b)-law would be the following:

b) Whoever judges that p and judges that $p \rightarrow q$, must/should also judge that q (§41).

Any theoretical sentence of any science can be used for setting norms for knowledge in the way suggested by the difference between (a) and (b). This in itself refutes 'the first prejudice' because not all theoretical sentences used for setting norms are part of psychology (§41). Turning from the psychologicists to earlier antipsychologicists, Husserl claims that the latter too missed the importance of the distinction between (a) and (b). This can be seen from earlier antipsychologicists' insistence on the idea that the essence of logic is the regulation of knowledge acquisition. Thus they missed logical laws in the sense of (a) (§41).

In the same context, Husserl also outlines what he regards as the right view on the relations between psychology and logical *Kunstlehre.* Only a subset of the rules of the logical practical-normative discipline (*Kunstlehre*) stand in need of psychological justification. This is the set of methodological, 'anthropological' (§43) prescriptions for generating and criticising knowledge. These are prescriptions that, implicitly or explicitly, are based on the limitations and resources of the human mind (§41). This subset of rules of logical *Kunstlehre* differs from both (a) and (b), even though the latter partly figure in the justification of these 'anthropological' prescriptions (§41).

Moreover, logical *Kunstlehre* seeks general norms (for all sciences), and thus it is not interested in deriving just any normative sentences from the theoretical sentences of just any science. In order to gain this generality, logical *Kunstlehre* derives its norms from theoretical sentences (laws) that concern the ideal conditions of the possibility of any theory or science. In other words, logical *Kunstlehre* derives its norms from 'pure logic' (§42).

In order to make the idea of this 'pure logic' more transparent, Husserl points out that science can be studied from two perspectives. Science can be investigated either as a certain kind of human activity or as a theoretical, objective content, i.e. as a systematically interrelated set of truths. The task of pure logic is to study the *form,* or *formal aspects* of this content. The ideal laws that pure logic arrives at through this investigation can subsequently be reformulated as (b)-norms. Husserl insists, however, that even such (b)-laws are 'ideal' rather than empirical. And thus they are to be distinguished sharply from all 'anthropological' prescriptions (§42).

In the light of these suggestions, Husserl can now also make more precise just where earlier normative antipsychologism went wrong. Its first error was to put too much emphasis on the opposition between laws of nature and 'normal laws', that is on the opposition between laws of nature and prescriptions. In this way, normative antipsychologism overlooked the more fundamental opposition between law of nature and ideal law (§43). Moreover, earlier antipsychologism also went astray in claiming that the opposition between 'true' and 'false' had no place in psychology. This was a mistake because truths are grasped in the process of knowledge acquisition, a process that can be investigated by psychology (§43). Finally, earlier antipsychologicists also erred in accusing psychologism of a *circulus in demonstrando* (see p. 44). A demonstrative circle is not involved because a derivation of logical laws from psychological laws does not use these logical laws as premises. Instead, the circularity in question is better described as a 'reflective circle': the derivation of logical laws from psychological laws uses these logical laws as derivation rules. While psychologism is guilty of arguing in this reflective circle, pure logic can avoid this circularity. Within pure logic, the sentences which any given deduction presupposes as derivation rules are not proven within that same given deduction; and sentences which are presupposed by all deductions are not proven at all. Rather they are postulated as axioms (§43).

H9.2 *Second prejudice*: Logic is concerned with ideas, judgements, inferences and proofs, and all these are psychological phenomena. Therefore logic must be based on psychology. *Refutation*: If this were true then the same reasoning would turn mathematics into a branch of psychology. But this view has been refuted already.

In order to refute 'the second prejudice', Husserl reminds his readers of the work of Lotze, Riehl, Frege and Natorp. Lotze and Riehl have shown that mathematics is a part of logic, and Frege and Natorp have argued forcefully that mathematics is not a branch of psychology. Combining these two lines of argument thus provides a strong case against the claim that logic is a part of psychology (§45).

Again Husserl proceeds from criticism to a partial outline of his own programme. Here he does so with respect to the relation between psychology and the ideal sciences (§46). Concerning arithmetic, he emphasises that pure number theory is no part or branch of psychology, even though numbers, sums and products refer back to mental acts of counting, adding and multiplying. Mathematical objects are found or 'identified' (*aufgewiesen*) in mental acts of a certain kind. Psychology studies these acts, while arithmetic studies the *ideal species 1, 2, 3, . . .* Put differently, numbers are ideal particulars, ultimate species of the genus 'number', and the laws of arithmetic are laws that are based on the ideal nature of this genus.

A similar distinction applies in the case of logic. Here too concepts (logical concepts in this case) are found or identified in certain kinds of mental acts. These acts are studied by psychology. However, pure logic studies terms like presentation, concept, judgement, inference, proof, theory, necessity and truth not as class terms for mental experiences and dispositions, but as concepts whose extensions are ideal particulars, species. Psychology and logical *Kunstlehre* (in some of its parts) take these same terms as class terms for mental experiences (§46). It is this distinction which earlier logicians had missed. In their treatment of judgements, these authors failed to draw a distinction between judgements as certain kinds of mental experiences and judgements as *units of ideal meaning*, or *sentences*. The ultimate particulars of the genus 'judgement' are ideal particulars like (the sentences) '$2 \times 2 = 4$' and '$2 \times 2 = 5$', not your act of judging that $2 \times 2 = 4$ and my act of judging that $2 \times 2 = 5$ (§47).

H9.3 *Third prejudice*: Judgements are recognised as true when one experiences them as self-evident. But self-evidence is a psychological phenomenon, a feeling. Therefore logic must study the psychological conditions for the occurrences of that feeling, i.e. it must find the psychological laws that link the occurrence of that feeling to prior or coexisting mental events. *Refutation*: Purely logical sentences say nothing about self-evidence and its conditions.

Husserl concedes that logical *Kunstlehre* should try to find psychological conditions for the occurrence of self-evidence. But, at the same time, he stresses that the relation between logical laws and self-evidence is ideal and indirect. Purely logical sentences say nothing about self-evidence and its conditions; they relate to self-evidence only in so far as sentences (a) and (b) are equivalent:

a) α is true
b) it is possible that someone judges with self-evidence that α is the case (§50).

Moreover, sentences of type (b) are not *psychological* sentences since the possibility in question is an ideal or logical modality, not a psychological one. In other words, the 'someone' in (b) refers not to a psychological subject but to 'some intellect from the set of all possible intellects' (§50).

Husserl rejects what he regards as the received view on self-evidence. According to this received view, self-evidence is a feeling that, under 'normal' circumstances, 'reveals' the truth of a judgement. Husserl objects that these 'normal' conditions have never been sufficiently specified and that it has never been explained why anyone should trust the feeling of self-evidence in the first place (§51).

Husserl makes three proposals concerning self-evidence. First, self-evidence is the *experience* of truth, not a *criterion* of truth. In other words, to experience that an assertion is in full harmony or agreement with an experienced state of affairs is to have self-evidence for that assertion. Thus, self-evidence is no additional ingredient of this experience. Second, truths are ideal species of the ideal genus 'truth', i.e. truths are ideal particulars. These ideal species are independent of whatever humans claim to be self-evident. And third, when one person claims that p is self-evident, whereas another person claims that $\neg p$ is self-evident, then one of them is wrong. Put differently, truth is prior to self-evidence (§51).

H10 A biological justification of logic and epistemology fares no better than a psychological one.

H10 defines Husserl's view on Avenarius's, Mach's and Cornelius's biological, or 'thought-economical', justification of logic and epistemology.

Husserl regards the basic ideas of Avenarius and Mach as sound. Organisms seek to adapt efficiently to their environment. That is, organisms seek to adapt to their environment in such a way that they can carry out the activities necessary for their survival and well-being with the use of as little energy as possible. Something similar can be said about science. Science seeks to arrive at an ever more efficient, an ever more thought-economical orientation in the realm of experience (§53). Thought-economic considerations even have a role to play in understanding purely deductive method-ologies. For instance, the replacement of number concepts with (empty) signs in calculations is a clear case of a thought-economic simplification (§54).

Nevertheless, pure logic cannot be justified by thought-economical considerations. Laws of logic are not justified when it is pointed out that their employment has survival value for the human species, or when it is shown that their employment makes human knowledge easier to unify. To argue in this way is to commit the fallacy of *hysteron-proteron*. The logical ideal of a deductively unified body of knowledge cannot be justified by the evolutionary trend towards a deductively unified body of knowledge. This is because invoking this trend is already to invoke the logical ideal. In other words, the validity of the ideal of rationality and unification is presupposed by thought economy, and it is not explained by it. We evaluate factual thought in terms of the ideal norm and *then* notice that factual thought often takes place *as if* it were guided by the ideal principle (§56).

Husserl concludes his criticism of psychologism and biologism by predicting that the sad state of contemporary philosophy will forestall a proper appreciation of his arguments. In the same context, he also lists philosophers that he regards as forerunners of his work. Kant, Herbart, Lotze, Leibniz, Lange and Bolzano are discussed in greater detail (§§59–61).

Part III: An outline of pure logic

Husserl concludes the *Prolegomena* with an outline of his projected new logical discipline, i.e. pure logic. As pure logic is meant to concern itself with the ideal conditions of the possibility of science, Husserl begins his outline with some general comments on the latter concept.

As Husserl sees it, a science is an objective and ideal unity, a system of interrelations. These interrelations hold between ideal or real matters (of fact) (*Sachverhalte*) on the one hand and between truths on the other hand. Matters (of fact) correlate with and are inseparable from truths. All matters (of fact) fall under the genus 'being as such', while all truths fall under the genus 'truth as such'. Matters (of fact) and truths are not identical since truths about truths are not truths about matters (of fact) (§62).

Husserl distinguishes between 'abstract' and 'concrete' sciences. Abstract, i.e. nomological and explaining sciences have the unity of a systematically complete theory. In other words, the laws of these sciences can all be deduced either from a single basic law or from a group of homogeneous basic laws (§63). Concrete, i.e. onto-logical and descriptive sciences lack such unity. Their truths are at most 'nonessentially' unified: either they all refer to the same kind of matter (as the truths of geography all refer to the earth), or they are united by a basic norm or value (as in the case of normative disciplines) (§64).

Husserl introduces the basic question of his pure logic as a generalisation of Kant's question concerning the ideal conditions of the possibility of experience. Pure logic investigates the ideal conditions of the possibility of scientific abstract theories. It takes these conditions in both a 'subjective' and an 'objective' sense (§65). Understood in the subjective sense, pure logic studies the conditions any intellect whatsoever has to fulfil if it is to acquire theoretical knowledge (§65). Taken in the objective sense, answer-ing the basic question of pure logic amounts to enquiring into the ideal conditions of the possibility of theoretical knowledge. Put differently, it amounts to enquiring into the ideal essence of a 'theory as such' (§66). Spelled out in greater detail, pure logic has three tasks. First, it clarifies those concepts which create unity within a theory, i.e. elementary forms of combination and formal, abstract concepts like object, matter of fact, singularity, plurality or number (§67). Second, pure logic seeks to discover the laws that are based on these concepts, laws concerning the objective validity of theoretical units composed of these concepts; this enquiry yields for instance the theory of inference, the theory of multitudes, or the theory of numbers (§68). Third and finally, pure logic develops a theory of possible theory forms, the goal here being to identify species of theory forms (§69). Such a project is analogous to, and an extension of, the theory of pure manifolds in mathematics (§70).

In this context, Husserl also comments on the relation between pure logic and mathematics. He claims that the mathematical treatment is the only properly scientific treatment of inferences and that philosophers have no right to reclaim this field of study. But he is quick to add that the mathematician is only an ingenious technician without ultimate insight into the essence of theories. It is the philosopher (*qua* pure logician and epistemologist) who arrives at such ultimate insight (§71).

In conclusion, Husserl proposes a further extension of the domain of pure logic, i.e. the study of the ideal conditions of the possibility of empirical science in general. This study clarifies the idea of probability (§72).

FREGE'S AND HUSSERL'S CRITICISMS COMPARED

Several similarities and differences of Husserl's and Frege's attacks on psychologism are worth pointing out.

A first noteworthy point is that almost all of Husserl's key arguments against psychologism can already be found in Frege's texts. The amount of overlap makes it likely that Husserl's criticism of psychologism was strongly influenced by Frege, indeed that Husserl simply took his arguments from Frege (Føllesdal 1958, Mortan 1961). A straightforward correspondence exists between the following key elements of Frege's and Husserl's cases against psychologism:

F1	——	H4–H9
F2	——	H4.1
F3	——	H9.2
F4	——	H4.2
F6	——	H9.2
F7	——	H2, H9.3
F8	——	H1, H3, H9.3
F9	——	H1, H3, H9.3
F10	——	H4, H4.3, H5, H7, H9
F11	——	H8
F13	——	H6, H9
F15	——	H8.3

There is no need to go through these parallels one by one. Let me here only comment on the parallel between F9 and H1, H3, H9.3. This parallel shows that Frege and Husserl are not divided over the question whether or not logical laws are primarily descriptive or primarily prescriptive. Both authors see logic as dividing into a descriptive and a prescriptive part, and both regard the descriptive part as primary. It is only when this parallel is overlooked, and when Frege is interpreted as a normative antipsychologicist, that their respective antipsychologisms appear to be different. Such a difference was suggested, *inter alia*, in Føllesdal's little classic *Husserl und Frege* (1958).[2] I also held the same mistaken view once, claiming that Husserl's arguments against normative antipsychologism were implicitly directed against Frege (Kusch 1989: 47–51). A careful reading of Frege's text reveals that such an interpretation is indefensible.

F17–F19, i.e. Frege's criticisms of *Husserl's Philosophie der Arithmetik*, have no direct parallels in Husserl's list of key theses. Nevertheless, they too can be found in Husserl's *Logische Untersuchungen*. In his Preface, Husserl distances himself from his earlier psychologism ([1900] 1975: 7), and in a footnote he withdraws his earlier critique of Frege's 'antipsychologistic position' ([1900] 1975: 172). As to F5, Frege's stricture on the use of the concept 'idea' (*Vorstellung*), Husserl does not follow Frege. Husserl continues to use this notion in his logic. However, in a later chapter of the *Logische Untersuchungen* Husserl too deplores the vagueness of the term and distinguishes fifteen different meanings of *Vorstellung* ([1901] 1984: V §44).[3]

This last point naturally leads to those Fregean ideas that have no direct counterparts in Husserl. Three such differences are worth noting.

First, we should note a terminological difference. Whereas Husserl attacks psychological interpretations of logic and epistemology as forms of 'psychologism', Frege, to the best of my knowledge, never used this term. Frege attacks 'psychological logic' and 'psychological logicians', not 'psychologism' or the 'psychologicists'. Though this is a rather minor difference, it is surprising to note that it has been overlooked even by as eminent a Frege scholar as Michael Dummett. Dummett writes that 'Frege launched a strong attack on what he called "psychologism"' (1978: 88).

Second, Føllesdal (1958: 40) has drawn attention to the fact that, even though Husserl and Frege employ similar arguments against psychologism, only Husserl considers these arguments as conclusive. Frege thinks that he cannot refute the psychologicist with knockdown arguments. Frege probably thought that only the completion of his entire project would provide a convincing argument against psychologism. The reason for Frege's caution is his conviction that logical argumentation can only proceed by deduction: 'The question why and with what right we acknowledge a law of logic as true, logic can answer only by reducing it to another

law of logic. Where that is not possible, logic can give no answer'
(1893: xvii). Thus, for Frege, the relativistic psychologicist who
denies the universally binding nature of logic cannot be refuted by
means of an explicit argument. Nor can one demonstrate to her
why an absolute notion of truth must be accepted. This would
presuppose that the critic (i.e. Frege) would be able to demonstrate
what truth is all about. But this is precisely where Frege is obliged
to stop, since he holds that 'what truth is, I hold to be indefinable'
(1969: 139). Husserl is less pessimistic in this respect and thus
deems it possible to refute relativism in all its forms. This, then,
explains why F12 has no direct counterpart in Husserl.

Third, note that whereas Frege reduces psychologism to idealism
and solipsism (F14), Husserl attacks psychologism as a radical form
of empiricism (H6). This opposition is noteworthy not least because
of a recent controversy in Frege scholarship. Michael Dummett
(1973: 684; 1978: 88; 1991: 80) has stressed repeatedly that Frege
was a realist who, through his attack upon psychologism, played a
part 'in bringing about the downfall of Hegelian idealism' (1973:
683). Others, most notably Hans Sluga (1976, 1980), have insisted
instead that Frege's antipsychologism was an attack on scientific
naturalism and that Frege would actually have been fifty years late
if he had intended to discredit Hegelian idealism.

Sluga's position, according to which Frege was indeed attacking
naturalism and empiricism, can be vindicated by noting that the
difference between Husserl's attack on psychologism as a form of
empiricism and Frege's attack on psychologism as a form of
idealism is merely terminological. Both Husserl and Frege see
psychologism as ultimately leading to relativism and scepticism.
This is because psychologism denies both the *third realm* of ideal,
Platonic entities and the *first realm* of physical objects and events.
Given Frege's and Husserl's own Platonistic viewpoints, the first
denial results in empiricism, and, once the second denial is added
to the first, the outcome is (solipsistic) idealism (of the individual
or of the human species). But whereas Husserl focuses on the first
denial and thus marks the resulting position terminologically as
empiricism, Frege attends more to the result of both steps and
speaks of psychologism as a position that ends up in idealism. Both
authors unite again, in viewing the outcome of both steps as
constituting a relativistic scepticism.[4]

4

THE CRITICISM OF
HUSSERL'S ARGUMENTS
AGAINST PSYCHOLOGISM
IN GERMAN PHILOSOPHY
1901–20

INTRODUCTION

It attests nicely to the enormous success of antipsychologism in this century that its early critics are largely forgotten. Almost all of these commentators focused on Husserl rather than Frege – for reasons that will be explained in Chapter 7 (see pp. 203–10). Husserl's *Prolegomena* were widely studied, praised by many authors and rejected by many others. In this chapter I shall focus on *critical* reactions to Husserl's *Prolegomena* between 1901 and 1920.

Many of these early critics were themselves highly original and prolific writers. The thoughts of most of them would merit no less of a detailed and sympathetic discussion than is routinely granted to Frege and Husserl. I hope that my brief summary of their objections will help to rescue at least some of them from total oblivion.

OBJECTIONS TO HUSSERL'S MAIN THESES

In many cases it seems artificial to separate attacks on one element of Husserl's antipsychologism from rejections of other ingredients of his overall argument. After all, since Husserl's main theses are interrelated, the critique of one particular thesis often implies opposition to other key assumptions as well. I shall deal with this problem in two ways. Some contested issues will be referred to several times, while other ideas will be brought up only once, despite the fact that they are all central to Husserl's anti-psychologistic argument as a whole. I shall quote more extensively than is common practice in scholarly work as I wish to convey a flavour of the polemical character of many criticisms. It also seems appropriate to make some key passages available to the anglophone reader, especially since most of the texts cited here have not yet been translated into English.

Normative antipsychologism, and logic as a normative discipline (H2 and H3)

Several authors took exception to Husserl's claim that logic as a normative-practical discipline (*Kunstlehre*) must be based upon logic as a theoretical science. Often, if not always, the same critics also defended normative antipsychologism as a sufficient defence against psychologism.

To shield a normative conception of logic was of special importance to the Southwest German school of neo-Kantian philosophers (Windelband, Rickert, Kroner). This school had long been committed to drawing the line between logic and psychology in terms of the value–fact opposition (e.g. Windelband 1884). Husserl's rebuttal of normative antipsychologism forced these neo-Kantians either to defend the is–ought distinction as a sufficient way of separating logic from psychology or else to explain why the value–fact opposition does not coincide with the is–ought dichotomy.

As early as 1904, in the second edition of his *Der Gegenstand der Erkenntnis*, Heinrich Rickert claimed that Husserl's attack on normative antipsychologism was much less convincing than Husserl's criticism of psychologism (1904: 88). However, only two later texts by authors of the Southwest German school of neo-Kantians, written by Rickert (1909) and Kroner (1909), reacted to Husserl's challenge in greater detail. I shall here concentrate on Kroner's more accessible paper, especially as Rickert endorsed Kroner's article in a footnote to his own paper (Rickert 1909: 196).

Rickert's student Richard Kroner agreed with Husserl that 'the meaning of logical sentences is not exhausted by their role as technical rules of thought'. But he did not accept Husserl's further claim that logical sentences were *about* ideal, abstract beings. Kroner proposed that logical laws were imperatives, and that these imperatives were founded on values. In other words, Kroner rejected Husserl's view according to which all normative disciplines were based upon theoretical sciences (1909: 241).

Kroner argued for this conclusion by showing that not all ought-sentences were founded on non-normative, theoretical sentences. On his view, only ought-sentences that expressed *hypothetical* demands fitted Husserl's analysis. For instance, the hypothetical ought-sentence (a)

a) If you want to ride a horse well, you ought to be able to control it, sit tight, etc.

indeed presupposed the theoretical, non-normative sentence (b)

b) Riding a horse well is possible only if one is able to control the horse, sit tight, etc.

However, *categorical* ought-sentences demanded a different analysis. The categorical ought-sentence (a′)

a′) The warrior ought to be courageous

was not based upon the theoretical sentence (b′) . . .

b′) It is part of the concept of the good warrior that he is courageous.

In the case of categorical ought-sentences, the order of presupposition was the other way around: the non-normative sentence (b′) derived its justification or meaning from the normative (a′) (1909: 242). To model the relation between (a′) and (b′) on the relation between (a) and (b)

> would be to practise moral philosophy in a Socratic fashion, i.e. it would imply a one-sided intellectualistic interpretation of the concept of value. Instead, the categorical demand that tells the warrior to be courageous is a demand that comes from her consciousness of duty, and it is the fulfilment of this demand which makes the value predicate 'good' applicable.
>
> (Kroner 1909: 242)

Kroner thought that the case of logic was similar to the case of morals. The highest logical norm was something like (a″)

a″) Every reasoner ought to think what is true

and this norm was primary with respect to (b″)

b″) It is part of the concept of the good reasoner that she thinks what is true.

And this analysis of the most basic logical norm also applied to all other logical norms (1909: 242). Thus, for instance, the non-normative sentence (b‴)

b''') Abiding by the Principle of Non-Contradiction is part of the notion 'thinking what is true'

was secondary with respect to (a''')

a''') Every reasoner ought to think what is true, and thus, among other things, she ought to abide by the Principle of Non-Contradiction.

The Southwest German neo-Kantians were not alone in opposing Husserl's arguments against normative antipsychologism. Rickert and Kroner were joined by Wilhelm Schuppe (1901: 18), Julius Schultz (1903), Heinrich Maier (1914: 313–38) and Johannes Volkelt (1918: 395).

For example, Schultz too repudiated Husserl's idea that normative sentences or disciplines depend upon theoretical sentences or sciences:

> our logician pretends that a normative sentence can be turned into a theoretical sentence by means of a simple transformation. 'An *A* ought to be *B*' he reformulates as 'only an *A* which is *B* has the attribute *C*'; and then he claims that the resulting sentence is purely theoretical and contains no normative element. That is really a curious sleight of hand! The conjurer shows us an empty hat, shakes it and then pulls – to our astonishment – a few piglets or a bouquet of roses out of the hat. Does not the credulous audience realise that the normative element has simply slid from the 'ought' of the first sentence into the '*C*' of the second?
>
> (Schultz 1903: 13)

Schultz regarded Husserl's pure logic as 'a stillbirth':

> No really, that would be a sad theoretical discipline that ran alongside the rule-giving discipline [i.e. normative logic] as if it were its shadow. The latter would say, for instance, 'deduce according to mode X', and the first would echo: 'the mode X is correct here.' On such meals the newborn pure logic will not be able to nourish itself! . . . Give us milk, Mr Husserl! Only a few drops! Otherwise your child will starve to death in front of your own eyes'!
>
> (1903: 14)

Schultz thus rejected the idea that a Husserlian pure logic provided the foundations for normative logic. As Husserl's most aggressive critic saw it, norms of logic needed a justification only when one started to have doubts about their validity. And under such circumstances one could supply justification in only two ways: either one showed that a given rule was a necessary product of one's biological and psychological makeup, or one showed that the given norm was central to scientific knowledge. But whichever of the two ways one happened to choose, Schultz contended, one did not thereby obtain necessary truths. Necessary foundations were out of the question because knowledge about our brains was empirical, and because scientific knowledge was revisable in all its parts (1903: 23).

The distinction between real and ideal laws (H4)

Many repudiations of H4 were inseparable from criticisms of other key ideas of Husserl's *Prolegomena*. Here I shall focus mainly on objections to Husserl's distinction between real laws (*Realgesetze*) and ideal laws (*Idealgesetze*). I shall summarise attacks on the act–content distinction, on truths-as-such and on Husserl's notion of self-evidence in the context of objections to H8 and H9.

The distinction between the real laws (of the empirical sciences) and the ideal laws (of logic and mathematics) was criticised in very general terms by Paul Natorp (1901: 282) and Dimitri Michaltschew (1909: 83). Other critics went into much greater detail. Several commentators maintained that H4.1, i.e. Husserl's argument that logical laws could not be psychological laws since the latter but not the former were inexact, was a *petitio principii* (Heim 1902: 27; Heymans 1905: 32–3; Lapp 1913: 53; Schlick 1910a: 409; 1918: 128). Schlick put the objection most succinctly:

> One sees immediately that one might with equal right infer the opposite [of Husserl's H4.1]: since logical structures, infer-ences, judgements and concepts undoubtedly result from psychological processes, we are entitled to infer from the existence of logical rules that there are perfectly exact psychological laws as well ... The proponent of 'absolute' logic cannot defend his position simply by claiming that all psychological laws are vague; for this amounts to a *petitio principii*.
>
> (Schlick 1910a: 409)

Schlick rejected the vagueness assumption even for those psychological laws that were not (also) logical: 'all processes in nature and mind occur according to laws, and these laws are without exceptions, just like the rules of formal logic. The laws are not inexact, our knowledge of them is insufficient – this is a huge difference' (1918: 128).

Heymans put the same objection slightly differently:

> It occurs in all inductive sciences that some of their parts . . . reach the deductive stage earlier than others and thus cease to be sciences of fact and become sciences of concepts (think, for instance, of the theory of gravitation in physics and astronomy). In an analogous way, within inductive psychology, some lawful relations (for instance those between . . . recognising and rejecting a contradiction) can be discovered earlier than others, and can be used as a starting point for deductive constructions.
>
> (Heymans 1905: 33)

Some of Husserl's critics also discarded H.4.2, i.e. they rejected the idea that laws of nature were probable and known by induction, whereas laws of logic were outside the realm of probability and known a priori. As concerned laws of nature, Moritz Schlick (1910a) and Willy Moog (1919) objected that not all laws of nature were merely probable. Schlick made this point by accusing Husserl once again of a *petitio principii*: 'He who regards logical principles as exact laws of thought [and thus as laws of nature] will of course deny that *all* laws of nature are merely probably valid' (1910a: 410). Moog held that Husserl's view of laws of nature was wrong even in the case of the physical sciences:

> There certainly are psychological and physical laws which have only an approximate validity. However, in the case of a law of nature like the law of gravity, it is inadequate to speak of a mere probability of its validity. It is equally wrong to restrict the natural sciences to the inductive method. Even though in the realm of the empirical sciences induction is more important than deduction, in the natural sciences inductive and deductive methods complement each other.
>
> (Moog 1919: 10)

Moreover, Moog felt that Husserl

confuses the material content of laws of nature with their meaning and sense. Even though a law of nature relates to the empirical world, has empirical content and is discovered empirically, a law of nature nevertheless does not have to be merely empirical. It can contain an a priori core . . . Neither is a law *for* the empirical world necessarily an empirical law, nor does a science that relates to the empirical world have to be a genuine [natural] science.

(1919: 13)

Husserl's characterisation of logical laws as known a priori met with even more opposition. According to Gerardus Heymans, all that epistemology could say, for the time being, with respect to a logical law such as the Principle of Non-Contradiction was that '*probably* all human beings reject contradiction' (1905: 66). Our knowledge of logical laws is more probable than that of other psychological laws only 'because we experiment, throughout our life, daily and every hour, with these elementary relations between phenomena of consciousness' (1905: 33).

Wilhelm Jerusalem was ready to admit that we are surer of the truth of mathematical and logical laws than we are of the truth of physical and biological laws. Nevertheless, he remained unwilling to treat mathematical and logical laws as known a priori. Mathematical and logical laws seemed more reliable because they 'are derived from judgements that have always proven to be true'. Moreover, Jerusalem suggested that 'psychologicists' like himself would proceed on the hypothesis that laws of logic were laws of nature:

We look upon ourselves as a part of nature. And thus we believe that the laws according to which our mental life develops, and which regulate our mental life, are laws of nature. Therefore we also assume that mathematical and logical laws too are laws of nature and that they are known not a priori but through experience. And so we seek to find the empirical origin of these laws. If we do not immediately succeed in this endeavour, we continue to try . . . That we are part of nature and that our mental development happens according to laws of nature, this for us is no dogma but a rule of method. And we follow this rule as long as it proves to be fruitful. *We* infer: no law of nature is known a priori. Logical laws are laws of nature. Logical laws are not known a priori. –

Husserl reasons completely differently. His syllogism goes as follows: no law of nature can be known a priori. Logical laws can be known a priori. Logical laws are no laws of nature. – But his minor premise is, for Husserl, not a rule of method but an arbitrarily posited dogma. He does not allow anyone to question this dogma.

(Jerusalem 1905: 103)

In the context of their objections to Husserl's conception of logical laws as laws known a priori, some authors also explained their own views on how our knowledge of logical laws is to be characterised. These authors tried to characterise this knowledge as being neither inductive nor a priori.

Julius Schultz suggested that one should start out in logic by following the example of geometry and construct different logical formal systems almost arbitrarily. The starting point could be different axioms that had on occasion been regarded as necessary. However, in a second step, one had to make a choice between different systems:

And it is here that *facts* of experience will be decisive. First, the 'true' logic will have to be based upon the general constitution of the human species; and second, it had better be necessary for existing sciences. In this way logical sentences are *not deduced from* these facts (that would indeed be absurd). Instead, we *test* the arbitrarily constructed tables of the a priori *with the help of* those facts. Only in this sense do psychology and the critique of science justify logic; and a justification in *this* sense does not lead to any inner contradiction.

(Schultz 1903: 29)

Ernst Dürr (1903), Hans Cornelius (1906), Leonard Nelson (1908), Wilhelm Schuppe (1901) and Christoph Sigwart ([1904] 1921) all agreed, *pace* Husserl, that human knowledge of logical laws was not a priori. According to Nelson, Husserl's denial that logical laws could be discovered and justified by psychology was based on an oversight. Only a psychological study of the human mind could show that the basic logical laws were the conditions of the possibility of our experience. Husserl overlooked that this proof did not *deduce* logical laws from psychological laws (1908: 170). Sigwart claimed that only the psychological analysis of our self-consciousness could lead to the discovery of logical necessity: 'If contradictions did not appear as factually impossible in our real, concrete train of thought, how could we ever come to deem them impossible?' (1904: 24). And Schuppe and Dürr denied that the distinction between a priori knowledge and inductive knowledge was exhaustive:

> The received opposition between empirical and a priori knowledge is rather unclear. By 'empirical knowledge' one understands sentences arrived at via induction. The opposite here is deduction . . . But by 'empirical knowledge' one also means something that is opposed to fiction and hypothesis: to become conscious of something that is given . . . That there is a salty substance is something no one can deduce a priori; it is knowledge based on experience. But this knowledge is not gained inductively; it is simply found . . . The objects of logic, even though they are not found in sense perception, are similar. They owe their being known to the reflection of thinking upon itself . . . And in so far as this coming to know [of logical determinations] is based upon finding something within the given, this coming to know can be called an experience.
> (Schuppe 1901: 14; cf. Dürr 1903: 543; similarly Cornelius 1906: 406)

As concerns H4.3, Schlick (1910a) challenged Husserl's claim that laws of logic did not imply the existence of matters of fact. Schlick maintained that psychological acts of judgement and logical sentences were intertwined, such that the logical sentence and its truth

> can never be found independently of the act of judgement; the logical sentence is included in the latter and results from it via abstraction . . . the logical sentence has its place only *in* the mental experience and does not exist outside it in any sense. The two cannot be separated; the judgement as logical structure, as 'ideal meaning' . . . comes to be, once one abstracts, within the real experience of judging, from all individual and temporal elements. And even though one can abstract from all individual-psychological factors, one cannot abstract from the psychological in general. In other words, one cannot understand logical sentences as structures without psychological quality. *Pace* Husserl, logical sentences imply the existence of experiences of judging. For if we take away, from any chosen judgement, everything which is psycho-

logical, we are left only with the matter of fact that the judgement expresses and upon which it is based.

(Schlick 1910a: 405; cf. Eisler 1907: 18)

Finally, I need to introduce two authors who censured Husserl for setting the ideal laws of logic too sharply apart from the real laws of human psychology. (We shall return to objections of this kind below and treat them at greater length.) Joseph Geyser, otherwise a strong advocate of Husserl's antipsychologism, missed in the *Prolegomena* an explanation of

how it comes to be that the soul's actual creation of thought processes leads, in general, to results that conform to the logical laws and norms ... there is no alternative to the explanation that somehow the logical realm gains *causal influence* upon thought processes. In so far as Husserl completely rejects any such causal influence, there remains a lacuna in his argument against the psychologicists.

(Geyser 1916: 226)

Melchior Palágyi went further and proposed that Husserl's sharp division between real and ideal laws led to relativism. Given the Husserlian view that logical laws were 'truth stars', outside space and time and totally remote from human thinking,

it is incomprehensible how our thought could reach a truth, a falsehood or any content whatsoever; after all, these contents are governed by ideal laws that have nothing in common with those real laws that govern, in a causal fashion, the coexistence and succession of real acts of thinking. In brief, knowledge of the truth would thus become impossible.

(Palágyi 1902: 42)

Palágyi found Husserl's assumption that the world of facts is governed by the principle of causality even more absurd. As Palágyi saw it, the principle of causality was itself an ideal law. And thus Palágyi could argue that Husserl was confused about the whole distinction between real and ideal laws:

In Husserl's conceptualisation, both kinds of laws blend into one another in such a way that one cannot take seriously the alleged unbridgeable difference between the two. But how then does Husserl differ from the 'psychologicists' whose unforgivable mistake is supposed to be their inability to distinguish correctly between real and ideal laws?

(1902: 46)

The psychological interpretation of logical principles (H5)

Philosophers who advocate psychological approaches to logic will naturally also question H5, Husserl's rejection of psychological interpretations of logical principles. However, only one author, Moritz Schlick (1910a), challenged Husserl's criticism of 'psychologistic' reformulations of the Principle of Non-Contradiction directly. As already seen above, Schlick held that logical sentences and acts of judging could not be separated from one another. From this it followed, according to Schlick, that Husserl's critique of Spencer's psychological reformulation of the Principle of Non-Contradiction missed its mark:

According to Spencer this principle is 'simply a generalisation of the universal experience that some mental states are directly destructive of other states'. This is completely right as long as one takes 'mental states' to refer to the right kind of conscious processes and as long as one takes into account that Spencer does not, of course, try to explain the factual effectiveness of the principle in thought. He just tries to explain how we arrive at the knowledge of his formulation and how we arrive at the knowledge of the validity of his formulation. Husserl only quotes the sentence that follows the above quotation, namely 'that the appearance of any positive mode of consciousness cannot occur without excluding a correlative negative mode; and that the negative mode cannot occur without excluding the correlative positive mode'. Husserl laments that this sentence is far from being a correct representation of the Principle of Non-Contradiction, and that it is a mere tautology. However, one cannot accuse Spencer of a serious mistake here, and one cannot accuse him of having missed the tautological character of his formulation. This is because Spencer himself continues . . . : 'the antithesis of positive and negative being, indeed, merely an expression of this experience'. The meaning of Spencer's formulation as a whole is not tautological; only the sentence that Husserl quotes and reproves is tautological.

(Schlick 1910a: 408)

Fallacies as counterexamples to psychological interpretations of logical laws (H7)

H7 was directed mainly against the Dutch psychologist and philosopher Gerardus Heymans. Husserl's main argument against a psychological interpretation of the laws of syllogistics was roughly the following inference:

> If the laws of syllogistics were (hardwired) psychological laws of thought, then no human reasoner could ever deviate from these laws.
> Human reasoners commit fallacies, i.e. they deviate from the laws of syllogistics.
>
> ---
>
> The laws of syllogistics are not (hardwired) psychological laws of thought.

In his reply, Heymans challenged Husserl's claim that fallacies were deviations from the laws of syllogistics. As Heymans saw it, someone who did not derive the right conclusion from given premises was confused about the meaning of the major, middle or minor terms, not lacking knowledge of the inference schemes. In the case of fallacies the causes of the deviation from the laws of syllogistics were

> as it were, *prior to* the thought processes. The premises are not the right ones, or are not clearly grasped or wrongly understood; but a principal difference in laws of thought [between laws of thought in the cases of correct and incorrect inferring] cannot be claimed to exist ... As concerns the question whether there are cases that can only be explained by assuming such a difference, one might say that the burden of proof is on the side of those who claim that there are such cases. As long as such cases have not been firmly established, the theory of knowledge can rest content with accepting the fact that people think according to logical laws.
>
> (Heymans 1905: 69)

Essentially the same reply was also suggested by Julius Schultz: 'the laws of thought do not lose their power over our brains when the common fallacies occur; fallacies are due to mistakes of memory or comprehension, they are due to mistakes that distort the meaning of the premisses' (1903: 26–7).

Scepticism, relativism and anthropologism (H8.1 and H8.2)

The core of Husserl's critique of psychologism was the following argument:

Sceptical relativism is self-refuting.
Psychologism amounts to sceptical relativism.

Psychologism is self-refuting.

Before turning to the critics' response to the second premise and the conclusion of this argument, it is worth mentioning that several authors also questioned the first premiss.

Doubts about Husserl's charge that relativism and scepticism were self-refuting doctrines were first expressed by Paul Natorp (1901). In his review of the *Prolegomena* Natorp hinted at the possibility that Husserl's arguments against relativism and scepticism were guilty of a *petitio*:

> [For Husserl] scepticism is . . . absurd. (But perhaps only for those who want strictly valid theories at all costs. The sceptic might say that he too wants such theories, but that he feels that they are an impossible ideal . . .). Husserl then studies scepticism and sceptical relativism in its individualistic form; he claims that 'as soon as this position is formulated, it is already refuted' – at least for those who understand the objectivity of logic. (But this is precisely what the sceptic denies.)
>
> (Natorp 1901: 274)

More detailed criticisms of Husserl's – and Rickert's (1892, 1904) – 'refutations' of scepticism and relativism were provided by H. Aschkenasy (1909), Hans Kleinpeter (1913: 45–6), Hugo Renner (1902: 4–5; 1905: 158–61) and Julius Schultz (1903).

For example, Aschkenasy (1909) contested Husserl's claim that the notion of a mind which did not abide by logical laws was nonsensical. While Aschkenasy granted that one could not form a '*clear idea*' (*klare Vorstellung*) of a consciousness with a different logic, he argued that philosophers were nevertheless justified to form the '*concept*' of such a consciousness:

> Epistemology has the right to operate with concepts that cannot, without contradiction, be realised in a clear idea . . . Such a concept is, for instance, the notion of the transcen-

dental object, i.e. the notion of a being which is independent of consciousness. Any attempt to represent the transcendental object in a mental idea leads straight into a contradiction. After all, it is part of the concept of consciousness that all its contents are immanent. The same observation applies to the concept of the epistemological [transcendental] subject. It cannot be thought, either. This is because the epistemological subject is meant to be a subject that can never become an object.

(Aschkenasy 1909: 393–4)

Moreover, Aschkenasy contended that the relativist could, without contradiction, deny the claim that logic, i.e. 'the norm', was absolute. All the relativist had to insist on was that even though 'every fact is justified by and through the norm, the norm itself can never be justified'. In the debate between the relativist and the absolutist, Aschkenasy suggested, the burden of proof was on the side of the absolutist:

> The relativist objects to the absolutist as follows: 'All you can rely upon is the fact that the norm happens to exist. But if you go further and claim that the norm is valid without condition, then I shall wait until you have proven this claim. But in fact you cannot establish this claim without arguing in a circle by proving the norm through the norm. And thus I cannot accept that the norm is the unconditioned presupposition of all consciousness.'

(1909: 397)

However, Aschkenasy's relativist did not claim that there could be a different truth, and that he could conceive of a different logic in any detail. He merely defended the possibility of a consciousness that was not governed by our logic:

> The relativist says this: 'Truth, i.e. reality, is that which forces me in a certain direction, and it is that which I cannot escape in so far as I come to know. There is only *one* truth, for I call "truth" all that which coerces me in this way . . . But I can posit – conceptually – the possibility that this coercion might not exist for a different consciousness. What I postulate in this way is *toto genere* different from what I find in my consciousness; and therefore the notion of truth is not applicable to the different consciousness that I posit. I thus do not claim that

76

a different truth is possible; for we can speak of truth only when we presuppose the very norm [i.e. the logic] that I am negating right now.'

(1909: 399)

Julius Schultz was especially concerned about the following argument of Husserl's *Prolegomena*:

If truth were relative to, and thus dependent upon, the human species, then, if the human species did not exist, there would be no truth. But then it would be *true* that no truth exists. And thus truth cannot be relative to, and dependent upon, the human species.

Schultz found this argument utterly confused:

I smell scholasticism! What do we mean when we say: 'in this or that case there would be no truth'? We hardly mean: 'there would *exist* the truth that, in that case, no truth *exists*'. This truth *exists now,* for *me* who happens to have a human constitution and who imagines this unreal possibility. The *present* truth states that, without subjects that are able to judge, there would be no judgement and no truth, but our opponent twists this present truth into the *hypothetical* truth that under certain conditions there would be no truths. Following Husserl's recipe one might as well argue: if no speaker existed, there would be no sentences; but then the sentence that no sentences exist would still exist.

(Schultz 1903: 31)

The independence theory of truth (H8.3 and H9.2)

Central to Husserl's attack on psychologism as a form of sceptical relativism was his assumption that truths-as-such existed, i.e. that truths existed that were independent of whether or not they were ever grasped by any reasoner. Schlick (1910a) baptised this assumption 'the independence theory of truth'. A considerable number of critics turned against this theory. (Brief rejections that I shall not take up here were Brentano ([1911] 1959: 180–1) and Gomperz (1908: 24–5).)

Since Husserl provided the clearest statement of the independence theory of truth in the context of his criticism of Christoph Sigwart, it seems only fair to start the summary of repudiations with this author. In the *Prolegomena* Husserl disagreed with Sigwart's claim that no judgement could be true unless it was actually thought by someone. Husserl regarded it as part of the meaning of the law of gravity that the law was true for all times, i.e. even prior to its discovery and regardless of whether it was ever formulated by any intellect.

Sigwart responded by accusing Husserl of conflating truth and reality:

> In the original sense of the terms, only assertions or opinions can be true or false. And assertions or opinions necessarily presuppose thinking subjects who entertain the opinions or utter the assertions. To postulate 'sentences' as independent essences is sheer mythology. In so far as Husserl speaks of 'contradictory facts' that cannot both be true, he conflates 'true' and 'real'. And thus Husserl lapses into the same conceptual confusion that the German Criminal Code is guilty of when it speaks of . . . 'pretence of false facts'. . . Only an opinion, a report about a fact, can be false. But a fact is simply there . . . When no judgements have been made, then there is nothing of which 'true' or 'false' could be predicated. Of course, the planets did move, already long before Newton, in a way that conforms to the law of gravity. However, before Newton formulated his theory . . . no true sentence about these movements existed within human knowledge. After Newton formulated the law of gravity as a sentence, this sentence became, due to its content, true for the past as well.
> (Sigwart [1904] 1921: 23)

Sigwart's critical footnote was expanded into a long article by his student Heinrich Maier (1914). Maier distinguished between two senses in which 'true' and 'false' could be predicated of judgements. Prior to Newton, the law of gravity was merely *hypothetically* or possibly true, i.e. it *would have been* true had it been pronounced. But 'only those judgements can be called *categorically* true which actually figure in acts of judging'. Put differently, for Maier truth was a relation between a 'transcendently given' fact and a judgement figuring within an act of judging. And thus it made no sense to speak of truth when one *relatum* was absent: 'It is true that the earth already circled the sun before Copernicus. But when understanding the words precisely, no one can seriously claim that the judgement "the earth circles around the sun" *had been* true prior to Copernicus' (1914: 324; cf. Schultz 1903: 25; 1907: 34–5).

Schlick followed Sigwart and accused Husserl of a conflation of 'truth' and 'reality': 'There is no truth of judgements such that this truth is independent of the judgements' existence in mental acts. Only the *facts* upon which true judgements are based are independent of us' (1910a:.403). However, Schlick went further than Sigwart by seeking an explanation for Husserl's alleged conflation:

> The mistake of the independence theory is based upon a fallacious distinction between ideas and objects of ideas. In the case of concrete ideas, say ideas of [physical] objects that I can [literally] grasp, this distinction makes sense; after all, I distinguish between the book lying in front of me on the table and my idea of that book. But, in the case of abstract ideas, object and content coincide, i.e. the object of the idea is nowhere to be found, except within that very idea. And thus logical sentences and acts of judging are absolutely inseparable.
>
> (Schlick 1910a: 407)

Husserl's distinction between the act of judging and the content of judgements was attacked by other critics as well. Wilhelm Jerusalem introduced his objection in the context of a defence of species relativism. Jerusalem focused especially on Husserl's claim that 'the same content of a judgement cannot be true for one species and false for another' ([1900] 1975: §36). Jerusalem replied:

> If the two species in question are totally differently organised, or 'constituted', then there are no contents of judgements that are identical for both. For some purposes one can distinguish between the act and content of a judgement, by reflecting on, or attending to, one or another of the two. But the act and the content cannot be separated in such a way that the one could remain constant while the other is changed. The act and the content of a judgement penetrate each other completely and every change in the act leads to a change in the content . . . Thus it is not absurd to restrict truth to human knowledge; what *is* absurd is rather to speak of identical contents of judgements in the case of differently organised species.
>
> (Jerusalem 1905: 104)

In the same context Jerusalem also accused Husserl of conflating 'truth' and 'reality' and claimed that the objectivity of
truth referred not to its ideality but rather to its 'intersubjectivity'
(1905: 109).

The earliest objector to the act–content distinction was Melchior
Palágyi (1902). Palágyi concerned himself foremost with constructing examples where a strict division between the act and the
content of a judgement would be impossible:

> Let us investigate, for instance, a sentence like 'I am thinking
> now' . . . Or let us study the combination of the sentences 'I
> am thinking now that I am thinking now'. In this [latter] case
> I reflect on my thinking with an act of thinking. How can it
> be possible to abstract from my thinking – when my thinking
> is the content of my thinking? I feel justified to claim that in
> such a sentence abstracting from the thinking person and
> her thought is impossible precisely because that from which
> we are asked to abstract forms the content of the sentence.
> And thus I have shown that Bolzano's and Husserl's demand
> that we should think the content of a judgement indepen-
> dently of the thinking act of a person cannot be fulfilled in
> such cases.
>
> (Palágyi 1902: 28–9)

Palágyi did not deny that the temporal act of thinking could be
distinguished 'from the sense that resides within it and that remains
the same for all times'. His point was rather 'that the nontemporal
sense is so linked to the temporal act that if the temporal act did
not exist then the nontemporal sense would not have any validity'
(1902: 29).

With Palágyi originated a further line of attack against Husserl's
independence theory of truth. According to this criticism, the
independence theory of truth led to relativism, scepticism and
agnosticism (cf. Michaltschew (1909: 93) and Lapp (1913: 42–64)).
Palágyi was especially upset about Husserl's claim (directed against
both Erdmann and Sigwart) that there could be species that were
mistaken about everything: 'But how could we then exclude the
possibility that we humans are such a species . . . ? We see where
the pursuit of Bolzano's ideas leads us. Husserl takes Bolzano's
mistaken thought of 'truths-as-such' very seriously and thus he ends
up in an incredible scepticism' (1902: 61).

Yet another objection to truths-as-such was suggested by Karl

Heim (1902: 8) and taken up by Michaltschew (1909: 397). Heim attacked the notion of possibility invoked when Husserl spoke of truths-as-such as 'ideal possibilities'. Husserl allowed for truths that might never be known, i.e. he allowed for possibilities that would never become actual. However, for Heim there simply were no such possibilities:

> [Husserl's] epistemology is correct only if it is logically justified to speak of mere possibilities that can never become actualities. The claim that something is possible, i.e. the claim that something can be present in consciousness, makes logical sense only if this something were already actual in someone's consciousness, or else if it is claimed that it will be actual in someone's consciousness in the future . . . Thus it is senseless to speak of mere possibilities that will never be actual.
>
> (Heim 1902: 8)

As will be recalled, Husserl's equation of psychologism with species relativism was directed mainly against Sigwart and Erdmann. I started this section with Sigwart's reply, but Erdmann's response still has to be reported. In a footnote to the second edition of his *Logische Elementarlehre* (1907), Erdmann regretted having been misunderstood by Husserl. Erdmann felt that a detailed discussion of Husserl's views would be fruitless in so far as his own and Husserl's views were too far apart: 'In such cases the decision does not lie in the hands of the conflicting parties, it lies with the neutral thinkers of the younger generation' (1907: 533).

However, Erdmann's argument for the hypothetical necessity of logic in the second edition differed slightly from the argument in the first edition. In an additional, new paragraph Erdmann linked his thesis to theological concerns and to a critique of rational psychology:

> We are unable to prove that the basic logical laws of our thinking . . . are the conditions and norms of all possible thinking. Thus we have to allow for the real possibility of a thinking that differs from ours. This concession has to be made, first of all, because science is not meant to exclude the religious convictions of religious consciousness . . . [i.e. science has no right to interfere with the belief that God may have a different logic]. Second, this concession also has to be made in so far as . . . it is no more than an empirical

81

experience *that* we think and an empirical experience of *how* we think. This experience is not changed by the fact that *we* are indeed bound to the conditions of our thinking, and that our valid thinking has to submit to the logical norms that we formulate. We are not even able to claim that our thinking will always be bound to these conditions and norms, for we have no right to assume that our thinking will be eternal. The days of the human species on earth are numbered, too . . . And even if the human species did not just belong to one period of the development of the earth or the solar system, even then we should not dare proclaim our thinking invariable. We could proclaim such invariability only if we were able to directly grasp the essence of our soul as an independent, invariable substance – in the way assumed by a rational psychology – and if we could deduce the invariability of our thinking. But this we are unable to do as long as we hold on to the idea that psychology can determine the stock and connections of psychological life processes only via observation – like any other science of facts. Finally, our thinking has developed out of less complicated forms of mental representation, and thus we have no right to rule out further development towards higher complexity of thought, a development that calls for different norms. Be it added, however, . . . that we have no reason to expect such further development . . . But here we are concerned not with probability but with possibility.

(Erdmann 1907: 531–2)

To conclude this presentation to criticisms to Husserl's independence theory of truth, it remains to be mentioned that there were also some philosophers who, by and large, agreed with Husserl's views but felt that these views could be argued for more precisely. Both Max Frischeisen-Köhler (1912: 15–17) and Richard Hönigswald (1914a: 80–3) fall into this category (cf. also Koppelmann 1913–18: 10–17).

Self-evidence (H8.3 and H9.3)

In Husserl's criticism of psychologism, the category of self-evidence figured in two ways. In the context of H8.3, Husserl claimed self-evidence for his thesis according to which no other species could have a different logic, and he countered doubts directed against this self-evidence with the rhetorical question: 'If we were not allowed to trust self-evidence any more, how could we make, and reasonably defend, any assertions at all?' (§40). In the context of H9.3, Husserl stressed that purely logical sentences said nothing about self-evidence and its conditions, and he rejected the use of self-evidence as a criterion of truth: 'One feels inclined to ask what the authority of that feeling [of self-evidence] is based upon, how that feeling can guarantee the truth of a judgement, how it can "mark a statement with the stamp of truth", "announce" its truth, etc.' (§51). In this second context, Husserl granted self-evidence a role only in the following 'ideal' sense: to every truth-as-such corresponded, ideally or conceptually, a possible judgement of some possible (human or nonhuman) intellect in which that truth was experienced as self-evident (§50).

Critics of Husserl's view on self-evidence attacked one or both of these lines of thought. In other words, some criticised the use of self-evidence in H8.3, while some objected to the rejection of self-evidence as a criterion of truth in H9.3. Others claimed that Husserl's views of self-evidence in H8.3 and H9.3 contradicted one another. And finally, several authors found Husserl's own use of the category of self-evidence simply confusing, unclear, metaphysical and psychologistic.

Natorp warned that Husserl's sentence 'truth is an idea that becomes an actual experience when instantiated in an evident judgement' could easily be 'misunderstood as metaphysics'. At the same time, Natorp expressed doubts whether such an interpretation would indeed be a misunderstanding: 'Or *should* it be understood as metaphysics?' (1901: 276–7). The notion of self-evidence in Husserl and his followers reminded Theodor Ziehen of 'intuition and intellectual perception in Schelling's sense' (1920: 307). And Wilhelm Wundt (1910b) lamented that Husserl never provided a clear definition of self-evidence.

According to Wundt, Husserl never gave satisfactory definitions of his key terms: in the *Logische Untersuchungen* 'every definition amounts to the explanation that the concept in question is a specific experience which cannot be defined at all. This observation also holds for that concept which plays the most central role in Husserl's logical investigations: the concept of self-evidence' (1910b: 611). Wundt suggested the following explanation for Husserl's alleged inability to define self-evidence:

Even stranger than the failure of psychologism is the fact that *logicism* [i.e. Brentano's and Husserl's position] fares no better. The latter fares no better despite its emphatic appeal to the self-evidence of logical laws. This is because logicism's appeal [to the self-evidence of logical laws] moves in a continuous circle: it declares logical laws self-evident, but then again it bases self-evidence upon the validity of logical laws. In order to escape this circle, logicism can do no better than explain that self-evidence is an ultimate fact which cannot be further defined. And since a fact can only be regarded as existing if it is somehow given within a perception [*Anschauung*, intuition], it is understandable that logicism treats immediate perception and indefinability as equivalent modes of justification . . . However, since every immediate perception is a psychological process, the appeal to immediate perception amounts to a relapse into psychologism.'

(Wundt 1910b: 623–5)

Heim, Kleinpeter, Moog and Schultz all felt that Husserl had gone wrong either in claiming self-evidence for his case against the 'psychologistic' sceptic or in employing the category of self-evidence at all. Heim objected that, given Husserl's own theory of the independence of truth, Husserl had no right to appeal to his feeling of self-evidence against the sceptic. Husserl's emphatic insistence on self-evidence 'might just as well be the language of a lunatic who emphatically praises his fixed idea as the only key to knowledge of the truth and who declares that everyone who disagrees is insane' (1902: 18). Moog saw Husserl's reliance on self-evidence as a residue of psychologism and insisted that logic and epistemology needed to make no reference to self-evidence at all (1919: 36). Kleinpeter made the same point more emphatically:

The basis of Husserl's whole philosophy suffers from a dilemma: on the one hand, he rejects all experience and all psychological considerations; on the other hand, he builds his whole system upon a psychological fact that is completely incompetent in logic. Husserl has remained a psychologicist in the worst sense of the term.

(Kleinpeter 1913: 40)

Schultz did not accuse Husserl of psychologism but he too deemed Husserl's reliance on self-evidence a crucial mistake.

According to Schultz one could not trust one's feeling of self-evidence because this feeling had proved to be highly unreliable in the past: 'since many sentences which were once regarded as apodictic have now been recognised as doubtful or mistaken, all evidence has to be taken to court' (1903: 28). For Schultz this court was staffed by biologists, historians and psychologists who worked towards a 'natural history of self-evidence' (1903: 6).

Schultz's last-mentioned suggestion was endorsed by Jerusalem: 'For us psychologicists the fact that the logical and mathematical sentences *seem* a priori self-evident is a problem, too. We seek to solve it through a cumbersome study of the historical development of human beings and mankind' (1905: 95). Jerusalem's criticism of Husserl's theory of self-evidence was directed primarily against Husserl's claim that 'truth is an idea that becomes an actual experience when instantiated in an evident judgement':

> In order to lay the foundations of pure logic, Husserl starts . . . from the fact that we make judgements whose correctness seems to us beyond doubt. He looks for the common feature of these judgements and thus he finds the 'idea of truth'. But he does not understand this 'idea' in the way in which every open-minded scholar will take it, i.e. as a tool of thought that was created by a human mind, as a tool that enables us to conceptualise briefly and intelligibly certain relations between the act and the content of a judgement. Instead, he interprets this idea, which allegedly exists in evident judgements, as an independent entity, as a *prius*, a προτερον τη φυσει, as something that is prior to all judgements, and as something that is the condition of all true judgements . . . Anselm thought he could strictly logically deduce the existence of God from the concept of God as the most perfect being. Husserl's method is similar. It is as if he were arguing: 'The idea of truth is given in the evident judgement. But this idea would not be the idea of truth if it did not guarantee the correspondence between judgements and matters of fact. Therefore the idea of truth which is given in evident judgements must have objective and absolute validity.'
>
> (Jerusalem 1905: 116–17)

Turning from repudiations of Husserl's own reliance on self-evidence to criticisms of his rejection of psychological self-evidence, two critics must be mentioned: Elsenhans and Schlick. (Cf. also Lapp (1913: 57–9) and Volkelt (1918: 287–8).)

Theodor Elsenhans sought to defend psychological self-evidence as '*the ultimate criterion*' in epistemology and logic (1906: 96), and he regarded Husserl as one of the few modern logicians who had tried to present a case against this criterion. However, Elsenhans questioned whether Husserl's formula 'truth is an idea that becomes an actual experience when instantiated in an evident judgement' really amounted to a genuine alternative:

> Do we really get rid of the view of self-evidence as 'a contingently added feeling'? Is there really any other way to speak of 'experience', of 'fit' or of 'actual experience' . . . than to take this experience as the experience of some *individual*, as the *psychological process* that occurs in singular thinking beings? . . . As soon as we regard self-evidence as an 'experience', be it that we regard it as an experience of the 'truth' itself, then the only conceivable place for this experience is *the singular individual.*
>
> (Elsenhans 1906: 97)

Schlick was especially concerned to point out that Husserl's two treatments of self-evidence, in H8.3 and H9.3, contradicted one another. As Schlick saw it, in H9.3 Husserl dismissed the very psychological self-evidence that Husserl himself relied on in his attack on scepticism and psychologism in H8.3 (1910a: 415–16; 1918: 123). In the earlier text, Schlick wrote:

> [Husserl's] absolute, independent truth would be unrecognisable in every sense. Even if it could, through a miracle, enter into the human intellect, how in the world could we recognise the truth as the truth? According to Husserl the criterion is *self-evidence.* At one point he begins a defence of the independence theory with the words: 'The following relation is self-evidently given [*durch Einsicht gegeben*]'; some pages later we read, as if to confirm the earlier claim: 'If we were not allowed to trust self-evidence any more, how could we make, and reasonably defend, any assertions at all?' But this obviously amounts to nothing else than a flight into the theory of self-evidence! It is beyond doubt that in these quoted sentences Husserl advocates 'the real theory of self-evidence', a theory that he himself rejects with the following

drastic words: 'One feels inclined to ask what the authority of that feeling [of self-evidence] is based upon, how that feeling can guarantee the truth of a judgement, how it can "mark a statement with the stamp of truth", "announce" its truth.' Nothing can hide the fact that our author here contradicts himself, not even the appeal to his distinction between the ideal possibility of self-evidence relating to 'sentences' and real self-evidence relating to *acts of judging*. After all, in this context we are dealing with factual, real knowledge of the truth, i.e. with real, psychological self-evidence. In fact it is only this real self-evidence that exists.

(Schlick 1910a: 415)

Thought economics (H10)

To conclude the presentation of objections to Husserl's key assumptions in the *Prolegomena*, it may be mentioned that his criticism of thought economics was also contested. Kleinpeter (1913: 39) remarked only generally that Husserl had failed to understand the central idea of Mach's theory, but Jerusalem went into somewhat greater detail:

An especially instructive example of the dogmatic character of Husserl's argumentation is his criticism of the principle of thought economy, a principle which Mach has formulated . . . [Husserl writes:] 'The ideal validity of the norm is the *precondition* of any sensible talk of thought economy . . . We notice the *hysteron proteron* . . . Pure logic is prior to all thought economy and it is absurd to base the latter on the former.' It is obvious how Husserl's argument goes . . . Why doesn't thought economy explain the origins and the validity of logical laws . . . ? Only because this would conflict with Husserl's dogma of the a priori nature of these laws. We psychologicists believe that logical laws are a result of the development of scientific thought and develop further together with scientific thought. We believe this because it is in agreement with a conception of mental life that has thus far always proven to be true. For us this belief is no dogma but a heuristic rule of method. Nothing shows that logical laws are a priori . . . My reading of Husserl's argument against thought economy suggests to me that the author tries to say this:

'Thought economy is a good, enlightening principle. It is useful for logic. But it cannot be used as a justification of logic because it cannot be found in my logical bible.'

(Jerusalem 1905: 97–8)

FURTHER ACCUSATIONS AND COMMENTS

Up to this point, I have focused on specific objections to particular elements of Husserl's antipsychologism in the *Prolegomena*. A summary of these specific objections does not, however, exhaust the topic of this chapter, i.e. the reception of Husserl's antipsychologism in Germany between 1901 and 1920. What needs to be added to the above summary is an overview of the more general comments and accusations that concerned Husserl's antipsychologistic argument as a whole.

A first frequent general charge was that Husserl's overall argument was unclear, and that Husserl's terminology was too esoteric. Some instances of this accusation we have already encountered above. Of those authors I have not mentioned before, Leo Ssalagoff lamented that Husserl never explained the guiding idea of his philosophy of logic (1911: 188); and Heinrich Lanz complained that Husserl had not given the kind of precise definition of psychologism which would make this philosophical mistake easy to identify in different philosophers (1912: 57).

Second, some authors contended that they had nothing to learn from Husserl's book, or else that some (or all) of Husserl's arguments had been presented before. Of the neo-Kantians, Paul Natorp hinted that Husserl's pure logic was but an insufficient version of neo-Kantian epistemology (1901: 270). He also claimed that Husserl had taken over some central arguments against psychologism from his (i.e. Natorp's) earlier article 'Über objektive und subjektive Begründung der Erkenntnis' (1887) (1901: 274). Privately, Natorp wrote that for the neo-Kantians Husserl's argument was 'an obsolete topic' (Holzhey 1986: 261), and later he publicly voiced the view that the neo-Kantians had 'nothing to learn' from Husserl's criticism (Natorp 1912c: 198). Similiar feelings were variously expressed by Busse, Heidegger, Heim, Jerusalem, Moog, Palágyi, Schuppe, and Wundt (1920). Ludwig Busse (1903: 155) claimed that Husserl's main line of argument could already be found in his book *Philosophie und Erkenntnistheorie* (Busse 1894), and Wilhelm Schuppe (1901: 20) made a similar suggestion with respect to his *Grundriß der Erkenntnistheorie und Logik* (Schuppe 1894). Wilhelm Wundt proposed that a determined rejection of psychologism had already been presented in the 1880s, when the first edition of his *Logik* was published (1920: 264–73). Heim saw Husserl's work foremost as a summary of earlier arguments for and against psychologism (1902: 1). Palágyi (1902: 9) hinted that Husserl had done little else but reformulate the ideas of Bernard Bolzano. Heidegger ([1912] 1978a: 19–20; cf. [1913] 1978b: 64) agreed with Natorp's assessment, but went further in including Frege as an important predecessor of Husserl. Frege's importance was also emphasized by Moog (1919: 7). And finally Wilhelm Jerusalem (1905: 93) took Husserl to task for not acknowledging his debt to Brentano.

Third, Aschkenasy, Dubs, and Natorp suggested that Husserl's list of culprits was not long enough: Aschkenasy (1909: 400–5) missed a critique of Simmel, Dubs (1911: 119–20) an attack on Dührung, Jevons, Kant, Meinong, and Windelband, and Natorp (1901: 227) a study of Lipps, Riehl, Schuppe, and Wundt.

Fourth, and more importantly, more than a dozen authors felt the need to deny emphatically that they, or other members of their respective schools, were advocates of psychologism. These authors can be divided into two groups: those that Husserl had explicitly accused of being psychologicists, and those that he had linked to psychologism without even mentioning their names. Of the first group, Cornelius (1906: 401–2; 1916: 48–9), Erdmann (1907: 32), Höfler (1905: 323), Lipps (1903: 78), Mach ([1904] 1988: 593–4), Meinong (1902: 197; 1907: 143), Sigwart ([1904] 1921: 23) and Wundt (1910b), all denied the charge at least for their own position. The second group consisted of writers that Husserl indirectly associated with psychologism. Husserl wrote in his preface that his antipsychologism became possible only once he had distanced himself from the doctrines of his teachers ([1900] 1975: 7); thus Husserl's teachers, Brentano and Stumpf, as well as their followers, e.g. Höfler, Meinong and Marty were all tied to the positions that Husserl rejected. Moreover, even prior to Husserl's *Logische Untersuchungen* the standard account of contemporary philosophy in turn-of-the-century Germany, volume 3 of Ueberweg and Heinze's *Grundriß der Geschichte der Philosophie*, had already presented the Brentano School under the heading 'psychologism' (1897: 274–6). Small wonder therefore, that all of these philosophers felt the need to stress that they had nothing to do with the relativistic psychologism that Husserl attacked (Brentano ([1911] 1959: 179–81), Höfler (1905: 323); Meinong (1902: 197), Stumpf (1907c: 33)). Husserl had also suggested that much of neo-Kantian philosophy amounted to a psychologism in disguise. Husserl never explained this link in detail but wrote that 'transcendental psychology too is psychology' ([1900] 1975: 102). Neo-Kantian philosophers were obviously angered by this remark. This much can be seen from the fact that both Natorp (1901: 280) and Rickert (1909: 222, 227) quoted this sentence, rejected the accusation and went on to turn the charge of psychologism around, i.e. turned it against Husserl himself.

Fifth, in turning the charge of psychologism (and relativistic scepticism) against Husserl himself, Natorp and Rickert did not stand alone. Indeed the accusation was made by almost twenty authors between 1901 and 1920: Busse (1903), Cornelius (1906), Eisler (1907), Heim (1902), Jerusalem (1905), Kleinpeter (1913), Kroner (1909), Lapp (1913), Maier (1908), Meinong (1913), Michaltschew (1909), Moog (1919), Natorp (1901), Nelson ([1908] 1973a), Palágyi (1902), Rickert (1909), Sigwart ([1904] 1921), Stumpf (1907c), Wundt (1910b). However, different authors disagreed over the question of what Husserl's psychologism (or relativistic scepticism) consisted in. Some regarded Husserl as a psychologicist because he supposedly based his pure logic upon the allegedly psychological notion of self-evidence (Heim 1902: 1, 18; Kleinpeter 1913: 40; Moog 1919: 35; Natorp 1901: 280; Sigwart [1904] 1921: 23; Wundt 1910b: 612). Others claimed that psychologism returned in Husserl's very criticism because of Husserl's idea that laws of logic are laws about ideal beings. Put differently, these authors maintained that any form of Platonism in logic was but a psychologism in disguise (Kroner 1909: 27; Moog 1919: 26–7; Rickert 1909: 195–6). A third group saw Husserl lapse into psychologism, scepticism and relativism because of his distinction between ideal laws and truths on the one hand, and real laws and events on the other. Members of this third group regarded this distinction as psychologistic or relativistic either because they thought that Husserl had failed to explain how ideal laws and truths could ever be known (Michaltschew 1909: 57, 83; Lapp 1913: 64), or because they felt that Husserl had not drawn this divide in a convincing way (Palágyi 1902: 42–55). And finally, according to a number of critics Husserl was a closet psychologicist in so far as he regarded his 'phenomenology', or 'descriptive psychology', as the proper place for foundational studies in logic (Busse 1903: 154; Cornelius 1906: 406; Jerusalem 1905: 131; Maier 1908: 360; Meinong 1913: 502; Nelson [1908] 1973a: 71; Rickert 1909: 227; Stumpf 1907c: 34–5).

Sixth, a number of writers added the further charges of 'scholasticism', 'aristocratic metaphysicism', 'mysticism', 'logicism' and 'formalism' to the accusation of psychologism. Varieties of the first three invectives appeared in Jerusalem (1905: 9), Lapp (1913: 42–3, 52, 59), Maier (1908: 53), Moog (1919: 27, 34), Sigwart ([1904] 1921: 24), Wundt (1910b: 580) and Ziehen (1920: 307); the formalism/logicism charge could be found in Natorp (1901: 281), Palágyi (1902: 1–9), Schultz (1903: 13, 19–20), Uphues (1903: 4) and Wundt (1910b: 516, 603). We have already encountered the accusations of mysticism and scholasticism above. But two examples of the formalism/logicism charge are well worth mentioning.

The formalism charge was developed in greatest detail by Palágyi. According to Palágyi, logic and epistemology were endangered not only by the psychologism of physiologist intruders into philosophy, but equally by formalistic tendencies in modern mathematics (1902: 12). In Husserl's sympathy for modern mathematical treatments of logic, Palágyi welcomed the attempt to free logic and philosophy from psychology but, in that very same sympathy, he also detected a mathematical imperialism: 'As one can see, mathematics is no less selfish than any of the other special sciences; mathematics too wishes to swallow logic completely. Logic is supposed to resolve totally into mathematics, and to this end it is supposed to renounce psychology' (1902: 5).

Wundt's accusation of logicism sought to unmask a different form of imperialism: 'Psychologism wants to turn logic into psychology, logicism wants to turn psychology into logic' (1910b: 516). However, Wundt regarded psychologism and logicism as philosophical positions that easily merged into one another. Modern 'scholastics' like Brentano and Husserl, Wundt alleged, ignored the advances of modern psychology and conceptualised the mind with the help of logical notions. Yet precisely for this reason, their attempts to separate logic from psychology were doomed to fail right from the start. All the scholastics could do was to combine the syllogistic subsumption of concepts with Hegelian dialectical moves through their reliance upon an undefined and unqualified notion of evidence, fall back into a 'nativistic psychologism' (1910b: 623).

CRITICISMS AND ACCUSATIONS: A SUMMARY

Perhaps the easiest way to summarise the various criticisms of, and accusations against, Husserl's attack on psychologism is to present the most significant criticisms in the form of a table (Figure 2). As this table makes clear enough, all ingredients of Husserl's case against psychologism were questioned repeatedly, and by many different authors. Especially Husserl's distinction between ideal and real laws, his independence theory of truth and his theory of self-evidence attracted the attention of his critics. It is also striking that almost half of the authors who commented critically on Husserl's arguments charged him with the very psychologism he had allegedly refuted.

Before leaving the reception of Husserl's case against psychologism, it might be appropriate to point out the significance of this reception for my overall argument in this study.

In this chapter we have returned to a time period in which the 'philosophical fact', i.e. the strong-modality statement

(*) Husserl is to be credited with refuting the psychologism of his German contemporaries

had a rather low modality. Writers between 1901 and 1920 disagreed with every single component of (*): they did not find Husserl's criticism original; they thought that his refutation of all, or parts, of so-called 'psychologism' begged too many questions; they charged Husserl with misconstruing all, or parts, of 'psychologism'; they reproached him for laying false charges against his colleagues; and they blamed him for having relapsed into psychologism himself.

Using the vocabulary introduced in Chapter 2, we might call Husserl's arguments the 'data' of the controversy over psychologism, and thus we might also say that the data of the debate over whether or not Husserl had refuted psychologism were *interpretatively flexible*. Put differently, there was no agreement among German philosophers at the time as to whether Husserl's doctrine, and different writers gave these arguments widely varying interpretations.

To establish the interpretative flexibility of the data at issue in a philosophical controversy is the second stage of a study in the sociology of philosophical knowledge (the first stage being the identification of a philosophical fact). In subsequent chapters I

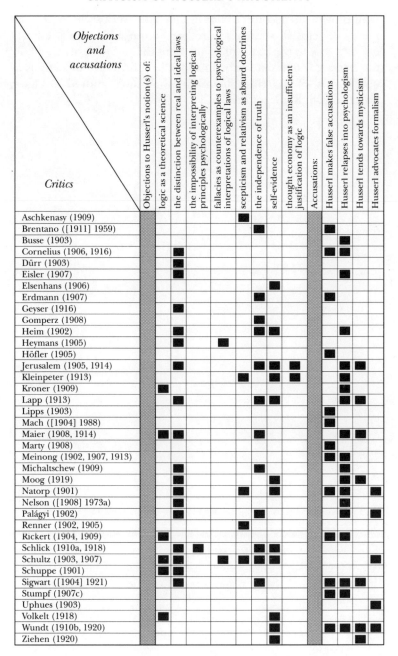

Figure 2 Objections to Husserl's attack on psychologism

shall provide an account of how the debate over psychologism was eventually closed, which closure mechanisms were involved and how (*) rose to the status of a statement that is widely accepted. By the same token, I shall explain why all of the above objections as well as most of the critics themselves were soon ignored and later, not surprisingly, forgotten.

5

VARIETIES OF 'PSYCHOLOGISM' 1866–1930

INTRODUCTION

In the last chapter I documented the way in which Husserl's arguments against psychologism were open to many different interpretations. In this chapter I shall go further and describe the interpretative flexibility of the very term 'psychologism' in German academic philosophy between 1866 and 1930. I shall show that there was no agreement among German philosophers at the time on what exactly constituted psychologism, and thus no consensus on who was to be regarded as a proponent of psychologism.

As will become obvious in what follows, the disagreement over the correct definition of psychologism was closely linked with a consensus on another question. With only very few exceptions, German philosophers agreed that psychologism was a serious philosophical error and that it needed to be exorcised from philosophy once and for all. Strangely enough, the consensus on this point has been completely overlooked by historians of philosophy. For instance, Herbert Schnädelbach claims in his much praised *Philosophy in Germany 1831–1933* that psychologism was the standard orientation of philosophers from the middle of the last century, and that Frege and Husserl were fairly isolated in their campaign against it (Schnädelbach 1984: 99).

In order to correct Schnädelbach's view on the one hand, and in order to display the interpretative flexibility of 'psychologism' on the other hand, I shall present the results of an analysis of about 200 philosophical texts (books and articles) published in Germany and Austria between 1866 and 1931.[1] All these texts use the term 'psychologism': they define the term, accuse other writers of being psychologistic and comment on the need for, or the structure of, the debate over psychologism. Although the procedure is unusual, indeed almost unknown in studies of the history of philosophy, I shall present most of my findings in the form of tables. To present my results in narrative form would make it difficult to convey and document the mass of accusations, criteria and definitions of psychologism. In order to complement the 'at a glance' perspective set out in tables and figures, I shall quote extensively from my sources. Citing these texts at some length will also serve to exemplify the style and tone of the debate.

ACCUSED AND ACCUSERS

In Chapter 4, we witnessed the strange spectacle of Husserl vigorously attacking psychologism or psychologistic tendencies in the thought of his contemporaries, only to be accused in turn of psychologism himself. Yet in being both an accuser and one of the accused, Husserl's situation was not unique in the German-speaking philosophical community during the first two decades of the twentieth century. Indeed, it is hard to find any philosopher during this period who did not share Husserl's fate. All of the major figures as well as their students and followers levelled the charge of psychologism against others, only to be dubbed psychologistic thinkers themselves, according to their colleagues' criteria. In the corpus I have analysed, no fewer than 139 writers are labelled 'psychologicists', and many of them in more than one text. In most cases, calling a philosopher psychologistic implied that his position was erroneous; only a few writers used the term 'psychologism' in a neutral or even positive sense. Most of the alleged 'psychologicists' were contemporaneous German and Austrian philosophers, but some were theologians (like R. Otto), historians (like Lamprecht), linguists (like Steinthal), historical philosophical figures (e.g. Protagoras, Suarez, Hume and Kant), philosophers of the nineteenth century (e.g. Bolzano) or British, French and American philosophers (e.g. Mill, Fouillée and James) (Figure 3).[2]

Obviously, many of these names will not be familiar to the contemporary anglophone reader. I shall not introduce these figures here, as my main purpose at this stage is to emphasise that the list of culprits was very long indeed. Several of the writers accused most often at the time will be discussed in greater detail in subsequent chapters.

Turning from the accused to the accusers, the list of authors

Avenarius	6	Hobbes	2	Otto	1
Bain	4	Höffding	1	Palágyi	1
Baldwin	2	Höfler	4	Petzoldt	1
Beneke	9	Horwicz	1	Protagoras	2
Bergson	1	Hume	8	Reid	1
Berkeley	6	Husserl	21	Richter	1
Bolzano	1	James	4	Rickert	4
Bouterwek	1	Jaspers	1	Riehl	1
Brentano	9	Jerusalem	4	Rosmini	1
Busse	1	Jevons	1	Schiller, F.C.S.	3
Calker	1	Jodl	2	Schlick	1
Cohen	2	Jouffroy	1	Schneider	1
Cohn	2	Kant	8	Schopenhauer	1
Cornelius	9	Kleinpeter	1	Schrader	1
Cousin	1	Kraus	1	Schultz	3
Democritus	1	Kreibig	2	Schuppe	4
Deneke	1	Krug	1	Schwarz	2
Dilthey	4	Külpe	1	Siegel	1
Dittes	1	Kuntze	1	Sigwart	9
Dreßler	1	Laas	1	Simmel	1
Dühring	1	Lachelier	1	Spencer	2
Ehrenfels	1	Lamprecht	1	Spengler	1
Eisenmeyer	1	Lange, C.	1	Spitta	1
Elsenhans	4	Lange, F.A.	3	Stallo	1
Epicurus	1	Lange, K.	1	Steinthal	2
Erdmann	8	Lask	1	Stöhr	2
Fichte	1	Lazarus	2	Stoics	1
Fouillée	1	Liebmann	1	Störring	1
Fowler	1	Lipps	20	Stumpf	7
Frege	1	Locke	6	Suarez	1
Fries	5	Lotze	2	Troxler	1
Frischeisen-Köhler	1	Mach	12	Uphues	2
Gomperz	2	Maier	1	Vaihinger	4
Göring	1	Marty	4	Verworn	1
Groos	1	Meinong	10	Volkelt	1
Gruppe	1	Miklosisch	1	Wahle	1
Hamilton	1	Mill, J.S.	13	Weisse	2
Hartmann, E. von	1	Müller-Freienfels	1	Wenzig	1
Hartley	1	Münsterberg	1	Windelband	2
Herbart	4	Natorp	2	Witasek	3
Herder	1	Nelson	1	Wundt	10
Heymans	11	Nietzsche	1	Zeller	1
Hillebrand	1	Ostwald	1	Ziehen	6

Figure 3 Authors labelled 'psychologicists' and the number of such attributions made by different writers

bringing the psychologism charge against others contains 61 philosophers.[3] Of these accusers, 22 were also numbered among the accused: Busse, Cornelius, Gomperz, Groos, Höfler, Husserl, Jerusalem, Kleinpeter, Külpe, Lipps, Maier, Meinong, Müller-Freienfels, Natorp, Nelson, Palágyi, Rickert, Sigwart, Stumpf, Windelband, Wundt and Ziehen. This does not mean, however, that the remaining 38 (accusers but not directly accused) managed to get off scot-free. The German philosophy of the day divided into fairly distinct schools, and thus all members of a given school could be charged with psychologism simply by calling one of the leading figures of that school a psychologicist. Thus anyone who regarded Rickert as a psychologistic thinker would also see his students Bauch and Kroner in the same light, and anyone who blamed Natorp for his allegedly psychologistic stance would thereby also denounce the philosophical position adopted by Natorp's colleague Cohen.

To bring out this 'guilt by association' aspect of the accusations, I have followed contemporaneous sources, i.e. the different editions of Ueberweg and Heinze (1902, 1906, 1951), which group the philosophers of the time into different schools. Figure 4 depicts the charges and countercharges of psychologism among philosophical schools in the form of a table.

Figure 4 shows that all major philosophical schools in Germany and Austria were involved in the merry-go-round of psychologism accusations and that, with the exception of the Neoscholastics and the followers of Rehmke, no school could escape the charge. Most active as accusers were the neo-Kantians (Marburg and Southwest German Schools), the 'experimentalists', phenomenologists and the Rehmke School. Among those who stood accused, phenomenology had a clear lead, but Wundt, Brentano and Meinong, as well as their students, did not lag far behind.

THE TEMPORAL LIMITS OF THE DEBATE

Examining the temporal distribution of psychologism charges can serve to provide us with something of a first, and rough, indication of the development of the controversy over time (Figure 5).[4] As Figure 5 indicates, the term 'psychologism' (as well as the accusation) made its first appearance as early as 1866. Nevertheless, it was only after Husserl's attack that the term gained popularity and that more and more philosophers set out to find psychologism in the

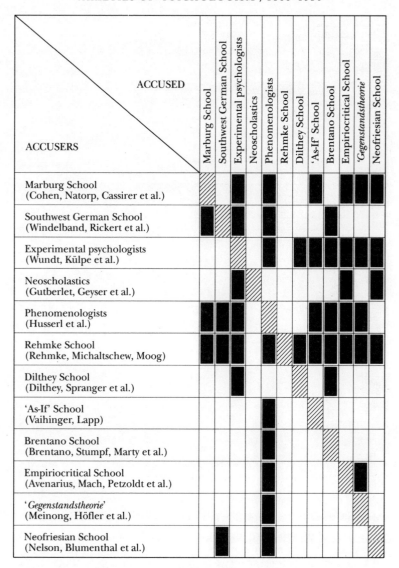

Figure 4 Charges and countercharges of psychologism among philosophical schools

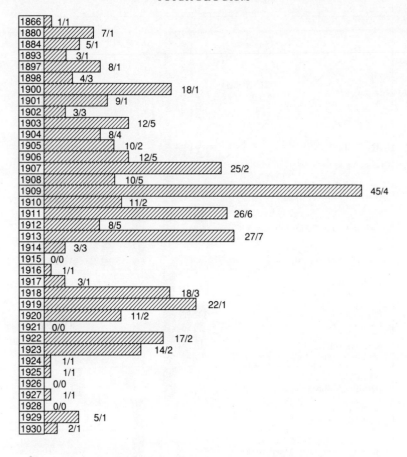

Figure 5 Numbers per year of writers labelled 'psychologistic' and number of texts per year in which such attributions occurred

works of their colleagues. Husserl's influence in giving 'psychologism' wider currency can also be seen from the fact that it was only after Husserl's book came out that the term began to appear in the titles of articles and books. For instance, in 1902 three books were published that carried 'psychologism' in their title, and more were to follow in subsequent years.[5]

Figure 5 also suggests that the hunt for psychologism took place mainly during the period between 1902 and 1914. Of the 80 accusing texts, 53 were published during this period. During the First World War such accusations came to a dramatic halt. The postwar period saw a brief revival of the hunt for psychologicists, but ultimately this revival too came to an end in the late 1920s.

'PSYCHOLOGISM' BEFORE HUSSERL

The term '*Psychologismus*' was first used by the Hegelian Johann Eduard Erdmann in 1866 in his *Die Deutsche Philosophie seit Hegels Tode*, an addition to Erdmann's *Grundriß der Geschichte der Philosophie*. Erdmann suggested the label 'psychologism' for the philosophy of Friedrich Eduard Beneke (Erdmann 1866). As a Hegelian, Erdmann certainly did not agree with Beneke's call for treating psychology as the basis of philosophy, but he did not engage in any detailed criticism of Beneke's philosophy.

Beneke had wanted to replace the philosophical speculations of Fichte, Schelling and Hegel with rigorous philosophical work. If philosophy was to be 'the highest science, the science of sciences' (Beneke 1833: 2), it would have to 'rely on the reality which is given to philosophy, i.e. *inner experience*' (1833: x). Beneke's goal was 'a new psychology' based upon 'a new psychological method' (1833: xv). This new science was to take the natural sciences as its model, but it was to surpass them in the degree of accuracy of its results. That is to say, Beneke held that the possibility of error was smaller in inner experience than in experience that relied upon 'the outer senses' (1833: 14).

Beneke's psychology was meant to study inner experience, analyse this experience into its simplest components and explain complex mental phenomena as resulting from an interplay of these components. Beneke rejected the older doctrines of mental faculties and innate concepts. Rather than simply assuming a faculty like 'understanding' (*Verstand*), psychology was to investigate thought 'in its origins and in its actions, and in its deepest basic factors'. To put it another way, thought was to be studied not as it occurs in the mature and educated soul, but in its development (1842: 26–8).

Beneke conceived of his new psychology as the centrepiece of philosophy: 'Knowledge of our self, i.e. psychological knowledge, is the central starting point; it is the basis of all other philosophical knowledge. What is more, all other philosophical knowledge can only be gained through this [psychological] knowledge' (1833: 14). More specifically with respect to the relation between logic and psychology, Beneke wrote:

We can influence the development of the human mind only according to the mind's own laws; and since the definition of these laws belongs to psychology, psychology is, as it were, the foundational science for logic, just as it is the foundational science for all other sciences.

(Beneke 1842: 16–17)

Logic as a whole was to be regarded as 'an applied psychology' (1842: 17).

The criticism of this 'psychologism', a criticism absent from Erdmann's *Die Deutsche Philosophie seit Hegels Tode*, begins with Wilhelm Windelband. In his *Die Geschichte der neueren Philosophie*, Windelband characterised psychologism as a constant companion of metaphysical systems: 'it amounts to treating metaphysical doctrines from the point of view of empirical-psychological justification, and its advocates all hold . . . that empirical psychology . . . is the basis of all philosophy' (1880: 387). Windelband listed several 'psychologicists', but he regarded Beneke as

the most consistent and most radical proponent of psychologism . . . Not only does he think, like Fries, that epistemology and all other disciplines are to be based upon psychology, he even denies that the task of psychology could be the identification of a priori knowledge; for him there is no a priori knowledge, and the topic of psychology is the history of the development of empirical consciousness.

(Windelband 1880: 393)

Windelband's polemics against this viewpoint came four years later in his paper 'Kritische oder genetische Methode?' Here Windelband presented Kant's introduction of the transcendental-critical method as the overcoming of psychologism and characterised all post-Kantian instances of psychologism, specifically Beneke, Fries and the *Völkerpsychologie* of Lazarus, Steinthal and Wundt, as unfortunate lapses. As Windelband saw it, psychologism used a 'genetic method', i.e. it relied upon empirical psychology and cultural history in order to prove that the axioms of logic, ethics and epistemology were universally valid. In other words, for Windelband's psychologicists to demonstrate that axioms were universally valid was to show no more than that they were accepted by all humans. According to Windelband, the hope of attaining universality in this empirical fashion was vain, however. The genetic method was 'the 'hopeless attempt' to justify, by means of an empirical theory, what is itself the precondition of every theory' (1884: 261). Windelband denied that one could find the same logical principles in all cultures, and proposed that only one element was truly ubiquitous: 'the drive for happiness'. And thus, our neo-Kantian concluded, psychologism had to end up in relativism and amounted to a philosophy of the 'mob' (*Pöbel*). Since psychologism would proclaim the drive for happiness as the only omnipresent element in human thought, 'it will be very popular with the mob . . . [And] . . . to submit philosophy to the judgement of the mob would be a sad end for the philosophical enterprise' (1884: 266).

Husserl's *Prolegomena* referred approvingly to Windelband's article, but the more immediate source for Husserl's usage of the term 'psychologism' was probably a study by his teacher Carl Stumpf entitled 'Psychologie und Erkenntnistheorie' (1892). According to Stumpf, German philosophy in the late nineteenth century suffered from a split between 'Kantian criticism of knowledge' (*Kritizismus*) and 'psychologism'. Stumpf defined these schools of thought as follows:

> We call . . . 'criticism' the conception of epistemology which tries to free the latter from all psychological foundations, and we call 'psychologism' (a term first used by J.E. Erdmann) the reduction of all philosophical research in general, and all epistemological enquiry in particular, to psychology.
>
> (Stumpf 1892: 468)

Stumpf wanted to overcome this opposition. For the most part, his paper was an attack on the neo-Kantian schools (especially the writings of Cohen, Windelband and Riehl). The attack was carried out by rejecting some central elements of Kant's philosophy.

Stumpf began by criticising Kant's doctrines of 'transcendental deduction' and of the 'schematism' of pure concepts of understanding. Transcendental deduction was meant to justify the application of categories to appearances, and the doctrine of schematism was intended to show how this application is achieved. Taking the doctrine of schematism first, Stumpf denied that Kant had succeeded in explaining how we apply categories to appearances. For instance, Kant claimed that the application of categories was made possible, and was governed, by the schemata of space and time, schemata into which the appearances ordered themselves (1892: 473). As Stumpf saw it, this move mistakenly separated categories like causality or substance from the notion of time (1892: 475).

Concerning Kant's transcendental deduction, Stumpf argued that no *general* justification for the application of categories, and thus for the creation of 'syntheses', was possible:

> If we ask the contemporary physicist why he identifies light with electricity, he will refer to specific properties of the appearances . . . The philosopher . . . must not overlook the fact that *specific* syntheses are obtained only by considering specific properties of appearances and their manifold combinations in space and time. But if, in each and every specific case, specific syntheses must be justified by reference to appearances, then we do not need any a priori justification; and indeed no a priori justification is even possible.
>
> (1892: 478–9)

Stumpf did not accept the Kantian rebuttal that, although specific, real laws of nature are dependent upon appearances, the *concept* of a law of nature is based exclusively upon understanding: 'Upon that which all specific laws of nature are based the concept of a law of nature too is based; for the latter is merely an abstraction from the specific laws of nature' (1892: 479).

Stumpf's emphasis upon the need for psychological investigations was more obvious in his second criticism of Kant, i.e. in his rejection of Kant's distinction between matter and form (1892: 481–93). Stumpf suggested here that every epistemological claim had to pass 'the test of psychology', and that Kant's distinction between space and time as the *forms* of perception, and sense qualities (like colours and sounds) as the *matter* of perception had failed this test: '*No claim can be epistemologically true and psychologically false* . . . The distinction [between form and matter] is psychologically completely indefensible, indeed it has hindered the progress of investigation considerably' (1892: 482). For instance, Kant had claimed that we can mentally subtract from the idea (*Vorstellung*) of a body everything belonging to sensation, retaining only the extension and form of this body. In Stumpf's view, numerous psychological investigations had shown this claim to be simply false (1892: 483).

Stumpf disagreed with the neo-Kantian idea that psychology and epistemology ought to be clearly separated from one another.

Nevertheless, he proposed that psychology and epistemology dealt with different problems. The task of psychology was to study the origin and genesis of concepts, whereas the goal of epistemology was the identification 'of the most general, immediately self-evident *truths*' (1892: 501). Over and above this identification, epistemology had no further goals:

> Assuming that this task has been carried out, i.e. that all of the most general and evident insights have been completely listed, formulated and classified, and separated from what merely appear to be axioms, then, I believe, epistemology has done all it can do with respect to the foundations of knowledge. I just do not understand what the question as to 'the conditions of the possibility' of such immediate truths could mean. All further investigation could only concern the *psychological conditions* under which such judgements occur in consciousness.
>
> (1892: 503)

Stumpf concluded by expressing a hope that would soon turn out to be vain: 'Hopefully psychologism and Kantian criticism will disappear from the agenda. And hopefully the abstract and fruitless factional politics that characterise Kantian criticism in particular will be replaced by detailed co-operation, a co-operation that befits the nature of the problems' (1892: 508).

In the period between Stumpf's 1892 paper and Husserl's *Logische Untersuchungen*, the relation between psychology and logic was discussed in several books and articles (*inter alia* Frege 1893, 1894). Few authors employed the term 'psychologism' as a label for their own or others' views, however (see Eisler 1899: 602; Elsenhans 1897: 212; 1898: 166; Enoch 1894: 512; Gutberlet 1898: 138–9; Güttler 1896: 9; Lasswitz 1893: 496; Münsterberg 1900: 19; Ueberweg and Heinze 1897: 274; Weinmann 1898: 242). In some of these texts, the positions labelled 'psychologistic' were treated as philosophical errors, in others they were presented in a neutral way, and in three articles views characterised as 'psychologistic' were considered the correct approach to the problem of the relation between psychology and philosophy.

A positive attitude towards 'psychologism' was taken by Elsenhans (1897, 1898) and Gutberlet (1898). Elsenhans held that 'the object of logic is part of the object of psychology and that we cannot find any difference between the ways in which these sciences treat of this object'. Therefore, Elsenhans concluded, 'logic is a part of psychology . . . [and] . . . there is no other way to solve the problems of logic than through a large measure of psychologism' (1897: 210, 212). In support of his view, Elsenhans referred not only to Stumpf (1892), but also to a passage in Theodor Lipps's *Grundzüge der Logik* (1893). As this passage would later be cited over and over again as the prime expression of 'psychologism', it is worth quoting in full:

> Logic is a psychological discipline since the process of coming to know takes place only in the soul, and since that thinking which completes itself in this coming to know is a psychological process. The fact that psychology differs from logic in disregarding the opposition between knowledge and error does not mean that psychology equates these two different psychological conditions. It merely means that psychology has to explain knowledge and error in the same way. Obviously, no one claims that psychology dissolves into logic. What separates the two sufficiently is that logic is a subdiscipline of psychology.
>
> (Lipps 1893: 1–2)

Interestingly enough, psychologism was regarded as a positive element also by the neoscholastic philosopher Gutberlet in 1898. Gutberlet called on neoscholasticism to combine 'the old ontologism' of Aristotelian and scholastic thought with 'the modern psychologism' of 'empirical psychology' (1898: 138). At the same time, however, Gutberlet rejected the tendency to treat all other sciences as part and parcel of psychology, and referred to 'a master of the logical algorithm', i.e. Frege, as a critic of this 'extreme psychologism' (1898: 139). Nevertheless, Gutberlet's partial endorsement of psychologism is striking in the light of his later writings, in which he saw 'psychologism' as the philosophy of Protestantism and as contradicting Catholic faith (1911: 147; cf. Eucken 1901: 2).

A neutral characterisation of 'psychologism' was given in Eisler's *Wörterbuch der philosophischen Begriffe und Ausdrücke* (1899) and in Ueberweg and Heinze's *Grundriß* (1897). Heinze introduced 'psychologism' in §35 of his book as follows:

> A number of thinkers find in psychology the basis of all philosophical sciences; in particular – *and here they differ from the Kantians – they find in psychology the basis for logic and*

epistemology. Brentano in particular has been influential among these philosophers, and his views have been developed further by his students.

Heinze went on to list Meinong, Marty, Husserl, Ehrenfels, Lipps, Uphues and Schwarz as proponents of this view (1897: 275–7).

Eisler defined 'psychologism' as 'the standpoint which regards psychology as the basis of all human sciences [*Geisteswissenschaften*], including philosophy'. Eisler mentioned Lipps, Brentano and Wundt, among others (1899: 602).

Despite these occasional positive or neutral characterisations of psychologism, most references to the term between Stumpf (1892) and Husserl (1900) were negative. One striking indication of the predominantly negative connotations of the term can be found in the fact that in 1899 Meinong sent a letter to Heinze asking not to be included in '§35. Psychologismus' (Meinong 1965: 140–2). Moreover, Güttler characterised psychologism as the 'dilettantism' that seeks to answer historical and metaphysical questions by means of empirical psychology (1896: 9), and Münsterberg saw psychologism as an excess in psychology. Münsterberg mentioned that psychology was often criticised for its 'claim to power' and continued:

> When this critical reaction ... turns against psychologism, which accepts no other reality than physical and psychological objects, then this reaction is not only well justified but psychology has plenty of reasons to sympathise with it. Only if psychology knows its limitations can it inspire trust, but not if it makes promises which it cannot possibly fulfil.
>
> (Münsterberg 1900: 13)

'PSYCHOLOGISM' AFTER HUSSERL

After the publication of Husserl's *Prolegomena*, uses, definitions and accusations of psychologism multiplied. Indeed, the number of references to the term is too large for us to follow these texts chronologically and one by one. In order to convey an impression of these uses, definitions and accusations, I shall provide (1) a survey of the different versions of psychologism, (2) an inventory of other 'isms' to which psychologism was linked, (3) a list of what different writers regarded as the key opponent of psychologism, (4) a list of writers who accepted 'psychologism' as a label for their own views, (5) a catalogue of definitions of and criteria for psychologism and (6) a survey of comments by various authors on the need for exorcising psychologism.

Versions of psychologism An initial perspective on the inflation that the term 'psychologism' underwent between 1900 and 1930 can be gained by examining the (grammatical) attributes with which the term occurred.

· First of all, writers distinguished between different forms of psychologism according to the fields of philosophy and the human sciences in which psychologism needed to be combated. Thus one finds 'psychologism' qualified as 'metaphysical', 'ontological', 'epistemological', 'logical', 'ethical', 'aesthetic', 'sociological', 'religious', 'historical', 'mathematical', 'pedagogical' and 'linguistic'.

Second, psychologism was also broken down into species according to the distinctive versions of psychologism that various schools were accused of proposing. Such adjectives included 'empiricist', 'aprioristic', 'sensualist', 'rationalist', 'critical-teleological', 'evolutionary', 'pragmatist' and 'transcendental'.

Third, versions of psychologism were distinguished on the basis of their age, their 'degree of truth' and the boldness with which they were supposedly put forward. That is to say, 'psychologism' could be 'old', 'new', 'false', 'true', 'objective (intersubjective)', 'justified' (*wohlverstanden*), 'one-sided/tendentious', 'extreme', 'moderate', 'universal', 'open', 'hidden', 'inverse', 'obvious', 'delicate', 'strict' and 'loose'.

And finally, we also find distinctions between 'intellectual' and 'emotional' psychologism, as well as between 'immanent' and 'transcendent' psychologism.

Bedfellows of psychologism In the last chapter, we saw that Husserl's German critics variously labelled his antipsychologism 'scholasticism', 'aristocratic metaphysicism', 'mysticism', 'logicism' and 'formalism'. The same delight in linking one abhorred 'ism' to further derogatory 'isms' can also be found in critiques of psychologism between 1900 and 1930. 'Anthropologism', 'biologism', 'Darwinism', 'empiricism', 'ethicism', 'existentialism', 'formalism', 'historicism', 'irrationalism', 'logicism', 'materialism', 'naturalism', 'ontologism', 'pessimism', 'positivism', 'Protestantism', 'relativism', 'scepticism', 'sensualism' and 'subjectivism' all appear as alternative characterisations of psychologism, as positions from which psychologism arises, as positions that result from psychologism, or as fallacies into which one easily slides when trying to avoid psychologism.

By far the most popular link was that between psychologism, naturalism and materialism. Typically, philosophers presented psychologism as the successor and heir to materialism. For instance:

> Psychologism is the form which naturalism had to adopt once materialism was rejected and an attempt had been made to replace philosophy by psychology.
>
> (Rickert 1902: 551)

> Basically we are dealing with the same abuse that occurred when, in the past, extrapolations were made from the lore of physics, and a complete *Weltanschauung* was constructed from it. What resulted was a shallow materialism that inevitably crumbled and fell apart as soon as it was confronted with the first serious philosophical questioning; psychologism was founded on the rubble of this ruin.
>
> (Münsterberg 1908: 88)

> The kinship between psychologism and materialism also surfaces at another point. Recall the materialistic fiction according to which it is not unthinkable that the history of the world and humankind was exactly as the history books tell us . . . but with the important proviso that no organism ever had the least spark of mental life. This consistent materialistic fiction has found its counterpart in the psychological fiction according to which the psychological processes . . . could occur exactly as they do occur . . . but without a single soul displaying the strange feature that we call 'consciousness'. As for materialism so also for psychologism . . . consciousness is a 'luxury' of nature.
>
> (P. Stern 1903: 67–8)

Windelband, in his *Die Philosophie im deutschen Geistesleben des XIX. Jahrhunderts* (1909) also treated psychologism as an offspring of materialism. However, Windelband went further by associating psychologism with other 'isms' as well. He discussed psychologism in a chapter entitled 'Positivism, Historicism, Psychologism' and presented this trio as arising from the earlier nineteenth-century movements of irrationalism, materialism and pessimism. Needless to say, all six positions were treated by Windelband as unfortunate and erroneous deviations from the true spirit of German idealism.

The link between psychologism, subjectivism and Protestantism was made in a speech by the Neoscholastic philosopher Gutberlet in a passage that deserves quoting in full:

> When I gave my first speech, from this same spot, on the occasion of the academic celebration of Saint Thomas Aquinas, I spoke about the relation between Saint Thomas and Kant. I characterised Saint Thomas as the philosopher of objectivity, as a Catholic philosopher, and the thinker from Königsberg as the philosopher of Protestantism. I sought to present the difference between them as a conflict between two opposed *Weltanschauungen*. Although this deep opposition may not always be obvious in the case of these two standard-bearers, the development of Kantianism and Protestantism up to the most recent past highlights this divergence. The subjectivism that Kant inaugurated has led, in the short period since my first lecture, with logical consequence to the denial of all objectivity; 'the dead are making headway'. In many quarters, pure phenomenalism, immanentism and psychologism are now presented as the highest and ultimate wisdom.
>
> (Gutberlet 1911: 147)

No less entertaining for the modern reader is Schwarz's suggestion that philosophy could only be put on to the right track by teaching it to avoid the twin errors of psychologism and ontologism:

> Ontologism is the mistake which seeks to derive from an existing being outside us that which can only be explained through the depth of infinity in us. Psychologism is the mistake which tries to derive from finite consciousness that which can only be explained through infinite consciousness reaching into finite consciousness.
>
> (Schwarz 1917: 6)

Schwarz regarded Schelling (!) as the conqueror of psychologism (1917: 8)

Dubs thought that the prima facie best defence for the psychologicist was to combine his position with Darwinism. Dubs suggested that the Darwinistic psychologicist regarded science, art, ethics and religion in general, and belief in the truth of psychologism in particular, as determined by the genetic makeup of humans, and as favourable in the struggle for survival. But in yet another amusing passage, we learn that even this best rationale for psychologism could be demolished:

But one thing is certain now: if the spirit of psychologism had governed human nature, science, art and ethics would never have developed; only pure brutish adaptation would have prevailed . . . Not ennoblement but brutality and cunningness in the struggle for survival would be the only goal of humankind! . . . ultimately one could beat psychologism with its own weapons, i.e. its own method. From the speculative perspective of psychologism, the [Kantian] criticistic idea of objective lawfulness and spirituality must, in its historical force, appear as the most superior product of adaptation. For [Kantian] criticism is firm and belligerent enough not to rest until psychologism is struck to the ground in the battle for survival.

(Dubs 1911: 123)

Finally, 'existentialism', 'ethicism' and 'biologism' remain to be accounted for. Moog coined 'existentialism' as a label for every position that held, or implied, that the logical realm could only be understood as depending on existing beings. Existentialism was inevitably tied to psychologism: 'Every existentialism depends openly or covertly upon psychologism, and it is to be rejected regardless of whether it presents itself as metaphysical or empirical, idealist or realist' (1919: 199). 'Biologism' was, for Moog, the most radical form of existentialism; it regarded logical laws as fictions that were useful for the survival of the human species (1919: 192). 'Ethicism' was a more moderate form of existentialism (and psychologism); ethicism regarded logic as the *morals* of thought (1919: 222).

Alternatives to psychologism   The list of bedfellows of psychologism is as heterogeneous as the list of positions that different authors regarded as the correct alternatives to psychologism is varied. Indeed, the catalogue of the latter is (at least) as long as the inventory of philosophical positions put forward in German-language philosophy between 1900 and 1930. This makes it impossible to provide here detailed characterisations of all of these positions. Some of them have been briefly introduced in Chapter 4, others have been mentioned earlier in this chapter, and still others will be introduced later on in this essay. We will confine our attention for the moment to the many different labels for the correct alternatives.

The most widely used and accepted term for the correct alternative was, as has already been seen, 'antipsychologism'. Neo-Kantian writers of various brands translated 'antipsychologism' as 'transcendental logic', 'idealism', 'German idealism', or 'Kantian criticism' (*Kritizismus*), and then went on to disagree over the question of just which interpretation of *Kritizismus* was to be chosen. For Rickert and his students, for instance, the correct interpretation of *Kritizismus* was 'logic as a pure science of values' (*reine Wertwissenschaft*). Phenomenologists held that 'pure logic' and 'transcendental phenomenology' marked the true antipsychologism; Rehmke's students swore by their teacher's 'fundamental philosophical science' (*Grundwissenschaft*), the neoscholastics by Thomas Aquinas's philosophy, and Meinongians by their master's '*Gegenstandstheorie*'.

In addition to these better known and therefore much debated alternatives, some other 'antipsychologisms' were also coined, but these were soon disregarded, or only caught the attention of a wider readership much later on. Let me mention and quote three of them.

Medicus held that psychologism could only be finally overcome through a return to Hegel. He granted that Husserl and the neo-Kantians had taken important steps towards defeating psychologism, but suggested that these steps were not yet sufficient:

> The empiricist presuppositions have not yet been completely eliminated: today's Kantians regard the philosophy of absolute action, i.e. dialectics, as nebulous outpourings. But they do so from the same motives that inform the psychologicists when the latter interpret the transcendental apperception, the brainless subject of the Kantian doctrine, as nebulous outpourings ... the necessary total implementation of the critical programme in its highest dialectical syntheses must, as with Fichte and Hegel, lead to the question of meaning, i.e. to the question concerning the content or meaning of being itself.
>
> (Medicus 1907: 72)

Adler, together with other early sociologists of knowledge, saw sociology as the effective remedy against psychologism. For Adler, psychologism amounted to the question 'How can the individual gain knowledge?' ([1925] 1982: 177). This position, Adler suggested, needed to be replaced by a sociology of knowledge that reinterpreted Kant's transcendental question concerning the conditions of the possibility of knowledge as a sociological one.

Finally, Scholz claimed that the victory over psychologism was due to the development of mathematical logic, or *Logistik*, as it was referred to in Germany at the time:

> Note what *Logistik* has liberated us from! We have to say something on this as well. Just recall the struggle against psychologism in logic, a struggle that, under Husserl's leadership, now has already been going on for a lifetime. This is a battle that has to be fought; but how little has been gained for positive logic in this battle. The non-*logistisch* opponents of psychologism have to date not managed to formulate even the 'principles' of logic in a flawless manner. *Logistik* has proceeded completely differently. It has formalised logic in such a way that a psychologistic interpretation of the formalised expression is a priori impossible.
>
> (Scholz 1931: 67)

Self-proclaimed psychologicists Among the qualifications of 'psychologism' listed above we also encountered the adjectives 'true', 'justified' and 'moderate'. Authors who used these attributes obviously did not feel that psychologism, in all its versions, was an erroneous philosophical view. Indeed, some authors even claimed that psychologism (rightly understood) was the best defence against psychologism (wrongly understood). Such authors, as well as others who accepted the label 'psychologism' without any qualification, deserve some attention, since they constitute the very few exceptions to the claim that German-speaking philosophers were agreed on the need to combat psychologism.

The first group of such writers were Brentano and his students Meinong, Marty and Höfler. They accepted the label 'psychologism' in the pre-Husserlian sense of Ueberweg and Heinze's *Grundriß der Geschichte der Philosophie*, but denied it in the Husserlian sense. In other words, they were willing to be called psychologicists, provided psychologism merely meant that psychology was the basis of, or central to, all of philosophy. But they denied that this position implied that logic and epistemology were mere parts of psychology, or that psychology was able to answer normative questions (Brentano [1911] 1959: 182–3; Höfler 1905: 322; Marty 1908: 6–18; Meinong 1913: 504). As Meinong put it:

> When 'psychologism' is used as the label for . . . a willingness and tendency to tackle problems mainly with psychological

tools, then psychologism does not deserve any reproach. . . .
In my own case, this is shown by the objective presentation of
my views in Ueberweg–Heinze . . . [But] if someone engages
in epistemology as if all knowledge had only a psychological
side, or if someone seeks to squeeze this second [nonpsycho-
logical] side into the perspective of psychological processes,
then he will have to bear the imputation of psychologism.

(Meinong 1913: 504)

A few other authors took a similar line: Cornelius (1923: 14), Eisler
(1902: 15; 1907: 19) and Linke (1924). For instance, Eisler attributed to Wundt a 'well-understood "psychologism"': 'The empirical
results of psychological investigations have strongly influenced his
philosophical views, and, second, inner experience has some
logical priority over outer experience' (1902: 15).

Lipps, one of the chief culprits for Husserl as well as for later
writers, defended himself by redefining both psychology and
psychologism:

In his fat but otherwise excellent book *Logische Untersuchungen*,
Husserl calls me a 'psychologicist'. I answer: I am a psychologicist – not towards the logicians, but towards the psychologists; I am a psychologicist towards those psychologists who
believe that one can do psychology without taking into
account logical, aesthetic and ethical facts – which are psychological facts. But I am not a psychologicist in the sense that I
would deny the independence of these facts. Indeed, I regard
the strict separation of the logical realm from the nonlogical,
psychological realm as one of the most important tasks of
logic. Psychology is the all-encompassing science. Even logic
is part of it, though it is not based upon psychology. Even
Husserl's logic is part of it.

(Lipps 1903: 78)

There were, however, some authors who were willing to call
themselves 'psychologicists' without any further ado. This usually
meant that they felt no need to distance themselves from the view
that epistemology and logic are part and parcel of empirical
psychology. Three of these authors, Heymans, Jerusalem and
Schultz, we have already encountered. Heymans suggested that the
'fight against "psychologism" in the normative sciences' was based
upon 'simple mistakes' (1922: 4). Jerusalem expressed his support

for 'the so-called psychologism, i.e. the line of thought which gives a psychological justification for logical truths and thus wants to turn the latter into psychological truths'. Jerusalem regarded 'this conception of, and work on, logical truths as the greatest advance that logic has made since Aristotle' (1905: 78). And Schultz predicted that the objections by 'recent "absolutists"' against 'the usual psychologistic justification of logic will not succeed' (1903: 1).

Finally, Mauthner suggested that a consistent Kantian epistemology should bear the title 'psychologism' as an 'honorary title'. For Mauthner, Kant had shown 'the anthropomorphism of every possible worldview'. And thus all normative questions had to go by the board: 'Once Kant directed his critique against knowledge itself, all rules and dogmas failed, and one had to confine oneself to a mere description. The critique of knowledge became ... elementary psychology, and this critique might be given the honorary title of "psychologism"' (1924, II: 257–8).

Definitions and criteria   Authors who were willing to regard themselves as 'psychologicists', however, formed but a small minority in German-language philosophy between 1900 and 1930. As indicated earlier, most philosophers regarded psychologism as a gross philosophical error that needed to be ruthlessly identified in the thought of their contemporaries. We have already seen how all philosophical schools participated in this merry-go-round of charge and countercharge, and how practically every single German philosopher, dead or alive, was unmasked as a proponent of psychologism. Not surprisingly, this merry-go-round was possible only because the criteria for attributing a psychologistic stance to another philosopher were extremely flexible. While the different schools agreed on the fact that psychologism entailed a mistaken grounding of philosophy in psychology, they disagreed sharply as to what constituted such a grounding.

I have summarised the bewildering array of definitions and criteria for psychologism in the form of a table (Figure 6). I will mention just a few of the most striking examples here. For Husserl, from around 1910 onwards, anyone who omitted to carry out the transcendental-phenomenological reduction could not advance beyond a psychologistic naivety. In like manner, the neo-Kantians thought that all philosophy that did not take its starting point from Kant, was psychologistic. For other writers, psychologism could be, among other things: any epistemology that did take its starting point from Kant; any use of the notions of 'self-evidence' or 'consciousness' in logic and epistemology; speaking of logic as a normative science of *Kunstlehre*; the failure to distinguish between the subject and the object, or the content and object, of knowledge; distinguishing between the subject and the object, or the content and object, of knowledge; any employment of notions like 'value' or 'obligation' in the theory of knowledge; every form of realism; the correspondence theory of truth; any attempt to separate different sciences in terms of either their objects or their methods; every definition of culture that made reference to human beings; or speaking of the natural sciences as a product of human culture. Indeed, even the attempt to draw a strict dividing line between psychology and philosophy by denying psychology the status of a philosophical discipline was psychologistic, or, more precisely, 'inverse psychologism'. Given this catalogue (not to mention numerous other criteria listed in Figure 6), one can easily see that it was well-nigh impossible for a philosopher in the early decades of the twentieth century to avoid being charged with psychologism.

Contemporary evaluations of the struggle over psychologism The various aspects of the debate over psychologism that I have tried to document above did not escape the attention of participants in, or observers of, the 'struggle'. For instance, as early as 1907, Eisler noted that 'there is hardly an antipsychologicist, from Kant up to Cohen and Husserl, who has not been accused of "psychologism" by some even more extreme thinker. In the end one no longer knows just who is a psychologicist and who isn't' (1907: 19). Baeumker wrote of the 'exaggerations' that proliferated in the fight against psychologism (1916: 87), and Steinmann observed that this 'catchword [i.e. psychologism] has lost all content since it has been used against almost *all* modern epistemological doctrines' (1917: 409). However, such disillusioned assessments were also controversial. Thus Eisler's claim 'one no longer knows who is a psychologicist and who isn't' infuriated Hönigswald. He claimed that anyone who held the proper neo-Kantian view of psychologism would always be in a perfect position to tell the guilty from the innocent (1908: 409).

Other writers lamented a situation in which German philosophy seemed to be deeply divided between psychologistic and antipsychologistic philosophical schools. Maier (1908: 50) defined these two movements following Stumpf's distinction between Kantian criticism and psychologism. Maier also echoed Stumpf's hope that this division would soon become obsolete. Driesch spoke of 'two camps that hardly understand each other any more' (1912: 8), and Mauthner suggested that contemporary philosophers 'divide into two camps according to whether they engage in epistemology from a *logical* or a *psychological* point of view'. And he went on:

> The fighters in both camps hurl insults at each other; the closer they are to the ranks, the more heated the language becomes; the leaders of both camps already know that the houses of both logic and psychology are only temporary places of refuge for our scientific collections of facts, and that these collections will one day be arranged differently and better.
>
> (Mauthner 1924, I: 446)

Aware of the danger that whatever they wrote on logic and epistemology would immediately be accused of the taint of psychologism, some philosophers tried to anticipate such criticism and to counter it by rhetorical means. Marty went for an *argumentum ad misericordiam* by drawing attention to the fact that characterising a philosophical position as 'psychologistic' was to label it in a 'disparaging' way (1908: 6). Rickert wrote that 'some good will' was needed if his work was not to be misinterpreted: 'Authors whose main aim is to criticise at all costs, since they lack the talent for original thought themselves, will find plenty of opportunities for carping at my work' (1909: 222). And Brentano attempted to escape the charge by exploiting anti-Catholic sentiments:

> Some have accused my theory of knowledge of psychologism; this is a neologism that makes many pious philosophers now cross themselves, pretty much like many orthodox Catholics on hearing the word 'modernism', as if these terms conjured up the devil incarnate.
>
> (Brentano [1911] 1959: 179)

Alas, German philosophers of the time were not taken in by these rhetorical strategies; none of them was successful in defusing criticism. Rickert was still accused of psychologism, and Marty's as well as Brentano's ploys were countered by Rickert's student

A philosophy is psychologistic if it:	
Key terms	Criteria
General	• regards philosophy as applied psychology (Eisler 1902: 15)
	• identifies epistemology with psychology of knowledge (Rickert 1904: 88)
	• applies psychology in the wrong place (Höfler 1905: 322)
	• attempts to derive all forms of necessity from psychologically experienced necessity (Spranger 1905: 16)
	• interprets the process of coming to know as a psychological process (Ewald 1906: 4)
	• denies general and independent norms and values (Ewald 1907: 288)
	• advocates subjectivism and relativism (Moog 1918: 302)
	• proposes a form of naive realism (Moog 1919: 84)
	• combines psychology and epistemology (Moog 1919: 230)
	• conflates genesis and validity (Clauberg and Dubislav 1923: 357)
Logic Logical laws Norms	• fails to distinguish between laws as norms and laws as general-necessary facts (Marty 1908: 7)
	• regards logical laws as a product of evolution (Gutberlet 1908: 2)
	• grounds logic in psychology or phenomenology (e.g. Rickert 1909: 227)
	• treats logic as a part of experimental psychology (Spitzer 1914: 132)
	• looks upon logic as a system of norms or conventions (Moog 1919: 219)
	• employs the notion of correctness in logic (Moog 1919: 284)
	• seeks to justify logical principles in terms of utility (Moog 1919: 192)
Judgements	• deems judgements to be psychological entities (e.g. Lipps 1903: 77)
	• conceptualises judgements as acts of acceptance (Moog 1918: 353)
	• denies psychology the right to clarify the notion of 'correctness of judgements' (Bauch 1918: 54)
Self-evidence	• uses the category of self-evidence in logic and epistemology (Natorp 1901: 20)
	• describes self-evidence as a feeling (Marty 1908: 8)
	• treats self-evidence as a criterion of truth (Marty 1908: 9)
Subject/object Consciousness	• takes its starting point from the individual consciousness (Cohen 1902: 510)
	• considers consciousness to be a shadow play of sensations, feelings and effects (Palágyi 1902: 3)

	• fails to separate the subject from the object of knowledge (Lipps 1905: 522)
	• calls logic a 'science of consciousness' (Dürr 1906: 274)
	• denies the transcendence of the object of knowledge (Dürr 1906: 271)
	• conflates objects with inner experiences (Meinong 1907: 143)
	• distinguishes between subject and object, the immanent and the transcendent realm, object and content; claims 'no subject without object' or 'no object without subject' (Michaltschew 1909: 29, 39)
	• assumes that the subject 'posits' (*setzt*) objects (Rickert 1911–12: 56)
	• attempts to derive epistemological consciousness from the objective world (Lanz 1912: 57)
	• conceptualises consciousness as something objective and factual (Lanz 1912: 54)
	• employs concepts like 'consciousness' or 'creating thought' (Groos 1912: 274)
	• tries to derive from finite consciousness that which can only be explained by infinite consciousness reaching into finite consciousness (Schwarz 1917: 6)
	• assumes that the central Kantian question was 'how does the individual acquire knowledge?' (Adler [1925] 1982: 177)
Kant	• fails to recognise the transcendental (phenomenological) ego-subject (Husserl [1929] 1974)
	• postulates unknowable things-in-themselves (Medicus 1907)
	• takes its epistemological starting point from Kant (Wundt 1914a: 315)
Morality	• treats self-evidence as a criterion of moral value (Marty 1908: 9)
Religion	• analyses moral, religious and artistic actions in purely psychological terms (Schwarz 1911: 279)
	• translates '(morally) good' as 'forced upon us by the natural laws of love' (Marty 1908: 8)
Theory of science	• downgrades the natural sciences by claiming that their knowledge is less reliable than the knowledge of psychology (Dürr 1906: 271)
	• regard laws of nature as norms of thought (Nelson [1908] 1973a: 191)
	• attempts to distinguish between different sciences either in terms of their objects or in terms of their methods (Moog 1919: 89)
	• defines culture (and thus the cultural sciences) with reference to human beings (Moog 1919: 122)
	• speaks of the natural sciences as a cultural product (Moog 1919: 128)
	• defines the natural sciences as those sciences that start from perception (Moog 1919: 163)

(continued)

Key terms	Criteria
	• deems the natural sciences superior to the human sciences in their methods and in the exactness of their results, and regards this difference as a logical difference (Moog 1919: 167)
Value Ought *Geltung*	• reduces value to interest (Meinong 1912: 9) • relies on the value of utility in epistemology (Moog 1913: 93) • uses notions like 'value' or 'obligation' in epistemology (Moog 1919: 221) • treats truth as a value (Moog 1919: 225) • employs the notion of *Geltung* (validity) in epistemology (Linke 1924)
Metaphysics	• adheres to Platonism (Kroner 1909: 27) • redefines psychology as a metaphysical science (Moog 1917: 10–12) • justifies logical principles on metaphysical grounds (Moog 1919: 186)
Varia	• conflates the immediate expression of a given thought with a report about this thought (Lipps 1905: 540) • looks upon 'the will to truth' as an a priori condition of knowledge (Nelson [1908] 1973a: 181) • distinguishes between primary and secondary qualities (Moog 1913: 99) • regards separating and uniting as activities of the soul (Rehmke 1918: 147) • talks of knowledge as corresponding to reality (Moog 1919: 84) • relies on the principle 'individuum est ineffabile' (Moog 1919: 112) • employs the distinction between discursive and intuitive knowledge (Moog 1919: 288) • attempts to dismiss or justify ideas by explaining their psychological origins (Jaspers 1919: 4) • explains ideas in terms of the biography of their author (Frischeisen-Köhler 1919–20: 31) • seeks to elucidate the creation of knowledge by examining the motives and goals of the creative individuals (Scheler [1925] 1982: 106–7)

Figure 6 Definitions and criteria of psychologism

Heidegger. Heidegger quoted Brentano's statement and then went on to write:

> We cannot and need not determine whether psychologism disturbs the mental balance of some 'philosophers'. As long as one aims for, and deems possible – *even in philosophy* – a research which is free of moods and value judgements, one can, with good reason, deny that calling a theory psychologistic amounts to an 'accusation'. Despite Brentano's disclaimer, his theory of judgements is psychologistic.
>
> (Heidegger [1913] 1987b: 122)

Heidegger's dissertation of 1913, which went to great lengths to unmask Brentano, Lipps, Maier and Wundt as psychologistic thinkers, must have come as something of a surprise to the contemporary reader. The selfsame Heidegger had written only a year earlier, 'we regard, at the present state of logical enquiry, any refutation of psychologistic aberrations as a superfluous enterprise' ([1912] 1978a: 20). This remark brings us, in conclusion, to different assessments of the question when, and to what degree, the psychologistic threat had been overcome. As early as 1908, Ewald had proposed that further warnings of psychologism were unnecessary (Ewald 1908: 231), and Natorp suggested in 1912 that the conflation of psychology with logic had 'already been overcome to a certain extent' (1912a: 94). In the 1920s, many authors wrote of the fight against psychologism as an issue of the past, and saw the real dangers to philosophy elsewhere (e.g. Hartmann 1928: x). But even at that late stage there remained authors who felt that the danger was far from over. Thus Cassirer wrote in 1927 that 'psychologism . . . still cannot be regarded as defeated. For although its form and justification have changed since Husserl's sharp and trenchant criticism, we must note that psychologism has, to a high degree, the ability to appear in ever new guises' (1927: 32). And Hönigswald complained in 1931 that

> people protest . . . that there is no longer any need to be on the defensive against 'psychologism' these days. That it's like kicking in an open door. They allege that psychologism is dead, and that anyone who revives the 'psychologism struggle' overlooks the real issues which confront philosophy today . . . [But] however resolutely one averts one's gaze from psychologism, it has not yet been overcome.
>
> (Hönigswald 1931: 4)

6

ROLE HYBRIDISATION
The rise of the new psychology

INTRODUCTION

The last two chapters described and analysed two series of texts. The first series consisted of the many different interpretations and criticisms, in German philosophy between 1901 and 1920, of Husserl's arguments against psychologism. The second series consisted of philosophical books and articles by German and Austrian philosophers, published between 1866 and 1930, which defined psychologism and accused a large number of philosophers of advocating psychologism. The analysis of this second series showed that agreement was reached neither on the proper definition of psychologism nor on the list of psychologicists.

In the remainder of this study, I shall provide a sociological explanation for these two series of textual events. Put in a nutshell, my explanation situates the debate over psychologism in the contemporaneous struggle over the status and proper location of the new (experimental) psychology. My explanation divides roughly into three parts, corresponding to Chapters 6 to 8.

The present chapter will focus on the rise and rapid expansion of the new experimental psychology from the 1870s until about 1914. This expansion took place mainly within philosophy departments, i.e. the early proponents of experimental psychology all held chairs in philosophy and typically presented their new discipline as a genuine philosophical project.

In the next chapter, I shall turn to the writings of those philosophers who perceived the expansion of experimental psychology within philosophy as a threat to their own views. Following the jargon of the time, we might call these writers 'pure philosophers'. I shall summarise their arguments for a strict separation between experimental psychology and philosophy, characterise their projects for a *philosophical, yet nonexperimental* psychology and describe their struggle for leadership in the assault on experimental psychology. In the same context, I shall also provide an overview of the experimentalists' responses to the pure philosophers' proposals and actions. Moreover, having looked at the various strategies used by pure philosophers for exorcising experimental psychology from philosophy, I can also give an answer to the question why Husserl's criticism of psychologism was so much more successful than Frege's.

Finally, Chapter 8 will explain why the debate over psychologism and the controversy over experimental psychology came to a simultaneous end during and after the First World War. The outcome of both debates is of course well known: philosophy and (experimental) psychology are now generally perceived as two distinct fields of study, and psychologism is typically regarded as a basic philosophical error.

THE RISE OF THE NEW PSYCHOLOGY IN NUMERICAL TERMS

One of the most important developments in German academic philosophy between 1880 and 1920 was the rise and institutional expansion of a new 'scientific' psychology, i.e. a psychology that borrowed at least some of its methods from the natural sciences. The dramatic extent of this rise and expansion is perhaps most easily brought out by looking at some numerical information on serial publications, psychological institutes and professorial chairs.

The number of serial publications in psychology published in German between 1880 and 1925 grew from three in 1880 to fifty-nine in 1925. The number of journals in general psychology rose steadily between 1885 and 1915, from one in 1885 to twelve in 1915, but levelled off subsequently. By 1900 there were several serial publications specialising in applied psychology; by 1925 they actually outnumbered journals and series in general psychology. While the number of parapsychology journals (two) remained constant over the period, the number of journals and series in psychiatry and psychoanalysis also increased steadily (see Figure 7).

As for the institutionalisation of psychology, the number of psychological institutes, divisions or seminars at German universities (including technical colleges) increased as steadily as the

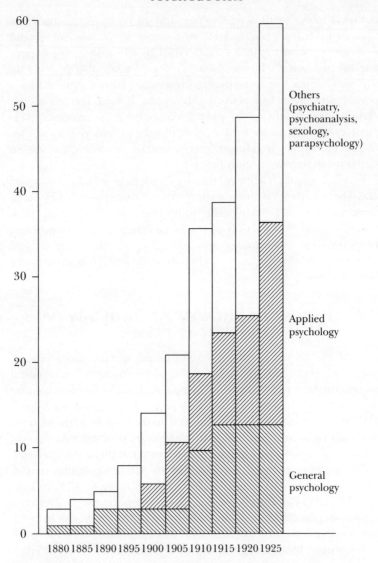

Figure 7 Number of serial publications in psychology published in German, 1880–1925
Source: Based on Osier and Wozniak (1984)

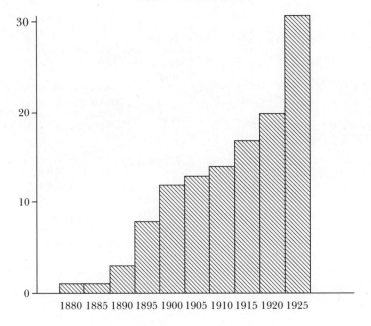

Figure 8 Number of German universities (including technical colleges) with a psychology institute, division or seminar
Source: Based on Geuter (1986)

number of serial publications in general and applied psychology (Figure 8). The founding of a psychological institute, division and seminar usually meant that the philosophy department, of which they were a part, could offer courses in experimental psychology and that at least some experimental research was carried out. The most famous of these institutes was of course Wundt's institute at the University of Leipzig; other important institutes were situated in Berlin, Göttingen and Würzburg.

The key figures behind these four leading institutes were Wundt (Leipzig), Ebbinghaus and Stumpf (Berlin), G.E. Müller (Göttingen) and Külpe (Würzburg). These five men, together with Brentano, set the agenda for the new field of study. Most of them were also highly successful teachers. Figure 9 depicts some of the central teacher–student relationships among the first and second generations of practitioners and/or advocates of experimental psychology in Germany.

I shall deal with the thought and career of these key figures shortly.

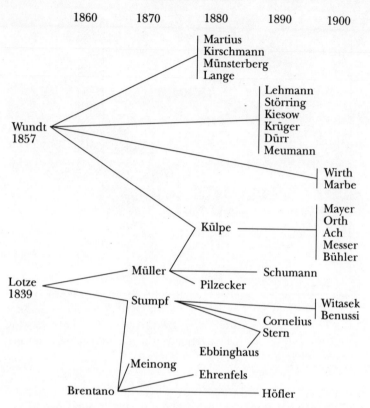

Figure 9 Key teacher–student relations among German philosophers/psychologists, by decade of habilitation, 1850–1909
Source: Ben-David and Collins (1966: 456), slightly modified

For the moment, note that the practitioners of the new (experimental) psychology worked in philosophy departments, and that between 1873 and 1913 the number of full professorships held by these 'psychologists' increased from one (i.e. Stumpf) to ten. According to the statistics of one contemporary witness, of the thirty-nine full professorships in philosophy in 1892, practitioners of experimental psychology held three; of the forty-two full professorships in 1900 they occupied six; while of the forty-four in 1913 they had already gained ten. Their share thus increased from 7.7 per cent to an impressive 22.7 per cent within the short period of twenty-two years (Frischeisen-Köhler 1913: 371). Of the ten practitioners of experimental psychology holding a philosophical chair at a German university in 1913 – Ach, Krüger, Külpe, Marbe, Martius, Messer, Meumann, G.E. Müller, Stumpf and Wirth – seven were first- or second-generation students of Wundt.

KEY FIGURES OF THE NEW PSYCHOLOGY

A number of philosophers, physiologists, and physicists were important sources for, and resources of, the new psychology.[1] Historians of psychology generally agree, however, that the credit for its institutionalisation goes to Brentano, Ebbinghaus, Külpe, G.E. Müller, Stumpf and Wundt.

Joseph Ben-David and Randall Collins (1966) have argued that it was mainly these figures who were instrumental in creating the new professional role of the physiologist-philosopher, a role that ultimately became the role of the new experimental psychologist. Ben-David and Collins propose that 'social factors' played a key role in the early history of modern psychology. According to these two sociologists, a new scientific field comes into existence only once a new 'professional role' has been created. In the case of psychology, the new role resulted from a 'role hybridisation': the founders of the new psychology found themselves in a situation where, on the one hand, physiology enjoyed a higher standing than philosophy and where competitive conditions were better in philosophy than in physiology, on the other. Therefore men like Wundt, Stumpf or G.E. Müller sought to bring physiological-experimental methods into philosophy, i.e. they sought to practise philosophy – or at least one of its subdisciplines, namely psychology – by physiological means.

It has been pointed out that the competitive conditions in German philosophy were not as good as assumed by Ben-David and Collins, and that specialisation in the new psychology was often also an attempt to seek the advantage which competence in a distinct scientific specialty could give in the highly competitive field of philosophy (Ross 1967; Ash 1980a). One can accept these corrections to Ben-David and Collins's argument without rejecting their idea that Wundt and other first-generation philosopher-psychologists actually developed – or at least advocated – a role for the philosopher that blurred sharp distinctions between philosophy and the natural sciences. To adopt this suggestion is imperative not least because the idea of the practitioners of experimental psychology as role hybrids figured centrally in both defences of, and attacks on, experimental psychology.

Wundt

There can be little doubt that Wilhelm Wundt (1832–1920) was the most important figure in the institutionalisation of psychology. As stated above, of the ten practitioners of experimental psychology holding a philosophical chair at a German university in 1913, seven were first- or second-generation students of Wundt. To this we can now add that Wundt's journal *Philosophische Studien* (1883–1903) was the first journal to publish mainly papers in experimental psychology, and that Wundt founded a psychology laboratory in Leipzig in 1879 that was soon to become the Mecca for anyone interested in the new psychology. Wundt's students included not only those listed in Figure 9; they also came from Great Britain (Spearman, Titchener), Russia (Bekhterev) and the United States (McKeen Cattell, Hall, Judd, Scripture, Stratton, Witmer, Wolfe). These students in turn founded new psychology laboratories in their respective countries, often modelled on Wundt's laboratory in Leipzig. By 1900 there were forty-three psychology labs in the US alone, and twelve of these had been founded by Wundt's students (Bringmann and Ungerer 1980b: 17).

Wundt's laboratory has been described as 'a knowledge factory' which had several features that we associate with experimental research today, such as hierarchical organisation and the institutional ownership of results (Ash 1980a: 262–3). Wundt himself wrote:

> The activity of the laboratory is divided into two departments: an introductory course, led each semester by one of the assistants in turn . . . and the more specialised work of the [institute's] members. . . . The plan for the more specialised work is determined in an assembly called for that purpose each semester on the opening day of the institute. The director first makes known the topics to be researched, both those carried over from previous semesters and those newly chosen. With respect to the latter, any special wishes of the individual older members who are interested in a particular topic are taken into account when possible. The members are then divided into separate research groups, each of which concerns itself with a specific topic . . . After deciding on the constitution of the groups, a leader is designated for each, usually an older member who has proven himself by assisting in other projects in previous semesters. The group later

assembles the results of the experiments, and, if they are suitable, prepares them for publication. The experimental protocols, by the way, are viewed as the property of the institute, whether the investigation is published or not.

(Wundt 1910a: 291–2; tr. Ash 1980a: 262–3)

Of the key figures in the early days of experimental psychology, Wundt was the only one lacking a formal philosophical education. Wundt studied medicine in Tübingen and Heidelberg. After his graduation, he briefly did physiological research with J. Müller and Du Bois-Reymond in Berlin, before becoming, from 1858 until 1864, von Helmholtz's assistant in Heidelberg. During this period Wundt developed his programme of a new experimental and cultural psychology and began work on his most successful book, the textbook *Grundzüge der physiologischen Psychologie*. This was first published in 1873, and subsequently went through six editions until 1911. After he had left Helmholtz in 1864, Wundt taught courses in anthropology and medical psychology before moving to Zurich in 1874, where he became professor of 'inductive philosophy'. Only one year later, Wundt was called to the chair of philosophy in Leipzig where he remained until his retirement in 1917 (Blumenthal 1985b: 22–3; Murray 1988: 200–1). In Leipzig, Wundt was highly successful as an academic lecturer and as a thesis supervisor: his lectures were attended by huge audiences – 630 students and visitors attended his afternoon lectures in 1912 (Blumenthal 1985b: 43) – and no less than 186 dissertations were produced in Leipzig under his supervision (Ash 1980a: 264).

The most characteristic feature of Wundt's conception of philosophy was his view that the days when philosophy could figure as the foundation of the natural and of the human sciences were gone. Instead, Wundt proposed that philosophy must be based upon the results of those sciences. Philosophy was to unite the general insights of the various disciplines into one consistent whole, and it was to investigate scientific methods and the conditions for the acquisition of knowledge (Eisler 1902: 8; Külpe 1920: 96). Wundt expressed this viewpoint most clearly in his writings on the classification of the sciences and philosophy (e.g. 1889b). There he claimed that philosophy and the other sciences had essentially the same content, suggesting that it was merely the *viewpoint* from which this content was studied that distinguished the two realms of knowledge. Whereas the various branches of science 'separate knowledge into a great number of individual objects of knowledge, the eye of philosophy is directed from the start towards the interrelation between all these objects of knowledge' (1889b: 48).

The task of philosophy with respect to this interrelation of knowledge was twofold: philosophy investigated the genesis of knowledge, and it analysed the systematic structure of given bodies of knowledge. Accordingly, philosophy divided into two 'basic sciences': the 'science of knowledge' and the 'science of principles'. The former was concerned with both the formal laws and the real content of knowledge. It comprised formal logic as well as 'general history of science' and 'pure and applied epistemology' (1889b: 53). The science of principles consisted of metaphysics as 'the general science of principles' on the one hand and 'the special science of principles' on the other. It examined the metaphysical assumptions underlying the different sciences. The special science of principles thus contained fields of study like 'general biology', 'general cosmology', 'philosophical psychology', 'ethics', 'aesthetics' and 'philosophy of history' (1889b: 54).

Wundt's general metaphysics aimed for a *Weltanschauung* that 'corresponds to the total scientific consciousness of a given time' (1904: 361) and that satisfied a given era's emotional needs (Eisler 1902: 10). Such scientifically oriented metaphysics was called 'inductive' by Wundt's one-time student Oswald Külpe in order to set it apart from the speculative and deductive metaphysical systems of German Idealism (Külpe 1920: 13). As Wundt argued in his metaphysical writings (Wundt 1889a, 1914a), the scientific results of his time forced reason first and foremost into adopting and developing three kinds of metaphysical ideas. The cosmological ideas were the assumptions of unlimited space, unlimited time, unlimited matter and an eternal chain of causes and effects. The two psychological-metaphysical ideas related closely to Wundt's psychological voluntarism: pure will was the essence of the human being, and all wills were ultimately related to one another in one total, ideal will. And finally, ontological ideas were, first, that the world was nothing but a totality of wills; second, that God was the all-encompassing worldwill; and third, that the development of the world was the development of the will of God.

Wundt's notion that philosophy presupposed the results of science was also central to his comments on the task and definition of logic. As the opening sentence of his *Logik* – 'Logic has to account for the laws of thought which are effective in scientific knowledge' (1906: 1) – already indicated, logic started from the existence of scientific knowledge.

In the context of the present study, Wundt's remarks on the relation between logic and psychology deserve, of course, special attention. Wundt placed logic between psychology and all other scientific disciplines. Logic was a normative discipline which sought to identify those combinations of ideas which were generally valid. Whereas psychology studied how humans *in fact* thought, logic investigated how one *had to* think in order to obtain scientific knowledge (1906: 1).

In some of his early writings on the relation between logic and psychology, Wundt sided with Theodor Lipps's position that, first, the laws of logic were 'the natural laws of thought itself' and, second, logic was 'the physics of thought' (Wundt 1882: 345). However, Wundt parted company with Lipps in wishing to make the normative character of this 'physics' explicit by calling logic a 'normative discipline' (1882: 345). In later writings, Wundt no longer sided explicitly with the 'physics of thought' thesis. But he remained committed to the idea that the psychological study of logical thought was the necessary first step in the development of any scientific logic. Although he did not regard this psychological study as a part of logic proper, he emphasised nevertheless that only a psychological study of thought could identify the special and unique features of logical thinking (1906: 11).

Wundt suggested that psychological analysis could pinpoint three features that distinguished logical thought from all other types of thinking: spontaneity, self-evidence and universality (*Allgemeingültigkeit*). First, as concerns spontaneity, Wundt held that logical thinking was experienced by humans as a free inner activity, that is as an act of willing. Thus logical laws of thought had to be understood as laws of the will (1906: 75). Second, logical thought had the special character of an inner necessity, a character which led one to ascribe immediate certainty to the combinations of ideas produced by logical thinking (1906: 76). Third and finally, the laws of (logical) thought had universality in two ways: they were evident for all reasoners, and their applicability was not restricted to any particular realm of objects (1906: 84–5).

The two last-mentioned features of logical thought, self-evidence and universality, allowed one to distinguish more clearly between psychological and logical laws. 'Logical laws of thought' were all those rules 'which contain regulations regarding that which is self-evident and universal in our thought'. Psychological laws lacked both self-evidence and universality. Moreover, while both psychological and logical laws of thought were arrived at through generalisation from, and observation of, factual thinking, only 'logical laws of thought are, at the same time, *norms* by means of which we approach factual thought and test its correctness' (1906: 88). However, this opposition between logical and psychological laws did not mean that no psychological concepts entered the vocabulary of logic. Wundt believed that, since logical laws of thought were identified within human thinking, and since logical thought was usually intertwined with other kinds of mental activities, the formulations and explanations of logical laws would always and inevitably contain psychological concepts (1906: 89).

In his classifications of the sciences, Wundt did not count psychology among the philosophical disciplines. Rather, psychology was one of the human sciences (*Geisteswissenschaften*). The human sciences were divided into three branches, 'the sciences of the mental processes', 'the sciences of the mental products' and 'the sciences of the development of the mental products'. Psychology together with psychophysics, anthropology and ethnology made up the first category; philology, economics, political science, law, theology, theory of arts and special methodology of the human sciences were 'the sciences of the mental products'; and the various historical disciplines belonged to 'the sciences of the development of the mental products' (1889b: 47). Arguing that mental processes were prior to mental products and their historical development, Wundt claimed that psychology was prior to, and the foundation of, all other human sciences (1889b: 44). Moreover, since psychology, especially experimental psychology, had various points of contact with physics and physiology, it also formed a bridge between the natural and the human sciences (Eisler 1902: 39). And finally, because of its historical indebtedness to both philosophy and physiology, modern psychology was also ideally placed to negotiate and act as broker between philosophy and the natural sciences (Wundt 1907a: 54–5).

According to Wundt, psychology was to be freed from metaphysical assumptions. One such traditional assumption was that the soul is a substance that underlies mental processes. Wundt rejected such 'substance theories of the soul' and contrasted them with his own 'theory of the actuality of the soul'. The latter amounted to the postulate that 'psychology has to interpret the facts of experience . . . within their own context, and without using any kind of metaphysical hypothesis' (1896: 36). To adopt the theory of actuality was to accept, first and foremost, that human experience did not by itself divide into 'inner' (psychological) and 'external' (physical) experience. 'Inner' and 'external' experience were no more than categories which humans imposed on their experience. Wundt suggested that an unbiased study of human experience revealed a dichotomy which differed from the opposition between internal and external experience: 'Every experience contains *two* factors which in reality are inseparable: the objects of experience and the experiencing subject' (1896: 12).

This opposition between objects and subject of experience was Wundt's key to the definition of psychology, and thus the key for distinguishing psychology from the natural sciences:

> Natural science seeks to determine the properties and the reciprocal relations among the *objects*. Thus natural science abstracts . . . from the subject . . . Psychology cancels that abstraction and thus it investigates experience in its immediate reality. It thereby reports on the relations between the subjective and the objective factors of immediate experience, and informs also on the genesis and the interrelations of the different contents of immediate experience.
>
> (Wundt 1896: 12)

In other words, Wundt submitted that both psychology and the natural sciences were empirical sciences, but that psychology studied 'the given' in its immediacy whereas the natural sciences looked at it merely 'as a system of *signs* on the basis of which one has to form hypotheses of the real nature of the objects' (1896: 23).

According to Wundt, one of the most important consequences following from this definition was that the different perspectives of natural science and psychology could not be reduced to one another: 'psychology is an empirical science *co-ordinated* with natural science, and the perspectives of both complement each other in such a way that only together do they exhaust the empirical knowledge open to us' (1896: 12). And thus the attempts of authors like Külpe, Münsterberg or Mach, all of whom saw psychology as reducing to physiology and biology, were misplaced.

Wundt also proposed that causality in psychology was qualitatively different from causality in the natural sciences. In other words, Wundt distinguished between 'physical' and 'mental causality', and claimed that 'no connection of physical processes can ever teach us anything about the manner of connection between psychological elements' (Wundt 1894: 43).[2]

In Wundt's view, three characteristics distinguished mental from physical causality. First, whereas for the natural sciences cause and effect were 'separate experiences, *disjecta membra*', in that the causal connection between two events 'comes only from the conceptual connection and treatment of experience' (1894: 43),[3] in psychology the connection between psychological elements was not a matter of theory but 'a fact of immediate consciousness' (1894: 108). To put it another way, Wundt suggested that, in the natural sciences, our knowledge of a causal connection between two events was based on invariant regularity on the one hand, and a theory connecting these – separate and distinct, Humean – events on the other. However, when, as psychologists, one knew a reason for an action, one relied neither on observation of a regular conjunction between two events nor on theories which established a conceptual connection (Mischel 1970: 7–8).

Second, mental causality could not be reduced to physical causality because the explanation 'of psychological processes is everywhere shot through with value determinations'. Such value determinations never occurred in causal explanations provided by natural science (1894: 98).[4] Wundt believed that explanation in psychology, as well as in other *Geisteswissenschaften*, always referred to normative standards of what was rational and appropriate (Mischel 1970: 8).

Third, psychological causality was distinct from physical causality because 'the formation of mental products which indicate a conscious purposive activity, in which there is a choice between various possible motives, requires a real consideration of purpose' (1894: 117).[5] In other words, Wundt held that the psychologist, in explaining human action and behaviour, inevitably had to bring in the goals and purposes of the agent.

Wundt thought that he had identified general laws of mental causality. He regarded these laws as the most general explanatory principles in psychology (Blumenthal 1985b: 40). The number of these principles varied in his writings over time; I shall here mention only the four principles listed in Wundt (1903b). They were a) 'the principle of creative resultants' (a complex mental phenomenon is more than the sum of its constituents); b) 'the principle of connecting relations' (every mental content is related to others from which it receives its meaning); c) 'the principle of increasing contrasts' (antithetical experiences intensify each other); and d) 'the principle of the heterogeneity of ends' (purposes and goals that human beings achieve often develop and arise within the attempt to achieve other, further goals) (Wundt 1903b: 778–90).

As the perspectives of psychology and natural science were radically different and not translatable into one another, psychology could not allow for the possibility that a physical cause could bring about a mental effect, or that a mental cause could bring about a physical effect. This stricture was Wundt's principle of 'psychophysical parallelism', which held that, although physical and psychological causal chains ran parallel to one another, they were neither identical, nor even comparable (Wundt 1894: 36; Mischel 1970: 10).

Wundt doubted the value of armchair 'introspection' (*Selbstbeobachtung*) as a foundation of psychological knowledge (e.g. Wundt 1888a; 1908b: 164; Danziger 1980a, 1980b, 1990). Nevertheless, he regarded 'inner perception' (*Selbstwahrnehmung*) of 'lower' mental processes such as sensation and perception as reliable provided it occurred under controlled experimental conditions (1908b: 163). Other areas of psychological study, and most notably the processes of thought, volition and emotion, Wundt eventually regarded as problem areas in which the experimental method could not be used effectively and fruitfully (Danziger 1980a: 247).

It was partly because of the perceived limitations of the experimental method that Wundt felt the need to stress that experimental psychology was not all of psychology. Another central area of psychological study to which Wundt contributed himself was *Völkerpsychologie*. The German term *Völkerpsychologie*, for which there is no established English translation, goes back to the von Humboldt brothers (Schneider 1990: 7). The first extensive programmatic outline for a *Völkerpsychologie* was sketched by the Herbartian philosopher Moritz Lazarus and the linguist Hermann Steinthal in 1860, in the leading article of their newly founded journal *Zeitschrift für Völkerpsychologie und Sprachwissenschaft* (Lazarus and Steinthal 1860). Wundt's own *Völkerpsychologie* was indebted to these authors, although his was a critically modified version of theirs. In his view, *Völkerpsychologie* should confine its research to three subject areas (1888b): language, myth and custom.[6] *Völkerpsychologie* studied universal-general features of the human mind, and such features could only be found in these three areas (1888b: 27). Moreover, Wundt was unwilling to reduce *Völkerpsychologie* to a mere application of individual psychology (1908b: 227–8). He emphasised that

> the conditions of mental reciprocity produce new and specific expressions of general mental forces, expressions which cannot be predicted on the basis of knowledge of the properties of the individual consciousness . . . And thus it takes both individual psychology and *Völkerpsychologie* to constitute psychology as a whole.
>
> (Wundt 1908b: 227)

First and foremost, *Völkerpsychologie* was needed for collecting objective data about psychological processes that could be reliably and objectively studied through neither introspection nor experiment: 'it is precisely at that point where experimental method reaches its limit that the methods of *Völkerpsychologie* provide objective results' (1908b: 227). These methods were the 'comparative-psychological', and the 'historical-psychological': the first compared phenomena of different cultures; the second compared different, successive stages of one and the same cultural phenomenon (1908b: 242).

Wundt called his psychology 'voluntaristic', and contrasted his 'voluntarism' with the 'intellectualism' of faculty psychology, associationism and Herbartian psychology. In Wundt's view, all of the latter suffered from the same defect: of all our mental experiences they concentrated exclusively on logical activities and their results, thereby failing to take account of volition and emotion (1908b: 150–8). 'Voluntaristic psychology', in Wundt's use of the term, was not meant to commit the opposite mistake of concentrating only on volitions. Rather, 'voluntarism' summarised three key ingredients of Wundt's psychology. First, different mental processes, like representing, feeling and wanting, were always mere aspects of a unitary event, and they were all equally basic; i.e. none could be derived directly from the other. Second, volition had a 'representative importance' for many other subjective processes, in so far as these other processes could often be most clearly detected when they were part and parcel of a fully fledged intentional and volitional action. And third, the fully fledged intentional and volitional action could serve as something of a paradigm for all psychological processes. This was because in the case of individual actions it was easy to see that they had the character of unique (i.e.

unrepeatable) and dated 'events'. Taking actions as the model of theorising in psychology could thus save psychologists from the temptation of believing that the products of mental acts – e.g. representations – could be exactly reproduced at different times (1908b: 161).

To conclude this overview of Wundt's philosophy and psychology, it is easy to agree with Ben-David and Collins that Wundt was indeed something of a 'role hybrid'. After all, Wundt entered philosophy as a trained physiologist; he introduced experimental methods into a philosophical discipline, namely psychology, and he contributed, throughout his time as professor in Leipzig, to both experimental psychology and various subdisciplines of philosophy. Moreover, Wundt adopted a view of philosophy according to which it was neither the foundation of, nor the ultimate arbiter between, the sciences. Instead, philosophy was to be 'inductive', i.e. tied to the scientific knowledge of its time, and the role of the arbiter was reserved for the new science, psychology.

Brentano

In Franz Brentano (1838–1917) we encounter a role hybrid of a rather different kind. Brentano started his academic career as an Aristotle scholar, submitting a dissertation in 1862 on Aristotle's notion of being. In 1864 Brentano was ordained a priest in Graz and assigned to a convent. In 1866 he became a lecturer, and in 1872 an extraordinary professor of philosophy in Würzburg, a position that he resigned together with his priesthood in 1873. From 1874 until 1894 Brentano taught in Vienna, first as a full professor until 1880, and subsequently as a lecturer. In 1894 he retired and moved to Florence.

Whereas Wundt was a physiologist who moved into philosophy, Brentano was a traditionally trained philosopher who sought to improve the low standing of philosophy in the intellectual field by linking it more closely to the more prestigious natural sciences. This attitude can already be identified in Brentano's *Habilitationsthesen* of 1866, the most famous of which is 'Vera philosophiae methodus nulla alia nisi scientiae naturalis est' (Brentano [1866] 1968).

Brentano's role in the history of twentieth-century psychology is difficult to characterise. His philosophy of psychology influenced a number of experimental psychologists, both directly and through the mediation of his students Stumpf, Husserl, Meinong and Marty. Brentano is seldom described as having been centrally involved in the institutionalisation of experimental psychology, however. He did not himself carry out any psychological experiments, and was occasionally depicted by experimental psychologists as being part and parcel of the kind of metaphysics from which psychology supposedly had to free itself (e.g. Wundt 1910b).

The best-known interpretations of both these sides of Brentano are due to E.B. Titchener (1909, 1921) and E.G. Boring (1950). As to Brentano's influence on the subsequent generation of psychologists, Titchener and Boring claim that it consisted mainly in the development of a psychology of acts, a psychology that allegedly stood opposed to a Wundtian psychology of contents (i.e. sensations). They also present him as lacking interest in, and failing to see the importance of, experimental psychology.

It is true that Brentano developed a psychology of mental acts, and that his work in this area soon became influential. What is less clear than Titchener and Boring seem to suggest, however, is whether his stress on the activity of the individual really did represent a fundamental difference from Wundt's work; after all, Wundt's voluntarism was meant to account for precisely such mental activity.

As far as Brentano's attitude towards experimental psychology is concerned, it is more easily shown that Titchener and Boring were simply mistaken in underestimating his interest in it. In fact, Brentano was as outspoken a proponent of experimental methods in psychology as any, and he publicly pressed for the founding of a psychology laboratory at the University of Vienna. Indeed, as Brentano reported in 1893, he asked the government for such an institute as early as the mid-1870s: 'If only the ministry had followed my suggestion back then, Vienna would have taken the lead ahead of all German universities' ([1893] 1968: 51).

Brentano's enthusiasm for experimental methods in psychology shows most clearly in his little-read text *Meine letzten Wünsche für Österreich*. There he suggested that the only remedy against the decline of philosophy would be 'the founding of an institute of psychology, an institute which should be entrusted only to someone who in her research follows the methods of the natural sciences' (1895: 33). Brentano claimed that without such an institute many central psychological investigations would remain undone (1895: 33). Moreover, he explained that even his own psychological project could not be carried out properly without the help of a psychology laboratory. The following passage highlights not only

Brentano's belief in the need for experimentation, but also succinctly summarises his view of the basic bipartite structure of
psychology:

> My school distinguishes between a *psychognosy* and a *genetic
> psychology* (in distant parallel with geognosy and geology). The
> first identifies all ultimate mental components that combine
> into the sum of mental phenomena, just as letters combine
> into the sum of words ... The second informs us on the laws
> according to which phenomena come and go. Since – due to
> the undeniable dependence of mental functions on the
> processes in the nervous system – the conditions [of the
> phenomena] are predominantly physiological ones, it is clear
> that psychological investigations must be intertwined with
> physiological studies. Prima facie it seems more plausible to
> suspect that psychognosy could completely ignore the physio-
> logical and thus do without all instrumental means. However,
> the aforementioned analysis of sensations ... can obtain its
> most essential successes only with the help of cleverly designed
> instrumental tools, and this is a psychognostic task.
>
> (Brentano 1895: 35)

Brentano also suggested that psychological work without the use of
experiments would inevitably lead to the kind of fruitless speculation of which he regarded Herbart as the chief representative
(1895: 36). And finally, Brentano polemicised against the idea that
experimental psychology should best be left to physiologists, and
thus be pushed outside philosophy proper:

> The systematic disciplines of philosophy are ... closely inter-
> twined. Perhaps I flatter myself here – but it has to be said
> that, on the basis of new psychological results, I have reformed
> elementary logic and I have provided a deeper insight into
> the principles of ethical knowledge. Similarly one could show
> for aesthetic and all other disciplines of philosophy that once
> they are separated from psychology they will wither like a
> branch that has been cut off from the trunk.
>
> (1895: 39)

Brentano's most influential writings on psychology were not the
above-quoted pamphlets, however, but rather his *Psychologie vom
empirischen Standpunkt* ([1874] 1924). This work consisted of two
volumes, one on the definition of psychology, and one on the

nature of mental phenomena. Four further projected volumes – on presentations (*Vorstellungen*), judgements, emotions and the will, the relation between the mental and the physical organism, and life after death ([1874] 1924: 1) – never appeared in print.

Brentano's distinction between two parts of psychology, 'psychognosy' and 'genetic psychology' has already been cited. In his *Psychologie* Brentano went on to suggest that psychognosy and genetic psychology differed in that only the former's results were self-evident, a priori and apodictic. The laws of genetic psychology, on the other hand, were mere inductive generalisations and thus inevitably inexact:

> There are two factors which preclude a precise formulation of the highest laws of mental succession: first, they are mere empirical laws, dependent upon the changing influence of physiological processes which have not yet been studied; and second, the intensity of mental phenomena, an intensity which plays an essential role here, cannot as yet be measured exactly.
>
> (Brentano [1874] 1924: 102)

The two most influential ideas of Brentano's *Psychologie* were undoubtedly his differentiation between inner observation and inner perception, and his distinction between mental and physical phenomena. *Observation* of inner mental phenomena was impossible. As observation implied full attention to the object observed, any observation of, say, an emotion would inevitably change the intensity of that emotion. What was possible, however, and what was indeed the basis of psychological knowledge, was inner *perception*. In inner perception, one did not attend fully to one's mental processes; rather one noted them 'incidentally' while remaining directed towards the primary objects of one's mental state or activity ([1874] 1924: 41).

Brentano's distinction between mental and physical phenomena is well known. The mark of mental phenomena was their intentionality:

> Every mental phenomenon is characterised by what medieval scholars called the intentional . . . in-existence of an object, and what we . . . would call the relation to a content, the direction towards an object (which here does not mean a real thing), or immanent objectivity. Every mental phenomenon

contains an object within itself, although not all do so in the same way. In a presentation something is presented; in a judgement something is being accepted or rejected; in love something is loved; in hatred something is hated, and in desire something is being desired.

([1874] 1924: 125)

It was this definition of mental phenomena as intentional experiences, or 'acts', which led Brentano and his students to the notion of psychology as a study of 'acts' or 'functions' rather than 'contents'. For Brentano, psychology was the study of mental phenomena ([1874] 1924: 27), and these mental phenomena were acts which had a content. The contents of such acts, however, i.e. sensations, concepts and thoughts, were the subject matter of other sciences rather than a topic for psychology (Bell 1990: 8).

Stumpf

Judging by the number of philosophy chairs that he held, Carl Stumpf (1848–1936) undoubtedly had the most successful career of all 'founding fathers' of modern psychology. Trained by Brentano and Lotze, Stumpf held chairs in philosophy in Würzburg, Prague, Halle, Munich and Berlin. He was appointed to a full professorship at the age of 25, and obtained the prestigious Berlin chair at the age of 46 in 1894.

Like Brentano, Stumpf emphasised the need for experiments in psychology, and like his teacher he also saw the new psychology as part and parcel of philosophy. He proposed, moreover, that psychology 'holds together all the different branches of philosophical research' (1907c: 90) and that recent progress in philosophy was mainly due 'to a psychology which has been carried out in the spirit of the natural sciences' ([1907a] 1910: 167). Furthermore, Stumpf explicitly rejected the idea that the introduction of experiments into psychology separated it from philosophy (1907c: 89). Add to this his insistence quoted earlier that 'no claim can be epistemologically true and psychologically false' (1892: 483), and it should be obvious that Stumpf's general view of philosophy made him another clear instance of a writer who was eager, or willing, to fuse the role of the philosopher with that of the natural scientist.

Nevertheless, Stumpf's attitude towards experimentation in psychology was somewhat ambiguous. While stressing the need for psychological experiments (1907c: 25), he did not himself engage much in experimental work. When the Prussian government in 1893 offered Stumpf a lavishly funded psychology institute in Berlin – with a budget double the size of Wundt's laboratory in Leipzig – Stumpf turned down the offer. In a letter to the ministry he wrote:

> I would like to suggest that, instead of such an institute as exists in Leipzig, just a psychology seminar be established, with the task of supporting and supplementing the lectures by means of laboratory exercises and demonstrations. The carrying out of scientific work for publication would naturally not be excluded, but would not be among the essential purposes of the seminar ... I am in any case of the opinion that large-scale research in experimental psychology has objective difficulties as well ... for my part I could not decide, now or later, to follow the example of Wundt and the Americans in this direction.
>
> (Quoted in Ash 1980a: 272)

Only a few years later, however, Stumpf changed his mind and petitioned repeatedly for more funds for experimental research (Ash 1980a: 273).

Stumpf's most influential writings were his *Tonpsychologie* (1883–90), as well as three longish articles, 'Psychologie und Erkenntnistheorie' (1892), 'Erscheinungen und psychische Funktionen' (1907b) and 'Zur Einteilung der Wissenschaften' (1907c). None of these were based on laboratory research; indeed, Stumpf actually became involved in a heated debate with Wundt about the psychology of sound, in which Stumpf placed the knowledge of the musical expert over and above knowledge obtained by psychophysical methods in the laboratory (Boring 1950: 365).

Stumpf's 'Erscheinungen und psychische Funktionen' was a highly influential restatement of Brentano's distinction between content and act, replacing these terms with 'phenomena' and 'function' respectively. Phenomena were sensory and imaginal data, whereas functions were, for instance, 'the noticing of phenomena and their relations, the combining of phenomena into complexes, the formation of concepts, grasping and judging, the emotions, the desiring and willing' (1907b: 4–5). Stumpf demanded that an adequate psychology should attend to both phenomena and functions, and he did so on the grounds that neither of the two categories could be reduced to the other (1907b: 10). Stumpf

also suggested that functions and phenomena could vary independently of one another (1907b: 15–38): function changed without a
change in phenomenon when, for instance, a formerly unnoticed
phenomenon became the object of attention, and a phenomenon
changed without a change in function when, for example, a room
got darker without the change being noticed.

Stumpf's 'Zur Einteilung der Wissenschaften' (1907c) contained
inter alia the suggestion that psychology should be distinguished
from three 'neutral sciences', to wit, 'phenomenology', 'eidology'
and 'general theory of relations'. The first was meant to study, with
experimental tools, phenomena and their interrelations (1907c:
26–32), the second was to investigate and list logical, axiological
and ontological categories (1907c: 32–7), and the third was to
concentrate on concepts like similarity, identity, dependence, as
well as part and whole (1907c: 37–42).

Ebbinghaus

In Hermann Ebbinghaus (1850–1909) we encounter an instance of
the role hybrid 'philosopher/physiologist' that differs from
Wundt's, Brentano's and Stumpf's versions of the new professional
role. Even though Ebbinghaus was trained as a philosopher – he
submitted a philosophical dissertation to the University of Bonn in
1873 – and even though he held philosophy chairs – in Berlin as
extraordinary professor (1886–94) and in Wroctaw as full professor
(1894–1909) – he did not feel the urge to contribute to more
traditional areas of philosophy. It was undoubtedly this attitude
which lead Dilthey and other 'pure philosophers' to oppose
Ebbinghaus's promotion to a full professorship in Berlin in 1894;
as Dilthey put it in a letter in 1893, to promote Ebbinghaus would
have meant 'a complete natural-scientific radicalisation of philosophy' (Dilthey and Yorck 1923: 165).

Ebbinghaus's exclusive attention to experimental psychology
also explains his activities as co-founder of the *Zeitschrift für Psychologie und Physiologie der Sinnesorgane* in 1890, and his active
involvement in the *Gesellschaft für experimentelle Psychologie*. The
Zeitschrift stood in opposition to the Wundtian programme of
psychology: its editors saw no need for a *Völkerpsychologie* that would
take over from experimental psychology once higher thought
processes were the subject matter; the *Zeitschrift* looked for legitimating support to figures in physiology rather than philosophy (Ash

1980a: 266); and it had little room for purely philosophical papers of the kind that Wundt's *Philosophische Studien* published alongside reports on psychological experiments.

Overall, Ebbinghaus's role in the early history of experimental psychology has been described as that of 'a leader without many publications' (Boring 1950: 389). His best-known work was a small but highly important book on memory *Über das Gedächtnis* (1885), in which he studied how the amount of material learned affected the ability to recall the material; how repeated learning strengthened memory; how the ability to remember decreased with increasing temporal distance from the learning process; and how direct and remote, as well as forward and backward associations strengthened or weakened the ability to remember (Boring 1950: 388). In later years, Ebbinghaus published *inter alia* on brightness contrast, colour vision and the testing of schoolchildren (Boring 1950: 389). In the eyes of many of his colleagues, Ebbinghaus's work showed that experimental psychology could indeed tackle the study of higher mental processes, and that no *Völkerpsychologie* was needed for that purpose (Külpe 1912b: 1074; Boring 1950: 388, 390).

Müller

Georg Elias Müller (1850–1934) has been called 'the first experimental psychologist' (Boring 1950: 379) and 'the experimenter's experimenter' (Blumenthal 1985a: 53). Both of these characterisations are meant to bring out two important features of Müller's work. On the one hand, Müller wrote only on experimental psychology. On the other hand, he did not agree with Wundt's idea that the experimental method in psychology had definite limits. For Müller, the experimental method could be applied to the study of all psychological processes, including such higher thought processes as memory and judging.

Müller studied philosophy with Moritz Drobisch, a Herbartian scholar, in Leipzig, and with Hermann Lotze in Göttingen. Müller submitted a dissertation on sensory attention in Göttingen in 1873. Five years later, Müller published his *Habilitationsschrift* on psychophysics, and on the basis of the success of the latter work he became Lotze's successor in Göttingen in 1881. Müller remained in Göttingen as full professor in philosophy until his retirement in 1921. From 1887 onwards the university granted Müller facilities for experimental work, and after 1891 the university also provided some funds for a laboratory. Contemporary sources suggest that Müller's laboratory was 'in many respects the best for research work in the whole of Germany', and that it was second only to the laboratory in Leipzig (Boring 1950: 374). The success of the laboratory can be seen, among other things, from the fact that the two other leading centres of experimental psychology in Germany at the time, i.e. Berlin and Leipzig, hired experimentalists trained by Müller.

Müller's contribution to experimental psychology was, and still is, admired for its precision and thoroughness. Typically, Müller would elaborate on the work of others, pushing their ideas further and giving them a higher degree of experimental and quantitative rigour. In this vein, he continued Fechner's work on psychophysics, Ebbinghaus's study of memory, McKeen Cattell's investigations into reaction times, Wundt's research on spatial localisation, Münsterberg's work on the sensory-motor theory of volition, Hering's theory of colour vision and Calkins's experiments on paired-associate learning (Blumenthal 1985a: 54).

In order to bring out Müller's differences with Wundt, Müller's bent towards physiological reductionism as well as his experimental study of higher thought processes must be mentioned. Müller's inclination towards physiological reductionism was already apparent in his dissertation. There he suggested that changes in the cortical blood supply are crucially involved in changes in attention. As blood was concentrated in different parts of the brain at different times, for instance, an experience would be enhanced if it were associated with a part of the brain in which such blood concentration occurred. Müller also sought to explain voluntary movement as resulting from an increased blood supply in certain brain areas. In subsequent years, he also tried to put psychophysics on a solid physiological basis by eliminating the mind–body dualism of Fechner (Blumenthal 1985a: 54–5). By the same token, Müller of course also rejected the Wundtian idea of mental causality.

Like Ebbinghaus, Külpe and others, Müller also rejected Wundt's notion that experimental psychologists were unable to study phenomena of thought (Külpe 1912b: 1074). Indeed, Müller continued and deepened Ebbinghaus's work in this area, soon becoming the leader in the study of memory. For instance, he refined the methods for the construction of nonsense syllables, studied various types of interference and inhibition, introduced the use of reaction times as measures of memory strength, and developed various new instruments (Blumenthal 1985a: 57).

Müller's impact on the field of experimental psychology can hardly be exaggerated. Boring wrote that 'as a power and institution he was second only to Wundt' (1950: 379), and for Blumenthal Müller was the major figure among those early psychologists who 'began strictly as experimentalists and remained, for the most part, steadfast in that activity throughout their careers . . . It is they who should be regarded as the true paragons of the new experimental psychology' (1985a: 52).

Külpe

Oswald Külpe (1862–1915) studied with both Wundt and Müller. Külpe began work on his doctoral dissertation under Müller in Göttingen, but completed it under Wundt in Leipzig in 1887. Although he dedicated his dissertation to Müller, in the following year Wundt appointed Külpe as his assistant. Külpe stayed in Leipzig until 1893 when he took up a position as professor of philosophy in Würzburg. Later, from 1910 until 1911, he held a chair at the University of Bonn, before moving on to the University of Munich.

As is to be expected from a student of both Wundt and Müller, Külpe was not only 'a careful technician' in his experimental work, but also a contributor to more entrenched philosophical disciplines – i.e. like Wundt, Külpe wrote extensively on logic and epistemology.

Külpe's name is of course best known in connection with the work of the Würzburg School, i.e. with the introspective-experimental study of higher mental processes of thinking. As pointed out by Danziger (1979), the Külpe-inspired work of that school must be seen as the outcome of Külpe's earlier 'repudiation' of Wundt. This repudiation of Wundt first took shape in Külpe's *Grundriß der Psychologie* (1893), and was developed by him in subsequent writings (Külpe 1894).

Külpe's central resources in his repudiation of Wundtian psychology were Richard Avenarius and Ernst Mach's views on science and psychology. Avenarius and Mach rejected the metaphysical dualism between the mental and the physical, claiming that 'experience' (*Erfahrung*) showed no such division. The two positivists nevertheless allowed for the possibility that experience could be investigated from two different points of views, i.e. either as *dependent* on, or as *independent* of the particular physiological system to which it belonged. The first viewpoint was that of the physical sciences, the second that of empirical, or scientific, psychology. In their conception of a scientific psychology, the notion of a physiological system was central for Avenarius and Mach. They demanded that psychological explanations be based on physiological principles, and that mentalistic concepts – that is, concepts presupposing the notion of an acting ego-subject – be excluded from psychology. As Mach and Avenarius saw it, such concepts had no basis in immediate experience. Both men saw it as the task of science to provide the most economical description of the interrelations among experiences, and Mach conceived of scientific laws as stating functional relationships between observables. Mach also held that the sciences were to be thought of as one hierarchical structure in which less general sciences were situated below more general ones. As progress toward greater thought economy meant the formulation of ever more general theories and laws, less general sciences were to be reduced to more general ones. With regard to psychology this meant that it should ultimately be reduced to physiology and biology (Danziger 1979: 210–12).

Because Külpe adopted the position of these positivist philosophers, he rejected, first, Wundt's notion of mental causality, second, the distinction between experimental and nonexperimental psychology and, third, the idea that there were areas in psychology to which the experimental method could not fruitfully be applied. Mental causality had to go because, like Avenarius and Mach, Külpe demanded that psychology relate the facts of experience to the 'corporeal', physiological or biological individual or organism. Only in this way, Külpe wrote in 1893, could psychology become a natural science: 'The objects of psychological enquiry would never present the advantages of measurability and unequivocalness, possessed in so high a degree by the objects investigated by natural science, if they could be brought into relation only with the mental individual' (1893: 4; tr. Danziger 1979: 209). For Külpe, mental processes had to be explained by physiology.

As Külpe wanted psychology to become a natural science, he had no sympathies for Wundt's distinction between two branches of psychology, experimental, physiological psychology and nonexperimental *Völkerpsychologie* (belonging to the *Geisteswissenschaften*). Nor did Külpe share Wundt's scepticism concerning the applicability of the experimental method to the study of higher mental processes. Encouraged by Ebbinghaus's study of memory, Külpe wrote that 'in principle there is no topic of psychological inquiry which cannot be approached by the experimental method. And experimental psychology is therefore fully within its rights when it claims to be the general psychology of which we propose to treat' (Külpe 1893: 12; tr. Danziger 1979: 213).

Once Külpe had a full chair in philosophy and his own laboratory in Würzburg, he and his students set out to study higher mental processes by experimental means. Such processes included judgement and problem solving. The methods used in these experiments were straightforward: tasks were set for experienced subjects, i.e. members of Külpe's research group, who then tried to solve the tasks. At the same time, these subjects made introspections on how they arrived at their solutions. In some experiments of this kind, reaction times were measured as well. The most famous result of these highly controversial experiments was of course the claim that there existed 'imageless thought', i.e. that many thought processes could not be accounted for by images and sensations alone. Külpe and his students spoke of 'conscious attitudes' (*Bewußtseinslagen*) and 'awareness' (*Bewußtheit*) in order to denote such unpalpable and unanalysable contents (Boring 1950: 403–6).

Although Külpe was undoubtedly the source of inspiration of much of the work of the Würzburg School (Ach, Bühler, Marbe, Messer, Orth, Watt), and despite the fact that his positivistic repudiation of Wundt had been the key opening move for that work, by 1909 he had changed both his physical location – accepting a chair in Bonn – and his philosophical outlook. Brentano's and Husserl's work was received positively in the Würzburg School, and eventually Külpe moved away from Machian phenomenalism and towards Husserlian phenomenology. (I shall return to this shift in Chapter 8.)

A science of one's own?

To conclude this brief review of the career and work of the six key figures in the rise of the new psychology, it is worth emphasising once more that they represented different versions of the role hybrid 'philosopher/physiologist' or 'philosopher/psychologist'. For instance, while all of them stressed the need for experimental work in psychology, not all of them engaged in such studies themselves. And while all of them held full professorial chairs in philosophy, two of them published only on experimental psychology, seeing no need to legitimate their position by writing also on more traditional philosophical topics.

These differences between the philosophers/psychologists were also reflected in their answers to the question whether psychology's progress, and its use of the experimental method, made it imperative that the institutional links with philosophy be cut. One can distinguish four positions with respect to this question.

Ebbinghaus claimed that psychology had indeed earned the title of a special science, and that it was to be independent of philosophy (Ebbinghaus 1907; cf. Hellpach 1906; Münsterberg 1914). For him the very possibility of further advances in psychology depended on its becoming 'an independent science primarily done only for its own sake' (1907: 185). As long as psychology remained a part of philosophy, Ebbinghaus feared, psychology would merely be a 'servant of philosophy', and would not live up to its full potential. Moreover, he alleged that psychology had already grown into a field of such breadth and complexity that it could not be properly advanced by anyone who taught and investigated various fields of philosophy alongside it (1907: 186).

A second position was close to that of Ebbinghaus but differed from it in distinguishing between two equally justified kinds of psychology: psychology as a special science, and psychology as a philosophical discipline. This position was advocated by Külpe in 1912. While Külpe agreed with Ebbinghaus that experimental psychology had already acquired the character of a special science, he also spoke of the need to retain a genuinely 'philosophical psychology':

> Of course a philosophical psychology will remain alongside the special science of psychology. The former [i.e. philosophical psychology] may certainly provide an orientation regarding, and a discussion concerning, the logical, epistemological and metaphysical problems and concepts, as well as the metaphysical continuations and conclusions [of experimental psychology].
>
> (Külpe 1912a: 264)

According to the third, Wundtian viewpoint, psychology was advanced enough to claim the title of a special science. However,

Wundt advised against any institutional separation. This view was based on his estimation that many psychological problems had close links with philosophical questions, and that psychological knowledge was important for philosophy. Wundt did not arrive at a clear statement of this view until 1913. In 1883 he was still calling experimental psychology a part of philosophy (1883: 617), while by 1896 he deemed it undeniable that psychology 'is well on the way to transforming itself from a subdiscipline of philosophy into an independent, positive science' (1896: 2). In 1903 Wundt wrote that 'psychology is – regardless of whether one counts it as a part of philosophy or not – for the philosopher an indispensable preliminary school' (1903c: 793–4). And in 1913 he added that the dependence relation was symmetric: the psychologist needed knowledge of philosophy just as much as the philosopher needed to be acquainted with psychological research (1913: 18). When Wundt concluded his 1913 pamphlet *Die Psychologie im Kampf ums Dasein* with the remark that psychology is 'both a subdiscipline of philosophy and an empirical basic science', he did not side with Külpe's plea for a distinction between experimental and philosophical psychology (1913: 32). Instead Wundt advocated the view that psychology as a whole should remain institutionally a part of philosophy, even though its advances justified one's calling it a special science.

Fourth and finally, Stumpf sharply rejected the suggestion that psychology should seek independence from philosophy. For Stumpf psychology – including experimental psychology – was the uniting element between, and the foundation of, the different philosophical disciplines. Moreover, Stumpf did not regard the use of the experimental method as compromising the philosophical character of psychology. While Stumpf conceded that some psychological studies were too specialised to be regarded as properly philosophical, he did not think that the existence of such studies called for an institutional or conceptual separation between psychology and philosophy: 'Although some individual [psychological] investigations are, and must be, nonphilosophical, psychological science as such and as a whole is not nonphilosophical' (1907c: 91).

AN OBLIGATORY CROSSING POINT

Although advocates and practitioners of the new psychology differed over the issues mentioned above, they as well as their students and followers agreed that psychology had become an obligatory crossing point for anyone interested in the advancement of culture, everyday life, philosophy and the sciences. Indeed, these writers regarded the new psychology variously as (1) a remedy against cultural decline, (2) as an auxiliary science for other disciplines, institutions and practices, (3) as the foundation of the *Geisteswissenschaften*, (4) as the key to progress in philosophy and (5) as the centre of philosophy itself.

Psychology and cultural decline   The crucial role of psychology in improving modern culture and society was stressed by Brentano and Heymans, among others. Brentano claimed that the present 'shattered social conditions' could be repaired on the basis of psychological expertise ([1874] 1924: 35). He expressed his hope that

> in this way, as well as in a thousand other ways, the influence of psychology would be the most beneficial. Perhaps only psychology can provide a remedy against the decline which, from time to time, interrupts the otherwise constantly ascending development of culture.
>
> (Brentano [1874] 1924: 31–2)

Part of this remedy was to be psychology's marshalling of arguments for a life after death ([1874] 1924: 37).

Thirty-seven years later Heymans was still using a similar line of argument. In his pamphlet *Das künftige Jahrhundert der Psychologie* Heymans spoke of the 'fragmented nature of our mental being': 'we want, simultaneously or successively, a thousand different kinds of things, but then again we want nothing from our whole heart or our whole soul' (1911: 18–19). Heymans listed statistical data to the effect that the divorce rate, the number of men changing jobs, and religious disorientation were all dramatically on the increase (1911: 19–23). Heymans had no doubt about which field of study would be of most help: 'Could it be that . . . our culture is already busy preparing itself a remedy and that this remedy is . . . psychology?' (1911: 26). For Heymans 'the expectation is justified that psychology will enable us to make faster and more regular progress in moral terms than ever before in the past' (1911: 46), and he predicted that the increasing importance of psychology in social life would be 'one of the most important moments in the history of mankind' (1911: 52). Not least, psychology would weaken materialistic worldviews by 'moving the mental realm from the periphery to the centre of *Weltanschauungen*' (1911: 49).

Psychology as *the* auxiliary science   Often proponents of the new psychology would also point to specific areas of life, and specific fields of science as realms to which psychological knowledge could be fruitfully applied. In the early decades of the new psychology such statements were largely predictions, hopes and promises (e.g. Brentano 1874), but by the second decade of the twentieth century the advocates of psychology were able to write extensive reviews of successful applications of psychology (e.g. Marbe 1912, Messer 1914b, Münsterberg 1912, 1914).

Brentano stressed above all the importance of psychology for politics:

> Since so far psychological doctrines have never been system-atically applied in the domain of the state, indeed, since the guardians over the people lack, almost without exception, all knowledge regarding psychological doctrines, one could say, with Plato and several thinkers of our own times, that, however much fame some statesmen have gained, no great statesman has yet appeared in history.
>
> ([1874] 1924: 30–1)

Marbe's much later review 'Die Bedeutung der Psychologie für die übrigen Wissenschaften und die Praxis' ('The importance of psychology for the other sciences and for practice', 1912) pre-sented psychology as the central 'auxiliary science' (*Hilfswissen-schaft*) for natural science, medicine, linguistics, philology, literary studies, aesthetics, history, pedagogy, jurisprudence, economics and philosophy, summarising some 200 psychological studies rel-evant for these areas.

Marbe did not mention the military in his review, but the utility and importance of psychological knowledge to the military was soon stressed as well. In 1911 and 1912 the *Archiv für die gesamte Psychologie* published two papers by a Captain Meyer on the 'ex-perimental analysis of mental processes involved in firing a hand-gun' (Meyer 1911, 1912b), and the *Zeitschrift für pädagogische Psychologie und experimentelle Pädagogik* devoted space to the same author's more programmatic statements on the need for a proper psychological training for officers (Meyer 1912a).

Psychology as the foundation of the *Geisteswissenschaften* Of the arts and sciences, supporters of the new psychology paid special attention to the human sciences (*Geisteswissenschaften*). We have already seen that Wundt regarded psychology as providing the foundations for the *Geisteswissenschaften*. Other authors concurred with this view. For example, Lipps equated psychology with the sum of all *Geisteswissenschaften*, proposing that fields of study deserve the title *Geisteswissenschaft* 'only if and in so far as they are psychological sciences' (1901: 6). Thus history was 'a psychological *explanatory* science, i.e. a science which subsumes individual facts under psychological laws' (1901: 8). Either the historians were themselves involved in the production of psychological laws, e.g. when finding regularities in sound shifts, or they applied psychological laws. And therefore 'it is just as certain that the historical sciences are psychological sciences as it is certain that they cannot function without their foundation, i.e. scientific psychology' (1901: 8). As Lipps saw it, this scientific psychology essentially included experimental psychology:

> experimental psychology is not *all of* psychology. But it is just as clear that it necessarily belongs within psychology . . . And we have to look at psychological institutes in the same way: not as *the only* condition, but as a necessary completion of the conditions under which psychology can be what it ought to be: – Not a queen of the sciences in the sense in which philosophy once aspired to this title, i.e. not a ruler. But a queen nevertheless.
>
> (Lipps 1901: 27–8)

Wundt's and Lipps's call for a psychological basis for the *Geisteswissenschaften* was taken up by the historian Karl Lamprecht, a colleague of Wundt in Leipzig and probably the most controversial historian in Germany around the turn of the century. Time and again (e.g. 1896, 1904, 1913a, 1913b) Lamprecht emphasised the need for psychological foundations for the discipline of history. According to Lamprecht, 'history as such is nothing but applied psychology, and thus it is clear that theoretical psychology must provide the main connecting thread for its inner understanding' (1904: 16–17). Psychology was 'the mechanics of the *Geisteswissenschaften*' (1904: 17) and all of its results and methods, 'starting already with the results, or at least the methods, of experimental psychology, are highly relevant for the methodological development of the *Geisteswissenschaften*' (1913a: 21).

Psychology as the key to progress in philosophy   Given the fact that most supporters, and key figures of the new psychology were philosophers by training, or else aspired to chairs in philosophy, it is not surprising that many of them stressed the significance of the new psychology for past and present progress in philosophy. This strategy was used by Wundt as early as 1863, i.e. at a time when he did not yet hold a position in philosophy. In his *Vorlesungen über die Menschen- und Tierseele* Wundt wrote:

> Since philosophy has returned from its last bold enterprise – the enterprise based on speculative thought – the view has been gaining ground that philosophical studies can be a foil for fruitful development only in sciences based upon experience. As philosophy returns to experience, so one philosophical science gains commensurately more and more attention; this is the science which is, more than any other, a science of immediate experience: I mean psychology. It cannot be ignored that the few independent studies in the area of philosophy which our time has produced belong mainly to the realm of psychology.
>
> (Wundt 1863: iii)

Wundt emphasised the philosophical significance of experimental psychology by giving the journal which was supposed to present the results of experimental research carried out in his institute the title *Philosophische Studien*. As Wundt later admitted himself, this title was meant to be a 'Kampftitel', a battle cry (1903b: 794; 1917: 571; 1920: 314). The title was intended to show 'that this new psychology claimed to be a subdiscipline of philosophy'. The title was also meant as a signal that experimental psychology had nothing to do with materialism, and that experimental psychology could not be equated with physiology (1920: 314).

Occasionally Wundt would also pursue another strategy for bolstering the status of the new psychology ([1907a] 1910: 54–5). The same Wundt who in 1863 had argued that experimental psychology resulted from the overcoming of idealistic speculation propounded some forty years later that the two areas of his psychology, experimental psychology and *Völkerpsychologie*, amounted to something like the culmination of recent philosophical and scientific history. Modern psychology carried within itself the true core of Herbart's, Schopenhauer's and Hegel's work, but it checked their ideas against the further influence of the positive sciences. Thus psychology was ideally placed to negotiate and act as broker between philosophy and the natural sciences.

Wundt's students agreed with the man whom they referred to as 'a modern Aristotle or Leibniz' (Külpe 1920: 95; Messer 1913: 248) in viewing psychological knowledge as crucial for philosophical work. Külpe feared that philosophical work would remain hopelessly abstract if it were not properly related to experimental psychology (1894: 292), and later he suggested that it was through his psychological knowledge that the philosopher possessed 'a centre in which all strands of conscious human activity join together' (1912b: 1071). And Marbe predicted that 'the time will come when one will look upon the study of psychology as being of equal importance to the philosopher as today one regards mathematics for the physicist, or physics for the chemist, or classical philology for the historian of ancient times' (1912: 69).

Several of the proponents of the new psychology pointed out furthermore that it was first and foremost *experimental* psychology which was the true motor behind philosophy's progress. Wundt (1863: iv–v) proposed that prior to the introduction of the experiment into psychology 'the discipline had essentially remained at the same point for centuries'. Münsterberg (1889: 1) too thought that it was the psychological experiment which had turned psychology into a progressive research project. However, the most famous slogan for opposing the old to the new psychology came from Ebbinghaus who wrote that '*psychology has a long past but only a short history.* It has existed and aged for millennia but it has hardly enjoyed a steady and continuous progress towards a more mature and richer form' (1907: 173; emphasis added). Such progress had become possible only once psychology had been turned into a laboratory science (1907: 185). Marbe claimed that traditional philosophical armchair psychology differed from experimental psychology as the work of the presocratic philosophers differed from the results and methods of modern natural science (Husserl [1911] 1987: 40). And finally Külpe proposed that only with the introduction of experiments into psychology had the latter become 'a universally valid science' (*eine allgemeingültige Wissenschaft*) in which 'contributions from opposite metaphysical and even epistemological viewpoints . . . can be easily and peacefully integrated'.

This meant that one could now speak of a 'mutuality of psychological work' that simply did not exist as long as psychologists were not using the experimental method (1893: 457–8).

Anyone who failed to see the great contribution of the new psychology to the progress in philosophy was prone to be ridiculed by the advocates of the new science. For instance, one defender of experimental psychology characterised philosophers sceptical of his field of study in the following way:

> There exist people who experience experimental psychology as uncomfortable: philosophers who have rested their mind on the pillow of rigid philosophical formulae and who regard every lively movement as an unjustified intrusion into their dream world; metaphysicians who engage in mental acrobatic tricks with the shadows of their thoughts and who are unable to stand the warm breeze of life and reality; literati who hate the arduous path of scientific research and who prefer to produce the shimmering coat of philosophical erudition by means of a few general sentences; ponderous supporters of old values who see in the new science the battering-ram which will pull down ramshackle edifices and doctrines into the dust; all these spirits of yesterday, all these who were raised in the verbal tricks of the past, all of them detect in experimental psychology their enemy.
>
> (Braunshausen 1911: 1)

Psychology as the foundation of philosophy To claim that the new psychology was largely responsible for recent progress in philosophy was one thing; to go further and claim that psychology was – or should be – the heart, or basis, of all of philosophy was of course quite another. Yet several writers took this further step and assigned the new psychology a dominant position within philosophy itself. Avenarius claimed not only that psychology-*cum*-physiology provided the key for a proper understanding of the human biological need for philosophy, but also that psychology belonged at the centre of philosophy itself. On the one hand, psychology enabled one to understand philosophy as resulting from the human psychobiological need to conceive of the world in the most economical and consistent way. On the other hand, psychology identified the two key concepts in terms of which one could and had to understand living within the real world. These terms were 'movement' and 'sensation' (Avenarius 1877: 486). And thus it turned out that in fact psychology itself provided the most economical way for understanding the world. This was justification enough for regarding psychology as the centre of philosophy (1877: 487).

A similar conclusion was reached by Krüger in a pamphlet entitled *Ist Philosophie ohne Psychologie möglich?* (Is philosophy possible without psychology?, 1896). Krüger was working under Theodor Lipps (1851–1914) at the time, who, as will be recalled, was *the* archetypal psychologistic thinker for many. Lipps was professor of philosophy in Bonn, Wrocław and Munich (1894–1914), and founder of the Psychological Institute in Munich, even though – like Brentano and Stumpf – he carried out little experimental research himself. I have already quoted earlier the notorious passage from his *Grundzüge der Logik* (1893) according to which logic was a psychological discipline. Krüger's pamphlet shows that Lipps's radical position had followers who perhaps pushed his position even further than he himself had intended. For Krüger, logic and epistemology were based upon psychology and were, as 'sciences of thought', part and parcel of psychology:

> The whole opposition between 'normative' and explanatory sciences is superficial and psychologically unjustified, because valid norms and obedience to them are just as much mental facts as is their violation. The task can only be to investigate psychologically what happens psychologically in both cases.
>
> (Krüger 1896: 22)

Moreover, Krüger claimed that philosophical disciplines like logic, epistemology, ethics and aesthetics were simply all

> parts and special areas of general psychology. They apply the latter's results to special areas and forms of mental life, and thus might be called *applied* psychology – as distinct from *pure* psychology – with which they will however, as just seen, always remain inseparably connected.
>
> (1896: 26)

No field of studies deserved the title 'philosophy' more than psychology. Indeed, empirical psychology not only formed the basis of all philosophy; for Krüger 'all *scientific philosophy* is empirical *psychology*' (1896: 28).

That this kind of enthusiasm for empirical psychology was not rooted out by Husserl's *Prolegomena* can be seen as we turn from

Krüger to Eisenmeyer's book-length study *Die Psychologie und ihre zentrale Stellung in der Philosophie* (Psychology and its central position in philosophy, 1914). Although Eisenmeyer did not equate philosophy and psychology, he deemed 'a scientific philosophy without psychology totally impossible' (1914: 22). According to Eisenmeyer, in every field of philosophical enquiry the starting point had to be the proper incorporation of psychological results, and to neglect these results could not but invalidate the philosophical study in question. This was because 'most of the laws of all philosophical disciplines are either straightforward psychological necessities or knowledge derived from them ... [Thus] all progress of the philosophical disciplines is tightly linked to the progress of our psychological knowledge' (1914: 34–5). Furthermore, Eisenmeyer asserted that it was only the relationship of all philosophical subdisciplines to psychology that justified our speaking of philosophy as *one* discipline. All of the subdisciplines 'have their common foundation in psychology, but otherwise each philosophical discipline is an independent structure, and only a few bridges lead from one to another' (1914: 22). For Eisenmeyer a philosophy not based upon scientific psychology was 'more or less beautiful poetry which has nothing in common with serious, sober and well-founded research' (1914: 36). The main body of Eisenmeyer's book consisted of arguments to the effect that each philosophical discipline was in fact dependent upon psychology. For instance, 'the laws of logic either are laws of psychology or result from psychological laws' (1914: 76). This was because it was a task of psychology to characterise and explain both logical and illogical behaviour (1914: 69). Epistemology was meant to identify the laws of our coming to know the world and ourselves, but these laws were, again, psychological laws. And thus epistemology was 'identical with the psychology of the process of coming to know' (1914: 80). Metaphysics was based upon psychology in so far as only psychological analysis could show that key metaphysical concepts were not empty (1914: 100). And finally, the history of philosophy presupposed psychology, because progress in philosophy was by and large based on progress in psychology (1914: 105). Eisenmeyer concluded: 'Wherever philosophical knowledge is not directly identical with psychological knowledge, it is built throughout upon psychological knowledge. Psychology is the central discipline for all of philosophy' (1914: 105).

Brentano and his students repeatedly voiced similar views. For

Brentano the 'roots' of aesthetics, logic and ethics all lay in psychology ([1874] 1924: 30). Marty suggested that the 'practical disciplines' of ethics, logic and aesthetics were related to psychology 'as medicine to theoretical biology, or agricultural science to chemistry' (1896: 79). He also held that metaphysics depended on psychology, since key metaphysical problems, for instance the question whether there were synthetic judgements a priori, could only be addressed by psychology (1896: 80). Marty defined philosophy as 'that area of knowledge which comprises psychology and all those disciplines that are linked to psychological research according to the principle of the division of labour' (1896: 82–3). Stumpf (1907c) by and large restated this view. The attempt to separate logic, aesthetics and ethics from psychology seemed 'nonsensical' to him, and he also rejected the idea that the introduction of experiments into psychology made its remaining within philosophy impossible: 'Why shouldn't philosophy rely on experiments wherever philosophy has use for them? Anyway, it wouldn't be the first time' (1907c: 89). The existence of voluntaristic, panmental and other psychology-based systems of metaphysics was proof enough for Stumpf that psychology was highly relevant for metaphysical studies (1907c: 90). And while Stumpf denied Krüger's claim that aesthetics, ethics and logic were merely 'applied psychology', he too insisted that they 'nourish themselves everywhere on psychological blood'. Stumpf also sided with Krüger in believing that it was psychology which 'holds together all these different branches of philosophical research' (1907c: 90).

7

ROLE PURIFICATION
The reaction of 'pure philosophy'
against the new psychology

INTRODUCTION

The last chapter provided a brief account of the rise of experimental psychology in Germany. For the concerns of the present study, two interrelated features of this rise are of special significance. First, the leading advocates and practitioners of the new psychology held chairs in philosophy departments. And second, these men introduced the new academic role – or 'role hybrid' – of being both a philosopher and an experimental scientist. Taken together, these two features explain, for instance, the enormous self-confidence of almost all of these philosopher-psychologists with respect to philosophy itself, i.e. their belief that the new psychology would be crucial to any future progress in philosophy.

Not all German philosophers were advocates and practitioners of the new psychology, however. In fact, between the 1870s and the 1910s a considerable proportion of German academic philosophers became increasingly hostile towards the new psychology. In particular, they resented the fact that the new psychology was sailing under the flag of a new, scientific philosophy; they opposed the idea that experimental psychologists were qualified to fill professorial chairs in philosophy; and they were annoyed by the suggestion that philosophers with no expertise in the new field were unscientific and antiquated. Even though these critics differed widely in their own philosophical positions, they had one central belief in common: they all thought it harmful to philosophy and its progress that experimental psychology should be regarded as part and parcel of philosophy. In other words, they believed that the role of the philosopher, as suggested by the academic success of experimental psychology, needed purification, i.e. these 'pure philosophers' argued that the role of the philosopher and the role of the scientific psychologist needed to be separated from one another and kept apart.

In this chapter I want to present the thought of these advocates of role purification. I shall begin by introducing the attitude to psychology of four leading figures of German pure philosophy at the time: Wilhelm Dilthey, Wilhelm Windelband, Heinrich Rickert and Edmund Husserl. I shall try to show how central parts of their philosophy were informed by their opposition to experimental psychology, and how they argued for the exclusion of experimental psychology from what they regarded as 'philosophy proper'. In the same context, I shall also indicate how advocates of experimental psychology reacted to these challenges by pure philosophy.

Subsequently, I shall summarise the debates on a petition which was initiated by the leading pure philosophers in 1913, and which demanded that no more experimental psychologists should be appointed to chairs in philosophy. The aggressive debates surrounding this petition show how much importance was attached to the issue of the status of experimental psychology.

Finally, against the background of the main body of this chapter, I can address a question which has remained in the air ever since I presented Husserl's and Frege's criticisms of psychologism in Chapter 3. This is the question of why Husserl's criticism was so much more successful than Frege's.

THE CLEANSING STRATEGIES OF
PURE PHILOSOPHY

My focus on Dilthey, Rickert, Windelband and Husserl rather than on some other pure philosophers – e.g. Eucken, Rehmke or Riehl – is easy to justify. Dilthey, the two neo-Kantians and Husserl were *the* leading figures of German pure philosophy between, roughly, the 1890s and the 1920s. These men were among the central initiators of the 1913 petition (with the exception of Dilthey who died in 1911); their work was more widely discussed than that of other pure philosophers; and they were regarded as leaders of important philosophical schools well into the 1920s. Moreover, and most importantly, their work was looked upon by both advocates and critics of the new psychology as constituting the main philosophical alternative to the kind of naturalised philosophy that Wundt and other experimentalists stood for.

Dilthey: Descriptive versus explanatory psychology

Wilhelm Dilthey (1833–1911) held philosophical chairs in Basle (1866–8), Kiel (1866–8), and Wrocław (1868–82), before becoming Lotze's successor at the University of Berlin (1882–1905). In Berlin Dilthey was actively involved in university politics; for our present concerns perhaps the most interesting point to mention is that in 1893 Dilthey was instrumental in bringing Stumpf – rather than Ebbinghaus or Wundt – to Berlin. As Dilthey wrote in a private letter at the time:

> The philosophical issue has now been laid to rest, and in a form that I regarded from early on as the most probable. Stumpf will come now . . . whereas previously he rejected the offer: my intervention has prevented the complete natural-scientific radicalisation of philosophy here.
>
> (Dilthey and Yorck 1923: 165)

In another letter Dilthey complained bitterly of Wundt's 'tastelessness' in failing to cite his (i.e. Dilthey's) work, and suspected that Wundt's behaviour was an act of revenge because of Dilthey's intervention on Stumpf's behalf (Dilthey and Yorck 1923: 189).

Dilthey's main theoretical reflections on the new psychology belong to the same period as his intervention in Stumpf's favour. In February and June of 1894, Dilthey read two papers at the Berlin Academy of Arts and Sciences on 'descriptive' and 'explanatory' psychology; subsequently he published these lectures under the title 'Ideen über eine beschreibende und zergliedernde Psychologie' (Dilthey [1894] 1974) in the Proceedings of the Academy. This article was to prove influential and controversial for the following three decades: the debates around it were to continue well into the Weimar period.

The subject of Dilthey's treatise was the distinction between two kinds of psychology, 'descriptive or analytical psychology' and 'explanatory or constructive psychology'.

Starting with explanatory psychology, Dilthey defined it as 'the deduction – out of a limited number of analytically discovered elements – of all facts that are given in inner experience, given in experiments, given in the study of other human beings, and given in historical reality'. Put differently, explanatory psychology proceeded in a 'synthetical or constructive' way ([1894] 1974: 158), and relied on the hypothetical-deductive method.

162

Dilthey questioned the adequacy of, and need for, the hypothetical-deductive method in psychology, suggesting that explanatory psychology had failed to develop any procedures which would allow for a choice between rival hypotheses:

> We first note the fact that every explanatory psychology is based upon a combination of hypotheses ... [hypotheses] which are unable to exclude other, alternative, hypotheses. Every such combination of hypotheses is still confronted by a dozen of others. A war of all against all rages in its area, and this war rages no less violently than in the field of metaphysics. There is nothing in sight, not even on the most distant horizon, which would have the power to decide this battle ... And thus no one can say whether this war of hypotheses in explanatory psychology will ever end and when this will be ... Hypotheses, everywhere nothing but hypotheses!
> (Dilthey [1894] 1974: 142–3)

As examples of such unsupported hypotheses in explanatory psychology Dilthey mentioned psychophysical parallelism, the assumption that all complex conscious phenomena can be reduced to lawfully interrelated atom-like elements, and the supposition that all psychic phenomena can be derived from sensations and feelings ([1894] 1974: 143).

As Dilthey saw it, explanatory psychology had mistakenly assumed that to follow the example of the natural sciences was to use the hypothetical-deductive method:

> We do not prove ourselves to be the true students of the great natural scientists by transferring their methods to our field but rather by adjusting our tools of knowledge to match the nature of our objects ... Nature we explain, mental life we understand.
> ([1894] 1974: 144–5)

Psychology did not need to rely on 'concepts obtained through hypotheses in order to establish a continuous connection between the great groups of mental facts' ([1894] 1974: 144). This was because mental phenomena and their interrelations were known in a direct and immediate fashion.

A further respect in which explanatory psychology was insufficient, according to Dilthey, was its one-sided attention to only a few mental phenomena. Explanatory psychology studied perception and memory as well as processes of association and apperception. But 'it does not take the human nature in its entirety and the latter's inner connection as its subject matter' ([1894] 1974: 156).

Dilthey also expressed scepticism about experimentation within explanatory psychology. While granting that the introduction of experiments into psychology had increased 'the power of explanatory psychology enormously', he denied that experimentation had led to the identification of any 'laws of the inner psychological [as opposed to the psychophysical] realm'. At best, experimentation could help in the description and analysis of mental phenomena ([1894] 1974: 165).

The failings of explanatory psychology reached further than psychology itself. This was because all *Geisteswissenschaften* as well as epistemology relied on psychological concepts and conceptions. And so the historian, linguist and epistemologist were all faced with the same unpleasant choice:

> Either the *Geisteswissenschaften* use the foundations that [explanatory] psychology offers, thereby themselves acquiring a hypothetical character, or they try and solve their task relying only on the ambiguous and subjective psychology of everyday life . . . In the first case explanatory psychology passes its completely hypothetical character on to epistemology and the *Geisteswissenschaften*.
>
> ([1894] 1974: 146)

Worse still, since so much of modern explanatory psychology was committed to psychophysical parallelism, and thus to 'a sophisticated materialism', explanatory psychology constituted 'a danger' for the jurist and criminologist in particular. For instance, modern schools in criminal law had proposed highly deterministic views of human action, and in doing so they had relied on the explanatory psychology of the Mills, Spencers and Taines that was to blame for this ([1894] 1974: 192–3).

To remedy the sad situation of both modern psychology and the *Geisteswissenschaften*, Dilthey suggested a new kind of psychology which he termed 'descriptive and analytical'. This psychology described 'the parts and interrelations which uniformly appear in every human mental life', and it described them 'as connected in a single interrelation which is experienced rather than [hypothetically] added'. Although in no way related to the natural sciences and their hypothetical-deductive method, descriptive psychology would use 'all means necessary to reach its goal', including analysis, experiment and comparison ([1894] 1974: 152). Unlike explanatory psychology, descriptive psychology would also use 'the works of geniuses', i.e. works of art, in order to study the forms of mental activity. Dilthey placed this latter kind of study far above psychological experiments ([1894] 1974: 180).

Descriptive psychology was analytical where explanatory psychology was constructive. Rather than constructing our mental experience out of hypothetically assumed elements, descriptive psychology analysed the always already given mental structures into their constitutive parts. In so doing, descriptive psychology provided us with apodictic results since 'every interrelation used by it can be definitely verified by inner perception' ([1894] 1974: 152). Here Dilthey was not too worried about objections to the reliability of introspection; he alleged that our ability to remember mental acts could serve as the firm foundation of our knowledge of these acts ([1894] 1974: 198).

Dilthey suggested that descriptive psychology – once properly developed – held considerable promise for philosophy, the *Geisteswissenschaften* and even explanatory psychology. Siding with Stumpf's 'Psychologie und Erkenntnistheorie' against the neo-Kantian positions of Cohen and Natorp, Windelband and Rickert, Dilthey held that all epistemology presupposed psychological concepts and ideas ([1894] 1974: 150).

As concerned the *Geisteswissenschaften*, Dilthey assured his readers that descriptive psychology would provide them with the same kind of firm foundation which, in the case of the natural sciences, was provided by mathematics ([1894] 1974: 193). Among other things, descriptive psychologists would dispel the danger of determinism by showing that the 'boring ... assumption of a psychological and psychophysical machine is [unproven]' and that the 'consciousness of spontaneity, livelihood and responsibility in the acts of willing' could not be explained away ([1894] 1974: 193).

Finally, Dilthey also emphasised the importance of descriptive psychology for explanatory psychology. While claiming that explanatory psychology 'has merely a heuristic value' ([1894] 1974: 193), he also submitted that explanatory psychology 'would receive from descriptive psychology a firm descriptive structure, a definite terminology, exact analyses and an important means of testing its hypothetical explanations' ([1894] 1974: 153).

Prima facie, it might seem that Dilthey in his 'Ideen über eine beschreibende und zergliedernde Psychologie' did not primarily attack *experimental* psychology, and did not object to the existence of experimental research within philosophy departments. Even a brief look at some of the reactions of Dilthey's contemporaries strongly suggests, however, that both experimental psychologists and pure philosophers made the connection between the rebuke of *explanatory* psychology and the rejection of *experimental* psychology. Dilthey sent copies of his article to a number of pure philosophers (Eucken, Natorp, Rehmke, Riehl, Stein and Windelband, among others), as well as to Ebbinghaus and Wundt. The replies – in letters to Dilthey – from the first group were very positive, even when their authors disagreed with Dilthey over some smaller aspects of his study. For example, Paul Natorp wrote of the pleasant surprise he had experienced when realising that Dilthey's ideas were similar to those of his own school: 'Not only in the negative part – the rejection of "explanatory" psychology – but also in the positive part [do we agree]' (9 March 1895; Lessing 1985: 201). The neo-Fichtean Rudolf Eucken was of the opinion that Dilthey's paper 'could bring new life to philosophy which otherwise resolves, and declines, into a study of historical detail, on the one hand and natural-scientific experimental psychology on the other hand' (10 March 1895; Lessing 1985: 204). Ludwig Stein praised Dilthey's work for having unveiled 'the illusions of psychophysics'; in Stein's opinion psychophysics had degenerated into 'a fanaticism of the experiment and a scholasticism of numbers' (26 March 1895; Lessing 1985: 218). And finally, the neo-Kantian Alois Riehl, having first applauded Dilthey's study, concluded his letter with the following paragraph:

> It is not only my own opinion, but the opinion of many and well-respected colleagues – and indeed, given your fitting critical judgement concerning the significance of psychological experiments, it is certainly your own view as well – that the interests of our science [i.e. philosophy] are severely damaged by the fact that one philosophical chair after another is surrendered to the psychophysicists. It is our duty to counteract this condition and its spread. And that is what I intend to do with all my powers. It would be correct to establish separate chairs for psychophysics; but it is unfair against the representatives of philosophy that the present system should continue – a system that has led to a situation

in which some holders of *first-class* philosophical chairs de-
grade philosophy in front of an audience that is unable to
judge for itself. I know this from experience.

(2 April 1895; Lessing 1985: 222)

The reaction of Dilthey's former colleague Hermann Ebbinghaus
was as scathing as that of the pure philosophers was positive. Dilthey
had asked Ebbinghaus for comments on his paper, and Ebbinghaus
replied not once but twice: with a letter and with a polemical article
in the *Zeitschrift für Psychologie und Physiologie der Sinnesorgane*
(Ebbinghaus 1896). In his letter, Ebbinghaus expressed his conster-
nation at Dilthey's 'unfairness *vis-à-vis* present-day psychology'.
Ebbinghaus was surprised that Dilthey had not chosen 'to leave
psychology to itself':

> You once mentioned to me that you were happy that Stumpf's
> entry into the faculty in Berlin would relieve you of your
> lecture course on psychology. I saw this as an admission that
> you no longer felt at home in this strongly growing discipline,
> a discipline which – as the Americans say – can no longer be
> done from one's lonely armchair.

(27 October 1895; Lessing 1985: 228)

In his 45-page public counterattack, Ebbinghaus accused Dilthey
of deficient knowledge of the past and present of psychology, of
ambiguities and of presenting trivialities as scientific or philosophical insights.

To begin with, Ebbinghaus pointed out that the relationship
between descriptive and explanatory psychology was never made
sufficiently clear by Dilthey. Some sections in Dilthey's paper
suggested that descriptive psychology was little more than a prepara-
tory step for the really important work of experimental psychology;
other passages implied that explanatory psychology had no future
and was best abandoned (1896: 170–3).

Second, Ebbinghaus accused Dilthey of reinventing the wheel in
criticising some aspects of association psychology and in emphasising the need for an analysis of mental states and processes.
Concerning the first issue, Ebbinghaus wrote that the defects of the
older association psychology had long been corrected. He regarded
those corrections as one of the two major advances in psychology,
the other one being the 'revolution which the introduction of
experiment and measurement has started' (1896: 177). In the same

context, Ebbinghaus also claimed that most of Dilthey's characterisations of explanatory psychology fitted only one philosopher-psychologist, namely Herbart (1896: 179), and that no modern psychologist would underwrite the mechanical notion of causality that Dilthey attributed to explanatory psychology (1896: 186). As to the second issue, the importance of analysis, Ebbinghaus reminded Dilthey of the title of James Mill's book, *Analysis of the Phenomena of the Human Mind*, and cited Mill's predecessor Thomas Brown with the words: 'The science of mind is in its most important respects a science of analysis' (1896: 182).

Third, Ebbinghaus argued that Dilthey was wrong in blaming explanatory psychology for its hypothetical constructions. To begin with, Ebbinghaus pointed out that every psychology, including Dilthey's own, would be forced to assume the existence of processes that could not be directly experienced (1896: 192–3). Moreover, Ebbinghaus regarded Dilthey's complaint that psychological hypotheses were vague and unsupported as 'a rhetorical exaggeration':

> Some of them can be made as plausible, and they can be verified just as well through their consequences, as good hypotheses of natural science. And it needs no argument to convince the unbiased observer that the possibility of exact verification has been enormously increased through experiment and measurement.
>
> (Ebbinghaus 1896: 198)

Ebbinghaus went on to write that 'the method of psychology, in its general outline, is in perfect order' (1896: 202). Finally, Ebbinghaus also rejected Dilthey's suggestion that the *Geisteswissenschaften* had the right to demand nonhypothetical foundations from psychology:

> one must ask with what right the *Geisteswissenschaften* can demand from psychology ... anything other than that which they themselves are capable of producing ... How secure are the explanations and the exclusiveness of hypotheses in the *Geisteswissenschaften*? They do not differ from those that figure in that psychology which Dilthey criticises.
>
> (1896: 204)

Given the harshness of Ebbinghaus's attack, it was perhaps not surprising that Dilthey declined Theodor Lipps's invitation to speak at a psychological congress in Munich in 1896. As Dilthey confided in a letter to a friend, he turned down the invitation because 'under no circumstances can I again sit in one room with Ebbinghaus since this would force me to exchange a greeting or a word with him' (10 March 1896; Dilthey and Yorck 1923: 210).

The neo-Kantians

The position of neo-Kantian philosophy towards the new psychology changed radically between the 1860s and the turn of the century. Initially, i.e. during the 1860s and 1870s, neo-Kantian philosophy aligned itself closely with both the physiology of the senses and the new experimental psychology. Wilhelm Windelband (1848–1915) and Hermann Cohen (1842–1918), the father figures of the two main neo-Kantian schools, studied under Lotze and Steinthal respectively, and both published in the *Zeitschrift für Völkerpsychologie und Sprachwissenschaft.* On that forum both expressed their support for a psychological study of ontological, epistemological and logical questions (Cohen 1866, 1868; Windelband 1875).

The interest in physiology and psychology shown by the important early neo-Kantian Friedrich Albert Lange (1828–75), the predecessor first of Wundt in Zurich (1870–73), and then of Cohen in Marburg (1873–5), was even stronger. Indeed, Lange could well have been mentioned in Chapter 6 as an important early advocate of experimental psychology. First, Lange provided the new psychology with one of its most central slogans: that it was to be free of metaphysical assumptions about the soul, i.e. that it was to be 'a psychology without a soul'. Second, Lange advocated a physiological-*cum*-psychological interpretation of the Kantian a priori, arguing that Kantian forms of perception, categories and ideas are grounded in the human physiological and psychological 'organisation'. Lange regarded the physiology of the sense organs as a 'developed or corrected Kantianism' and praised Hermann von Helmholtz's ways of employing Kant's views as no more than 'heuristic principles'. And third, Lange used a physiologically reinterpreted Kant as a weapon against materialism. He reasoned that the category of matter is no more than just another necessary product of our 'organisation'; i.e. that matter is a thing-for-us rather than a thing-in-itself (Lange 1866).

Of the various critical views on the new psychology developed within the neo-Kantian movement (see e.g. Köhnke 1986; Schmidt 1976), the best known were those of Windelband and Rickert.

Wilhelm Windelband succeeded Wundt in Zurich in 1876, and later taught in Freiburg, Strasbourg and Heidelberg. Even though Windelband's views on the usefulness of the new psychology for philosophical research changed over time, in one respect his position remained constant: from his inaugural lecture in Zurich in 1876 onwards he demanded that psychologists should not hold chairs in philosophy. Eventually, Windelband even became notorious for ridiculing the role hybridisation of the philosopher and the experimentalist.

The title of Windelband's inaugural lecture in Zurich was 'Über den gegenwärtigen Stand der psychologischen Forschung'. In it Windelband proposed to deal with 'the old query concerning the relation between philosophical and empirical research' (1876: 3). He suggested that in the present age this question was most urgent with respect to psychology (1876: 4). Windelband claimed that psychology had never been interested in metaphysical or epistemological questions. Instead, the interests of metaphysics and epistemology had kept psychology within philosophy: 'The fact that metaphysics, and the epistemology linked to it, had to rely essentially on the results of psychology understandably brought it about that philosophers seized upon this science with special energy and sought to exploit it for their interests' (1876: 12). The Windelband of 1876 thus conceded that philosophy needed psychology. However, precisely for this reason he hoped that psychology would eventually receive its own professorial chairs:

> The more we are convinced that in the central project of all sciences, a project which philosophy must direct, psychology has an especially important and decisive task, the more we must cling to the demand that it can fulfil this task only if it first and foremost exists independently and without presuppositions . . . and thus we should consider whether under these conditions the time hasn't arrived . . . to institute independent chairs for psychology.
>
> (Windelband 1876: 13)

Looking back on the closing decades of the nineteenth century thirty-three years later, Windelband's perception of the role of psychology within philosophy was much more negative. He claimed that the 1880s and 1890s had been a time of philosophical decline and that the interest in psychology and physiology, together with the interest in historical relativism, was to blame for this sad state. He also thought that historical relativism was reinforced by psychology's central role within philosophy: 'This [historical] relativism ... sympathised with psychology because the latter's causal explanation of facts could provide neither criteria for truth nor criteria for the good: psychologism proved to be a comfortable basis for resting content with changing historical facts' (1909: 89).

While emphasising that the new psychology was an 'important achievement', and while still admitting that psychology was closer to philosophy than any other empirical discipline (1909: 91), Windelband deplored that its effect on the development of philosophy in the nineteenth century had been damaging. In particular, Windelband derided experimentalists in philosophical chairs:

> For a time it was thought in Germany that one was close to being qualified for a philosophical chair as soon as one had learned to press electric buttons in a methodological way, and as soon as one could numerically prove by means of well-ordered and tabulated series of experiments that some people get ideas more quickly than others.
>
> (Windelband 1909: 92)

Windelband called this kind of work 'a psychologistic substitute for philosophy' and went on to explain that such pseudophilosophy was welcomed by some political circles precisely because it bracketed the 'great problems of life, the political, religious and social questions' (1909: 92).

Today, Windelband is of course less remembered for these assaults than for his distinction between 'idiographic' and 'nomothetic' sciences (Windelband 1894). It is not difficult to see, however, that the first topic is connected to the second.

Windelband's famous rectorship speech, 'Geschichte und Naturwissenschaft' (1894), was an attempt at classifying the sciences. Having first distinguished between philosophy and mathematics, on the one hand, and the empirical sciences on the other hand, Windelband then addressed the question of how to distinguish further among the latter. One of the main reasons why he rejected the traditional distinction between *Geisteswissenschaften* and *Naturwissenschaften* was that it did not allow for a clear-cut classification of psychology: 'with respect to its subject-matter it can only be classified as a *Geisteswissenschaft* and, in some sense, as the basis of

171

all other *Geisteswissenschaften*; yet its methodological conduct is, from beginning to end, that of the natural sciences' (1894: 9–10). Therefore, Windelband searched for a new criterion for dividing up the empirical sciences, a criterion that would place empirical psychology firmly on the side of physiology, physics and biology. This new criterion was 'the formal character of the goals of knowledge acquisition' (1894: 11). Most of the sciences that traditionally had been classified as natural sciences searched for general laws, i.e. they were 'nomothetic sciences' or 'sciences of laws', whereas most of the sciences that traditionally had been classified as *Geisteswissenschaften* searched for 'particular historical facts' and thus were 'idiographic sciences' or 'sciences of events' (1894: 11–12). Judged by these criteria, empirical psychology was a nomothetic science.

Windelband's speech had two major implications for psychology. The first was that it seemed appropriate to classify psychology with physics rather than history or philosophy. This reclassification contradicted of course the Wundtian view that psychology stood between the *Geisteswissenschaften* and the natural sciences and thus could act as a fair broker between them. The second was a rejection of Wundt's and Lamprecht's notion that the historical sciences must rely on the results of scientific psychology:

> It is indeed strange how limited are the demands of the historical sciences upon psychology. The historians have never been impeded by the notoriously, extremely imperfect degree to which the laws of mental life have so far been identifiable: historians have known just enough – on the basis of natural knowledge of human nature, tact and ingenious intuition – to understand their heroes and their actions. That should make us think; and it makes doubtful whether the recently envisaged mathematical-natural-scientific formulation of elementary mental processes will produce a result for our understanding of real human life that is worth mentioning.
>
> (Windelband 1894: 23)

Heinrich Rickert (1863–1936), the second leader of the Southwest German School, held chairs in Freiburg, where he was succeeded by Husserl in 1916, and Heidelberg, where his predecessor had been Windelband. Rickert's work on concept formation was – like Windelband's classification of empirical sciences – an argument against any special role for empirical psychology with respect to the *Geisteswissenschaften*.

Rickert (1896, 1899, 1913a) argued that the crucial difference between *Kulturwissenschaften* and *Naturwissenschaften* was the way in which both fields of empirical study form concepts. No science attempted to 'copy' (*abbilden*) reality, rather scientific knowledge acquisition was a process of 'reorganising' (*umbilden*) and 'simplifying'. This process needed 'a principle of selection' and this principle was but the characteristic way in which perceptual data were transformed into concepts (1899: 30–1). Natural science sought to form '*general* concepts', concepts under which many different particulars could be subsumed: 'To come to know nature means indeed to form general concepts' (1899: 32). Cultural sciences, however, were characterised by a different method of concept formation: 'They want to present reality itself which is after all never general but always individual, and which – as soon as it is considered in its individuality and particularity – marks the borderline for every natural-scientific concept' (1899: 37).

Rickert believed that this difference in concept formation was more fundamental than Windelband's distinction between 'sciences of laws' and 'sciences of events'; for instance, the search for general laws in the natural sciences was but one way in which generalising concept formation expressed itself (1899: 38).

In order to characterise the two distinct ways of concept formation further, Rickert focused on the difference between the subject matters of the two fields of empirical study, i.e. on nature and on culture. What distinguished nature from culture was that cultural objects and processes embodied, or were intimately related to, values. When humans conceptually reorganised perceptual data from the perspective of human values, they constructed culture, whereas when they conceptually reorganised perceptual data without a value perspective, they constructed nature (1899: 20–1). This difference between culture and nature was linked to the opposition between the two ways of concept formation. This was because – typically – the general had little cultural value whereas the particular or the individual had the highest cultural value:

> The cultural importance of a reality does not derive from what it has in common with other realities; instead, its cultural importance is due to that which distinguishes it from others.

That reality which we construct as culture we also always construct as the particular and as the individual.

(Rickert 1899: 45)

Moreover, natural science and cultural science had different kinds of objectivity. Whereas the objectivity of natural science was built upon the exclusion of mere opinions and values, the objectivity of cultural science in general, and history in particular, was due to the 'universal validity of cultural values' (1899: 51).

From the point of view of this general framework, Rickert then went on to draw a number of conclusions with respect to empirical psychology.

First of all, empirical, scientific psychology was no cultural science. It aimed for general concepts and laws, and it did not study reality from the perspective of values (1899: 36). More precisely, psychology was that part of natural science which studied realities which filled time but not space (1899: 32–4).

Second, the subject matter of the cultural sciences must not be defined as consisting of mental or psychological processes and products: 'the mere presence of the mental element does not yet constitute a cultural object; after all, mental life can also be studied as nature' (1899: 25). Put differently, the subject matter of the cultural sciences did not coincide with that of psychology; psychology studied nature whereas the cultural sciences ultimately studied values.

Third, scientific psychology was of little use to the historian. Like the artist, the historian too needed to be a 'connoisseur of human nature', but no more:

Art does not want to conceptually grasp mental life in general, it wants – as far as possible – to grasp mental life intuitively in its particularity; and this ability is completely independent of knowledge of scientific psychology. The same holds for the 'psychology' which the historian needs.

(1899: 41)

Rickert called this latter psychology – which he distinguishes elsewhere from Dilthey's descriptive psychology (1913a: 478–80) – 'historical psychology' (1899: 42).

Moreover, Rickert suggested that relying on scientific social psychology committed the historian to neglecting great historical personalities. And this neglect was politically dangerous as it lent support to

> a materialistic historiography which marks only the extreme endpoint of the whole development . . . It depends for the most part on the specific wishes of social democracy. Since the guiding cultural ideal here is democratic, it creates the tendency, in the past as well as in the present, to regard the great personalities as inessential and to accept only that which comes from the masses.
>
> (1899: 60)

Fourth, the objectivity of the natural sciences was not superior to the objectivity of the cultural sciences and philosophy. For Rickert, the inverse was true because the objectivity of values was the ultimate and highest objectivity. While it was true that natural science had produced remarkable 'objective cultural values', it was the cultural sciences and philosophy which were ultimately the judges in matters of values. The cultural sciences studied values through history, and philosophy attempted to construct 'a comprehensive system of objective cultural values' (1899: 67). Natural science being just one cultural value among many, it was the Rickertian philosophy of values which was the true foundation of all sciences.

Windelband's and Rickert's writings on psychology and the classification of the sciences received a lot of critical attention. The following four writers exemplify the main directions of criticism.

Stumpf took issue with Windelband's way of writing the history of late nineteenth-century philosophy. As will be remembered, Windelband saw this era as one of decline precisely because experimental psychology took centre-stage within philosophy. Stumpf agreed with Windelband only with respect to the claim that 'between Hegel's death and the present there undoubtedly occurred a catastrophe'. For Stumpf, however, this catastrophe consisted entirely of the materialist doctrines of Feuerbach, Vogt, Büchner, Marx, Engels and Stirner (Stumpf [1907a] 1910: 164). Moreover, it was scientifically based philosophy, the work of Fechner and Lotze, which overcame 'this unphilosophical direction – and materialism is always unphilosophical'. Turning against Windelband, without mentioning him by name, Stumpf continued:

But the low didn't last long. It is incorrect to say, as a well-known historian has done, that the second half of the nineteenth century was a nonphilosophical era full of positivism, an era that has only now been overcome. The upswing started as early as the sixth and seventh decade. It was then that Lotze and Fechner opened a new path. They were indeed indebted to idealistic philosophy. But the power which enabled the physician Lotze and the physicist Fechner to create new and viable ideas came from a specialist's natural-scientific training. Both tried – with decisive success – to bring this knowledge to bear on that area [of philosophy] that had been neglected from Kant to Hegel: psychology.

(Stumpf [1907a] 1910: 165)

Note here that Stumpf referred to Windelband as a historian rather than a philosopher, and that he did not mention the neo-Kantian Lange.

Marbe was especially concerned to challenge Rickert's views on psychology and the classification of the sciences (in Rickert 1896). Marbe felt that Rickert's remarks on psychology were 'completely off target':

One cannot settle the issue of what is, or is *not*, the subject matter of psychology by way of a formal discussion. If it is true that the mental processes are concomitants of certain bodily processes in the nervous system, and if it is impossible to find purely psychological laws, then there is no alternative to assigning mental processes to the bodily processes which correspond to them. The subject matter of psychology consists *in fact* not only of the mental realm but also of part of the bodily realm.

(Marbe 1898: 278)

In general, Marbe proposed that Rickert's 'many factual mistakes' were due to his 'formal method':

A fruitful theory of science must gather information about the object and the method of the individual fields of knowledge in an inductive way. And it must thereafter evaluate the experiences gained in this way from the standpoint of general logic and the theory of knowledge.

(1898: 279)

William Stern accepted Rickert's reasoning to the conclusion that empirical psychology was a theoretical natural science, and that psychology could not be the foundation of the *Geisteswissenschaften*. Nevertheless, Stern felt that Rickert had paid insufficient attention to the ways in which the theories of scientific psychology could be useful to the historian. Using one of Rickert's own examples, Stern conceded that

> the psychopathological phenomenon 'megalomania' is a problem of natural science, whereas Nero's individual deeds are a problem for the historian. However, our understanding of Nero is greatly improved once we understand the individual causal connection of his acts as a case to which the general phenomenon 'megalomania' applies.
>
> (W. Stern 1903: 213)

Stern also thought that the psychological category of 'mass hysteria' could illuminate the medieval crusades, that laws of psychological association were of help to the linguist, and that the way one wrote history would be influenced by one's views on such psychological theories as voluntarism, intellectualism, determinism or indeterminism (1903: 213).

Finally, Schlick repudiated what he regarded as the central idea of both Windelband and Rickert, namely that 'the difference between the mere stuff of experience or the collection of data, on the one hand, and lawful knowledge, on the other hand', could be used to demarcate the historical sciences from the natural sciences. According to Schlick, natural science did not ignore the 'purely factual, "historical" data' since it sought to explain actually happening events in the real world': 'when the physicist says "I know the most general laws of nature", then this means nothing else but: "I am able to penetrate into the individually given events most deeply".' Furthermore, history too struggled for knowledge of laws, 'and only in so far as it succeeds should one ascribe to it any value for knowledge' (1910b: 124). Schlick proposed a new way of distinguishing between two kinds of concept formation. According to this proposal, natural science was the science of quantities, whereas philosophy was the science of irreducible qualities. And *within* philosophy, it was psychology as the science of 'the first, and immediately given qualities' which was 'the philosophical science par excellence' (1910b: 131).

Husserl's phenomenology

All of Edmund Husserl's (1859–1938) writings, both those published during his lifetime and those published posthumously, bear ample witness of his constant preoccupation with psychology (see e.g. Drüe 1963; Kockelmans 1967). Here I shall focus only on those of Husserl's published reflections on the new psychology that were widely noticed during the first two decades of this century.

Husserl's attitude towards the new scientific psychology is more complex than that of the neo-Kantian philosophers. After all, Husserl pursued a twofold strategy with respect to the new psychology. He argued that the new psychology in its present state could not be a fundamental discipline within philosophy, and that experimental psychology was beset with grave problems and weaknesses. He also tried to enrol the support of proponents of the new psychology by suggesting that if only they were to build their psychology upon his phenomenology, they would remain in the closest possible contact with philosophical disciplines.

Phenomenology as descriptive psychology The most natural starting point for our review of Husserl's views on psychology is the introduction to volume II of the *Logische Untersuchungen*. It was this programmatic text which led several of Husserl's early critics to accuse him of relapsing into psychologism.

The introduction to volume II explained how the philosopher should study the conditions of the possibility of logic. To study these conditions was to investigate meanings; it was, more precisely, to study meanings 'as they are embedded in concrete mental experiences' ([1901] 1984: 8). The new discipline which Husserl attempted to introduce, i.e. phenomenology, took its starting point from these complex experiences, analysed them into their parts, and attended especially to those aspects of mental experiences that were essentially involved in judgements and in knowledge acquisition. As the *Prolegomena* had argued, the logician was interested not in 'the psychological judgement, i.e. the concrete mental phenomenon, but in the logical judgement, i.e. the identical meaning of an assertion' ([1901] 1984: 8–9). Husserl did not take this statement back, but added now that one had to distinguish between the logical, 'ideal analysis' and 'phenomenological analysis'. The latter was no part of the 'very own domain of pure logic', although the interests of the logician in clarity and precision were served by the work of the phenomenologist. Logical meanings were given at first only in 'subjective realisations' and in an 'imperfect form'; later they could be raised above this imperfect level by the work of phenomenology: 'It is the purpose of phenomenology to provide us with a sufficiently wide-ranging descriptive . . . understanding of mental experiences as is necessary to give firm meanings to all fundamental logical concepts' ([1901] 1984: 9–10).

The analytical and descriptive work of phenomenology was not only related to logic, however:

> Pure phenomenology represents an area of neutral investigations, an area in which different sciences are rooted. It serves to prepare the ground for *psychology as an empirical science.* It analyses and describes (especially as a phenomenology of thought and knowledge acquisition) the experiences of presentation, judging and coming to know, experiences which in psychology must find their genetic explanation, i.e. their exploration according to interrelations subject to empirical laws. In addition, phenomenology discloses the 'sources' from which the ideal laws of *pure logic* 'spring'.
>
> (Husserl [1901] 1984: 7)

And third, the purposes and motives of phenomenology were also identical with those of epistemology ([1901] 1984: 12).

In passing, Husserl called his phenomenology a 'descriptive psychology', even though he immediately added that this same title had already been used for other psychological projects and thus did not serve well to characterise his own work ([1901] 1984: 24). Husserl was willing to admit, however, that phenomenological reflection on one's mental experiences was beset by the same kinds of problems with which other descriptive psychologies were struggling: attending to one's own mental experiences might change their quality, and the 'narrowness of consciousness' put limits on the number of experiences that one was able to reflect on simultaneously ([1901] 1984: 15).

Finally, it deserves to be mentioned that Husserl anticipated the objection that his phenomenological – or descriptive-psychological – clarification of the possibility of logic constitutes a lapse into psychologism. He met this objection by stressing that his project did not make logic dependent on psychological *theories* concerning the causal relations between mental states. Instead phenomenology provided merely 'a certain class of descriptions' which formed the 'preliminary stage' for both the theories of logic and the theories of empirical, explanatory psychology ([1901] 1984: 24).

As mentioned in Chapter 4, critics of Husserl's *Logical Investigations* were unimpressed by this disclaimer (Busse 1903: 154; Cornelius 1906: 406; Jerusalem 1905: 131; Maier 1908: 360; Meinong 1913: 502; Nelson [1908] 1973a: 71; Rickert 1909: 227; Stumpf 1907c: 34–5). Now we can add that many experimental psychologists were also unenthusiastic about Husserl's offer to provide their field of study with a new foundation. This lack of enthusiasm – to put in mildly – was expressed by no less a critic than Wilhelm Wundt himself.

Wundt accused Husserl not only of psychologism but also of 'logicism' (*Logizismus*), that is of an attempt to turn psychology into a subdomain of logic. In recent decades, Wundt alleged, this tendency had been represented most strongly by Brentano and his students, and here Husserl merited special attention: Husserl 'seeks to transform psychology into a reflective analysis of concepts and words' (1910b: 519). Husserl's goal was not just to exorcise psychologism from logic, his goal was to exorcise psychologism from psychology as well: 'He accepts only logic into his psychology . . . His psychology without a soul is at the same time a psychology without psychology' (1910b: 580).

On Wundt also showed little inclination to accept Husserl's claim that phenomenological analysis clarified important concepts for both psychology and logic. The concepts which Husserl selected for his study were 'the scientifically unchecked concepts of vulgar psychology and these concepts do not become the least bit more psychologically scientific by this detour through purely logical conceptual analysis' (1910b: 579).

On Wundt's reading of Husserl, 'the phenomenology of thought' did not study phenomena of thought as these were given to consciousness. Instead, phenomenology investigated the 'linguistic form' of such phenomena of thought. What made things worse, these linguistic forms were not studied from the perspectives provided by the psychology, or history, of language but rather from the viewpoint of a logical meta-reflection on the results of grammar (1910b: 603). Unfortunately, this procedure ignored the basic insight that meanings are not stable (1910b: 607), and thus disqualified phenomenology as a foundation for empirical psychology (1910b: 603–4).

Phenomenology and experimental psychology Just how deeply Husserl was angered by Wundt's criticism can be seen directly from a posthumously published text written in 1913, and more indirectly from his article 'Philosophie als strenge Wissenschaft' ([1911] 1987). The posthumously published text was the draft for a new preface to the second, 1913 edition of the *Logische Untersuchungen* (Husserl 1939). In that draft Husserl called Wundt 'one of the worst psychologicists' and went on to claim that Wundt's interpretation of the *Logische Untersuchungen* was completely misguided and due to a superficial reading of the text: 'One cannot read and understand the *Logische Untersuchungen* the way one reads and understands a newspaper' (1939: 334). Some of Husserl's polemics against Wundt in this draft appeared exaggerated even to his student Eugen Fink, and thus Fink chose to delete from his edition of the draft preface 'about two printed pages of sharp polemics against W. Wundt that are *without* topical relevance' (1939: 331).

The main body of Husserl's 'Philosophie als strenge Wissenschaft' was an attack on naturalised philosophy and experimental psychology. Husserl contrasted two candidates for the title of a strictly scientific philosophy: his own phenomenology, and a naturalised philosophy with experimental psychology at its core. Needless to say, Husserl tried to show that phenomenology alone had a claim to this title. At the same time, Husserl stuck to his earlier claim that it was only by building on the results of his phenomenology that empirical – or experimental – psychology could become a genuine science.

Husserl had several complaints against the notion of psychology as the basis of other areas of philosophy. Husserl first pointed out that a science of fact cannot give foundations for normative disciplines ([1911] 1987: 12–13).

Second, Husserl claimed that all of natural science including psychology was epistemologically 'naive'. Natural science did not ask what justified our belief in the existence of psychophysical nature, it simply took this existence for granted. Since it was the proper task of epistemology to search for a justification of our belief in psychophysical reality, the notion of a 'natural-scientific epistemology' was 'absurd' (*Widersinn*) ([1911] 1987: 15). Husserl believed that with respect to 'epistemological naivety', psychology did not differ from any other natural science. Psychology too was committed to the existence of physical entities; psychology studied mental states and events as belonging to 'human and animal consciousnesses [*sic*] which in turn are linked to human and animal bodies' ([1911] 1987: 13).

Third, current experimental psychology was '*de facto* unscientific' (1911: 20). This was because it had neglected the tasks both of a 'direct and pure' descriptive analysis of consciousness and of a clarification of key concepts. Lacking such analysis and such clarification, the descriptive and explanatory concepts of experimental psychology were no more than 'coarse class concepts' ([1911] 1987: 18). For the same reason, experimental work lacked theoretical guidance, and its results remained without explanation. And thus Husserl felt compelled to compare experimental psychology to social statistics:

> One might say that experimental psychology relates to original psychology [i.e. the descriptive analysis of consciousness] as social statistics relates to original social science. Such statistical research collects valuable facts, and it discovers valuable regularities; but it does both only indirectly. The interpretative understanding and the real explanation of these facts and regularities must come from an original social science, that is from a social science which brings social phenomena to direct givenness and which studies their essence. Likewise, experimental psychology is a method that may be able to find valuable psychophysical facts and regularities; but these must remain without any possibility of a deeper understanding and an ultimate scientific use unless a systematic science of consciousness steps in to investigate the mental realm in an immanent way.
>
> (Husserl [1911] 1987: 18)

Husserl went on to deplore the fact that 'experimental fanatics' derided as 'scholastics' those psychologists who, like Stumpf, Lipps and Brentano, had noticed the insufficiency of experimental psychology ([1911] 1987: 20).

Fourth, experimental psychology erred in its attempt to model itself on the natural sciences. It talked as if mental phenomena were similar to physical objects: it spoke of their real properties, their causal relations and their observation by differently situated observers. Husserl stressed, however, that the essence of mental phenomena allowed for no such talk and for no such analysis:

Everything that we call . . . a mental phenomenon is, as such, a phenomenon and *not* [like physical] nature . . . To attribute a nature to phenomena, to search for their real parts or causal interrelations – all this is pure absurdity; it is no better than to look for the causal properties of numbers.

([1911] 1987: 28–30)

And fifth, experimental psychology overlooked the distinction between particulars and essences in the mental realm. It was because experimental psychologists had no understanding of essences that they failed to see the importance of phenomenology for their work ([1911] 1987: 32).

To appreciate this point of Husserl's argument, we need to take into account that the Husserl of 1911 had modified his conception of phenomenological analysis. Phenomenology was now strictly set apart from descriptive psychology, and this for two reasons: first, phenomenology studied 'pure' consciousness and, second, it investigated essences rather than facts. Put differently, phenomenology did not study mental experiences as being *about* real objects 'out there', and it did not study mental experiences as belonging to a physiological, biological or physical system. Moreover, phenomenology sought to determine the essences of mental phenomena, it tried to identify what, say, all acts of perception have in common.

Husserl called the method for the identification of essences 'perception of essences' (*Wesensschauung*) ([1911] 1987: 32). Perception of essences occurred when the phenomenologist reflected on her own mental acts. Husserl denied that his trust in such reflection had been undermined by earlier criticism of introspection. Phenomenological reflection was not touched by this criticism, because phenomenological reflection and introspection were different methods: introspection was directed at facts whereas phenomenological reflection was directed at essences ([1911] 1987: 36). Furthermore, Husserl also found unjustified and exaggerated experimental psychologists' tendency to reject all forms of introspective self-observation ([1911] 1987: 21).

Finally, by identifying the essences of phenomena of pure consciousness, phenomenology provided not only the foundations for epistemology, it also supplied the foundations for descriptive psychology (which in turn was the theoretical basis of experimental psychology). Essences of phenomena of *pure* consciousness became essences of phenomena of *empirical* consciousness as soon as one reintroduced the assumption that all consciousness was the consciousness of human beings (or animals) with real, physical bodies:

> phenomenology and psychology ... are both dealing with consciousness ... even though they do so in a different 'attitude'; we can express this by saying that psychology is dealing with 'empirical consciousness', with consciousness in the attitude of empirical experience, with consciousness as something which exists in the context of nature; phenomenology, however, is dealing with 'pure' consciousness, i.e. with consciousness in the phenomenological attitude.
>
> ([1911] 1987: 17)

Descriptive psychology of psychological essences – or, as Husserl would later say, 'eidetic psychology' – was in turn the foundation for experimental psychology: it provided the latter with the concepts and categories that interpreted and guided experimental studies.

Because of this intimate connection between phenomenology and eidetic psychology, Husserl could argue that – at least potentially – psychology was closer to philosophy than was any other science. Of course, this close relation existed only once psychologists came to accept the phenomenological method:

> [only] if psychology builds upon a *systematic* phenomenology ... will the enormous experimental work of our time ... bear fruit. Only then will one again be able to admit ... that psychology stands to philosophy in a close, nay, in the closest possible, relation.
>
> ([1911] 1987: 39)

Though Husserl did not make this point explicitly, the structure of his argument implied here that an experimental psychology with such awareness of phenomenology need not even be expelled from philosophy. Husserl criticised the appointment of experimentalists to philosophical chairs only for those areas of psychology that were no closer to philosophy than are chemistry or physics ([1911] 1987: 40).

Wundt did not continue the exchange with Husserl but two experimentalists, Georg Anschütz and August Messer, the first a student of Lipps and Wundt, the latter a member of Külpe's Würzburg School, did reply to 'Philosophie als strenge Wissenschaft' at greater length.

Anschütz was particularly unhappy about Husserl's allegation that the concepts of experimental psychology were 'coarse'. Anschütz claimed that 'exact psychology' would always differentiate its concepts further and that experimentation helped to bring about such differentiation. Not only did Anschütz deny Husserl's accusation, he also went further and turned the complaint around: 'it is precisely that movement which believes that one can do without experiments which often works with such "coarse class concepts"' (1912b: 10). Anschütz mentioned Brentano, Cornelius and Lipps as representatives of this 'movement'. He concluded with the hope that Husserl would arrive at a more balanced treatment of experimental psychology by familiarising himself with 'all special fields of the more recent exact psychology' (1912b: 10–11).

Messer too suspected that Husserl was unfamiliar with experimental psychology, and wondered how Husserl could otherwise have failed to provide proof for his claim regarding the 'coarse concepts' of modern psychology (1912: 117). Furthermore, while granting that normative sciences were independent of psychology, Messer felt that Husserl had done nothing to discredit the view that psychology was the foundation of both metaphysics and the *Geisteswissenschaften* (1912: 118). Moreover, Messer dismissed Husserl's reproach according to which experimental psychology treated mental phenomena as thing-like entities. Messer credited Wundt with having exposed this mistake long ago (1912: 119–20).

Messer also rejected the idea that every psychological claim presupposed the existence of physical nature. He claimed that Husserl's phenomenology itself was the needed counterexample. Phenomenology did not make such ontological commitments *and* phenomenology was a kind of psychology (1912: 119). This claim brings us to the heart of Messer's analysis. As he saw it, Husserl's phenomenology was indeed a viable and important project, but it did not transcend the limits of psychology. Messer granted that the phenomenologist did not seek to study the peculiarities of a particular mental act, and that the phenomenologist did not attempt to fix such a mental event 'in the context of nature'. But Messer denied that these two moves of abstention distinguished the phenomenologist from the empirical psychologist. The psychologist still acted within the boundaries of his discipline even when he went beyond the particular, temporal event. Like the phenomenologist, the psychologist too aimed for '*general* knowledge'; and, like the psychologist, the phenomenologist had better be interested in coming to know 'reality' (1912: 123). Messer concluded that phenomenology could not be separated from psychology, and that it was, as 'pure psychology', psychology's most basic part (1912: 124).

Transcendental phenomenology and psychology   Although Messer's appraisal of Husserl's phenomenology was much more flattering than Wundt's criticism, it is not difficult to appreciate why Husserl could not accept Messer's interpretation, either. Since Husserl claimed a foundational status for phenomenology regarding not only psychology but also philosophy, accepting that phenomenology was a part of psychology would have left him wide open to the psychologism charge. And thus it does not come as a surprise that Husserl began his next major publication, the *Ideen zu einer reinen Phänomenologie und phänomenologischen Philosophie*, with an explicit rejection of Messer's evaluation ([1913] 1950: 4).

In the *Ideen*, Husserl made a new effort to clarify the double role of phenomenology as both the nonpsychological foundation of psychology and the fundamental discipline of philosophy. He now explained that phenomenology related to psychology as geometry related to the natural sciences ([1913] 1950: 4). More precisely, 'transcendental phenomenology' was set apart from psychology by two criteria. First, whereas psychology was a science of facts, phenomenology was a science of essences. And second, whereas psychology was a science of realities and dealt with phenomena that ultimately were part of the spatiotemporal world, phenomenology was a science of 'irrealities', a science of phenomena that were 'cleansed' of all ontological commitments to the existence of a spatiotemporal world. Husserl expressed this idea also by saying that the realm of phenomenology was the result of two 'reductions': 'eidetic reduction' and 'transcendental reduction'. The first led from facts and phenomena to essences, and the second from worldly realities to pure phenomena. And thus Husserl could write that 'our phenomenology is not an eidetic science (*Wesenslehre*) of real but of transcendentally reduced phenomena' ([1913] 1950: 6).

Moreover, all eidetic sciences – e.g. phenomenology, pure logic and mathematics – were independent of sciences of fact. Facts of psychology had as little bearing on phenomenology as facts of physics had on mathematics. However, sciences of fact were dependent upon eidetic sciences. And this for two reasons. First, all empirical sciences were dependent upon logic and mathematics. And second, 'every fact includes a stock of *material* essences and the eidetic truth belonging to each of these pure essences represents a law to which the factually given particular, just like every possible particular, is bound' ([1913] 1950: 23). As in his earlier programmatic paper, Husserl again spoke of a 'perception of essences' (*Wesensschauung*) and likened it to sensual perception ([1913] 1950: 52).

Finally, on the basis of this view of the relationship between sciences of essences and sciences of facts, Husserl held that

> phenomenology is the authority for the methodologically basic questions of psychology. Whatever phenomenology establishes the psychologist must accept as the condition of the possibility of all his further methodology ... Whatever conflicts with the results of phenomenology is *principally psychological absurdity*.
>
> (Husserl [1913] 1950: 193)

Messer remained unconvinced by Husserl's book-length attempt to argue anew for a sharp divide between phenomenology and psychology. In an update on his evaluation of Husserl's work, an article published in 1914, Messer still missed in Husserl's work the proof 'that modern psychology doesn't know of the immanent analysis of essences'. Messer now suggested that especially the Würzburgian 'psychology of thought', a school to which Messer himself belonged, could claim competence in this area:

> With this method [i.e. of the Würzburg School] the phenomenological method – as Husserl himself, his students and his followers use it with respect to psychological objects – harmonises only too well ... One notices precious little of the abyss that according to Husserl separates phenomenology from *all* psychologies.
>
> (Messer 1914d: 64)

While Messer granted Husserl that the two reductions indeed set phenomenology apart from psychology, he felt that 'this separation is only of purely theoretical significance, and is in fact completely irrelevant for the practice of research'. And thus Messer upheld his earlier verdict that phenomenology '*is psychology – indeed it is psychology's most basic part*' (1914d: 66).

Other proponents of the new psychology (e.g. Jerusalem 1914,

Elsenhans 1915, Steinmann 1917) were harsher in their judgements. Elsenhans proposed that Husserl's *Ideen* left the interpreter only two alternatives: either Husserl's phenomenology was metaphysics or it was a form of descriptive psychology. And Elsenhans regarded the latter interpretation as more charitable. Husserl's

> strict division between a world of 'pure essences' and a world of empirical facts . . . is the boldest of metaphysical hypotheses. And thus it is not surprising that Husserl's phenomenology is so often mistaken for an empirical descriptive psychology. It is not only Husserl's own earlier mode of expression which has contributed to this, it is also the reluctance of authors . . . to take this step towards a realism of concepts.
>
> (Elsenhans 1915: 240)

Jerusalem praised 'Husserl's strong psychological talent' but deplored the fact that Husserl declined to accept this title. In Jerusalem's opinion, Husserl was 'a psychologist in spite of himself' (1914: 90). Nevertheless, Jerusalem would have nothing of Husserl's '*Wesensschauung*'. In his view Bergson, among others, had shown that the mental realm was characterised by constant change. And thus it was impossible to identify permanent and stable essential structures. What appeared to Husserl to be such essential structures of the mental realm, were, in Jerusalem's view, the products of 'associations that have become fixed, and of social condensations' (1914: 92). And thus Jerusalem suggested that the phenomenological *Wesensschauung* be replaced with evolutionary and sociological studies (1914: 93).

Pure philosophy and the new psychology

As the examples of Dilthey, Windelband, Rickert and Husserl make clear, the philosophies of these best-known figures of the late nineteenth and early twentieth centuries were in part – to say the least – arguments against the new psychology *as a genuine philosophical project*. The rise of the new psychology was not an event that merely coincided with the development of the philosophy of these leading pure philosophers; rather it was an event that shaped their very philosophical agenda.

The examples cited above also make clear that pure philosophers reacted to the new psychology in different ways. While all of them sought to reject its claims to being in some sense fundamental to both philosophy and the *Geisteswissenschaften*, they nevertheless differed over two issues: they disagreed over how distant from philosophy the new psychology was; and they disagreed over the question which purely philosophical project should replace experimental psychology both within philosophy and as the basis for the *Geisteswissenschaften*.

Concerning psychology's distance from philosophy, Dilthey remained somewhat vague, whereas Rickert saw the new psychology as being no closer to philosophy than any other empirical science. Windelband granted empirical psychology the title to being proximate to philosophy; and, provided that empirical psychology were to take its starting point from phenomenology, Husserl seemed to promise it even some sort of philosophical status.

With respect to the replacement issue, Dilthey proposed a new kind of empirical-descriptive psychology as both the basis of philosophy and the foundation of the *Geisteswissenschaften*; Rickert and Windelband suggested that a theory of values combined with practical, common-sense psychology would do for the *Geisteswissenschaften* what experimental psychology had promised but not delivered; and Husserl presented his phenomenology as the foundation of philosophy and empirical psychology.

Obviously, these proposals did not just compete with the various projects of advocates and practitioners of the new scientific psychology, they also competed against one another. Here I shall not delve into the many texts in which our pure philosophers and their students criticised each other. There were two main strategies to such criticisms. First, the critic from one school of pure philosophy, say school *A*, could claim that the project of another school *B* amounted to nothing new, and was in fact just a variant of what the founders of *A* had pronounced long ago. This, for instance, was Natorp's strategy with respect to both Dilthey and Husserl (Lessing 1985: 201; Natorp 1901, 1917–18). Second and more importantly, the critic could try to weaken the appeal of *B* by pointing out that it contained a disguised psychologism of sorts and thus constituted an insufficient barrier against the new psychology. We have earlier seen how Natorp and Rickert used this strategy against Husserl's *Prolegomena*; here I might add that Rickert employed it also against Natorp. Commenting on Natorp's philosophy of mathematics, and especially on Natorp's idea that numbers are 'posited' by pure consciousness, Rickert called Natorp's position 'a rationalistic psychologism . . . which is worse than the empiricist psychologism' (1911–12: 58).

The competition between the various projects of pure philosophy explains why the psychologism accusation was not only directed against proponents of the new psychology, but also levelled against various pure philosophers. Although, as seen earlier, different schools differed on how they defined psychologism, for pure philosophers at least psychologism always had the negative connotation of signalling a defeatist attitude towards the role hybridisation proposed by proponents of the new psychology. And thus, being accused of psychologism was a threat to the pure philosopher's standing in his community. One had to defend oneself against the charge, and one had to turn it against the accuser.

POWER POLITICS?

The petition and its background

The debate over the status of the new empirical psychology and especially the status of experimental psychology peaked in 1913. The immediate cause for this was a petition signed by 107 philosophers in Germany, Austria and Switzerland, demanding that no more philosophical chairs should go to experimental psychologists. The events that led up to this petition centred around Marburg. In April 1908, the faculty in Marburg created an extraordinary professorship which it sought to fill with an experimental psychologist, either G.F. Lipps or E. Jaensch. The Ministry of Education repeatedly rejected this proposal over the next three years on the grounds that the new professorship had been meant for historical and systematic philosophy rather than psychology. Nevertheless, the faculty was unwilling to follow Cohen's and Natorp's suggestion and fill the position with yet another neo-Kantian, i.e. with Ernst Cassirer. The conflict between the two philosophers and the faculty reached its height when Cohen retired in June 1912. The faculty now put two experimental psychologists at the top of the list for Cohen's former *Ordinarius* chair and appointed E. Jaensch in the fall of the same year (Holzhey 1986, I: 19–22). When even a student protest had no effect, Natorp went public and wrote an article in the daily *Frankfurter Zeitung*. He complained bitterly of the fact that again a professorial chair in philosophy had been 'surrendered to a special science which has no more to do with philosophy than any other special science'. He also criticised that in this way the Marburg School had effectively been destroyed, and he suggested, somewhat enigmatically, that there were political reasons for these developments (Natorp 1912b). At the same time Natorp, Husserl, Rickert, Windelband, the neo-Kantian Alois Riehl (Berlin) and the neo-Fichtean Rudolf Eucken (Jena) drew up the aforementioned petition, collected signatures for it and submitted it to all German-language universities and ministries of education. In so doing, they followed an idea which Husserl had suggested to Natorp early in 1911, that is they founded some kind of 'professors' union' (*Professorengewerkschaft*) against experimental psychology (letter by Natorp, 26.4.1911, in Holzhey 1986, II: 398).

In order to make the subsequent debate over the petition accessible, it is necessary to quote it in full (tr. Ash 1980b: 407–8).[1]

Statement

The undersigned teachers of philosophy at institutions of higher education in Germany, Austria and Switzerland see themselves as having cause to make a statement (*Erklärung*) directed against the filling of chairs of philosophy with representatives of experimental psychology.

The working area of experimental psychology has increased to such an extent with the highly gratifying advance of this discipline, that it has long been recognised as an independent field which demands the full energy of a scholar. Nonetheless, independent chairs have not been created for it; instead, professorships of philosophy have been filled with men whose activity is to a great extent or exclusively dedicated to the experimental investigation of mental life. This becomes understandable when one looks back to the beginnings of this discipline, and certainly it was unavoidable earlier that one scholar represented both fields at once. With the progressive development of experimental psychology, however, this situation has resulted in inconveniences for all concerned. Especially philosophy, for which interest among students is steadily growing, is severely damaged by the removal of chairs dedicated to her alone. This becomes all the more disquieting since the working area of philosophy is steadily growing larger, and since students should not be deprived of the opportunity to obtain systematic direction from their professors as well as about general questions of worldview and philosophy of life, especially in these philosophically troubled times.

The undersigned see it as their duty to point out to philosophical faculties and also to state educational authorities the disadvantages for the study of philosophy and psychology which grow out of this situation. In the common interest of both disciplines it must be taken carefully into consideration that philosophy retain its position in the life of the universities. Experimental psychology should therefore be supported only by the establishment of its own professorships, and everywhere where previously philosophical professorships are occupied [by psychologists] new chairs of philosophy should be created.

The complaint was of course far from new. Indeed, the allegation that experimental psychology had nothing to do with philosophy was almost as old as experimental psychology itself. For instance, a reviewer of the first volume of Wundt's journal *Philosophische Studien* doubted in 1882 whether the experimental reports it published were of any '*philosophical* interest' and suggested 'physiological' or 'psychophysical studies' as a more appropriate title (Horwicz 1882: 498). Another author, Karl Güttler, wrote a monograph entitled *Philosophie und Psychologie*, demanding that experimentalists should leave the philosophy departments. He quoted Külpe and Münsterberg, who had earlier called for separate chairs for psychology, and he wholeheartedly agreed with their suggestion that no one could cope with the overburdensome task of being both a philosopher and an experimental psychologist (1896: 22–7). Güttler also fielded a political argument against experimental psychology as a philosophical discipline. To replace pure philosophy by psychology would leave the students without a proper 'general education' (*Allgemeinbildung*), and thus without the argumentative skills necessary to '*restrict* . . . and . . . *combat* the wrong goals' of social democracy. Güttler also sided with another author's pamphlet (Dippe 1895) in proposing pure philosophy as the 'immune system of the academically educated against modern diseases of thought' (1896: 28).

Moreover, already prior to Natorp's article in the *Frankfurter Zeitung*, pure philosophers had taken their plight to widely circulating dailies and monthly magazines. R. Lehmann wrote in *Die*

Zukunft in 1906 that the general growth in philosophical interest squared badly with the tendency to fill ever more philosophical chairs with experimental psychologists. Lehmann asked rhetorically whether the resulting decline in academic philosophy would 'continue until the present generation has reached rock bottom and until a new generation will come forth' (1906: 487). And to mention a third example, in 1909 the *Frankfurter Zeitung* gave its front page to an article by Paul Hensel. The main theme of Hensel's article was that the career prospects of young philosophy graduates in Germany were endangered from two directions at once: by Catholic philosophers and by experimental psychologists. Hensel deplored the fact that a number of professorial chairs had been reserved for Catholics, and he deemed it 'shameful' that one could find psychophysicists lecturing on philosophical topics. Hensel saw the Thomists and the psychologists as forming an unholy alliance against German Idealism. He believed that 'the whole psychophysics can easily find a place in the system of St Thomas' but that between German Idealism and Thomism there can 'at most be a *truce* but no peace' (1909: 2).[2]

Wundt's intervention

The 80-year-old Wundt was the first proponent of experimental psychology to react in print to the pure philosophers' petition and, productive as ever, his reply grew into a little book, published under the title *Die Psychologie im Kampf ums Dasein* (Psychology struggling for survival, 1913). Wundt's book defended and attacked on two fronts: against the philosophers' 'get psychology out of philosophy' stance (1913: 2), and against some psychologists' desire to 'get philosophy out of psychology' (1913: 3).

To begin with his comments on the petition, Wundt was not convinced that its wording should be taken at face value. The petition had expressed concern for the further development of experimental psychology as well as for the advancement of philosophy. Wundt acknowledged that 'some participants in the protest action are honest in their defence of the interests of psychology', but he doubted whether the same could be assumed of one particular signatory,

> an excellent representative of historical philosophy who once remarked that occasionally someone is thought to be qualified for a philosophical chair as soon as he has learnt to press

electric buttons in a methodological way, and as soon as he can numerically prove by means of well-ordered and tabulated series of experiments that some people get ideas more quickly than others.

(Wundt 1913: 5)

Though Wundt did not mention Windelband by name here, his readers knew of course to whom he was referring. Furthermore, Wundt commented in detail on the petition's way of speaking of *experimental* psychology, rather than of psychology in general. To Wundt this suggested that psychology was being equated with experimental psychology:

The petition demands exclusively the elimination of *experimental* psychology from the philosophical curriculum . . . Does this mean that, at the present state of science, only experimental psychology qualifies for the title of psychology? . . . Do not the philosophers know about the existence of this area [i.e. *Völkerpsychologie*]? . . . Or do they deem it so insignificant that it does not need to be mentioned alongside experimental psychology?

(1913: 7)

Wundt also suspected that the philosophers' opposition to experimental psychology was due to a prejudice against experimentation. Wundt formulated this prejudice thus: 'Experimentation is a philistine art; thus the experimental psychologist is at best a scientific artisan. But an artisan doesn't belong among the philosophers' (1913: 9).

Turning from his philosophical to his psychological opponents, Wundt again made criticisms without mentioning names. In this context too, however, his target was easy to identify. After all, Wundt addressed all the arguments of his own former student, Oswald Külpe's paper 'Psychologie und Medizin'. There Külpe had suggested the distinction between philosophical psychology and another branch of psychology that – because of its empirical and experimental character – should become a separate natural science. While Külpe did not deny the existence of many close ties between experimental psychology and philosophy, he argued nevertheless that 'the combination of psychology (as a special science) with philosophy is beyond the capacity for work, the talent and the inclination of a *single* human being' (1912a: 266). In Külpe's view, the continuation of the status quo could only lead to 'dilettantism' in philosophical questions. Külpe went so far as to express understanding for the pure philosophers' opposition to this 'invasion of specialists' (1912a: 267). Having discussed a number of psychopathological studies allegedly lacking in psychological sophistication, and having emphasised the need for a psychological component in the training of medical doctors, Külpe suggested that experimental psychology should lobby for chairs in the medical faculty (1912a: 190–263).

Wundt spent more time rejecting Külpe's ideas than attacking the pure philosophers. First of all, he was unimpressed by Külpe's plea for a psychological education of medical doctors. In his view, the only kind of psychology the general practitioner needed was 'practical psychology . . . which, like every ingenious talent, is partly innate, partly acquired through practice' (1913: 11). Wundt was ready to admit that the psychiatrist needed more than just this practical talent, but he saw no reason for moving empirical psychology into the medical faculties. Instead he suggested that not all of psychology need be an academic, i.e. university-based, subject, and that psychiatrists might receive their psychological training in asylums (1913: 15).

Wundt also addressed the 'stress complaint' (*Überbürdungsklage*), i.e. the claim that the psychologist was overburdened by the demands of being both an experimental psychologist and a philosopher. Addressing the philosophers, Wundt remarked coldly that those 'who have never themselves experimented can hardly be regarded as competent judges of this question' (1913: 9). Turning to Külpe's similar concern, Wundt was scarcely less ironic. He reminded his readers that the 'stress complaint' was first raised with respect to schoolchildren, then made its way into student circles and had now 'captured even the philosophers, both the non-psychologists and the psychologists' (1913: 17). Wundt went on to predict that psychologists would soon have cause for an 'out-of-work complaint' if indeed they were to break away from philosophy (1913: 21).

Wundt's main worry was that an institutional split between philosophy and psychology would soon turn experimental psychologists into mere artisans. On his count, almost half of all of the psychological literature extended into metaphysics and epistemology (1913: 18). And 'the most important questions of psychological education are so closely linked to epistemological and metaphysical questions that one cannot imagine how they could ever vanish from psychology' (1913: 24). Wundt also rejected the American model of having separate psychological institutes as being ill-suited to Germany: an independent psychology would give exclusive attention to practical application, and this would not fit the emphasis on theoretical work typical of the German university system (1913: 26).

Wundt reproached Külpe for equating empirical psychology with experimental psychology, just as he had done with the signatories of the petition. He was especially critical of Külpe's (and the Würzburg School's) 'psychology of thought' and denied their experiments the status of 'experiments in the scientific sense' (1913: 28–30; I shall return to this criticism in the next chapter).

Finally, Wundt outlined his own view of the relation between psychology and philosophy, and he made a number of suggestions for future action. As Wundt saw it, psychology was 'both a part of the science of philosophy and an empirical *Geisteswissenschaft*; and its value for both philosophy and the empirical special sciences resides in its being the main negotiator between them' (1913: 32). In terms of action, Wundt proposed that the larger universities should have three chairs in philosophy, one for 'the systematic disciplines', one for the history of philosophy, and one for psychology (1913: 34). Moreover, since good work in psychology presupposed a sound background in philosophy,

> one should not accept any candidate for the *Habilitation* who is a mere experimentalist, and who is not a man with both a psychological and a philosophical education, preoccupied with philosophical interests; and the philosophers as well as the psychologists themselves should work towards a situation in which faculties propose – for those philosophical chairs that are meant to represent psychology – only such men as are also able to represent philosophical disciplines effectively and independently.
>
> (1913: 38)

A number of pure philosophers and experimental psychologists soon rushed into print with their reactions to Wundt's book. One of the first came from Rickert in the *Frankfurter Zeitung*. Rickert was less than enthusiastic about Wundt's intervention. In Rickert's opinion, Wundt's book was likely to 'cloud' the central issue. He also deplored Wundt's 'personal attacks which are hidden and thus hard to grapple with' (1913b: 1). Rickert was especially concerned to point out that the disagreement over the petition, and thus over the question of whether experimental psychologists should be appointed to professorial chairs in philosophy, was not just a disagreement *among philosophers*:

> In any case, Wundt's brochure [*sic*] must not be understood to imply that our petition results from a struggle between two different 'schools of thought' *within philosophy*, one of which counts psychology as a part of philosophy and one of which does not; and thus it must not be concluded that the most 'objective' procedure would be to fill one part of philosophical chairs with 'pure' philosophers and another part with experimental psychologists.
>
> (Rickert 1913b: 2)

To back up his position, Rickert mentioned that some experimentalists had supported the petition, he referred to Külpe, and he claimed that even Wundt sided with the signatories *in so far* as Wundt too wished to '*keep one-sided, specialised researchers away from philosophical chairs*' (1913b: 2).

Marbe's headcount

Wundt's *Die Psychologie im Kampf ums Dasein* did not remain the only book written in response to the petition. Wundt's former student, and Külpe's ex-colleague in Würzburg, Karl Marbe, published a long analysis of the petition, *Die Aktion gegen die Psychologie: Eine Abwehr*. Without doubt, both Wundt's and Rickert's texts had already been polemical, but Marbe's contribution was unusually scathing even by the acerbic standards of the German academic environment.

Marbe began by acknowledging that science could not function without a constant struggle for survival between ideas and schools of thought. Nevertheless, he felt that in this 'struggle for life in science', the pure philosophers' petition marked a new level of 'suppression' in that it sought not only 'to damage the academic career of many scholars', but also 'to stop young scholars from turning to a certain field'. Marbe promised his readers proof that the 'very cleverly worded "petition" . . . is in fact meant to suppress psychology' (1913: 3–4).

Like Wundt, Marbe too commented on the petition's focus on 'experimental psychology', but from a different angle. As Marbe interpreted the petition, its wording suggested that only non-experimental psychology had a right to remain within philosophy. To Marbe this suggestion was out of phase with the development of 'modern psychology':

> Just as one cannot oppose experimental physics in order to further physics, so one cannot oppose 'experimental psychology' and still wish to promote psychology – although, of course, experimentation does not exhaust either all of psychology or all of physics. *The campaign is thus in fact directed against modern psychology.*
>
> (Marbe 1913: 16)

To increase the plausibility of this claim, Marbe reminded his audience of 'Windelband's spiteful comments on psychology' (1913: 6).

Marbe not only focused his attention on the wording of the petition, he also undertook to analyse the competence of its signatories. He deplored that there were several nonphilosophers among the signatories and that the petition was not sent to every university-level philosophy teacher. He added that the connoisseur of the philosophical literature found in the petition 'the only memorable literary achievement of some of the undersigned names', and that Rickert had even miscounted the number of signatures (107 rather than 106) (1913: 14). From here Marbe went on to a little statistical exercise: he wished to show that the signatories formed only a minority among professional philosophers, and that they were incompetent to judge questions regarding modern psychology.

Restricting his investigation to the full professors among both signatories and nonsignatories, Marbe pointed out that only 40.9 per cent of all full professors at German-language universities signed the petition (1913: 16). Furthermore, while only 7 per of the signatories had published on modern psychology and only 25 per cent had taught courses on psychology, during the last ten years, the respective numbers of *non*signatories were 51 per cent and 43 per cent (1913: 17–22). Marbe's conclusion: '*Those who have signed the "petition" are, taken as a whole, less competent in questions of psychology than those who have refrained from signing*' (1913: 22).

Turning to Rickert and Windelband, Marbe took up two of their arguments against experimental psychology as a philosophical discipline. He flatly denied that modern psychologists were incompetent in philosophical questions. He also emphasised that 'the scientific reputation of the Windelband School, which works most intensively against psychology, is greatest within that school itself'. Marbe went on to write that in the contemporary philosophical literature one found, 'aside from the occasional obvious rubbish, an infinite number of contributions which have been as often rejected as they have been accepted' (1913: 27). In addition, Marbe addressed the worry that modern psychology might be too scientific, unable to provide guidance in matters of *Weltanschauung*, and conformist in political matters. He replied that

> the more scientific the personality of an academic teacher, the more he is familiar with real science and the more self-critical and duty-conscious he is, the less he will be ready to abuse the lectern for a propaganda of his *Weltanschauung*. It may well be the case that this will sometimes make him less of a political troublemaker than another who mixes politics and religion with science. But that should not be held against him as an allegation.
>
> (1913: 27)

Marbe did not have to wait long for replies by pure philosophers. And the pure philosophers who did respond to his polemical onslaught answered in style. Hensel asked whether anyone would expect to find signatures in cuneiform script under a petition by judges protesting against the filling of judges' positions by Assyriologists (1913: 2). The phenomenologist Geiger too thought that no one could have expected the experimental psychologists to sign anyway: 'After all, the representatives of experimental psychology profit from the current state of affairs . . . whereas, e.g. a man like Husserl . . ., in part because of this state of affairs, is still today without a budget-funded chair' (1913: 754). Geiger also denied the philosophical value of the experimentalists' work on volition (1913: 755) and accused Marbe of conflating 'the interests of the representatives of a science with the interests of that science itself'. Just as Galileo and his followers succeeded even though university chairs were in the hands of their Aristotelian opponents, so experimental psychology too had to prove its mettle without relying on an academic power base: 'deeper reflection has never seen the progress of a science depend upon the careers of its representatives' (1913: 754).

Commenting on Marbe's tables and statistics on the psychological activities of signatories and nonsignatories of the petition, Hensel remarked that 'the bustling industriousness with which they have been compiled must make evident to every unbiased reader just how necessary Rickert's petition has been' (1913: 2). And defending himself directly against Marbe's accusation that his lecture course in psychology was really a course in the history of literature, Hensel wrote that it was difficult to convince 'heads with little training in philosophy' of the need for a historical psychology. Hensel concluded: 'You [i.e. Marbe] have no reason to tell yourself: *O si tacuisses, philosophus mansisses.* One can only remain what one has been in the past' (1913: 2).

The Lamprecht–Simmel controversy

The third main intervention on behalf of experimental psychology came from the Leipzig historian Karl Lamprecht. As mentioned in the last chapter, Lamprecht regarded modern psychology as the foundation of historical studies, and even wrote that 'as such, history is nothing but applied psychology' (1904: 16). Lamprecht published a piece in the semi-popular *Die Zukunft*, entitled 'Eine Gefahr für die Geisteswissenschaften' (1913a). Georg Simmel, who thought that Lamprecht's writing constituted 'sabotage by Wundt' (letter to Rickert, 3 June 1913; Gassen and Landmann 1956: 111), replied in the same journal (Simmel 1913), and this reply in turn sparked a further public rejoinder from Lamprecht (1913b).

Like Marbe, Lamprecht also thought that the petition was a novel way of advancing one kind of philosophy at the expense of others. Unlike Marbe, Lamprecht felt that this was an event of historical significance: it broke with the ideals of Protestantism, i.e. with the ban on attempts to silence one's opponents, and it also constituted 'a hitherto, in this proportion, unseen intrusion of power politics into what one might call university politics' (1913a: 18).

Lamprecht offered some historical reflections on the present state of philosophy. All indications were that Germany was about to experience another era of idealism, and that there existed a strong need for a new systematic *Weltanschauung*. Unfortunately, however, 'pure philosophy' had done little to contribute to this new project. The only project that had gained wider currency in the *Geisteswissenschaften*, Lamprecht thought, was Rickert's system of values. Lamprecht showed no sympathy for this 'impotent' project.

The only way to stop its further spread was to strengthen psychology within philosophy:

> let us assume that this doctrine of absolute values would develop further from its presently shown impotence into a total system – of course a system of metaphysical character; let us assume that a new, great poetry of metaphysical concepts would grow out of it; what then would be the result for the further development of the *Geisteswissenschaften*, provided that, at the same time, psychology had been pushed into the role of a special natural, or even medical, science? There can be no doubt: the *Geisteswissenschaften* would fall completely under the spell of that poetry.
>
> (Lamprecht 1913a: 23)

Indeed, Lamprecht believed that a victory of pure philosophy would lead to a situation in the *Geisteswissenschaften* not unlike the situation of the natural sciences in the 1830s and 40s when the latter were 'dominated by Schelling's philosophy of nature' (1913a: 24).

In his reply 'An Herrn Prof. Karl Lamprecht' (1913), Simmel made three points. First, he denied Lamprecht's claim that German philosophy tended to be dominated by one philosophical system. Simmel rather perceived an ever increasing diversity (1913: 230–1).[3]

Second, Simmel disputed Lamprecht's thesis regarding the enormous importance of experimental psychology for the *Geisteswissenschaften* as well as for philosophy. Claiming to have followed the achievements of experimental psychology for twenty-five years, Simmel confessed to be unable to name,

> aside from Fechner's law and its development and some of those occasional contacts and stimulations that happen among all sciences, any positive or even negative significance of these psychological experiments for the specifically philosophical projects. Indeed, perhaps no other natural science in its present state has as little significance for these projects as has experimental psychology.
>
> (Simmel 1913: 231)

And third, Simmel used the political argument that we have already encountered in Güttler (1896) (cf. Simon 1913: 2):

> where the young are no longer offered philosophy, the best elements turn to other sources that promise to nourish their

deepest needs: to mysticism, or that which they call 'life', to social democracy, or to literature in general, to a misunderstood Nietzsche or to a sceptically coloured materialism. Let us not delude ourselves about this: the German universities have largely lost the innermost leadership of youth to powers of this kind. It is certain that the transition from philosophy in the older sense to experimental psychology is not the only cause for this change ... But this replacement of genuinely philosophical chairs by experimental-psychological chairs gives this change increasing support.

(1913: 233)

Experimental psychology and psychologism

Even with this exchange, the controversy over the petition did not die down; indeed it continued pretty much until the outbreak of the First World War.[4] The above should suffice, however, to convey an impression of the content and style of the exchanges.

The debate over the 1913 petition was, as indicated above, merely the climax of a series of interventions for and against the appointment of experimental psychologists to philosophical chairs. As the arguments for both sides made clear enough, pure philosophy aimed for a purification of the role of the philosopher whereas many proponents of the new psychology sought to defend the status quo in which the roles of the philosopher and the experimentalist could coincide in one scholar.

It is especially noteworthy that the debate over the petition coincided with the peak in the number of texts accusing philosophers of psychologism. By this stage in my argument, this should hardly come as a surprise. From the point of view of pure philosophy, to combat psychologism and to argue for role purification amounted to one and the same project. For the pure philosopher, the language game 'refutation of psychologism' was superimposed on the language game 'why experimental psychology is not entitled to philosophical chairs' and superimposed on the language game 'which project of pure philosophy works best as a justification for regarding experimental psychology as a nonphilosophical project'.

From the perspective of a proponent of the new psychology, the situation was less clear-cut. Some tried to disentangle their opponents' position by challenging 'refutations of psychologism', and thereby attempted to argue for the inclusion of experimental psychology within philosophy (e.g. Schlick 1910b; Eisenmeyer 1914). Others accepted some version of refutations of psychologism but denied that such refutations had any bearing on the institutional status of experimental psychology (e.g. Wundt). And a third position by and large accepted the pure philosophers' position (e.g. Külpe).

Finally, it needs to be emphasised that, as the controversy went on, the two positions on the institutional status of psychology did not drift towards any kind of compromise. The late contributions to the debate were just as extreme as the early interventions.

WHY HUSSERL – AND NOT FREGE?

The issue of role hybridisation versus role purification in the case of German philosophers in the late nineteenth and early twentieth centuries can also serve as the key for understanding why Husserl's arguments against psychologism were widely discussed whereas Frege's arguments were by and large ignored.

The important point to note here is that, for many German pure philosophers, the dangers of 'logical mathematicism' (Rickert 1911–12: 27) were no less severe or real than the dangers of psychologism. The logical algebra of Boole and Jevons had been given a cold reception by German philosophers in the last two decades of the nineteenth century, and this scepticism continued well into the twentieth century (see Bühl 1966; Pulkkinen 1994). Hans Sluga has suggested that this hostile reaction was due in part to 'a feeling of insecurity in the face of the unusual and hermetic appearance of the new logic', in part 'it was fear of the incursion of mathematics into an area that traditionally had been integral to philosophy' (1980: 74).

J. Geyser saw as

> the weakest point of mathematical logic (*Logistik*) ... its tendency towards the purest formalism. It extracts the quantitative elements from all qualitative parts of the content of the world, and thus treats the characteristics of the content of concepts as empty elements of an arithmetical addition ... And thus qualitative relations have no place in *Logistik*. The latter may well be the special logic of mathematics, but it can never be the general logic of scientific knowledge in general.
>
> (Geyser 1909b: 132)

Geyser also ruled that mathematical logic could only claim the prize of greater clarity – compared with other methods in logic – 'if it lowers itself down to us who are not familiar with the secrets of higher mathematics and speaks to us not in the parlance of the mathematicians but in the simple language of general scientific thought' (1909b: 143).

Natorp praised mathematical logic for its attacks on empiricism, psychologism and nominalism in general, and he applauded Frege in particular (1910: 3). However, this acclaim was immediately followed by the accusation that the project of mathematical logic was circular:

> Logic is supposed to be a deductive science; however, it certainly is part of logic to establish the laws of the deductive method and to justify the necessary and general validity that the latter [i.e. the deductive method] lays claim to. But can the formulation and justification of a logical method be provided by that logical method itself? That is absurd.
>
> (Natorp 1910: 5)

Natorp also held that the mathematical-logical calculus operated with meaningless symbols and that such machine-like operation was unworthy of the philosophical logician (1910: 7).

Rickert's attack on the intrusion of mathematics into the realm of logic also mentioned Frege; Rickert too applauded Frege's criticism of psychologism in mathematics (1911–12: 30). Rickert went on to argue that logic needed to be clearly set apart from mathematics and that, after the defeat of psychologism, the greatest threat to 'the independence of logic' came from 'a direction that one might call logical mathematicism' (1911–12: 27). Rickert sought to show in detail that logic and mathematics belonged to different ontological categories: whereas mathematical idealities (*Idealitäten*) have being (*Sein*), logical idealities 'have validity' (*gelten*) (1911–12: 78). More specifically with respect to numbers, Rickert wrote that 'the object of mathematical research is numbers, not the concept of number'. The concept of number is one of the central subjects of philosophical, nonmathematical logic (1911–12: 75).

Rickert's student Martin Heidegger belaboured the same point: with *Logistik*

> there arises for logic a new task of demarcation. In order to provide a solution, I think that the first thing necessary is to

show that *Logistik* does not extend beyond mathematics, and that it is unable to reach the truly logical problems. For me the weakness of *Logistik* resides in its uses of mathematical symbols and concepts (especially the *concept of a function*), a use that conceals the meanings as well as the changes in meaning of judgements.

(Heidegger [1912] 1978a: 42)

Especially interesting from the point of view of a comparison between Husserl and Frege is the fact that Husserl too regarded mathematical logic as a nonphilosophical enterprise. In 1891, Husserl reviewed Ernst Schröder's *Vorlesungen über die Algebra der Logik* (Schröder 1890) and took the author to task for failing to provide a study of the mental processes involved in deduction. As the young Husserl saw it, the mathematical logician did not provide a philosophical analysis of what the logical-mathematical algorithm is a surrogate for (Husserl [1891a] 1979).

Husserl made the need for a clear divide between the philosophical and the mathematical logician even more explicit in the *Logische Untersuchungen*. While acknowledging that mathematical logic was a discipline in its own right and not to be derided by philosophers, he nevertheless reduced the mathematical logician to a mere 'technician': he was 'not the pure theoretician but merely the ingenious technician, the designer . . . Just like the practical mechanic constructs machines . . . so the mathematician constructs theories.' It was only the philosophical logician who could provide 'the essential insight' into the mathematicians' doing: 'It is only through the work of philosophical research that the work of the natural scientist and the mathematician is completed in such a manner that pure and true theoretical knowledge is achieved' ([1900] 1975: 254–6).

In light of how widespread these attitudes were among philosophical logicians, it is perhaps not surprising that they felt little inclination to take their cue from a mathematician's criticism of psychological logic. To most of them this would have meant applying a cure that was as dangerous as the disease. Frege did little to alleviate this fear – e.g. he did not make suggestions for a division of labour between the mathematical logician and the philosophical logician. Moreover, it can hardly have helped Frege's case that when thrashing Frege's *Begriffsschrift* in 1880, Schröder concluded by praising 'the philosopher' Wundt (!) for dedicating fifty-two pages of his *Logik* (Wundt 1880–83) to the logical calculus. For Schröder, Wundt was the first philosopher to take proper notice of the '*mathematical reform of logic*' (Schröder 1880: 94).

There were other obvious differences between Frege and Husserl as well. With the exception of three years in Göttingen, where he obtained his Ph.D., Frege spent most of his academic life at the University of Jena. Frege did not attempt to form any 'school', and it is likely that he turned down the offer to become a full professor in 1896 (Bynum 1972: 42). In Frege's days the University of Jena was a university with a great past but a humble present. Schiller, Fichte, Schelling and Hegel had taught there several decades earlier, but by the 1860s Jena had fallen behind other German universities. In 1869 it had no more than 500 students, only five chairs in the humanities and one professorship combining the fields of mathematics, physics and astronomy (Sluga 1984: 331). In 1901 it still had no more than 700 students, and it was the second smallest of the twenty-one universities in the German Reich. In 1874, when Frege returned to Jena from Göttingen, Jena became the last German university town to be connected to the German railway system. Moreover, Jena was considered a 'summer university', and during the second half of the 1870s rumours that its closure was imminent persisted (Kreiser and Grosche 1983: 331–2).

Husserl, on the other hand, received his academic training at the big and leading universities of his day. He studied astronomy, physics and mathematics in Leipzig, Berlin, Vienna and Halle, and befriended, and impressed, some of the leading figures in both mathematics (Weierstrass) and philosophy (Brentano, Stumpf). From 1901 onwards he was extraordinary professor of philosophy in Göttingen, and even though G.E. Müller did his best to slow Husserl's career (Schuhmann 1977: 90), Husserl did eventually become *Ordinarius* in Freiburg, succeeding Rickert. Already before the publication of his *Logische Untersuchungen*, Husserl had established contacts with several of the leading neo-Kantians, e.g. with Paul Natorp.

It thus seems obvious that the different reception of Frege's and Husserl's arguments against psychologism was strongly influenced by their location both geographically and academically. Whereas Frege was an isolated mathematician and had little contact with the German philosophical scene, Husserl was a well-established member of the philosophical-academic community.

The differences in the argumentative style of Frege's main attack on psychological logic (foremost in the *Grundgesetze*) and Husserl's attempted refutation of psychologism (in the *Prolegomena*) are also unmistakable and dramatic.

First, the two onslaughts on psychological logic differ of course in that Frege devoted a mere fourteen pages to the criticism of psychological logic, whereas Husserl used a whole book for the same purpose. Moreover, Frege attacked only a single author in the *Grundgesetze*, whereas Husserl criticised more than twenty both directly and indirectly. No doubt, to the German philosophical reader, Husserl's offensive must have appeared much more *gründlich* than Frege's.

Second, Frege's criticism of Erdmann has rightly been characterised as 'merciless and satirical' (Bynum 1972: 35). While Frege granted that Erdmann's *Logik* was 'not totally without significance' (1893: xix), the tone of his comments suggested a different view. Erdmann's position was judged to be full of 'conflation' (1893: xvii); he was 'stuck in a psychological-metaphysical quagmire' (1893: xx, xxii), an 'unclear writer' (1893: xxiii), 'on the wrong track' (1893: xxiv), guilty of 'almost the worst possible conflation' (1893: xxv), and his book was 'bloated with unhealthy psychological fat' (1893: xxv). Overall, the reader was left with the impression that Frege felt contempt and disgust for his opponent, and that he was out to teach him an easy and obvious lesson.

Judged from a rhetorical perspective, the tone of Husserl's criticism was much more effective and compelling. To begin with, Husserl found words of praise even for those philosophers that he criticised harshly and at great length: Mill's treatment of logic was 'valuable' ([1900] 1975: 19); Drobisch was 'excellent' (*trefflich*) ([1900] 1975: 50); Lange's logic 'wise' (*geistvoll*) ([1900] 1975: 101); Sigwart 'important' (*bedeutend*) ([1900] 1975: 106, 138), 'excellent' (*ausgezeichnet*) ([1900] 1975: 107) and displaying 'so much acumen' (*Scharfsinn*) ([1900] 1975: 138); Heymans' work was 'interesting' ([1900] 1975: 116); Erdmann 'excellent', 'of outstanding merit' (*verdient*) ([1900] 1975: 149) and 'outstanding' (*hervorragend*) ([1900] 1975: 157). Husserl also referred to Brentano and Stumpf indirectly 'as the men ... to whom my scientific education owes most' ([1900] 1975: 7). Husserl even denied that 'psychologism' was meant as a term with negative connotations: 'I am using the expressions "psychologicist", "psychologism", etc. without any derogatory slant' ([1900] 1975: 64). And having chastised Erdmann's ideas as 'absurd', Husserl went on to explain that 'absurd' too was used 'without any slant' ([1900] 1975: 153). Furthermore, at one point Husserl presented his antipsychologism as a compromise formula between the earlier normative antipsychologism and psychological logic ([1900] 1975: 168).

Moreover, Husserl introduced his antipsychologism as a philosophical stand that he too found difficult to adopt. Put differently, Husserl presented himself as a humble convert to antipsychologism, as a convert who attacked others only because they held variants of his own former views:

> I had started from the predominant conviction that, just like logic in general, so also the logic of deductive sciences would have to receive its philosophical clarification from psychology ... I now publish these attempts towards a *new foundation of pure logic and epistemology*. They arose during many years of work. In so doing, I hope that the independence with which I cut my own ways off from the predominant logical movement will not be misunderstood. Especially I hope not to be misunderstood with respect to the substantial motives that guided me. The course of my development has brought it about that I have put a long distance between myself and the logical basic views of those men and works to whom my scientific education owes most ... And as concerns the frank criticism that I level against psychologistic logic and epistemology, I would like to remind the reader of Goethe's idea that 'one relates towards nothing with greater harshness than towards those errors that one has just given up'.
>
> (Husserl [1900] 1975: 7)

And indeed, while speaking favourably of his opponents, Husserl also attacked them in a harsh and scathing way. For instance, he spoke of 'the low of purely logical insights in our time' ([1900] 1975: 80), 'the low of *scientific* philosophy' ([1900] 1975: 214), and he accused his opponents time and again of 'prejudices', 'conflation', 'equivocations', '*metabasis eis allo genos*', '*hysteron-proteron*' and – this being Husserl's favourite – 'absurdity' (*Widersinn*). In sum then, Husserl's text combined praise with criticism, whereas Frege's text was simply scornful.

Frege's and Husserl's criticisms of psychologism also differed in the following, third, respect. Frege did not mention any other philosopher either as a possible ally or as a predecessor of his position. Rather than speaking of philosophical allies, Frege wrote that he would need the support of other *mathematicians* in order to defeat the psychological logicians (1893: xxvi). Here too Husserl's textual strategy differed radically from Frege's. Although Husserl wrote in his preface that he arrived at his antipsychologism independently of others, he nevertheless included a whole chapter on his antipsychologistic predecessors, spoke of his indebtedness to 'great thinkers of the past' and mentioned Kant, Leibniz, Herbart, Lotze, Lange and Bolzano in particular ([1900] 1975: §§58–61). The tendency to relate his work to Kant was especially prominent throughout the book. Note, for instance, that the very title 'Prolegomena' alluded to Kant's *Prolegomena zu einer jeden künftigen Metaphysik* ([1783] 1979), and that already Husserl's posture of the humble convert was reminiscent of Kant's famous awakening from 'dogmatic slumber' (Kant [1783] 1979: 10). It is also noteworthy that Husserl presented his pure logic in a Kantian guise, i.e. as a quest for the ideal conditions of the possibility of abstract theories (§§65–6), and that he called his antipsychologism 'idealism' ([1900] 1975: 215). Last but not least, Husserl referred approvingly to the contemporaneous neo-Kantians Natorp, Riehl and Windelband ([1900] 1975: 94, 160, 172). It is true that, as mentioned earlier, Husserl found psychologism in Kantian as well as neo-Kantian ideas ([1900] 1975: 102), but his attempt to present himself as close to the neo-Kantian project – a project dominant in German philosophy at the time – was unmistakable.

Fourth, and finally, Husserl's success was undoubtedly also due to the fact that he linked his criticism of psychologism to a criticism of the dominance of experimental psychology in philosophy departments. In a longish footnote Husserl contested Külpe's claim that logic was one of the best-developed areas of philosophy. Husserl went on to suggest that real progress in logical studies would come about only once philosophical logicians had adopted a careful piecemeal approach to the logical foundations. Doubting that this suggestion would be followed, Husserl went on to write:

> This kind of thinking [i.e. an approach based on small steps] can already be found everywhere in philosophy; however, as I have learnt to appreciate, this kind of thinking goes mostly in the wrong direction: the best scientific energy is directed at psychology – psychology as an explanatory natural science which should not interest philosophy any more than should

the sciences of the physical processes . . . I am pleased about the otherwise promising development of scientific psychology, and I take a strong interest in it – but not as someone who expects any kind of *philosophical* clarification from scientific psychology.

([1900] 1975: 214)

8

WINNER TAKES ALL
Lebensphilosophie and the triumph of phenomenology

INTRODUCTION

In the last four chapters, we have followed the controversies over psychologism and over the philosophical status of experimental psychology. We have seen that these two debates were connected; for instance, arguments against psychologism often were, at the same time, arguments against the appointment of experimental psychologists to philosophy chairs. It remains to be explained why these disputes were eventually abandoned, and why phenomenology and its views on psychologism and experimental psychology emerged as the winner.

My explanation emphasises two causal factors, the effects of the First World War and the mentality of the Weimar Republic. The war brought about an atmosphere in which attacks on one's colleagues were regarded as utterly inappropriate. Moreover, the war also led to a clear division of labour between pure philosophers and psychologists: while pure philosophy concentrated on the ideological task of celebrating the German 'genius of war', experimental psychology focused on the training and testing of soldiers.

I shall characterise the change in mentality of the postwar period which Germany's defeat brought about, and analyse the effect of this change upon pure philosophy and experimental psychology respectively. Put in a nutshell, both academic pure philosophy and experimental psychology had to cope with, and accommodate to, an intellectual environment that was hostile to science, rationality and systematic knowledge.

Pure philosophers used two strategies for surviving in this atmosphere, and often in tandem: they attacked the '*Lebensphilosophie*' which formulated the new mentality, or else they presented themselves as its true leaders. Rickert, the leading neo-Kantian during the Weimar period, chose the offensive, whereas phenomenologists like Scheler opted for alignment. As the second strategy proved far more successful, phenomenology became more and more dominant. Thanks to this predominant position, phenomenology could subsequently impose its view on the history of the pre-war philosophical disputes.

At the same time, the project of a naturalistic philosophy with experimental psychology as its central pillar quickly lost support. Advocates and practitioners of experimental psychology therefore had to find new ways of justifying their work. Many of them continued their wartime involvement with applied psychology. This choice was encouraged by the state and industry which funded new chairs in psychology only in the practice-oriented technical universities. Psychologists eager to remain within philosophy departments adopted a strategy of siding with the (earlier) enemy: they rejected what they now called the 'atomistic' pre-war tradition of experimental psychology, and they openly embraced and adopted the earlier much ridiculed philosophical psychology of Dilthey and Husserl.

WAR AND PEACE

When war broke out in August 1914, academic hostilities within the German Reich ceased immediately. The German *Kaiser's* exclamation '*Ich kenne keine Parteien mehr, ich kenne nur noch Deutsche*' (I no longer know of parties, I only know of Germans) was not only hailed in the political sphere, it was also celebrated in the trenches of academic warfare. In throwing themselves wholeheartedly behind the war effort university professors joined other intellectuals like Thomas Mann, Gerhart Hauptmann, Stefan George or Robert Musil, all of whom greeted the war enthusiastically (Hepp 1987: 149). So great was the general sense of a new beginning that even the times of German antisemitism seemed finally over. No less a person than Hermann Cohen was ready to travel to America in order to convince Jewish organisations of the full integration of Jews into German society (Zechlin 1969: 89). Intellectuals of all kinds rushed their patriotic pamphlets to the printing press, and gave thousands of public lectures. Rudolf Eucken, for example, gave thirty-six lectures in one year alone (Ringer 1969: 182). Almost without exception, German intellectuals praised the newly found unity of society, and 'the ideas of 1914'. This expression was first introduced by the economist Johann Plenge, who wrote:

> When we celebrate this war on a future day of remembrance, that day will be the feast of the mobilisation. The feast of the second of August . . . That is when our new spirit was born: the spirit of the tightest integration of all economic and all political powers into a new whole . . . The new German state! the ideas of 1914!
>
> (quoted in Ringer 1969: 181)

Old enemies could now be found signing the same petitions; for example, a petition in support of maximum war aims was signed by no fewer than 352 university professors (Ringer 1969: 190), and Eucken's, Lamprecht's, Windelband's and Wundt's signatures can all be found under the notorious 'Aufruf der 93 an die Kulturwelt' (Appeal of the 93 to the cultured world). This *Aufruf* was meant to 'protest against the lies and insinuations with which our enemies try to besmirch Germany's pure cause'. It claimed that 'those who present the world with the ignominious spectacle of rushing Mongols and Negroes against the white race, those have least right to present themselves as defenders of European civilisation'. The appeal concluded with a defence of German militarism:

> It is not true . . . that a war against our so-called militarism is no war against our culture. Without German militarism German culture would have vanished long ago from the face of the earth. . . . German army and German people are one. Today this consciousness unites 70 million Germans regardless of their education, their station, or their party.
>
> (quoted in Hepp 1987: 207–8)

'The genius of war': Pure philosophy goes to war

Pure philosophers were among the leading propagandists for the German cause. Many of them gave public lectures and published books and articles both on the meaning of war in general, and on Germany's role in the present struggle.[1]

Of the neo-Kantians, Paul Natorp was the most prolific writer with altogether three books (1915, 1918a, 1918b). In Natorp's view, unlike her enemies, Germany was fighting the war in order to achieve and guarantee freedom for all states and for all human beings. It was because Germany had gone to war for the freedom of all, and was fighting 'out of our deepest love for peace', that Germany's stand was 'morally superior' to that of other nations (1915: 63). As Natorp saw it, it was time for Germans to oppose the 'meanness' of their enemies 'with the only language that is appropriate here: the unmistakably clear language of the fists. This language is justified by the eternal truth: Whoever lies, deserves a beating.' The language of fists did not come natural to Germans, Natorp alleged, but Germany had to learn this form of communication in order to fulfil its world-historical task: 'today *we* are those who fight for eternal moral justice' (1915: 64–5). While other countries had conquered the world, Germany had made important philosophical discoveries (1915: 77). And thus Germany alone had developed, and in part already implemented, the ideal society based on reason. This new society was a combination of 'socialism and "militarism"', an 'inner organisation [of society] . . . based on the autonomy of rational will'. It was a society in which the rational individual identified with the interests of the whole of society (1915: 83–5). 'For this goal Germany must win the war – win the war or die!' (1915: 90).

Similar themes were developed by the leading neo-Kantian philosopher in Berlin, Alois Riehl (Riehl 1915). Like many other German philosophers of the time, Riehl presented the war as a struggle between culture and civilisation. Already before the war this opposition had played a key role in criticisms of modernity (Elias 1978; Ringer 1969). Now the distinction between culture and civilisation was used in order to justify Germany's superiority over the Allies. Riehl introduced the distinction in the following way:

We call civilisation the sum, and the use, of all those means that make our external life more simple and more beautiful. Central parts of civilisation are the social conventions, the style and equipment of our flats, as well as technical inventions which multiply our powers and put external nature at the service of our will: wireless telegraphy, aeroplanes, Zeppelins. Even intellectualism, i.e. the training of our understanding, is no more than civilisation, it is merely something external. But culture creates the soul for this body. Culture is an internal notion, culture arises from the inner, spiritual content of life, and no progress in the external shaping of life, no sophistication of conventions, can play the role of culture ... Thus we can well understand how the highest level of civilisation can coincide with a low in true, inner culture.

(Riehl 1915: 315)

In Riehl's view, French, British and Russian society stood for civilisation, whereas Germany displayed a high level of culture: 'This war is in fact a cultural war (*Kulturkrieg*). We fight in this war in order to preserve and improve our culture, and we know that thereby we fight for the culture of humankind' (1915: 325). Riehl also rejected the idea of some British and French intellectuals that Germany needed to be liberated from its militarism. For instance, Riehl lamented that Germany's enemies had failed to consider 'whether we even want to be freed from our so-called militarism' (1915: 320). Like Natorp, Riehl saw the present war as proof for the contention that modern society need not be a mere sum of individuals:

> In these early days of August of last year, during the early days after the outbreak of the war, our whole nation experienced an inner renewal ... The endangered fatherland had called upon our highest moral powers, it was as if we all had become purer and better. Whatever damage the long peace might have caused in us, this damage now seemed to vanish like something foreign ... One people and one spirit, thus the whole nation rose in wonderful unity. This means that a nation (*Volk*) is more than the sum of citizens.
>
> (1915: 316–17)

A third neo-Kantian worth mentioning here is Rickert's student Bruno Bauch. Bauch's review (Bauch 1915) of Wundt's main war contribution (Wundt 1915) demonstrated nicely how former academic enemies had now become friends. Bauch did not go so far as to call Wundt a philosopher, but in other respects Bauch was full of praise and admiration: Wundt was 'a true German' (1915: 305), his characterisation of the British was 'masterful', and his whole work a model of 'the spirit of German truthfulness and German character ... that hopefully will one day again be useful to the whole of cultured humankind' (1915: 310).

Bauch's article 'Vom Begriff der Nation' (1916–17) was openly racist and antisemitic. I have already quoted a key passage of the

215

notorious 'Appeal of the 93 to the cultured world' which protested that Germans as 'the white race' were forced to fight against 'Mongols and Negroes'. Indeed, this complaint continued to play a key role throughout the war. By 1916, when enthusiasm for the war started to wane, and even Rudolf Eucken had to deliver his patriotic speeches to half-empty lecture theatres (Lübbe 1974: 183), racism combined with scapegoating: it now became a public concern whether 'enough' Jews were dying in the war (Zechlin 1969: 528). Bauch's 'Vom Begriff der Nation' was an attempt to provide a philosophical justification for the revival of antisemitism. According to Bauch, the unity of the German nation was a unity of blood and skull:

> The common blood is the unifying bond in the natural existence of a nation . . . If it were to happen that after many generations an anthropologist stumbled over my skull then either he would recognise it immediately as the skull of a German or else he would be regarded as a bungler . . . when in these our harsh times our warriors fight the enemy in a tough, hard and merciless way, when these same warriors, in the peace of the reserve, till the fields and house of the enemy, assist the latter's wife in troubles and illness, share their bread with his children, socialise with them friendly and lovingly, share in their sufferings and joys like their own fathers would do, teach them games, or even sing the enemy's child a German Christmas song – then most people in the enemy's land will find this incomprehensible and miraculous. But we say simply of our warriors: 'This is blood of our blood'.
>
> (Bauch 1916–17: 142)

In Bauch's view, Jews were not part of the German nation. They were 'ethnic strangers' (*völkische Fremdlinge*) and their language 'not our language' (1916–17: 147).

Turning from the neo-Kantians to the phenomenologists, it is important to emphasise that no one was as successful with his wartime writings as was Max Scheler, a student of Rudolf Eucken, but a convert to phenomenology.[2] Scheler's wartime articles filled three volumes, *Der Genius des Krieges und der deutsche Krieg* (1915a), *Krieg und Aufbau* (1916) and *Die Ursachen des Deutschenhasses* (1919). Scheler's wartime writings made him famous in Germany almost overnight (Hartmann 1928: xiii), and they laid the foundation for

Scheler's – and phenomenology's – leading position in the Weimar period.

The central and recurring theme of Scheler's war books was the idea that war created 'communities of love': 'The ultimate objective telos of war . . . is first and foremost: the formation and extension of one or another of the many forms of true units of love – units that as 'a people', 'a nation', etc. are the opposite of mere factually or lawfully shaped communities of interests' (1915a: 10). Because war enhanced love among human beings, war was more valuable than peace. Peace 'unites human beings in a merely external fashion; this is because peace turns people into atoms and separates them from one another' (1915a: 89). And since war was the most effective way of forming communities of love, fighting in war became a religious obligation. Because of the Fall and original sin, God had placed the morality of war as a necessary transitional phase before the morality of love: 'war thereby remains a positive and essential part of God's order of redemption' (1915a: 97).

Scheler also used metaphors of health and illness to describe the benefits of war. War

> throws out the terrible tensions of hatred, jealousy, anger, revenge, fury and disgust – feelings that in peacetimes are suppressed into the deeper strata of the soul – and thus war re-establishes the precondition for a truer mutual respect and sympathy among nations. In this way, war constitutes a psycho-therapy of nations.
>
> (Scheler 1915a: 100)

And the same held for the individual as well; Scheler sided with Binswanger's suggestion that neurotic young men were cured 'by the great cleaner "war"' (1915a: 365).

According to Scheler, war had been beneficial to the development of technology, science, the arts and philosophy. For instance, it was war which had led to the populating of many parts of the world. Furthermore, the development of weaponry had encouraged and guided the development of technology: 'The weapon has preceded the tool, and almost all of the older and the more recent higher mechanics has been created in support of technologies of war and fortification' (1915a: 46).

Given Scheler's belief in war as the father of intellectual achievements, it does not come as a surprise that he failed to see a conflict of interest between the military and the university as far as the

217

distribution of resources was concerned. Pouring money into universities and academies would lead to unfortunate cuts in military spending, and – in any case – it would not deliver the goods: 'With the exception of the short stretch from Kant to Herbart in Prussia, the whole of European philosophy since Descartes has . . . arisen outside of the state universities . . . Sword and spirit can form a beautiful, worthy couple' (1915a: 141–2). Militarism was thus the best guarantee of cultural progress (1916: 171–2).

Somewhat surprisingly, Scheler did not only defend German militarism but also proposed a new form of patriotism, i.e. 'European patriotism'. He sketched this patriotism in two ways. First, he explained that, despite its national traditions, European science had led to one common European worldview. This worldview corresponded to 'the European structure of mind which orders the possible phenomena of nature and soul according to the possibilities of their *active control*' (1915a: 276–80). Scheler believed that the European view of the world was closer to the world-in-itself than any other worldview (1915a: 283). Second, Scheler demarcated the new European patriotism also more directly by appealing to the feelings of soldiers at the front:

> The *patriotism of Europe* – it will be born for the first time in the blood and iron of this war! . . . You German soldiers out there in the field, you now see for the first time Cossacks, Indians, people from Canada, Newfoundland, Australia, New Zealand, you see Arabs, Persians, Turks, Japanese, Maoris and Negroes throwing stones . . . Take a good look at them! Have sympathy with the suffering of the living creature even during the harshest of battles! Do respect the nobler pain of the human animal in all your enemies – the human animal out of which the human being was born! Honour the 'whites' out of which the European has emerged – but do feel love for the French, the English, and the singing and fighting Serbs . . . And do not forget in the case of the Russian that he too wishes to obey Jesus our Lord . . . ! That is the gradation of feelings that you should adopt.
>
> (1915a: 282)

Scheler supposed that Germany was fighting for this European – or rather: 'West European' – worldview or spirit. The German cause was 'holy' in so far as Germany defended West European culture against Russia (1915a: 340). Nevertheless, Germany's war was also justified in so far as Britain was concerned: in this case it was a war against capitalism, against the taste of the bourgeoisie and against the flight from reality (1915a: 75).

Even though it was regarded as inappropriate during the war to criticise the views of fellow German philosophers publicly, Scheler's enthusiastic endorsement of war as the father of all culture and science did meet with occasional resistance. Helmut Falkenfeld, a student of Rickert, welcomed Scheler's patriotism, but denied Scheler's writings the status of a 'philosophy of war'. Falkenfeld was especially annoyed by Scheler's suggestion that men like Kleist, Hölderlin, Fichte and Hegel 'became only through war what they were'. Falkenfeld criticised this suggestion by claiming that he could list countless numbers of careers that had been cut off by war (1916–17: 100). It also seems natural to assume that some papers by other authors which rejected the idea of war as a beneficial cultural force were indirect criticisms of Scheler's ideas (e.g. Cohn 1914–15; Mehlis 1914–15).

Publications such as those cited above radically changed the agenda for German philosophy. The question how pure philosophy related to the natural sciences and the *Geisteswissenschaften* was no longer the crucial issue; instead the topics to be addressed, both in public lectures and in pamphlets, were Germany's role in history and the meaning of war and suffering. Some of the resources of earlier intra-academic struggles could be employed in the new problem area: whereas earlier culture had to be defended against the materialism of naturalistic philosophy, it now was being defended against the materialistic or utilitarian spirit of the British. And where German Idealism had earlier been the model of a non-naturalistic philosophy, it could now be drawn upon to characterise a society in which the good of the community was prior to the good and the rights of the individual.

'Between the clergyman and the medical doctor': Psychology goes to war

Advocates and practitioners of experimental psychology had several strategies for proving their mettle during the war.

A first strategy was indistinguishable from the *modus operandi* of pure philosophers. Some advocates and practitioners of experimental psychology drew on their knowledge of ethics or the philosophy of history, and argued that Germany was morally superior to other nations. This strategy is evident for instance in Oswald Külpe's little book *Die Ethik und der Krieg* (1915). The defence of militarism presented there did not differ much from arguments used by, say, Natorp or Scheler.

A second strategy was to write a patriotic political speech or pamphlet, without any philosophical or scientific pretensions. A clear example is Wundt's 'Über den wahrhaften Krieg' (On true war, 1914b). This pamphlet was a straightforward tirade against the British: Britain was the 'main culprit for this world-fire'; it had 'turned the war into a world war' (1914b: 13); British government and British people were equally guilty (1914b: 17); both displayed a 'reckless egoism' in their actions (1914b: 22); Britain waged war 'against every single German' (1914b: 29); and it had 'left the group of civilised states, at least for the duration of this war' (1914b: 29). For all this Britain would have to be punished severely after Germany's victory:

> Concerning England we will have to say: 'she to whom much has been given, from her much can be demanded'. Given that she is just a small island state, England has a much too heavy load of colonies. She will have to pay us dearly from her abundance if then a just distribution of the colonial work of culture is to result from the present war.
>
> (Wundt 1914b: 35)

The third strategy was to employ *Völkerpsychologie* and analyse differences between the *Volksseelen* of Germany and its enemies. Not surprisingly, Wundt and some of his students engaged in this project at some length. Wundt's booklength study *Die Nationen und ihre Philosophie: Ein Kapitel zum Weltkrieg* (The nations and their philosophy: a chapter on the war, 1915), undertook to probe – '*sine ira et studio*' (1915: 5) – the '*Volksseele*' of the French, British and German nations, respectively. In his analysis, Wundt drew on war songs, typical forms of behaviour and dominant philosophies. The last-mentioned source was justified by reference to Fichte's famous quip according to which 'one's philosophy shows what kind of human being one is' (1915: 11); Wundt believed this insight especially apt when applied to nations. As concerned France, Wundt suggested that Descartes had been its only remarkable philosopher (1915: 23). More characteristic for French thinking, however, was the philosophy of more recent French materialists. In

Wundt's eyes, they advocated a philosophy of self-love that reso-
nated well with the French *Volksseele*: 'The moral thinking of the
[French] *Volksseele* is a sophisticated egoism which, in decisive
moments, can turn into an energetic altruism. But behind this
altruism there lurks, as a hidden motive, the need to show off'
(1915: 35). Wundt's assessment of the British was more scathing.
As evidenced by the philosophy of Hobbes, Locke, Berkeley, Hume
and Spencer, the British tended towards 'a reckless materialism'
(1915: 44), and their thinking was often 'cumbersome, clumsy,
shallow rather than clear . . . sprawling rather than deep' (1915: 45,
47). When discussing Hume's philosophy, Wundt deplored its
'psychologism' (1915: 51–3).

These conclusions were checked against a study of war songs.
Comparing the Marseillaise, 'Rule Britannia', and 'Wacht am
Rhein', Wundt claimed that the highest values of the French were
'honour and fame', of the British 'power and dominance' and of
the Germans 'reliability . . . loyalty and duty' (1915: 125–9). In the
case of the French, Wundt showed some sympathy for their alleged
emphasis on honour, and praised them, for instance, for the way
in which they conducted themselves in arguments. Whereas
Germans had a tendency towards dogmatism, the French were
always ready to concede the partial truth of opposite views (1915:
131). The British, however, deserved no praise for their discursive
behaviour. In the company of others, the Englishman 'either
prefers not to talk at all, or, since silence is experienced as
inappropriate, talks only about trivial and obvious matters'. This
was because the British were 'a *replete* nation', used to their
dominance in the world, and unwilling to take risks (1915: 135–7).[3]

A fourth strategy was to apply psychological knowledge to wartime
pedagogy. August Messer's paper 'Der Krieg und die Schule'
(1914a) is a typical representative of this genre of wartime writings
by psychologists. Messer meant to advise teachers on how to adjust
to the new conditions. First and foremost, Messer drummed into
teachers a sense of their importance. Worried that they might
prefer the role of the soldier to that of the pedagogue, Messer wrote
that 'what you have to do as educator and teacher is *not* inferior to
fighting with the weapon'. After all, it was in German schools that
the German culture was passed on to the next generation (1914a:
529). Moreover, Messer wanted teachers to develop 'a firm moral
standpoint' with respect to the war (1914a: 530). Teachers should
present the World War as a 'necessary . . . tool for the preservation

of an absolutely necessary moral value-in-itself': German culture (1914a: 532). Despite his emphasis on the need for patriotism and feelings of disgust for the enemy, Messer was worried by the possibility that excessive hatred would harm the emotional development of German children. In order to avoid emotional harm, the teacher ought to make sure both that students did not hate the individual Russian, Frenchman, or Englishman, and that the students knew of resistance to the war within the enemies' population (1914a: 535).

The fifth and most widespread strategy for contributing to the war effort was to engage in military psychology. Before the outbreak of the war, little work had been done in this area, and the writings of the aforementioned Captain Meyer (1911, 1912a, 1912b) had not stimulated others. Once the war was under way, this changed quickly. Work in military psychology, or 'military psychotechnics' swept aside most other research projects. As one famous witness remarked in 1918: 'If anyone had told me [before the war] what kinds of things would go on in my institute during these war years, I would have shaken my head in disbelief' (Stumpf 1918: 273). Much of this work was never published, but some contemporary sources provided long lists of wartime research projects (Stumpf 1918; Rieffert 1922). Experimental psychologists developed aptitude tests for pilots and co-pilots, drivers of military vehicles, wireless operators, machine gunners and gun-layers, among others. They studied causes of aeroplane accidents, the influence of high-altitude flying on the psyche of the pilot, the sense of balance in pilots, the perception of sound direction, the reaction times of soldiers working in sound measurement units, the psychological processes during the firing of handguns, the psychology of aiming and precision bombing, the fatigue resulting from wearing gas masks, the effectiveness of camouflage, the psychology of soldiers shot in the head, brain damages, the loss of abilities and their recovery, the psychology of amputees, the effects of war on mental life, war neuroses, the psychological effects of prostheses, malingerers, the reintegration of injured soldiers into working life, war-dogs, and the proper organisation of the army.

Even this impressive list was not long enough for some writers. Theodor Ziehen wanted to extend the idea of aptitude tests for army personnel to army commanders as well. As a first step in this direction, Ziehen published a *Psychologie großer Heerführer* (Psychology of great army commanders, 1916). This study was

meant to identify the properties that make for a successful com-
mander. Ziehen regretted not being able to test current army
leaders in the laboratory, as 'our living army commanders have
more important things to do than to play the role of an experimental subject in a psychological laboratory' (1916: 6). In
order to compensate for this difficulty, Ziehen proposed two
methods: the analysis of historical reports on the character of army
commanders, and the use of (French!) studies on the abilities of
successful chess players.

Some advocates and practitioners of experimental psychology
tried to capitalise on the alleged success of military psychology by
demanding permanent positions for psychologists within the army.
According to Franz Janssen (1917) such new posts were necessary
in order to test all recruits, and in order to develop aptitude tests
for all services within the military. Janssen was especially concerned
to integrate social psychology into military psychology. Only once
the psychologist had entered the army on a permanent basis would
there be

> a psychology of leadership, a psychology of how to make
> soldiers enthusiastic, of how to influence smaller and larger
> military units in the field, in the various situations of marching,
> during rest, in the trenches, during drumfire, on patrol, a
> psychology of attack, of resisting, withdrawing, and much
> more.
>
> (Janssen 1917: 108)

Max Dessoir's *Kriegspsychologische Betrachtungen* (1916) wished to see
the psychologist at the front rather than in the reserve. Soldiers
welcomed the psychologist as someone 'between the clergyman
and the medical doctor ... [as someone] who really tries to
understand them'. And what was more, psychology could help win
the war by making true the general opinion 'that we shall win the
war because we have the stronger nerves' (1916: 3–5).

Finally, be it noted that the experimental character of German
psychology could also be translated into a further reason for feeling superior to the British. As the physiologist-psychologist Max
Verworn argued in his book *Die biologischen Grundlagen der Kultur-
politik: Eine Betrachtung zum Weltkriege* (The biological foundations
of cultural politics: a study on the World War, 1915), Germany was
superior to Britain because the former but not the latter was able
to 'think experimentally'. As Verworn saw it, in Britain '"science" is

looked upon as a harmless but somewhat dopey pastime' (1915: 44). British politicians had not learnt to properly calculate the results of their actions, and thus they had not learnt to appreciate the German wisdom according to which 'honesty is the best policy' (1915: 47). British politics was still based on the unscientific assumption 'My country, right or wrong', and action based on this maxim had caused the present war with all its sufferings: 'The war is the result of the lack of experimental thinking in the leading circles of England. This war is a disgrace for English education' (1915: 55).

THE TRIUMPH OF PHENOMENOLOGY: PHILOSOPHY AND PSYCHOLOGY IN THE WEIMAR REPUBLIC

It is easy to appreciate that a war on the scale of the First World War had to lead to a suspension of academic hostilities. It is less obvious why, once the war was over, German and Austrian philosophers did not return to either the hunt for psychologicists or the debate over the status of experimental psychology. Prima facie, philosophers would have had ample reasons for such a return to the pre-war agenda: no consensus had been reached on the definition of psychologism; on who was to be regarded as a psychologicist; on who was to be credited with having delivered the central arguments against psychologism; on whether experimental psychology was a philosophical discipline; and on whether the roles of the experimental psychologist and the role of the philosophers should, or could, be combined. Moreover, experimental psychology continued to be practised within philosophy departments until the 1940s. And finally, during the Weimar Republic, there still appeared the occasional article or book that claimed to introduce new elements into the psychologism issue. For instance, Theodor Ziehen's *Lehrbuch der Logik auf positivistischer Grundlage* (1920) could have been regarded as psychologistic by anyone's criteria – Ziehen came out defending Sigwart, Wundt, Erdmann and Lipps (1920: 205) – but it was largely ignored. Willy Moog's *Logik, Psychologie und Psychologismus* (1919) provided not only an excellent summary of earlier arguments pro and contra Husserl, but also claimed to have caught yet more philosophers red-handed. Again, and unfortunately from Moog's point of view, there was no outcry. Although he did get the odd favourable review (Morgenstern 1920–21; Endriß 1921), Moog's work remained below the threshold of wider philosophical attention, and Moog could do no better than become a historian of ideas subsequently. Last but not least, Paul Hofmann (1921) and Martin Honecker (1921) each submitted a book-size proposal for a compromise between pure logic and psychologistic logic. Thus Hofmann's *Die Antinomie im Problem der Gültigkeit* argued that Erdmann and Husserl were equally entitled to their respective views. The structure of the human mind forces us simultaneously into thinking that the laws of logic are dependent on the human organism and into believing that they are outside space and time.

The challenge then is to explain why no return to the pre-war agenda occurred, and why Husserl and phenomenology were soon regarded as having been right both about psychologism and about the relationship between philosophy and psychology. In order to explain these facts, we need to start from the general mood and mentality of Weimar culture.

The Weimar mentality

It will not come as a surprise to historians of German twentieth-century philosophy and science that I invoke the antiscientific mentality of Weimar culture as a causal factor in the change of agendas. After all, the mentality of German academics in the Weimar era plays a pivotal role in two classics of the history of science. F.K. Ringer has studied it in his book on the decline in social and political influence of the German university professor between 1890 and 1933 (Ringer 1969), and Paul Forman has emphasised its importance for understanding the German physicists' interest in developing and propagating an a-causal mechanics (Forman 1971).

Already prior to the war, many leading intellectuals had repeatedly voiced their scepticism about the modern world. Typically their doubts were couched in terms of the 'culture versus civilisation' opposition. While granting that technological progress made life more comfortable to many, 'German mandarins' argued that such improvements in civilisation would not lead to improvements in moral and spiritual values. Indeed, most of them supported the view that culture as the realm of philosophy, art, religion and morals would inevitably decline as a result of technology, mass production, democratisation and secularisation. For them it seemed inevitable that an increase in the 'external' quality of life would have to bring about a decline in Germans' appreciation of 'higher values'. In good part, the enthusiasm of German academics for the war was due to the hope that the war would bring about a radical change. To many the war had initially promised to be the great purifying experience, an experience in and through which Germany would rediscover its culture, and recognise the futility and superficiality of the modern technological world.

With Germany's defeat these expectations were shattered and theories of decadence and decline were reinforced. The feelings of helplessness, impotence and pessimism were intensified by the poor living conditions of academics during the Weimar Republic. Inflation wiped out savings, most university teachers lived in poverty, travel became impossible, and not even libraries could afford to buy even the most basic handbooks and journals. In 1923, when inflation reached its peak, the University of Freiburg fired 35 per cent of its teaching staff. At the same time, however, the number of students rose to dramatically new levels. The number of students at German universities increased from 61,000 in 1914 to 72,000 in 1918, and to 112,000 in 1923. It hardly needs mentioning that the students suffered even more than did their teachers, and that their career prospects were very bad indeed. Talk of an 'academic proletariat' was both widespread and an adequate description of conditions at the time (Ringer 1969: 52–75).

Given these conditions, it was only natural that terms like 'decline', 'crisis' and 'alienation' entered everyone's vocabulary. Crisis talk quickly turned against technology and science. A 'neo-romantic, existentialist "philosophy of life"' – to use Forman's term – became the fashion of the day, and 'the scientist was the whipping boy of the incessant exhortations to spiritual renewal, while the concept – or the mere word – "causality" symbolised all that was odious in the scientific enterprise' (Forman 1971: 4). Science was accused of a 'destruction of the soul', pronounced guilty of the current 'world crisis' and declared responsible for 'the whole of intellectual and material misery bound up with that crisis' (Max von der Laue, quoted in Forman 1971: 11). Science was seen as paving the way for 'the ultimate intellectualisation', for 'the disenchantment of the world' and for an 'all suffocating determinism' (Ernst Troeltsch, quoted in Forman 1971: 17). Many of these sentiments received their most forceful formulation in Oswald Spengler's *Untergang des Abendlandes* (Decline of the West, 1918), a book that had sold more than 100,000 copies by 1926. For Spengler, the *Kausalitätsprinzip* of science was the central ingredient of the

Western, 'Faustian', world-feeling. Western culture was on its way to self-destruction (Forman 1971: 31–7).

Faced with such accusations, scientists had a choice between resistance and accommodation. To choose the path of resistance meant to defend the scientific enterprise and to combat irrationalism, mysticism, occultism, spiritualism and theosophy, among others. This path was chosen, for instance, by Max Planck and Arnold Sommerfeld. The more common reaction of scientists to the antiscientific climate was a strategy of accommodation. Advocates of this line accepted the central charges, declared a state of crisis for their discipline, and tried to remodel their thinking along the lines suggested by Spengler and other advocates of *Lebensphilosophie*. Accommodation meant abandoning causality, atomism and technology, and praising the value of intuition, holism and community. By 1929 this ideology had even found its way into the opening pages of the *Handbuch der Physik*. And Richard von Mises told an audience in 1920, that 'the age of technology' was on its way out, and that physicists were striving for 'new intuitions of the world'. Physics was taking up again 'the question of the old alchemists . . . numerical harmonies, even numerical mysteries play a role, reminding one no less of the ideas of the Pythagoreans than of some of the cabbalists'. Von Mises even agreed with Spengler's thesis that Western culture was in terminal decline, and doubted that its successor would 'continue the exact sciences in our sense' (Forman 1971: 51).

In embracing the central charges, and in declaring themselves in crisis, the physicists did not stand alone. 'Crisis' became the central measure of success for any field of study; one of the key texts of the period, Martin Heidegger's *Sein und Zeit*, even formulated this criterion explicitly: 'The value of a science depends on the degree to which that science is *able* to undergo a crisis in its fundamental concepts' (1927: 9). Small wonder, therefore, that crisis talk spread quickly to all fields. The cases of physics and mathematics are described in detail in Forman's little classic, and Ringer draws attention to some key texts in medicine, linguistics and economics (Ringer 1969: 385–7).

From *Lebensphilosophie* to phenomenology

Both Ringer and Forman single out one philosopher, Oswald Spengler, as *the* central philosophical figure in Weimar Germany.

For the aims of their respective studies this simplification does no harm. Spengler's formulation of the theory of decline was by far the most widely read and the most often attacked. For present purposes, however, Ringer's and Forman's procedure will not do. To see why, we only need to note that Spengler was a *Privatgelehrter* without an academic affiliation, and without any influence in matters of university politics. Even though his was a considerable intellectual influence on a whole generation of German intellectuals, Spengler never acquired an academic power base.

In order for us to understand the reshaping of academic philosophy during the Weimar Republic, we have to look beyond Spengler. We need to understand how phenomenology came to be identified, *at least within academia*, with many of the very same themes and claims that were first brought to everyone's attention by Spengler's book. Here lies the key to phenomenology's success in the Weimar Republic, and here we shall find the explanation why the Husserlian view on both psychologism and experimental psychology entered our textbooks and our histories of philosophy.

The ingredients of *Lebensphilosophie* Before the publication of Heidegger's *Sein und Zeit* in 1927, Karl Jaspers, Max Scheler and Oswald Spengler were most often cited as the main living representatives of what was called '*Lebensphilosophie*' by friends and foes alike. Spengler's *Untergang* appeared in 1918, and Jasper's *Psychologie der Weltanschauungen* in 1919. In Scheler's case selecting one central text is slightly more difficult. I have given a summary of Scheler's highly successful wartime writings above. These writings catapulted him to national prominence. Scheler (born in 1874) had been a student of Eucken, but had regarded himself as a phenomenologist since the turn of the century. In 1919 he became a full professor at the new university in Cologne. Scheler was a highly prolific writer throughout his career. His main work was his *Formalismus in der Ethik und die materiale Wertethik* (1913–16), but this long and technical work was much less influential than Scheler's collection of articles *Vom Umsturz der Werte*. Of this anthology, Scheler's programmatic article 'Versuche zu einer Philosophie des Lebens: Nietzsche – Dilthey – Bergson' ([1915b] 1972) serves best as an introduction to his concern with *Lebensphilosophie*.

In 'Versuche zu einer Philosophie des Lebens', Scheler suggested that the new century had witnessed the beginnings of a new kind of philosophy, a '*philosophy of life*'. At the present time, this new way of thinking was still 'vague' but already it could be called 'a demand of the time' and 'the longing of a new generation'. As a first approximation to its content, Scheler distinguished it from two other conceptions of philosophy with which it could perhaps be confused. The philosophy of life had nothing to do with popular philosophy (*Populärphilosophie*), i.e. the project of making philosophy accessible to the masses. Nor should the new 'thought style' be misunderstood as being *about* life, as taking life as its ready-made or already existing *object*. As Scheler saw it, whenever a philosopher treated something as a ready-made or existing object, he would have to relate to it 'as [something which is] basically dead'. Accordingly, the 'of' in the expression 'philosophy of life' did not indicate a *genitivus objectivus*, but 'a *genitivus subjectivus*, that is, a philosophy out of the plenitude of life, indeed – to put it more sharply: *a philosophy out of the plenitude of the experience of life*' ([1915b] 1972: 313).

Put differently, the life studied by the new philosophy was the life that became visible 'in the process of experiencing itself', it was what revealed itself in experience. Here is how Scheler himself summarised the 'content' of the new philosophy:

> The 'content' of the new philosophy is this: whatever opens itself to us immediately in experience itself as *contents*; whatever reveals itself *in* thinking and perceiving of the world; whatever [reveals itself] *in* wanting and acting, and *in* suffering from resistances (and the world reveals itself to the wanting, acting and suffering being only through such resistances); whatever strikes us in the emotions of love and hatred as contents, values and meanings regarding world, man, God, woman, art, etc.; whatever new religious worlds and values open themselves to us in prayer, premonition and belief . . .; whatever in this most immediate and tightest intercourse with the universe and with God seems to stand before us – and what is already gone and dead, indeed destroyed and void once it has become lived life [*gelebtes Leben*].
>
> (Scheler [1915b] 1972: 314)

As the title of Scheler's article already indicates, he regarded Nietzsche, Dilthey and Bergson as three central prophets of the new philosophy of life. Nietzsche's central contribution had been to enlarge the meaning of the concept of 'life'. We owe to Nietzsche a notion of life as 'an action which flows on infinitely and which constantly increases its own value', a concept of life which is so broad as to incorporate both 'God and the dead world' ([1915b] 1972: 314).

For Scheler, Dilthey's importance for the philosophy of life derived from his theory of historical understanding and his criticism of explanatory psychology. Dilthey sought to understand humans of the past 'out of the totality of their life', out of 'the structure of their experience' ([1915b] 1972: 319). Dilthey discovered that a straightforward understanding of a human being of another culture or historical period was not possible. Since historians would always have their own 'structure of experience', they would always be tempted to interpret the historical figures in their, i.e. the historians' own terms. And this tendency would become irreparable once historians sought help from modern natural-scientific psychology. Natural-scientific psychology was itself a historical product, and its categories were thus applicable only to modern men and women. The past could not be understood based on the atomism of modern science (1915b: 320–1).

Scheler spent more time on Bergson than on Nietzsche and Dilthey together. He began his discussion of the French philosopher by emphasising that German philosophy could not accept all of Bergson's results. For instance, Bergson's view of logic betrayed a 'misological [sic] psychologism'. And Bergson's work on the perception of space was coarse by comparison with the studies of Husserl and other phenomenologists. After this initial cautioning, however, Scheler endorsed wholeheartedly what he regarded as Bergson's new attitude to the world and the soul; indeed, Scheler suggested that Bergson had opened a 'new basic direction which differs from all other thinking of the modern era' (1915b: 324).

This is how Scheler described Bergon's 'new attitude':

This philosophy relates to the world through the gesture of the open and upward-moving hand, through the eye that opens freely and widely. This is not the squinting and critical look of Descartes . . . and it is not the Kantian eye out of which the mental beam – which is controlling and alienated as if it came from 'another' world – strikes forth onto things and runs through them. The human being that philosophises here is free of the anguish that gives birth to the modern calculation of things, and free of the proud sovereignty of the 'thinking pipe' which – in Descartes and Kant – is the source

230

and the emotional a priori of all theories ... Here every
thought is informed not by the will to obtain 'control',
'organisation', 'exact determination', 'fixation' – here
thought is imbued with the movement of sympathy.

([1915b] 1972: 325)

Scheler also recommended Bergson's opposition between science
and philosophy, and defended the distinction between understanding (*Verstand*) and intuition.

'Science' ... looks on the world 'as if it were an enemy' ...
'Philosophy' looks on the world as an object for a possible
marriage in intuition and love. 'Science' works according to
the a priori models of understanding ... 'Philosophy' works
'to measure' by trying to follow the natural contours of things.

([1915b] 1972: 325)

'Understanding', according to both Bergson and Scheler, was but
a 'system of selecting factors', developed during evolution. Understanding was also the foundation of science and thus science could
not but be an instrument for controlling and exploiting the world
([1915b] 1972: 326). To leave this orientation behind, that is, to
relate to the world through intuition, was not to be passive,
however. Rather the attempt to relate to the world in a non-
exploitative way demanded '*intensive mental* effort and exercise'
([1915b] 1972: 327).

Scheler was especially eager to protect the concept of intuition
from neo-Kantian objections, and to emphasise its proximity to, if
not identity with, phenomenological *Wesensschau*. Neo-Kantians
would want to know just how the philosopher of life would know
that 'in "intuition" he touches Being [*Sein*] itself and, as it were,
holds it in his arms'. According to Scheler, Bergson and German
phenomenology would best reject such doubts out of hand. Criteria
for our coming to know the truth would be needed only where the
truth was not already self-evidently given. Criteria could be asked
for only where doubt was meaningful. Thus the Kantian 'adopts the
attitude of the doorman towards the world ... whereas all true
philosophy is the guest who uses every open door in order to grasp
it' ([1915b] 1972: 325).

Scheler concluded by stressing that the philosophy of life was still
only in its beginnings, and that it would take 'the more exact, strict
– German – methods' to develop it further. Here Scheler referred

231

explicitly to Husserl's *Ideen* but added that it would be premature
to introduce the contribution of phenomenology at this stage:

> I have remained silent since the work in the group of the
> friends of phenomenology is of such high standards that it
> needs, for the moment at least, a measure of peacefulness.
> Any echo to our talk in the public realm would only interrupt
> this work much too early.
>
> ([1915b] 1972: 339)

Nevertheless, Scheler was ready to predict that once the philosophy
of life was properly developed, 'the European human being' would
step out of the 'prison' of understanding, civilisation and technology ([1915b] 1972: 339)

We now turn from Scheler to Oswald Spengler's *Untergang des
Abendlandes* (1918). Spengler started with the self-confident assertion that his philosophy was not 'one among other possible and
logically justified philosophies, but, as it were, *the* natural philosophy of our time, a philosophy that all others have only vaguely
anticipated' (1918: vii). Moreover, Spengler claimed that his study
was the 'first attempt ever' to predict history (1918: 3). According
to him, Western culture had reached its final stage of decline, i.e.
'civilisation'. This final stage of Western culture was characterised
by rationalism, technology, big cities, democracy, cosmopolitanism,
humanism, pacifism, emphasis on human rights and scepticism.
Spengler predicted that this phase of civilisation would usher in the
ultimate decline of Western culture into total dissolution, primitive-
ness, and enfeeblement between the years 2000 and 2200. His
prediction was based on a comparison between the patterns of
development of Egyptian, ancient Greek, Arabic and Western
culture (1918: 72–8, 'Tafeln zur vergleichenden Morphologie der
Geschichte'). Spengler's use of the distinction between culture and
civilisation was of course a familiar theme. Spengler called civilisation the 'inevitable *fate* of every culture' and went on to explain
that civilisation followed culture like 'death follows life, fixedness
follows development . . . mental old age follows . . . mental child-
hood'. Civilisation marked 'an *end* without return' (1918: 44).

Spengler defended his comparative method by referring his
reader to Goethe's work on the morphology of plants. Indeed, he
claimed that his philosophy was primarily indebted to Goethe's
'unknown' philosophy (1918: 69). Spengler's central move was to
interpret cultures as organisms:

Cultures are organisms. Cultural history is their biography. The available ... recorded history of Chinese or ancient culture is morphologically the exact parallel to the history of a human individual, of an individual animal, tree or flower. If one wants to get to know their structure, one can rely on the comparative morphology of plants and animals, for it has long since provided the proper methods for such endeavour.

(Spengler 1918: 150)

Throughout his book, Spengler contrasted the Goethian morphological investigations to the study of causal relations in nature. For instance,

all ways of understanding the world can, in the end, be called morphology. The morphology of the mechanical and the extended realm, i.e. that science which discovers and orders natural laws and causal relations, is called systematics. The morphology of the organic, of history and of life, of all that which carries direction and fate within itself, is called physiognomics.

(1918: 145)

Systematics was dominant within the natural sciences, whereas physiognomics could be found in historical studies. And the natural sciences were based on 'understanding' whereas history relied on 'intuition' (*Anschauen*):

One can be trained to become a natural scientist, but the historian is *born* as such. The latter understands and penetrates instantly, out of a feeling that cannot be learnt, that cannot be influenced, that is not obedient to the will, and that occurs only rarely in its highest forms. On the other hand, analysing, defining, ordering, dividing into cause and effect, all these are things anyone can do if only one chooses to do them. The one is work, the other is creation. Form and law, simile and concept, symbol and formula have a very different organ. What surfaces here is the difference between *life and death*, between begetting and destroying. Understanding, i.e. the concept, kills when it 'comes to know'. It turns what is known into a rigid object that can be measured and divided into parts. Intuition infuses its objects with a soul.

(1918: 147)

According to Spengler, Kant and Aristotle were the philosophers of understanding, whereas Plato and Goethe were the philosophers of intuition. Or, in Spengler's own words: 'Plato and Goethe accept the secret, Aristotle and Kant wish to destroy it' (1918: 174). Plato and Goethe did not try to analyse 'words' like 'destiny, undoing, chance, fate, purpose . . . No hypothesis, no science can touch upon that which one feels when losing oneself in the meaning and sound of these words. They are symbols, not concepts' (1918: 164). Aristotle and Kant, on the other hand, developed a systematic philosophy, at the heart of which was 'a logic of the *inorganic* and the rigid' (1918: 164). This type of philosophy was based on 'fear of the world' (*Weltangst*), it was full of '*hatred* against that which cannot be understood', and it aimed at 'submission, [and] mecha- nisation' (1918: 174). It sought to neutralise the inevitable contin- gencies of life by conceptualising chance as 'that which has *not yet* been brought into the scope of a physical formula' (1918: 214).

Spengler did not hesitate to declare contemporary *Katheder- philosophie* the heir of Kant and Aristotle. Contemporary philosophy put on 'a scientific costume', 'a learned mask'. It was a 'philosophy of facts that smiles [arrogantly] when confronted with metaphysical speculations' (1918: 50). And almost all of its representatives wished to avoid becoming involved in society:

> Nothing is easier than to cover up one's lack of ideas by founding a system. But even a good idea is worth little when voiced by a dunderhead (*Flachkopf*) . . . What all philosophers of the most recent past lack is a decisive position in real life . . . What insignificant persons they are! What mundane intellectual and practical horizons do they display! How come that it arouses near pity in us to imagine that one of them should prove his intellectual mettle as a statesman, diplomat, organiser on a large scale, leader of some powerful colonial, commercial or traffic company? . . . No doubt one has lost sight of the ultimate purpose of philosophical effectiveness. One confuses it with sermon, agitation, glib style, or speciali- sation. The perspective of the bird has been surrendered to that of the frog.
>
> (1918: 58–61)

Spengler was especially scathing with respect to experimental psychology. In his opinion, it would be better to spend one's time

on 'constructing an aeroplane engine than on a new and superfluous theory of apperception'. According to Spengler, the development of new theories of the will or new interpretations of the notion
of psychophysical parallelism was a 'job' at best, 'but it is not
philosophy' (1918: 61). Indeed, he went so far as to write that 'today
some inventors, diplomats and bankers are better philosophers
than all those who engage in the dull handicraft of experimental
psychology' (1918: 62). Spengler's contempt for experimental
psychology derived in part from his cultural relativism. According
to this view, philosophy, arts, science and moral values were all
relative to cultures: 'There are no eternal truths. Every philosophy
is an expression of its time' (1918: 58). 'There is no number as such,
and there can be no number as such. There are several number
worlds since there are several cultures' (1918: 85). 'We find as many
mathematics, logics, physics, as there are great cultures' (1918:
412). 'There are as many morals as there are cultures, no more and
no less' (1918: 471). Just as philosophy, arts, science and moral
values were relative to cultures, so also, for Spengler, were conceptions of the human soul. And it was the basic mistake of modern
psychology that it had overlooked this historical relativity: 'The
conception of the soul depends on the spirit of the *respective
language*' (1918: 409). 'Every culture, and every epoch of every
culture created its own conception of the soul. And each of them
mistook its conception for the soul of humankind in general'
(1918: 412). Spengler submitted that every culture or epoch had
expressed its own inner essence, its own 'soul', in its view of the
individual human soul. Thus it was only to be expected that in the
recent history of Western – '*Faustian*' – culture, the human soul was
centred around the will. Other, earlier, cultures, like the ancient
Greeks, did not know of the will. The same was true of the triad of
thinking, feeling and wanting. Modern psychology had to think of
them as functional centres, and was forced to conceptualise their
interrelations on the model of mathematical functions. But this
whole style of thought was foreign to the Greeks (1918: 412).

Spengler was also highly critical of the fact that modern psychology wanted to be a natural science:

No [modern] psychology has so far doubted the following
sentence: there is a soul the structure of which can be
analysed scientifically; my soul *is* whatever I isolate – via a
critical observation of my conscious acts of existence – as

mental elements, functions, complexes. Nevertheless, the strongest doubts should have arisen here. Is an abstract science of the mental possible at all? . . . The 'will' [for instance] is no concept at all, it is a name, an original word like 'God', a sign for something of which we are immediately and inwardly certain without, however, being able to describe it . . . Soul has nothing to do with space, object, distance, number, limit, causality – and thus it has nothing to do with concept and system . . . To analyse the soul by means of abstract thought is even less feasible than to analyse a Beethoven theme with the help of a scalpel or an acid. Not even the soul itself can 'know' something about itself.

(1918: 405–6)

Spengler was eager to show that modern psychology had indeed conceptualised the soul and its activities by means of spatial metaphors. As such spatial metaphors he mentioned, among others, the concept of a threshold of consciousness, or the distinction between conscious and subconscious. Spengler wrote that 'the psychologist does not even notice that he is playing the physicist. No wonder that his procedure coincides so well with the ridiculous methods of experimental psychology' (1918: 408).

The third key text of *Lebensphilosophie* in the early years of the Weimar Republic was undoubtedly Karl Jaspers' *Psychologie der Weltanschauungen* (1919). The stodgy style of the book was a far cry from the flowery and polemical language of Scheler and Spengler, and several central themes of Scheler and Spengler – like the culture vs. civilisation opposition, the notion of cultural decline, the attack on natural science – were missing from Jaspers' work. Nevertheless, with its emphasis on the contingency of the human condition, with its Kierkegaardian stress on the 'moment' (*Augenblick*), death, struggle, chance and guilt, as well as with its attack on rationalism, Jasper's study could easily be read as congenial to Scheler's and Spengler's concerns.

Jaspers called his study a '*psychology* of *Weltanschauungen*'. This raises the question what Jaspers meant by 'psychology' and how this psychology related to philosophy. As Jaspers outlined early on in his book, 'philosophy' was used as a label for two rather different activities. The first of these two activities was the creation or preaching of new *Weltanschauungen*, the second was a 'universal treatment' of different realms, such as the domain of the sciences, the domain of valid or invalid entities, the domain of society, or the domain of the human being. Jaspers baptised the first type of activity '*prophetic philosophy*' and opined that strictly speaking it alone deserved the title 'philosophy'. Philosophy as 'universal treatment', on the other hand, was nothing but an umbrella term for the disciplines of logic, history of philosophy, sociology and psychology. These 'philosophical disciplines' differed from 'prophetic philosophy' in that they did not offer any *Weltanschauungen*, and in that they did not evaluate the objects of their study (1919: 2).

Interestingly enough, the criterion of neutrality was used by Jaspers as a precautionary defence of his psychology of *Weltanschauungen* against the accusation of psychologism. As Jaspers told his reader, psychologism was the belief that 'the representation of psychological facts' could serve as a justification or as a criticism of aspects of these facts. In so far as his psychology made no such evaluations, it was protected from the charge of psychologism, Jaspers felt (1919: 4).

In order to situate his work within psychology, Jaspers claimed that many psychologists had neglected the task of answering the basic psychological question: 'what characterises the human being' (1919: 5). In order to answer this question, psychology had to recapture a sense of the 'psychological whole or totality' (*das psychologische Ganze*). And this was where the psychology of *Weltanschauungen* would come into its own. It 'walks along the limits of our psychological life to the extent to which this life is accessible' (1919: 6). The basic starting point of this psychology would be

> the living experience . . . in which we let our own ego enlarge, dissolve and again contract. It is a pulsating life of extending and contracting, of surrendering and preserving one's self, of love and loneliness, of floating together and of fighting, of determining, contradicting and melting, of collapsing and rebuilding.
>
> (Jaspers 1919: 7–8)

Despite his insistence that the psychology of *Weltanschauungen* was no evaluative enterprise, Jaspers allowed for the possibility that it would use the opposition between 'sincerity' and self-deception:

> Sincerity (*Echtheit*) [is] a basic concept of interpretative psychology . . . The final opposition is this: the individual turns towards the contents of *Weltanschauung* . . . for their own

237

sake, they find an adequate resonance in his existence, he grasps them as something essential, as something authentic, as something absolute; or else he has adopted these contents – without noticing it – only as auxiliary means, as useful ideologies for other purposes. He then deceives himself about himself in his *Weltanschauung*.

(1919: 36)

According to Jaspers, the main inspiration for the psychology of *Weltanschauungen* had come from Hegel, Kant, Kierkegaard, Nietzsche and Weber. As contemporary reviewers were quick to point out, the idea of a typology of *Weltanschauungen* was of course also indebted to Dilthey's philosophical and historical studies (e.g. Stein 1920–21: 124).

The details of Jaspers' typology of *Weltanschauungen* need not concern us here. He regarded the subject–object opposition as an 'original phenomenon', and he structured his investigation accordingly into a typology of 'attitudes' of the subject, and 'worldviews' (*Weltbilder*) qua objects. Jaspers' contrast between intuition and 'the rational attitude' reminds one of similar pronouncements by Scheler and Spengler. Concerning the rational attitude, we are told that it

> moves inevitably in oppositions . . . intuition (*Anschauung*) is something which is alive. Intuition is infinite, and contains within itself what, for understanding, are oppositions. Intuition is flowing and overflowing. The limiting forms of *ratio* introduce a *solidifying net* into this living intuition . . . Rational work is a continuous destruction of the living although the fixed structures may become tools for new forms of life . . . The *effects of the rational attitude* are thus twofold: 1) it introduces *relations, clarity, connections* . . . 2) it brings *solidification and death*.

(1919: 71–4)

With respect to the 'immediate attitude', i.e. the attitude of 'the moment' (*Augenblick*), Jaspers wrote that it was 'the medium for all liveliness'. Its development was impeded, however, by rational self-reflection:

> The more the human being tries to shape himself in a rational way, the more grows the tendency to turn every momentary

experience, every temporally determined reality into a means for something else . . . Reflecting on ourselves we often live more in the past or in the future; we try to avoid the present.

(1919: 108)

Another central theme of Jaspers' book was the study of 'borderline situations' (*Grenzsituationen*). These were situations of 'struggle, of death, of chance and of guilt'. They were 'essential' to the human condition, and forced the individual into choosing attitudes and worldviews. On Jaspers' account of these situations, each of them had 'an antinomic structure' (1919: 232):

> Each of these cases – struggle, death, chance, guilt – is based on an antinomy. Struggle and reciprocal help, chance and meaning, guilt and the consciousness of ceasing to be guilty, are tied to one another, and the one does not exist without the other.
>
> (1919: 256)

Humans could react to these antinomies in three ways: they could let themselves be destroyed by them, they could 'dodge' them, and they could 'gain strength' through them (1919: 240).

Jaspers implied that much of systematic philosophy was, as it were, an attempt to 'dodge' the antinomies of life. Jaspers' pet concept for studying this philosophical dodging – or 'philosophism' (Stein 1920–21: 129) – was '*Gehäuse*' (case, shell, box, casing). Such shells were rational interpretations of the world, interpretations which compromised the severity of the borderline situations. They provided philosophers with a 'comfortable house to live in'. All *Gehäuse* were the product of rationalism:

> What all *Gehäuse* have in common is *rationalism*. . . Rationalism is the type of thinking that remains in the realm of that which is delimited and which can be delimited; it is the type of thinking which grasps everything with the understanding [*Verstand*] and which therefore sees nothing.
>
> (1919: 306–7)

Jaspers was especially critical of one brand of *Gehäuse* philosophy, a brand that he called 'value absolutism' (*Wertabsolutismus*). Few contemporary readers will have failed to identify the target: Jaspers' colleague in Heidelberg, Heinrich Rickert. Indeed, Jaspers' description of the philosopher as hiding in his shell could even be read as an allusion to Rickert's – real and not just metaphoric – agoraphobia. It seems that Jaspers even used a conversation between himself and Rickert in order to show that value absolutism must ultimately collapse into nihilism:

> One value absolutist once said to a young man who was in a painful life situation, and full of disappointment, as if to console him: 'Think of the absolute values!' But a slightly self-ironic smile after this serious appeal showed that here too a nihilism threatened.

> (1919: 325)

Jaspers went on to contrast the philosopher of value absolutism with the emerging prophetic philosopher. The absolutist would always strive for logical consistency in his *Gehäuse*. The developing prophet, however, would face 'crisis and desperation' openly, and thus he would realise that logical consequence was not the highest value: 'Instead he will be an irrationalist, critic, questioner and – through a sudden turn-over – will become a prophet' (1919: 353). The same point was hammered home through a distinction between 'three types of human existence': the 'chaotic human being' would be guided by impulse and chance; the 'consequent human being . . . is a rigorist, an obstinate mule, a fanatic, a logicist'; and finally, the 'demonic human being' would accept the fragmentary nature of the human condition, face up to the antinomies of the borderline situations and be unpredictable in his actions (1919: 354–5). Jaspers implied that Kant was a demonic thinker in so far as the three critiques are nothing but 'gigantic fragments' (1919: 358). The new imperative for the genuine human being would be this: 'You should *live* and live through your stages to ever new crises' (1919: 361).

The success of *Lebensphilosophie* in the Weimar Republic   The success of *Lebensphilosophie* has been described by historians more than once (e.g. Ringer 1969; Forman 1971). Between 1918 and 1923 the first volume of Spengler's book went through thirty print runs, and between 1923 and 1926 the revised edition saw another thirty printings. By 1926 more than 100,000 copies had been sold. The typical reaction of the German professor to the book was something like 'of my discipline Spengler understands, of course, not the first thing, but aside from that the book is brilliant'

(Forman 1971: 30). Put differently, even though the German professor would attack Spengler over details of his argument, 'as far as one's mood was concerned ... one was convinced of the truth of Spengler' (Löwith 1986: 25).

Spengler's correspondence too gives a good indication of the scale of his success (Spengler 1966). As early as November 1918, Georg Misch, a professor of philosophy and student of Dilthey, reported to Spengler that he had seen the book at Georg Simmel's house and that

> the title and the idea of a morphology of history appealed to me, because my thoughts about the logic of the history of the mind, derived from Goethe and Dilthey, crossed at this middle point. My expectations have now been fulfilled beyond all measure.

Misch was also interested in winning Spengler over to academic philosophy: 'In spite of your disapproval of professors of philosophy, may I enquire whether you would be inclined, in principle, to take over a chair in philosophy?' (Spengler 1966: 69; letter of 8 November 1918). Other, less illustrious admirers informed their master 'that they had all received new eyes', that his book 'has become the "fashion" among the educated, [that] finally all the learned have had to read it' (1966: 85), and that in German universities 'there has scarcely been a lecture course in which the lecturer at the start does not make some allusions to *The Decline of the West*' (1966: 100). Spengler himself wrote to his friends that his book 'has a wide circulation' (1966: 71; 18 December 1918), and that Georg Simmel had called the book 'the most important philosophy of history since Hegel' (1966: 81; 25 June 1919).

Spengler's success was not hampered by the considerable number of books, pamphlets, articles and public lectures that were directed against him by philosophers and historians. The most famous of such attacks came from the journal *Logos*, the central periodical of pure philosophy. In 1920 *Logos* dedicated a special number to refutations of Spengler's philosophy and history (volume 9, 1920–21). The reaction of the learned public to such attacks comes out succinctly in the following anecdote. While Husserl was 'railing against Spengler' from the lectern, the students in the auditorium all had the *Untergang* lying in front of them (Kraft 1973: 89). Indeed, at least initially, Spengler was immune to criticism voiced by academic philosophers as his contempt of academia was especially popular. For instance, in Berlin students ridiculed the stodgy philosophy of the neo-Kantian Riehl and of the psychologist Stumpf: 'In Berlin ist die Philosophie mit Stumpf und Riehl ausgerottet worden. [In Berlin philosophy has been destroyed root and branch, *Stumpf und Stiel*]' (Scholem 1981: 21).

Attacks on Spengler coming from philosophers and psychologists often betrayed their authors' earlier involvement in debates over psychologism. Thus Spengler was accused of psychologism (Sternberg 1922: 107) and of conflating 'true' with 'taken-to-be-true' (*Fürwahrhalten*) (Messer 1922: 109). Such accusations did no longer carry the day in the Weimar Republic, however. In 1923, the historian of philosophy and psychology, Richard Müller-Freienfels suggested that *Lebensphilosophie* should bear the title 'psychologism' as an 'honorary title'. As this sympathiser of *Lebensphilosophie* saw it, the new philosophy at last gave proper heed to the contribution of the human constitution to knowledge. The same was true, in Müller-Freienfels's view, of invectives like 'sociologism' and 'biologism' (1923: 80–3). Dilthey's student Max Frischeisen-Köhler too contended that the time should be over where new lines of enquiry could be stopped in their tracks by labelling them psychologistic. For all its weaknesses, *Lebensphilosophie* 'is a first courageous attempt to leave for a new trip on the infinite ocean which surrounds the small island of the self-content, secure, universally valid, logical-formal knowledge' (1921: 113, 136).

Jaspers and Scheler did not have the same public success. Nevertheless, Jaspers' book 'was read a great deal at the time' (Jaspers 1957: 34), and Scheler has been described, by contemporaneous sources, as 'one of the most distinguished brains of the time', as having been 'on the lips of everyone who was interested in intellectual life' (Scholem 1977: 173), as 'a star of the first magnitude . . . a philosopher of the age' (Spiegelberg 1960: 227) and as 'the leading figure . . . "the most typical expression", and "the clearest representative", of German philosophy' (Misch 1931: 2).

Lebensphilosophie **and the decline of neo-Kantian philosophy** Of the various projects of pure philosophy, it was neo-Kantian philosophy that was most threatened by the new philosophy. First of all, Scheler and Jaspers singled out neo-Kantian philosophy as the central enemy, and Spengler saw Kant as the adversary of his hero Goethe. Second, Scheler's and Spengler's attacks on science too were bad news for neo-Kantian philosophy. After all, many neo-

Kantians were concerned primarily with explaining the conditions of the possibility of scientific knowledge. Third, the neo-Kantian philosophy of the *Geisteswissenschaften* was also in the line of fire. Spengler's morphology squared badly with Windelband's and Rickert's philosophical historiography, and his historical and cultural relativism was a direct denial of the neo-Kantian *Wertabsolutismus*.

It certainly did not help the neo-Kantian cause that the offensive came at a moment when the two leading schools had just lost key members to death and retirement. Windelband and Emil Lask, Rickert's most promising student, both died in 1915, Cohen in 1918 and Natorp in 1924. Windelband's chair in Heidelberg went to Rickert, but Cohen's professorship was taken over by the 'experimentalist' Jaensch, and Husserl succeeded Rickert in Freiburg. Little surprise, therefore, that talented and ambitious students of the neo-Kantians – men like Hans-Georg Gadamer, Nicolai Hartmann and Martin Heidegger – abandoned the project of their teachers and joined the ranks of the phenomenologists. This erosion left Rickert as the main spokesman for the Southwestern School, and Ernst Cassirer, the student of Cohen and Natorp, as the main heir to the Marburg School.

Cassirer did not engage the new philosophical movement in a running battle, and he did little to accommodate his work to the Weimar mentality. Cassirer was a highly prolific writer, and his writings on Kant's philosophy (1918), the history of epistemology (1920), the philosophy of mathematics and physics (1921), the philosophy of symbolic forms (1923, 1925b, 1929) and the Enlightenment (1932) earned him the respect and the recognition of his colleagues. Thus in 1919 Cassirer was called to two philosophical chairs (Hamburg and Frankfurt), and in 1930 a commission formed to fill a prestigious chair in Berlin placed Cassirer well ahead of Heidegger and Hartmann (Farias 1987: 123). Nevertheless, Cassirer's scholarly work did not capture the imagination of Weimar students, and, at least before 1929, Cassirer made no attempt to combat the views of those philosophers that were more successful in this respect. Only in 1929 did Cassirer deviate from his earlier silence on *Lebensphilosophie* by engaging in a public debate with Heidegger over the correct interpretation of Kant. During this famous 'Davos debate', Cassirer tried to rehabilitate neo-Kantian philosophy by rejecting what he regarded as fashionable caricatures ('neo-Kantianism is the scapegoat of recent philosophy', Cassirer in

Heidegger 1991: 274). He also defended a traditional understanding of Kant's project against Heidegger's attempt to turn Kant into
a metaphysician of human finitude. While reports vary on whether
or not this encounter ended in hostility (Pos 1949; Hamburg 1964;
Cristaudo 1991), there can be no doubt that it was Heidegger who
continued to be looked upon by German university students as 'the
secret king in the realm of thought' (Farias 1987: 126).

Rickert's publications during the Weimar Republic are more
relevant to the present study. Rickert and some of his students both
attacked the philosophy of life and sought to accommodate to it.
Two years after the publication of Spengler's *Untergang*, and one
year after Jaspers' *Psychologie der Weltanschauungen*, Rickert tried to
do for *Lebensphilosophie* what Husserl had done only twenty years
earlier for psychologism: write the book-length 'refutation' to
which friends and foes alike would have to refer subsequently.
Rickert's *Philosophie des Lebens* (1920) was a frontal attack on what
Rickert called the 'fashion philosophy' of the day: the attempt 'to
build the whole *Weltanschauung* and *Lebensanschauung* on the
concept of life' (1920: 5). Rickert's book was similar to Husserl's
Prolegomena in that he too accused the defendant of inconsistency,
in that he reduced the defendant to one or two 'isms' ('intuitionism' and 'biologism'), and in that he identified seeds and symptoms
of these philosophical diseases in many different writers.

Under the label 'intuitionism' Rickert opposed the view that
philosophy must be based upon an intuitive grasp of the world, and
that philosophy must be freed from the strait-jacket of systems,
principles and concepts. Rickert saw this idea arising out of the work
of Bergson, Dilthey and Husserl. For us it is especially interesting
to note what Rickert had to say about phenomenology: 'It is true
that Husserl does not have a philosophy of life. Nevertheless, his
thought shows an affinity with it, and it is perhaps precisely this
affinity to which he owes a great part of his success' (1920: 28).
Rickert was thinking here foremost of Husserl's '*Wesensschau*'; he
regarded it as being similar in kind to Goethe's intuitive morphology.
Moreover: 'If any further proof for the affinity [between phenomenology and *Lebensphilosophie*] was needed, we could refer to Max
Scheler who is a follower of Husserl and a self-proclaimed philosopher of life' (1920: 29). In Husserl's phenomenology Rickert also
found another motive for 'intuitionism', namely the latter's hostility
to systems and principles:

We need the system in order to extract the theoretically

developed world cosmos from the world chaos ... [In
Husserl's work] not only are the outlines of a cosmos missing,
but the mere *Wesensschau* of isolated phenomena ... will
never lead to any cosmos either. Husserl can hardly deny this.

(Rickert 1920: 45, 50)

The main target of Rickert's attack on intuitionism, however, was
Scheler and not Husserl. He quoted key passages from Scheler's
praise of intuition in his paper 'Versuche zu einer Philosophie des
Lebens: Nietzsche – Dilthey – Bergson' ([1915b] 1972), and went
on to write:

Such sentences certainly *sound* very beautiful, they are eminently 'modern' and spoken out of the deepest soul of many.
Indeed, these sentences might well formulate what draws
many to the philosophy of life. The attitude towards life of a
human being that only 'lives', i.e. that *enjoys* life, is described
very seductively. Especially unphilosophical characters will
find that convincing since it suggests to them that they could
be true philosophers if only 'the limits of their concepts were
overflown'.

(1920: 52)

Rickert himself was less excited. Scheler's article betrayed 'a lack of
principles, i.e. the worst of all philosophical diseases' (1920: 56).

As Rickert turned from the critique of intuitionism to the
rejection of 'biologism', Scheler continued to be one of his main
targets. Biologism, for Rickert, was the view that 'biology alone ...
is able to provide the concepts for all of philosophy' (1920: 75).
Rickert found this view clearly expressed in Scheler's wartime
writings. Given Rickert's earlier involvement in the struggle over
the position of scientific psychology within philosophy, his argument against biologism does not come as a surprise:

The general assumption [of *Lebensphilosophie*] is obviously that
a natural science is capable of guiding us theoretically in
questions regarding values ... [But] biology as a natural
science does not take a stand [with respect to values]. For
biology, life and death, health and disease are different facts,
not bearers of value and non-value.

(1920: 118, 126)

And thus Rickert concluded that biologism was no better than
'materialism', 'psychologism' and 'historism' (1920: 180).

In his *Philosophie des Lebens,* Rickert did not spend much effort on the refutation of Spengler and Jaspers. Spengler was mentioned only in a footnote since allegedly his thinking 'is of such un-scientific capriciousness that one cannot speak about it in a scientific context'. Rickert's main point of criticism was that Spengler's attempt to predict the course of history was indebted 'to one of the rationalistic prejudices of the Enlightenment' (1920: 33). Jaspers' reproach of system philosophy, i.e. Jaspers' *Gehäuse* theory, was mentioned but quickly dismissed as 'self-refuting' (1920: 153).

The *Philosophie des Lebens* did not remain Rickert's last word on the 'fashion philosophy' of the day. In a series of further papers (1920–21, 1923–24a, 1923–24b), as well as in his *System der Philosophie* (1921), he repeated and developed his arguments against *Lebensphilosophie.* These writings do more than just criticise *Lebensphilosophie,* however. They also show how Rickert tried to accommodate it in his own philosophy. He approvingly quoted views that the world war had led 'to a radical turn in European culture' (1923–24a: 305), he applauded the '*overcoming of intellectualism*', i.e. the overcoming of a one-sided reliance on under-standing (*Verstand*) (1923–24a: 307), and he cited a report accord-ing to which the students of the day posed the following demands: 'we do not want science, we want religious certainty, beautiful vision, we want nourishment and confirmation for our con-structive instincts' (1923–24a: 308). Rickert tried to give some such 'beautiful vision' in his *System der Philosophie.* In fact, Rickert sought to convince his readers that 'philosophy of life is actually philo-sophy of values' (1921: 316). To make this equation compelling, Rickert courageously took up one of Scheler's central concerns: the philosophy of sexual love (cf. Scheler 1913). Rickert submitted that the study of the realm of values was not exhausted by the traditional philosophical disciplines of logic, aesthetics, epistem-ology and ethics. The neglected values were linked to 'complexes of persons' (1921: 395). Moreover, these values made up 'the meaning of life' for the 'average person' (*Durchschnittsmensch*) (1920: 397). According to Rickert these values were 'love values' and they demanded their own field of study:

> We should not only think here of sexual love . . . The love we
> have in mind here always has a particular character . . . love
> of one's mother, . . . love of one's child, love of one's home,

love of one's fatherland . . . The science of love values . . . we shall call *erotics*, and we shall place it alongside logic, aesthetics and ethics.

(1920: 398)

Rickert went on to analyse some of these values and ended with a praise for sexual love as the 'good in which future values combine with values of the present' (1920: 409).

Rickert's '*eroticism*' was warmly applauded by one influential reviewer of the book, the educationist-psychologist Eduard Spranger (1923–24: 196). Some other philosophers – mostly Rickert's students – endorsed either his attack on *Lebensphilosophie* and phenomenology, or his *System*, or both (e.g. Faust 1927; Liebert 1924; Sternberg 1920). On the whole, however, Rickert succeeded neither with his attack on *Lebensphilosophie* nor with his attempt to present his own philosophy as its true heir. His arguments were only rarely addressed, and when they were mentioned at all they were rejected as attempts to discredit a 'deep longing of our time' (Frischeisen-Köhler 1921: 135) or dismissed as the typical product of the 'philosophy of science', of a 'cleverly constructed machine which spins around its wheels noisily and with much energy but which turns out surprisingly few useful products' (Müller-Freienfels 1923: 64). The same critic deemed it 'impossible to understand how Rickert can use the label "fashion philosophy" for a movement [i.e. *Lebensphilosophie*] that has arisen with spontaneous necessity all over the cultural world'. And Müller-Freienfels concluded:

> Only those people who are dressed in much outdated coats complain about 'fashion' . . . If *Lebensphilosophie* is a 'fashion' then all of the great movements of world history have only been 'fashions' and it is easy to live with the accusation. For this is already clear today: *Lebensphilosophie* . . . is already an important cultural force, and its effects cannot be predicted.
>
> (Müller-Freienfels 1923: 138)

We have to understand why Rickert's assault on, and accommodation to, *Lebensphilosophie* could not succeed in the Weimar Republic. The causes for this can best be brought out by contrasting Rickert's failure with respect to *Lebensphilosophie* with Husserl's success with respect to psychological naturalism.

First, I have already mentioned that of the four leading figures of pre-war neo-Kantian philosophy – Windelband, Rickert, Cohen, Natorp – Rickert was, by 1924, the only survivor. I have also drawn attention to the fact that some key professorships were lost to other schools of thought, and that in part due to this development neo-Kantian philosophy no longer offered secure career prospects. Moreover, the most productive and undoubtedly most talented of all neo-Kantian philosophers alive at the time, Ernst Cassirer, did not seek to engage phenomenology or other schools in argument.

Second, when Husserl attacked 'psychologism' in 1900, a majority in the community of academic philosophy had a vested interest in the cleansing of philosophy departments of experimental psychologists. In 1920 most of the philosophical community was able to unite, too, but only against a threat coming from outside academic philosophy: Spengler. But aside from the common fear of a new rise of nonacademic philosophy – a situation familiar to German philosophy from the previous century – German academic philosophers of 1920 did not have a common interest to oppose *Lebensphilosophie* in all its forms.

Third, because there was no common interest in opposing *Lebensphilosophie* there also was no competition over who provided the best arguments against it. If there was competition at all, it was competition over who would best accommodate to the Weimar mentality. And to accommodate to this mentality meant avoiding the traditional academic 'rituals' of unmasking inconsistencies, self-refutations, and 'isms'. Thus if Rickert did expect his criticism to be the focus point of arguments for and against *Lebensphilosophie*, he was bound to be disappointed.

Fourth, in a climate hostile to rationality, *Verstand* and logic, one could not expect to carry the day by rational refutations. In this respect, Rickert confused the mentality of the first decade of the century with that of the third. For Jaspers, Scheler, Heidegger, as well as their followers, Rickert's logical arguments rendered logical finesse suspect. The seemingly quick success of the self-refutation arguments spoke against the logician and the employment of logical reasoning, not against *Lebensphilosophie* and relativism. In Heidegger's lectures, for example, Husserl's and Rickert's self-refutation arguments were referred to as a 'joke' (Heidegger 1981: 163).

Fifth, it seems a reasonable conjecture to suppose that the sixty-year-old neo-Kantian professor's sudden conversion to eroticism did not strike members of the younger generation as especially convincing. The attempt to fish in Scheler's pond was a bit obvious and clumsy, especially as the treatment of the topic in terms of neo-Kantian value philosophy was hardly exciting.

And sixth and finally, Rickert could not succeed in his attack on phenomenology. Due to the efforts of Husserl, Scheler and Heidegger, phenomenology was on its way to becoming the most attractive academic *Lebensphilosophie*.

***Lebensphilosophie* and scientific philosophy** Even given the general antiscientific climate of the Weimar Republic, it is surprising how little there remained of Wundt's project for constructing an inductive metaphysics. Almost no one of the better known philosophers referred to Wundt's work in logic, epistemology and metaphysics, and no one bothered to even criticise him for his scientific orientation. Indeed, Wundt was so completely out of date that authors like Scheler or the historian Ernst Friedell could even remember him with a few friendly words. In a long article on contemporary German philosophy, Scheler characterised Wundt as 'the last great systematic philosopher of German philosophy'. Scheler felt compelled to provide an explanation for Wundt's lack of influence:

> One reason for the negligible influence of this excellent researcher and scholar in philosophy might be that his epistemology and his metaphysics suffer from great vagueness and uncertainty, and that the whole of his philosophy – despite its overload of scholarship – is colourless and bloodless.
>
> (Scheler 1922: 273)

In the light of the aggressive and insulting style in which Scheler characterised other philosophers, especially the neo-Kantians, this criticism of Wundt must be regarded as very mild indeed. Wundt was treated in the same way by Friedell. After dismissing Hermann Cohen's philosophy as 'dialectical card-sharpening' Friedell turned to Wundt and continued:

> Another kind of professors' philosophy [*sic*] but more fruitful and pleasant was Wilhelm Wundt's comprehensive work. According to his own definition, philosophy is 'the general science which has to unify the general results of the individual sciences into a consistent system'. Thus the philosopher would be only some kind of collector and registrar, clarifier

and summariser . . . That is a very unambitious mission and Wundt has fulfilled it satisfactorily.

(Friedell 1931: 1391)

Friedell went on to object, however, to Wundt's 'philistine' work, 'the shy care with which he avoided all quick and courageous thoughts', 'the pedantry of his presentations' and his 'petit bourgeois spirit' (1931: 1392–3).

To authors like Scheler and Friedell, the project of the Vienna Circle undoubtedly appeared as nothing more than another variation on the Wundtian project. The authors of the Vienna Circle did not have a following in German academic philosophy, and their attempts to change the tide were not successful. It is easy to see why.

First, Otto Neurath's book-length attack on Spengler's *Untergang* (Neurath 1921) did not deviate much from other contemporaneous reproaches. Neurath pointed out that Spengler had no proof for his decline thesis (1921: 161), and that his cultural relativism was self-refuting (1921: 204). Neurath called Spengler 'a treasure chest for anyone who seeks excuses for unscientific behaviour' (1921: 206), and dedicated his book to the 'young people who today often toil with Spengler and waste much effort on him' (1921: 213). Needless to say, there was no reason why Neurath's criticism should work where similar ones by dozens of other academic philosophers had failed before.

More interesting for our concerns is the famous pamphlet *Wissenschaftliche Weltauffassung: Der Wiener Kreis*, written by Neurath, Carnap and Hahn, and published in 1929. In this pamphlet the authors pronounced a new scientific worldview in opposition to 'metaphysical and theologising thought' (1929: 301). This scientific worldview was

> characterised . . . by its basic attitude, its point of view and direction of research. The goal is *unified science*. The endeavour is to link and harmonise the achievements of individual investigators in their various fields of science. From this aim follows the emphasis on *collective efforts*, and also the emphasis on what can be grasped intersubjectively; from this springs the search for a neutral system of formulae, for a symbolism freed from the slag of historical languages; and also the search for a total system of concepts.

(Neurath et al. 1929: 306)

The reader was also told that there were 'no unsolvable riddles', that metaphysical statements were empty of meaning, and that intuition could not stand on its own (1929: 306–7). Philosophy had to abandon its centuries-old dream of being 'a basic or universal science alongside or above the various fields of the one empirical science', and it was to confine itself to a clarification of assertions (1929: 316).

All of these claims of course flew straight in the face of what the German educated public expected to hear from philosophers. That such pronouncements did not resonate in German academia, indeed that they were ignored rather than criticised, was to be expected.

It is worthwhile noting those elements of the pamphlet, however, which catered to some of the contemporaneous intellectual and emotional needs. Already the subtitle 'the Vienna Circle' can be read as such an element. After all, whereas the philosophy of the pre-war era had been the philosophy of 'schools', the philosophy of *Lebensphilosophie* was pretty much a philosophy of 'circles'. The model for such circles was the 'George Kreis', a circle of followers and friends of the poet Stefan George. Whereas 'school' had signalled common adherence to the doctrine of one master, 'circle' suggested a looser grouping with a common attitude rather than with a common master or a common theory. As we shall see below, phenomenology presented itself in just this way. One finds these elements also in the text of the *Wissenschaftliche Weltauffassung*. Thus we are told that the circle of men called together by Schlick 'produced a fruitful inspiration', and that their 'attitude towards questions of life also showed a noteworthy agreement' (1929: 304). The pamphlet also emphasised the political aspirations of its members, thus rejecting any suggestions that theirs was yet another *Professorenphilosophie*:

> For instance, endeavours toward a new organisation of economic and social relations, toward the unification of mankind, toward a reform of school and education, all show an inner link with the scientific world-conception; it appears that these endeavours are welcomed and regarded with sympathy by the members of the Circle . . . we have to fashion intellectual tools for everyday life, for the daily life of the scholar but also for the daily life of all those who in some way join in working at the conscious reshaping of life.
>
> (1929: 304–5)

Note also the emphasis on life in the last sentence of the pamphlet: 'The scientific world-conception serves life, and life receives it' (1929: 318).

The attempt to accommodate to the mentality of the 1920s can also be recognised in a curious paper by Moritz Schlick, 'Vom Sinn des Lebens' (1927). Schlick found this meaning in play because

> the core and ultimate value of life can lie only in such states as exist for their own sake and carry their satisfaction in themselves . . . There really are such activities. To be consistent, we must call them *play*, since that is the name for free, purposeless action, that is, action which in fact carries its purpose within itself.
>
> (Schlick [1927] 1979: 114)

Schlick went on to locate play in youth, implying that 'the meaning of life is youth' ([1927] 1979: 123). Interestingly enough, in the course of developing this train of thought, Schlick underlined both the importance of *Lebensphilosophie* ('This notion of creative play will be accorded a major part in the life-philosophy of the future' ([1927] 1979: 116)), and the significance of metaphysics. The invocation of 'a metaphysical viewpoint' in order to justify the 'affirmation of youth as the true meaning of existence' was especially curious. Schlick opined that in as different cycles as those of 'plants and animals . . . galaxies and atoms' it was always 'the fruit which provides the meaning of the whole cycle' ([1927] 1979: 127). No doubt this type of analogical, or intuitive, reasoning would have been to the liking of Spenglerites, had it not been for Schlick's other, more sober, scientifically oriented papers.

The success of phenomenology Having shown that neither neo-Kantian philosophy nor scientific philosophy gained a wide following in the Weimar era, I shall now explain how phenomenology rose to the position of the dominant philosophy. Phenomenology triumphed because Scheler and Heidegger – both of whom had aligned themselves with phenomenology already before and during the war – succeeded in presenting their thought as *the* academic-philosophical answer to Spengler, and as *the* academic *Lebensphilosophie*.

Husserl's own position towards *Lebensphilosophie* was ambivalent at best. Like Rickert and Schlick, he too was ready to bow to the gods of the day. For instance, in 1925 Husserl wrote a preface to a

German edition of speeches of Gautama Buddha. In this short text Husserl spoke of the 'degenerate culture' of the present and the need for 'mental purity and sincerity' and an 'overcoming of the world'. He also hoped for 'a new type of human "holiness" . . . [that would] awaken new powers of religious intuition and . . . contribute to a deepening of Christian intuition' (1925: 125–6). Nevertheless, Husserl attacked Spengler from the lectern (Kraft 1973: 89), and in public lectures in 1931 he denounced Heidegger's and Scheler's work as 'anthropologism and psychologism', and as 'aberrations that do not even reach the true philosophical dimension' (1931: 164, 179).

Scheler's evaluation of Husserl's work was not exactly enthusiastic, either. Scheler called Husserl's transcendental phenomenology 'a curious turn', 'the major obstacle for the construction of a metaphysics on the basis of a theory of essences', and a partial return to Berkeley, Kant and Natorp (Scheler 1922: 311).

In the light of these quotations, we need an explanation for why Scheler and Heidegger called themselves 'phenomenologists' at all, and how 'phenomenology' could cover projects as different as those of Husserl, Scheler and Heidegger. We may also ask how Husserl – and Husserl alone – came to be credited with the refutation of psychologism. I shall provide an answer by focusing on Scheler.

Scheler was the key figure in phenomenology during the early Weimar Republic, and his assessment of the history of philosophy in Germany between 1900 and 1920 has become the generally accepted view of this period (see e.g. Schnädelbach 1984). As mentioned before, Scheler was a student of Rudolph Eucken, a neo-Fichtean philosopher in Jena. Many of Eucken's pre-war writings touched upon themes and issues that by hindsight can be regarded as anticipating *Lebensphilosophie* (e.g. Eucken 1896). Scheler wrote both his doctoral dissertation and his *Habilitationsschrift* under Eucken. Scheler's *Habilitationsschrift* was on *Die transzendentale und die psychologische Methode*, and it was published shortly after Husserl's *Prolegomena*, in 1901. In this study, Scheler opposed psychologism, which for him meant 'the claim that the specifically philosophical disciplines are parts of psychology' (1900: 320). While rejecting the attempt to naturalise meaning and logic, Scheler also criticised 'the transcendental method' of Kant and the neo-Kantians. According to Scheler, the transcendental method had produced results of two kinds: sentences that could in principle be falsified by experience and sentences that could not be refuted in this way. As Scheler saw it, all sentences of the first kind had turned out false, whereas sentences of the second kind had proved to be empty and sterile (1900: 285).

It is natural to assume that Scheler's hostile attitude towards neo-Kantian and naturalistic philosophy led him to regard phenomenology as an ally. His Catholicism was undoubtedly an additional factor in his alignment with Husserl. Catholic philosophy and German Idealism were usually perceived as irreconcilable systems of beliefs and Kant's philosophy was often opposed to that of Thomas Aquinas (Eucken 1901). Phenomenology, on the other hand, had a background in scholasticism. Be this as it may, during the first decade of the century Scheler started calling himself a phenomenologist and adopted central ideas from Husserl's *Logische Untersuchungen*. For Scheler, phenomenology was a search for essences, a search based on *Wesensschau* or 'eidetic intuition' rather than on transcendental-reductive, 'constructive' arguments.

Scheler was instrumental in forging a strong link between 'intuition' of the Bergsonian variety and Husserl's 'eidetic intuition' (of the *Logische Untersuchungen*). I have earlier quoted several key passages from Scheler's widely read article 'Versuche zu einer Philosophie des Lebens: Nietzsche – Dilthey – Bergson' ([1915b] 1972). This article shows that for Scheler phenomenology was part and parcel of *Lebensphilosophie*.

One may well doubt whether Husserl could ever have convinced many Weimar readers of such a link between phenomenology and *Lebensphilosophie*. Scheler, however, had an excellent position for establishing this link. He was both a self-proclaimed phenomenologist, and one of the most prolific advocates of *Lebensphilosophie*. His wartime writings had earned him a high degree of visibility, and he was a brilliant lecturer and a fascinating – 'demonic' – figure (Gadamer 1977: 71). Throughout the 1920s, Scheler's influence grew steadily among postwar philosophy students, and some of their teachers. Indeed, as quoted earlier, several contemporary sources agree that Scheler was *the* most influential philosopher in Weimar Germany before Heidegger's sudden rise.

In Scheler's usage, 'phenomenology' was synonymous with '*Sach*-philosophie' (Scheler [1922] 1973). '*Sache*' and '*Sachlichkeit*' were key buzzwords in Weimar Germany. Neither term has a direct equivalent in the English language. Depending on the context, '*Sache*' translates as 'thing', 'object', 'matter', 'issue' and 'fact', and 'Sachlichkeit' is usually rendered as 'factuality', 'functionality' or 'objectivity'. In the Weimar period, to study '*Sachen*' meant to investigate 'real things' and 'real problems'; it signalled disgust for artificially created (philosophical) pseudoproblems; it suggested re-establishing contact with the real world by viewing it in an unprejudiced manner; it was equivalent to rejecting ornament and needless sophistication; and it flagged a strong preference for 'seeing' over 'constructing'. Given these links and connotations, it is easy to appreciate how the phenomenological battle cry '*Zu den Sachen selbst!*' could be presented as summing up the aspirations of the era.

Scheler was successful in convincing his listeners and readers that phenomenological *Sachphilosophie* contrasted with the 'traditional philosophies of standpoints and schools'. Allegedly, for these schools, philosophical reflection did not start from the *Sachen* but rather from the texts of some famous dead philosopher. This approach ushered in 'school fossilisation, alienation from intuition and from reality, and a secret and tricky terminology' ([1922] 1973: 265). Put differently, 'one whets the knives, without ever cutting anything' ([1922] 1973: 266). For Scheler, neo-Kantian philosophy was *the* paradigm case of a standpoint philosophy: it had its secret language, it confined itself to epistemology and methodology ([1922] 1973: 266), and it reflected on the sciences rather than on the *Sachen* themselves ([1922] 1973: 269). Scheler was especially biting when it came to the Marburg School and the Southwest German School. The '*Scientificismus*' [*sic*] of the Marburg School was without comparison, and Cassirer's historical studies were 'attempts to rape history' ([1922] 1973: 285). Windelband's and Rickert's attempts to draw a distinction between the *Naturwissenschaften* and the *Geisteswissenschaften* were 'philosophically without any foundation' ([1922] 1973: 287), and their work overall was '*much inferior*' even to that of the Marburg School. Windelband's and Rickert's philosophy consisted of only 'a few extraordinarily poor and thin basic thoughts' and thus 'it must be regarded as a *problem* for the psychology of culture how this *most empty* of German Kantian schools could become so widespread in our country'. Scheler suspected that part of the explanation was that this philosophy demanded only 'a *minimum* of thinking work' and asked his reader to compare his assessment of Southwest German philosophy with Windelband's nasty comments on experimental psychology ([1922] 1973: 290).

Phenomenology differed from neo-Kantian philosophy not only in so far as it was a *Sachphilosophie*. Phenomenology was special also in being free from the strait-jacket called 'unity of a *school*'. Scheler admitted that all phenomenologists had in various degrees been 'stimulated' by Husserl but he denied that this stimulation extended beyond a common 'philosophical attitude . . . a new *techne of the seeing consciousness*'. One could not become a phenomenologist by learning a set of doctrines, but only by 'continuously *practising*this attitude of consciousness' ([1922] 1973: 309). Because phenomenologists shared no less, but also no more than this common attitude, phenomenology allowed its practitioners a wide variety of *Weltanschauungen*, a diversity of religious convictions, a range of more and less systematic approaches, and shifting transcendental and psychological methods ([1922] 1973: 311).

To characterise phenomenology in this loose way had two obvious advantages. On the one hand, it allowed Scheler to keep phenomenology as a label for his own thought – and thus underline the continuity of his own work – without having to present himself as Husserl's student or follower. On the other hand, the loose definition also served as an invitation to anyone who wanted to be in touch with the new thinking to call his or her work 'phenomenology'. Put differently, Scheler offered a paradise on the cheap: in order to call oneself a phenomenologist (and thus in order to escape the verbal abuse that Spengler practised in his writings), all one needed to give was a vague commitment to the *Sachen* and to intuition. This was an offer that not many were able to refuse.

Scheler's interpretation of the recent history of philosophy was no less successful than his invitation to adopt the label 'phenomenology'. On Scheler's account *Sachphilosophie* began with phenomenology, and phenomenology dated from the beginning of the century. Husserl's *Logische Untersuchungen* with its refutation of psychologism marked the entry to a new era ([1922] 1973: 266). This historical claim was motivated by several interests.

First, it downgraded the work of Husserl's and Scheler's neo-Kantian competitors. As Scheler presented the matter, the neo-Kantian schools had been 'in inevitable decline' for some time, and they were still around only owing 'to the law of historical inertia' ([1922] 1973: 279). Exclusively to emphasise Husserl's success in the refutation of psychologism was to attribute to phenomenology alone one of the most crucial, and most hotly contested prizes in the recent history of philosophy. Needless to say, other schools claimed the title for their heroes (Faust (1927) for Rickert, and Cassirer (1925a) for Natorp). But as phenomenology emerged as the most influential philosophy of the Weimar era, its students adopted Husserl's and Scheler's rather than Cassirer's view of history.

Second, to locate the beginning of the new *Sachphilosophie* in the year 1900 had the additional advantage of downgrading Spengler's claim to innovation. Despite all the scorn that Scheler poured over Rickert and other neo-Kantians, he agreed with them at least in their rejection of Spengler. Spengler's thinking 'stood opposed to *all* contemporary serious philosophy' and it was no more than a 'last distant echo of romantic historism' ([1922] 1973: 324).

Third, Scheler's praise for Husserl's work of 1900 was also a method for downgrading Husserl's subsequent writings, i.e. it was a way of building Husserl a monument *in the past – and only in the past*. I have already quoted Scheler's critical assessment of Husserl's transcendental phenomenology, and that Husserl's renewed attack on psychologism in 1929 in his *Formale und transzendentale Logik* went without much notice. As Scheler reminded his readers in 1922, 'so-called "psychologism", which once seemed a danger to philosophy, is today principally overcome' ([1922] 1973: 302–3).

Fourth, declaring the threat of psychologism a thing of the distant past had the additional advantage of enabling Scheler to express his interest in recent psychological research freely. Scheler advocates especially the work of the Würzburg School, Spranger, Jaspers and the Gestalt theorists ([1922] 1973: 303).

And fifth and finally, a general agreement that Husserl's arguments against psychologism were sound also helped Scheler in the promotion of his version of the sociology of knowledge (Scheler [1924] 1980). For Scheler social factors determined which parts and aspects of the world or the '"pure" realm of meaning' would become known. To claim anything stronger, i.e. that reasoning and perception could be shaped by social position, was to be guilty of 'sociologism (which is a counterpart of psychologism)' ([1924] 1980: 58). Versions of sociologism were Poincaré's 'conventionalism', Durkheim's 'positivistic "sociologism"', and Marxist 'technicism' ([1924] 1980: 62, 115).[4]

Scheler succeeded in his attempt to translate the interest in *Lebensphilosophie* into support for phenomenology. Phenomenology became the philosophy of the period. Indeed, its success was acknowledged even by its most outspoken critics. For example, in 1925 the neo-Thomist Herbert Burgert wrote:

> Husserl has compared himself to the greatest thinkers of the past . . . He is the Messiah who after centuries of longing and searching has brought the whole truth . . . A fanatical congregation has originated, the number of converts is on the increase, and the infidels are not just pitied as blind, but branded and despised as despicable and dishonest.
>
> (Burgert 1925: 226)

Towards the end of his paper, Burgert added, however:

> But let us not forget the good that has been done by Husserl. This good is the defence of theory-free *Wesensschau* against Kantian constructions, the struggle against the mere 'whetting of knives' as Lotze called it, i.e. the reduction of philosophical knowledge to logic and epistemology.
>
> (1925: 230)

Moreover, in a lengthy criticism of Husserl and phenomenology, Rickert's student August Faust reported in 1927 that 'the word "phenomenology" has become a slogan; it serves as a code name for the many degenerate forms which even a good thing will bring forth once it has become the fashion of the day' (1927: 26). Faust also lamented that the slogan 'zu den Sachen selbst' was calculated to remind one of 'neue Sachlichkeit', 'the latest catchword in European painting' (1927: 28). And in 1932 two critics observed that 'there can be no doubt that the word "phenomenology" . . . has become an overstretched concept' (Illemann 1932: 1), and that

> one may justifiably claim that with the appearance of Edmund Husserl's 'Logische Untersuchungen' in 1900 . . . there began a new phase in German philosophy . . . Since then, the word 'phenomenological' has, as it were, become for almost all philosophy of our time the expression of a new mental attitude.
>
> (Schingnitz 1932: vii)

Needless to say, with less critical authors Husserl and Scheler fared even better.

Last but not least, Scheler was also successful with his interpretation of the history of German philosophy during the first two decades of the twentieth century. One recent history of German philosophy reports that Husserl and Frege 'were fairly isolated in their campaign against [logical psychologism]', and that 'Edmund Husserl . . . is the great figure . . . with whose work Max Scheler and Martin Heidegger were associated in the final suppression of psychologism' (Schnädelbach 1984: 99). Clearly, such assessments stand in a tradition of writing the history of German philosophy that was first introduced by Scheler in the 1920s.

How psychology ceased to be a threat

The overall argument of this study up to this point has been this: the philosophical debate over psychologism was caused by pure philosophers' opposition to experimental psychology. If this argument is correct then – *ceteris paribus* – a general lack of interest in psychologism should be accompanied by less anxious attitudes among pure philosophers towards experimental psychology.

The reality of the Weimar period was as my thesis predicts. Although occasionally authors in the Weimar era labelled some thinkers psychologistic, the large-scale hunt for psychologism, as witnessed in the pre-war period, was not reopened after the war (see Figure 5, p. 100). At the same time, attacks on experimental psychology ended as well. Experimental psychology was no longer perceived as a threat. I shall now explain why indeed it no longer needed to be perceived in this way.

The end of the expansion within philosophy departments During the years of the Weimar Republic, advocates and practitioners of experimental psychology failed to increase, or even maintain, their pre-war share of professorial chairs within philosophy departments. While the prestigious chairs in Bonn and in Wrocław were recaptured by pure philosophers, experimentalists were unable to conquer any vacant chair (Geuter 1986). By 1930, dissatisfaction among psychologists reached the point where they copied the methods of their former enemies and sent a petition to all ministries of education. The petition demanded that 'philosophy, education and psychology must be represented in every German university through separate full professorships' (Erklärung 1931).

New lectureships and chairs for psychology were introduced during the 1920s but almost exclusively in applied psychology. By 1931, there existed six chairs designated 'full professor in psychology', but most of them were located in technical universities

(*Technische Hochschulen*) and commercial academies (Ash 1980a: 282). Between 1918 and 1928, nine technical universities introduced courses and research in 'psychotechnics'[5] and educational psychology (Dorsch 1963; Geuter 1986).

This institutional development went hand in hand with a reorientation in research. Increasing numbers of psychologists turned to applied psychology. This rise of applied psychology expressed itself quickly in terms of publications. By 1925 serial publications in applied psychology outnumbered those in general or 'pure' psychology by a ratio of two to one (see Figure 7, p. 124). The change relative to the pre-war years can also be seen by focusing on individual psychologists. For example, Karl Marbe, a student of Wundt and Külpe, had done important work in the psychology of thought in the first decade of the century, but during the Weimar Republic he worked on the psychology of advertising, forensic psychology, the psychology of accidents, and aptitude tests for train conductors, insurance agents, prison guards, dentists and surgeons (Marbe 1961). In 1922, in a speech to the 'Society for Experimental Psychology', Marbe suggested that psychology should emphasise its practical significance, and he claimed that 'an intervention on behalf of psychology will be positively received by governments since their demand for practically useful, specialised psychologists becomes ever louder' (1922: 150). As the new positions in technical universities showed, Marbe had interpreted the mood of administrators correctly. Indeed, applied psychology had been encouraged by politicians since before the war. For example, when opening the congress of experimental psychology in Berlin in 1912, the mayor of the capital asked his audience for 'substantial and solid psychological results, especially in forensics, medicine and education (Goldschmidt 1912: 97).

This reorientation of experimental psychology marked a defeat for the Wundtian view of the psychologist. As we saw in Chapters 6 and 7, according to Wundt the psychologist needed a substantial familiarity with philosophical positions: 'The most important questions of psychological education are so tightly linked to epistemological and metaphysical questions that one cannot imagine how they could ever vanish from psychology' (1913: 24). The practical psychologist had no use for such 'epistemological and metaphysical questions'. Wundt had argued against the 'Americanisation' of German psychology repeatedly, and at an early stage. In 1903 he withdrew his support for his student Ernst Meumann's

Archiv für Psychologie, because 'in the issues published thus far, a total of 873 pages have been devoted to education but only 715 pages to all other areas of psychology' (Bringmann and Ungerer 1980a: 70). And in a paper of 1910, 'Über reine und angewandte Psychologie', Wundt predicted that a growth in educational psychology would turn 'pure psychology' into 'applied pedagogy' (1910c). Although Wundt's prediction did not come true in this dramatic form, it is clear that psychologists involved in advertising and aptitude tests could not make a strong case for competence in epistemology, logic or aesthetics. No surprise therefore, that when psychologists petitioned governments for more chairs in 1930, they explicitly granted that areas as extensive as psychology and philosophy could not 'be taught and studied by one and the same person' (*Erklärung* 1931).

Crisis talk   It is clear that the antiscientific mentality of the Weimar Republic was damaging for the project of a psychology modelled on the natural sciences. The reactions of proponents and practitioners of psychology to this hostile environment resemble those of the physicists and mathematics studied by Forman (1971). A first obvious strategy of accommodation was to declare one's discipline in crisis. Psychologists used this strategy extensively but they did not agree on what the crisis consisted in, and how it ought to be overcome.

In this respect, the crisis talk of the Weimar era followed an earlier pattern. In the late nineteenth century philosophers had identified grave but different crises in psychology. For instance, R. Willy, a follower of Avenarius and Mach had analysed 'Die Krisis in der Psychologie' in 1897 in a three-part article, and the neo-Thomist C. Gutberlet followed suit in the following year (Gutberlet 1898). For Willy the crisis was brought about by excessive metaphysical ballast, whereas for Gutberlet it was due to a lack of metaphysical assumptions.

Psychologists had also seen their discipline under threat and in crisis during the attack by pure philosophy. Writing in 1915, Felix Krüger (1915) suspected that the current crisis of psychology was due to the fact that pure philosophy had made contempt for experimental psychology 'a fashionable attitude': 'This fashionable attitude of contempt for psychology often expresses itself in a comical way as when today beginners in some fields of philosophy of mind or cultural research assure us that they investigate these mental worlds from all kinds of perspectives, problem-historical, object-theoretical, value-structure-philosophical, of course also phenomenological, *but not* psychological. Especially all links with experimental psychology they reject as shameful' (1915: 25). Nevertheless, Krüger suspected that there also was a real crisis within psychological theorising. This crisis consisted of psychology's individualistic and static orientations (1915: 38).

Many authors during the Weimar period agreed with this view. Others, however, located the causes of crisis altogether elsewhere. Thus the philosopher Jonas Cohn blamed the 'great distress' of psychology on the existence of an 'abyss' between the '"exact" work of the experimentalist' and the '"empathetic", "interpretative" psychology of the historian, educator and poet' (1923–24: 51). The same theme was central to Eduard Spranger who spoke of a 'phase of most severe shocks in the foundations of psychology'. Spranger feared that this phase would lead to the development of two separate kinds of psychology, explanatory psychology and interpretative psychology (1926: 172). In 1926 Karl Bühler reported that 'one can already read in the daily newspapers that psychology is in crisis. And those who write those things are probably right, even though no two of them will have had the same thing in mind. Often it is claimed summarily that the *naturalistic, sensualistic, mechanistic,* atomistic conception of mental life of the second half of the nineteenth century has failed, and that as yet no new unifying approach has taken its place' (1926: 455). Bühler accepted this evaluation, but he added some further causes for the current crisis. Such additional causes were Spranger's thinking and behaviourism. As Bühler saw it, it was behaviourism 'which has made the crisis of psychology acute' (1926: 459).

Psychologists knew of course that their crisis talk was a concession to the *Zeitgeist.* For instance, writing in 1926, Erich Jaensch admitted that 'talk of a *crisis* in psychology, a crisis that takes effect foremost in Germany' was not without justification. But Jaensch added that the crisis proclamations were largely due to 'a widespread tone of voice and manner of speech of our time' (1927: 92).

Phenomenology and experimental psychology While psychologists' adoption of crisis talk shows that they reacted to the hostile environment by accommodation, it does not tell us much about the changes in psychological research itself. Nor does it explain why theoretical, non-applied, psychology stopped being a threat to pure philosophy. Such an explanation, however, is not difficult to give. Weimar psychology was no longer a danger because it aligned itself closely with pure philosophy and its pre-war projects for a pure, philosophical psychology.

This reorientation had actually begun prior to the war, especially with regard to phenomenology. During the early years of the century, Külpe and his collaborators in Würzburg had begun to question Wundt's assumption that thinking could not be studied by experimental means. The Würzburg School's method for studying thought processes was a combination of traditional armchair psychology with modern laboratory technique.[6] The process of introspection was distributed over two psychologists: the experimental subject would observe and report his mental experiences, whereas the experimental organiser (*Versuchsleiter*) would evoke the experience, record the subject's report, and possibly ask for further clarifications. For instance, the experimental organiser might ask for the subject's experiences once it heard the sentence '2 + 5 = 8', and then record the answer. This method was first applied by Karl Marbe in order to find out 'which experiences must be added to one or several conscious processes in order for them to rise to the level of judgements' (Marbe 1901: 15). Marbe's result was a negative one: there was no type of mental experience such that it was a necessary and sufficient condition for the occurrence of a judgement, i.e. for 'conscious processes such that the predicates "correct" and "false" can be meaningfully applied to them' (1901: 10).

In order to defend the credibility of their results and the reliability of their method, Külpe and his colleagues needed a theoretical underpinning. They also needed a vocabulary for the description of thought processes. In this situation, several members of the Külpe School, including eventually Külpe himself, turned to phenomenology and other strands of introspectionist philosophical psychology. For instance, August Messer used Theodor Lipps' distinction between 'immediate' and 'mediate memory' in order to defend introspective reports. Mediate memory would be active recall of an earlier event, and thus selective and distorting. Immediate memory, however, would be the residue that remained in consciousness for a short while after the occurrence of a mental experience. It was reliable and observable, and its nature was not altered by its being observed (Messer 1906: 17). Messer also referred to Husserl's work in arguing that the experience of meaning and intending could not be reduced to sensations (1906: 186; cf. Messer 1907: 417–25).

The reliance on Husserl reached its peak in Karl Bühler's three-part 'Tatsachen und Probleme zu einer Psychologie der Denk-vorgänge' (1907, 1908a, 1908b). The first part began with a praise for Husserl's methodology in the *Logische Untersuchungen*:

> Husserl has recently developed an original and very fruit-ful method, a kind of transcendental method. In general terms, he assumes that the logical norms can be fulfilled and then asks himself what this allows us to infer about the processes that must be regarded as the bearers of these law-fulfilling events.
>
> (Bühler 1907: 298)

Bühler went on to claim that his study of 'the *hic et nunc* of what is experienced while thinking' would prove Husserl's assumptions true (1907: 299). In the main body of his study, Bühler sought to identify 'the ultimate experienced units of experiences of thinking'. According to Bühler, these units were 'the consciousness that . . .', i.e. 'thoughts' that did not need to be represented in consciousness as sensations, ideas or emotions (1907: 329). In talking about these thoughts, Bühler and his experimental subjects, other Würzburg psychologists, used Husserlian terminology.

The strong link between the Würzburg School and phenomen-ology was not missed by other writers at the time. Ernst von Aster commented that 'Bühler's . . . experiments are . . . an attempt to check and to confirm Husserl's phenomenology in an experimental way' (1908: 62). It also seems natural to suspect that Wilhelm Wundt's highly polemical reaction to Bühler's work in particular was fuelled not only by Bühler's denunciation of Wundt's 'writing-desk experiments' but also by Bühler's usage of a philosopher who in Wundt's opinion had developed 'a psychology without psychol-ogy' (1910b: 580). Wundt wrote a long criticism of Bühler's papers, and declared the Würzburg experiments 'sham experiments'. According to Wundt, the Würzburg experiments violated all four criteria for good experimental work: 1) the observer was not able to determine the occurrence of the process to be observed, 2) the observer was not able to follow the process without disturbing it, 3) the observation was not repeatable and 4) the conditions of the occurrence of the observed process could not be varied (1908a: 329–39). Bühler replied by accusing Wundt once more of 'writing-desk' judgements (1908a), to which Wundt retorted by denying that 'the Leipzig laboratory [is] but an aggregate of desks' (1908a: 446).

The Würzburg paradigm established phenomenology firmly within experimental psychology. Despite Wundt's warnings of Husserl's alleged attempts to turn psychology into some form of logic, Külpe, Bühler and Messer would continuously rely on some of Husserl's central concepts and ideas.

Another important inroad for phenomenology into psychology was provided by Karl Jaspers. In his pre-war work on psychopathology Jaspers relied on 'the phenomenological direction of research' explicitly (e.g. Jaspers 1912). Jaspers distinguished between an 'objective' and a 'subjective' psychology: the former would study 'objective symptoms' as well as the dependence of mental life on physiological processes, the latter would investigate 'mental life as such'. Subjective psychology was close to, or even identical with, phenomenology: 'The first step [of subjective psychology] is to identify and classify mental phenomena, and to engage in this work is to bring forth "phenomenology"' (1912: 393). In his plea for subjective psychology, Jaspers used the phenomenological appeal for freedom from theory and prejudice:

We must leave aside all traditional theories, psychological constructions or materialistic mythologies of brain processes; we turn towards what we can understand, grasp, distinguish and describe in real thought. As experience teaches us, this is a very difficult task. This strange phenomenological freedom from prejudice is not an original possession but a laboursome acquisition.

(Jaspers 1912: 395)

On Jaspers' account, phenomenology had many of those 'intuitive' aspects on which its popularity during the Weimar Republic would soon rest: 'Phenomenology cannot convey its results purely discursively. The phenomenologist must count on the reader not only to *think* along, but also to *see* along . . . This seeing is not a sensory seeing but an understanding-interpretative seeing' (1912: 396). It is clear that such explicit endorsement for phenomenology from one of the key figures of *Lebensphilosophie* additionally paved the way for phenomenology into Weimar psychology.

Most important of all, however, for the outstanding position of phenomenology within Weimar psychology was the success of

Gestalt psychology. The four principal members of the Berlin School in Gestalt psychology, Wertheimer, Köhler, Koffka and Lewin, were all students of Carl Stumpf, Husserl's teacher and Brentano's disciple. Moreover, Gestalt theorists in Graz and Prague too were first- and second-generation students of Brentano (von Ehrenfels, Meinong, Benussi) (Smith 1988). Husserl's terminology did not have the same crucial position in Gestalt theory as it had in, say, Bühler's psychology of thinking, but for Gestalt theorists there certainly was a continuity between their own work and phenomenology. Thus it was not artificial for Kurt Lewin to point out in 1927 that key concepts of Gestalt theory could be mapped onto Husserl's terms 'essence' (*Sosein*) and 'phenomenological epoche':

> To infer from the experience of a single instance to the universally valid law corresponds to the inference from an '*example*' to a 'type' – a type that is invariant with respect to historico-geographical space-time co-ordinates. This progression is not comparable to the advance from several members of a set to the entire set; rather, it consists in the transition from '*this instance*' *here and now* to '*such an*' instance . . . The concept of type involved here bears a certain similarity to the notion of '*essence*' in phenomenological logic. The type is also characterised by its essence (*Sosein*) and not by its existence (*Dasein*), and the advance from the individual example to the type in the empirical sciences (and correspondingly from the individual experimental instance to the law) shows certain features equivalent to the phenomenological *epoche* (the 'bracketing' of existence').
>
> (Lewin [1927] 1992: 394)

Dilthey's return: Psychology and *Lebensphilosophie*　Not all of the major psychologists of the Weimar Republic linked their work to phenomenology, however. Indeed, some key figures, like Erich Jaensch and Felix Krüger rejected phenomenology as a 'surrogate' for scientific psychology (Krüger 1924: 37) and claimed that the unbiased description of the immediately given experience had been standard practice in experimental psychology long before Husserl (Jaensch 1927: 129). Here it is very indicative of the intellectual climate of the time, that psychologists who did not emphasise their proximity to phenomenology felt the need to stress their allegiance to the work of another pure philosopher and his psychology. And thus Weimar psychology saw the return of a project that had been pronounced dead and superfluous by a leading experimental psychologist, Hermann Ebbinghaus, in 1896: Dilthey's interpretative psychology. While it must have been shocking to older members of the experimentalists' community, it was not implausible for psychologists to return to Dilthey's suggestions. In an intellectual climate where the credibility of work in the sciences and arts depended on its proximity to *Lebensphilosophie*, Dilthey's psychology was a natural choice. After all, Dilthey had Scheler's, Spengler's and Jaspers' approval: Scheler ranked him among the forerunners of *Lebensphilosophie*, Spengler adopted his historical relativism and his criticism of experimental psychology, and Jaspers' *Psychologie der Weltanschauungen* was read as an elaboration of Dilthey's typology of worldviews.

The leading advocates of this Dilthey revival were Felix Krüger, Wundt's successor in Leipzig, and Eduard Spranger. In 1915, Krüger had still noted his scepticism with respect to Dilthey's work (1915: 113), but this caution made way to a full-fledged endorsement by 1924. In 1924, Krüger claimed that Dilthey's criticism of the method of experimental psychology had been correct and that psychologists should follow Dilthey's recommended methodology:

> Everywhere in psychology one must first precisely describe that which appears in pure form; one must compare it and analyse it as completely as possible before one undertakes to conjecture its conditions, and before one determines its laws . . . In this regard, Dilthey's methodological demands are . . . correct.
>
> (Krüger 1924: 36)

Krüger also held that a proper understanding of individuality and personality was possible only by relying on Dilthey's concept of 'psychological structures':

> His theories of the 'structural interrelation' between all mental life and certain important products of intellectual culture have not yet been exhausted as far as their truth is concerned. These theories have anticipated the main results of most recent research. These results point us to the idea that mental events – especially when they produce formations of

meaning – cannot be grasped by means of understanding, or on the basis of the prejudices of a mechanistic atomism and associationism. Mental events can be understood strictly empirically only as events of life.

(1924: 32)

Krüger applauded especially Dilthey's idea of 'the *holistic* character of mental life': 'What is given to consciousness never forms a mere aggregate. Its distinguishable parts and sides do not relate to one another in the form of sums; instead they are always combined into a whole and directly related to this whole' (1924: 33). Krüger found in Dilthey also the resources for an attack on what he regarded as the excessive intellectualism of Gestalt psychology. For Krüger, Gestalt psychology neglected the role of feelings in the structuring of experience: 'The holistic character of all experience (*Erleben*) expresses itself first and most strongly in feelings' (1924: 34). Of course such criticism was well aimed given the antirationalist thrust of Weimar culture.

Despite all this approval, Krüger did not side with Dilthey's suggestion that there could, and perhaps should, be two different brands of psychology:

Judged by the standards of science it is unacceptable that in the long run there could be several, principally different psychologies side by side . . . From the perspective of the task, there can be only *one* science of the forms and laws of mental reality.

(1924: 56)

This feeling was not shared by other disciples of Dilthey, however. Writing in 1926, the educationist-psychologist Eduard Spranger could already list five different proposals for how the two different brands of psychology should be labelled: '1. explanatory vs. interpretative psychology, 2. inductive vs. 'insight-based' [*einsichtig*] psychology, 3. psychology of elements vs. structural psychology, 4. meaning-free vs. meaning-related psychology, 5. natural-scientific vs. *geisteswissenschaftlich* psychology' (1926: 172). The last three oppositions were used by Spranger himself.

Spranger felt the need for a *geisteswissenschaftlich* psychology on the grounds that the individual and her culture were inseparably intertwined: 'Subject and object [i.e. culture] can only be thought of as related to one another. When emphasising the objective side, we speak of *Geisteswissenschaft* . . . When stressing the side of the individual subject, however, we speak of psychology.' Whereas *Geisteswissenschaft* would study either factual historical communities or else ideal norms and laws, *geisteswissenschaftlich* psychology would investigate the individual's embeddedness in communities and her ways of adhering to ideal demands. 'One sees here that psychology in this sense can only be done in close contact with objective *Geisteswissenschaft* . . . We therefore speak explicitly of *geisteswissenschaftlicher Psychologie*' (1924: 7).

Geisteswissenschaftlich psychology had been neglected in recent years, Spranger alleged. This was because modern psychology had excessively relied on natural science: it studied the relation between body and mind, in its psychophysical research it presupposed results of physics, and its concept formation was modelled on the physical sciences. By the last accusation Spranger meant that modern psychology allegedly sought to find the ultimate elements of mental life. Thus modern scientific psychology had been a 'psychology of elements', of 'mental atoms' (1924: 9).

The weakness of this type of psychological thought was most apparent to Spranger – and like-minded thinkers like Theodor Erismann (1924, 1926) and Ludwig Klages (1920) – once it was contrasted with the psychology of the poet and the political historian: 'When we try to illuminate psychologically the decision of a historical figure, we do not dissolve it into ideas, feelings and wants; we only ask for the motive which became decisive, and we situate it within a historical context of meaning and value; the rest is taken for granted unless abnormal disturbances occurred' (1924: 11).

Spranger compared the atomistic procedure of the psychology of elements with the vivisection of a frog: 'When we cut up a frog, we learn about its inner structure, and we can come to know, through conjectures, the physiological function of its organs. But we should never expect to be able to put the parts together again, and to be able to re-create the living frog. Likewise, the synthesis of mental elements into the mental whole does not capture the meaningful context of life in its relation to its whole intellectual environment' (1926: 12). With this and other analogies, Spranger argued that the natural-scientific psychology of elements depended on the psychology of structure, i.e. *geisteswissenschaftlich* psychology (1926: 19).

As seen above, Dilthey's *lebensphilosophische* emphasis on feelings could be used as a weapon against the alleged intellectualism of

Gestalt theory. Gestalt theorist themselves, however, did not present their thinking as in any way opposed to Dilthey. On the contrary, Wertheimer, Köhler and others went out of their way to hammer home that Gestalt theory was in line with the Diltheyan themes of 'wholeness', 'anti-atomism', 'type' and 'structure'. And this task of persuasion was not too difficult as this very terminology was part and parcel of Berlin Gestalt theory almost from the start. This comes out nicely in the following summary of a lecture by Wertheimer in 1913:

a Aside from chaotic, therefore not, or not properly, apprehensible impressions, the contents of our consciousness are mostly not summative, but constitute a particular characteristic 'togetherness', that is, a segregated structure, often 'comprehended' from an inner centre . . . To this the other parts of the structure are related in a hierarchical system. Such structures are to be called 'Gestalten' in a precise sense.

b Almost all impressions are grasped either as chaotic masses – a relatively seldom, extreme case – or as chaotic masses on the way to sharper formation, or as Gestalten. What is finally grasped are 'impressions of structure' [Gebildefassungen]. To these belong the objects in a broad sense of the word, as well as relational contexts [Beziehungszusammenhänge]. They are something specifically different from and more than the summative totality of the individual components. Often the 'whole' is grasped even before the individual parts enter consciousness.

c The epistemological process – knowledge in a precise sense – is very often a process of 'centring', of structuring, or of grasping that particular aspect that provides the key to an orderly whole, a unification of the particular individual parts that happen to be present.

(quoted in Ash 1985: 308)

In their public presentations of their ideas, members of the Berlin School went much further. Wertheimer typically began his papers with a criticism of how modern science had distorted experience and then went on to present Gestalt theory as the best remedy (Leichtman 1979: 48). Wertheimer and Köhler called pre-war psychology 'dead', 'dry', 'meaningless', 'empty', 'static' and 'fragmented' (Ringer 1969: 377), and Wertheimer used a Spengler-ian theme (Spengler 1918: 405) when promising a philosophy in which the world is like 'a Beethoven symphony, and we would have the possibility of grasping from a part of the whole something of the structural principles of that whole' (quoted in Ash 1985: 322).

The presentable psychologist Psychologists like Krüger, Spranger, Wertheimer and Köhler were welcomed by pure philosophy, and especially by philosophers of *Lebensphilosophie* and phenomenology. Indeed, far from being an intellectual challenge and threat for pure philosophy this type of psychology was a wonderful advertisement and an inroad for philosophy into the science faculties. In 1920 Köhler suggested an extension of Gestalt theory into physics, and claimed that there were 'suprasummative' physical processes, i.e. physical processes the quality of which could not be derived from their parts (Ash 1985: 316). Although Köhler denied that such speculations were influenced by 'romantic-philosophical' thinking, the type of natural philosophy suggested here could hardly lack success at a time when even Köhler's most outspoken psychological critic, Erich Jaensch, wanted to 'place a garland on Schelling's forgotten grave' (1927: 120). Little surprise therefore that in 1922 there was no opposition by pure philosophers to Köhler's appoint-ment as professor in philosophy and as head of the Psychological Institute. This new psychology did not even encounter opposition when in 1922 its budget was increased more than 600 per cent and came close to passing that of the Physical Institute (Ash 1980a: 286).

Given the scale of the accommodation of German psychologists, it seems only natural that in 1929 the *Gesellschaft für experimentelle Psychologie* dropped the 'experimental' from its name and added the word 'German' (Ash 1980a: 286). This would have been unthinkable twenty years earlier but now it was merely a most appropriate expression of the reshaping of psychological knowl-edge and research that had taken place. 'Experimental psychol-ogy' now rang too much of a 'natural-scientific psychology of elements'. 'Experimental psychology' reminded one too much of times when at least some philosopher/psychologists had aimed for a renewal of philosophy by means of a natural-scientific method-ology and a naturalistic theory of the human mind. No one wanted to be reminded of this past.

SUMMARY AND
CONCLUSIONS

Ohne Furcht vor dem Odium der Peinlichkeit, neigen wir
vielmehr der Ansicht zu, daß nur das Gründliche wahrhaft
unterhaltsam sei.

(Thomas Mann, *Der Zauberberg*)

Anyone writing on German philosophy is easily infected by German
scholars' passion for detail. I am no exception to this rule. Lest my
book be understood and appreciated only in my culture of origin –
'whose natives could [not] be *bored*' (James 1890: 192) – I had better
begin my conclusions with a summary of my overall argument.

In this book, I have written the history of one key episode of
modern philosophy from the viewpoint of the sociology of philosophical knowledge. In order to make plausible the suggestion that
sociological reconstructions of philosophical knowledge are possible and illuminating, I have focused on one philosophical statement of high credibility and shown in its case how, as Latour and
Woolgar once put it, 'a hard fact can be sociologically deconstructed' (1986: 107). The philosophical statement that I selected
was the claim that psychologism is a mistaken and self-refuting view,
and that Husserl (and Frege) are to be credited with having shown
this to be so. I called this statement a 'philosophical fact' because
it fulfils the criteria of 1) being widely accepted, i.e. being
incorporated into the standard textbooks, 2) being such that it
cannot be ignored or bypassed whenever one works in the respective field, and 3) being capable of use without further argument to
support new statements.

My sociological-historical account of the change in modality of
this statement followed the five-part format of SPK outlined in
Chapter 2. Given the initial identification of a philosophical fact

272

(Stage 1, Chapter 1), the next step was a return to the historical record, i.e. a return to the period in which the selected statement and its subclauses were first formulated and had a weak modality, or low plausibility (Stage 2). In my case this meant going back to German philosophy between, roughly, the 1870s and the 1920s, and identifying a series of texts that developed various accounts of what psychologism consisted of, and of who was to be regarded as a psychologistic thinker. I explained the technical content of both Frege's and Husserl's attacks on psychologism at some length (Chapter 3). Subsequently, in Stage 3, I demonstrated the interpretative flexibility of the arguments put forward against psychologism, and of the key concept of psychologism itself. I showed that there was no agreement among German philosophers between 1900 and 1914 on whether Husserl's arguments against psychologism were successful, on how psychologism was to be defined, and on who was to be judged a psychologicist (Chapters 4 and 5). In the two subsequent chapters (6 and 7), I went on to provide a sociological explanation for the existence of different interpretative strategies in terms of social interests. I described the conflict of interest between advocates and practitioners of experimental psychology and pure philosophy, and showed that moves in the language game 'refuting psychologism' typically were, by the same token, moves in the language game 'the cleansing of philosophy departments from experimental psychologists' (Stage 4). And finally, I gave a sociological explanation of why the debate over psychologism and over the philosophical status of experimental psychology ended around 1914, and why Husserl emerged as the central figure in the refutation of psychologism (Stage 5). Central in this last step, and last chapter, were the ideas that the First World War led to a redivision of labour between pure philosophy and experimental psychology, that the antiscientific mentality of the Weimar Republic weakened the support for the project of a naturalistic philosophy, and that phenomenology was more successful in adjusting to the new climate than any other philosophical school.

Obviously, philosophers and sociologists will want to know whether I take the case study reported above to have any general implications for (meta-)philosophy or the sociology of (scientific) knowledge. While I do not think that case studies can ever establish any philosophical or sociological thesis conclusively, I do believe that they may strengthen or weaken our intuitions regarding

273

substantial theoretical, philosophical and sociological issues. I shall now try to set out some of the hypotheses, criticisms and ideas that I take to be supported by the above study in this weak sense.

First and foremost, my study reinforces the notion that philosophical knowledge, like any other form of knowledge, has social variables. Sociologists of knowledge can provide sociological explanations of why one group of philosophers is more likely to accept a given belief than another group. Such explanations will invoke purposes, goals, interests, social order and social action. In proposing such explanations, sociologists do not reduce philosophical knowledge to power, and do not treat arguments as a mere ideological smokescreen for social interests. Instead, they explain the differential weighting of cognitive goals, beliefs, arguments, styles of reasoning, values and data.

Second, any case study in the sociology of knowledge can only identify some of the social variables of the knowledge under scrutiny. There are simply too many such variables. In my case study, for example, I have attended to the following social factors: the opposed professional interests of pure philosophers and experimentalists in expanding their influence within philosophy departments; the competition between different schools of pure philosophy; the mentality of the Weimar era; and adjustment strategies to a hostile intellectual environment. Other sociologists of philosophical knowledge will hopefully go further and study other social variables in these same texts, such as the social imagery used (cf. Bloor [1976] 1991), or social-psychological factors (cf. Köhnke 1986).

Third, I emphasised in Chapter 2 that a case study in the sociology of philosophical knowledge should adhere to the strong programme in the sociology of knowledge, and thus aim for symmetry regarding its explanations. In other words, the beliefs and arguments of all of the different sides in a controversy should be taken to have social variables, not just the beliefs and arguments of those who turned out to be the losers. I realise, however, that no symmetrical account of a philosophical controversy can guard against being read in a nonsymmetrical fashion by latter-day partisans of one of the philosophical positions under scrutiny. Thus, when presenting the material in this book to different audiences of philosophers, I have noticed that advocates of 'The same old story' interpret the arguments for a naturalistic philosophy as a mere smokescreen for experimental psychologists'

274

lusting for professorial chairs. Supporters of the revolt against antipsychologism, on the other hand, regard the projects for a nonexperimental, philosophical psychology as no more than badly disguised moves to turn back the clock and hinder progress. There is little, as far as I can see, sociologists of philosophical knowledge can do to stop their strong-programme explanation from being turned into a weak-programme account, according to which social factors are significant only when scientists or philosophers deviate from the path of reason.

Unfortunately, the issue of symmetry and neutrality is even more tricky than the last paragraph suggested. Indeed, there might be definite limits to this impartiality. It is relatively easy for the sociologist of knowledge to remain neutral in disputes that concern issues far removed from central tenets of the sociology of knowledge itself. For instance, the sociologist can study debates over gravity wave detectors without being drawn into the controversy herself. Impartiality is more difficult to maintain, however, once the controversy under investigation is fully, or in part, about ideas and arguments that either provide support for or undermine the sociology of knowledge itself. The case study presented here is a case in point. Many arguments used today against the 'strong programme' or 'the empirical programme of relativism' are close relatives or heirs to the arguments invented by neo-Kantians, phenomenologists and Frege against psychologism. Given my own stated adherence to the strong programme, the reader will not be surprised to learn that I am more impressed by the force of Ellis's, Lipps's and Schlick's defences of psychologism, or by Jerusalem's psychologism-cum-sociologism, than by Husserl's or Frege's attacks. Although I have taken great pains to present the positions fairly and in a balanced way, the attentive reader will undoubtedly be able to identify places where my account resembles the viewpoint of a participant in the dispute.

Fourth, my case study also has another implication for the sociology of scientific knowledge. Even the very best case studies in this field of scholarship suffer from two weaknesses: they follow traditional, whiggish history of science in focusing on the 'scientific geniuses', and they do not sufficiently explain the closure of scientific debates. The most important book of historical scholarship within the sociology of scientific knowledge, Shapin and Schaffer's *Leviathan and the Air-Pump* (1985), is a case in point. The seventeenth-century controversy over the experimental form of life is structured as a clash and power struggle between two great figures, Boyle and Hobbes. Shapin and Schaffer's treatment of these men differs from earlier history in so far as they treat them not only as geniuses of knowledge but also as skilful politicians. But they do not break with the assumption that the history of science is the history of great men. Moreover, *Leviathan and the Air-Pump* confines itself to showing that both Boyle and Hobbes developed consistent positions, and that both sought to enrol political support for their respective projects. Shapin and Schaffer do not even try to explain why Boyle ultimately triumphed over Hobbes.

However much my own work is indebted to Shapin and Schaffer's marvellous work, I feel that my study of the psychologism controversy avoids the two weaknesses mentioned. I show in some detail why the controversy ended, and why it resulted in the victory of phenomenology. I also explain that only retrospectively did the psychologism dispute become a struggle between Husserl and the rest of the philosophical community, i.e. that Husserl's emergence as the great lone fighter was an artefact of how history was rewritten by the victorious party of phenomenologists. My study suggests that the absence of closure explanations and the focus upon great men is an accidental rather than an essential feature of the recent sociology of scientific knowledge.

Finally, one way in which I motivated my project in Chapter 1 was to suggest that it is of some interest to metaphilosophical enquiries regarding the structure and causes of philosophical disagreements. In conclusion, we can now formulate a number of metaphilosophical hypotheses concerning the shape and structure of philosophical controversies. Being derived from a case study of only one controversy, these hypotheses might easily and quickly turn out to be wrong, but bold and falsifiable hypotheses are better than none. Some might also regard these hypotheses as trivial, but then in a virginal area like the metaphilosophy of philosophical knowledge this can hardly be avoided.

1 Philosophical controversies are decidedly more fuzzy than controversies in the natural sciences. Often it is only with hindsight that we can identify the members of the groups and camps that disagreed. This is because, compared with natural scientists, philosophers are much less inclined to co-operate with one another, even if the other holds a similar view with respect to the contested issue. Usually, even individuals who are on the same

side of the divide, as we see it today, can be found accusing one another of providing insufficient arguments against the common opponent, thus attacking one another for being closet advocates of the joint enemy's position. Or, to put this observation into the now popular warfare idiom: philosophers' wars are wars of all against all, rather than clashes of two armies.

2 Like controversies in the natural sciences, philosophical controversies are often cases of boundary work. Controversies in philosophy are often triggered when parts or the whole of the philosophical community feel endangered by the success and appeal of one or several antidisciplines. In such cases, philosophers then start to search for hidden tendencies in each other's work, tendencies that allegedly provide an insufficient defence against usurpation. To study German philosophy of the late nineteenth and early twentieth centuries is especially telling in this respect, not least because the Germans have a special way of doing things with words. After all, we owe to the Germans such marvels of philosophical terminology as psychologism, mathematicism, scientism, sociologism, biologism and historicism. And this list is by no means exhaustive. Typically, the criteria for attributing any of these 'isms' are highly idiosyncratic, thus ensuring that the charge can make numerous rounds.

3 The focal point of philosophical controversies can be, and typically is, a very small number of books and articles. To become such a focal point, a text must be bold in its accusations, preferably short, and highly rhetorical. The sharper the tone, and the more straightforwardly the book provides its readers with a catchphrase to which it can subsequently be reduced, the better (cf. Husserl's equation of psychologism with sceptical relativism).

4 In philosophical controversies, charges of relativism, irrationalism, total scepticism and the like occupy a much more central role than in other sciences. This is in part due to the fact that philosophical controversies are followed by a wider audience of scholars in other fields and by the public at large. Strengthening one's position in the eyes of these wider audiences by linking one's opponents' views to unreason and moral defect is a temptation that philosophers feel no need to resist.

5 Philosophical controversies are abandoned rather than resolved. They are not laid to rest because one side eventually succeeds in persuading its opponents by means of what all sides accept as facts and arguments. Rather, philosophical disputes end because

one or both sides lose interest, or because general cultural trends, political events, or death weaken or extinguish one side in the controversy.

6 The 'canon' of classical texts in philosophy is determined by the victorious parties in controversies, and is thus shaped by contingent historical factors. Because of a variety of social and political factors, we now regard Frege's and Husserl's writings as the key texts on the issue of psychologism; analytical philosophers opt more strongly for Frege, Continentalists are more interested in Husserl. It is easy to imagine, however, that history could have taken a slightly different turn, such that naturalism would have triumphed over *Lebensphilosophie*. *Ceteris paribus* we would then be reading today the writings of Jerusalem, Schulz, Stumpf and Wundt *as philosophical classics*, and Continentalists would be travelling to Japan to read Wundt's unpublished papers rather than to Louvain to study Husserl's manuscripts. Perhaps one of the most important achievements of the sociology of philosophical knowledge is indeed to remind us of this contingency.

NOTES

1 PSYCHOLOGISM: AN INTRODUCTION

1 Unless otherwise indicated, all translations from German sources are my own.
2 Two recent reruns of the familiar story in Anglo-American philosophy are Brockhaus (1991) and McCarthy (1990).
3 It also deserves to be mentioned that the exact determination of a philosopher's alleged psychologism, or then the defending of a philosopher against the charge of psychologism, can amount to a busy industry. The case of the early Husserl, prior to Frege's criticism, is the most notorious instance, but Mill scholarship has recently been catching up fast. See Christopher (1979), Musgrave (1972), Nordquest (1979), Richards (1980), Scarre (1989), Skorupski (1989).
4 I take the latter expression from Hintikka (1981).
5 Anti-Fregean and anti-Husserlian rebels have also started to rewrite the history of philosophy, bringing to light figures that were regarded as heretics as long as antipsychologism was conceived of as infallible. See e.g. Meyering's attempt to rehabilitate von Helmholtz (Meyering 1989) and Kitcher's work on Kant's transcendental psychology (Kitcher 1990).
6 Haack (1978: 238), cf. Engel (1991: 293).
7 See e.g. Metzke (1949), Hoffmeister (1955), Apel and Ludz (1958), Schmidt (1969), Brugger (1988), Müller and Halder (1988), Janssen (1989).
8 See e.g. Du Troit (1983), Dummett (1991), Føllesdal (1982), Mohanty (1964, 1982), Smith and McIntyre (1982), Kusch (1989).

2 TOWARDS A SOCIOLOGY OF PHILOSOPHICAL KNOWLEDGE

1 Much stressed by Skinner (1969).
2 See Nyíri (1974), Collins (1987, 1989), Bloor (1983, [1976] 1991), Köhnke (1986). See also Ben-David and Collins (1966), Collins and Restivo (1983). Cf. also Lamont (1987). Peckhaus (1988) points in the

same direction. Amsterdamska (1985) applies similar ideas to the history of linguistics. Obviously, a complete presentation of such enquiries would have to go back at least as far as Marx; perhaps it would even have to return to the Enlightenment or, further still, to the ancient Sophists (Hamilton 1974; Kerferd 1981). For a criticism of some earlier approaches, see Appendix 1.

3 Markle and Petersen (1981), Collins and Revisto (1983), Pinch and Bijker (1984), Collins (1983, 1985), Shapin and Schaffer (1985), Latour (1987), Hull (1988), Engelhardt and Caplan (1987), Brante and Elzinga (1990). See also Beauchamp (1987), Giere (1987), McMullin (1987).

3 PSYCHOLOGISM REFUTED?

1 For the correct view, see Pietersma (1967: 318), Philipse (1989: 70–1), Dummett (1991: 225). For the mistaken interpretation, see e.g. Føllesdal (1958: 49), Kitcher (1979: 246), Kusch (1989: 47–51).

2 See note 1 to this chapter.

3 Cf. Føllesdal (1958: 30–4).

4 For most philosophers, the parallels between Frege's and Husserl's antipsychologism are secondary issues. More important is the question whether or not their criticisms are valid. For a brief summary see Appendix 2.

For a criticism of Frege's act–content distinction, see Hannay (1979). For defences of Mill, see Bloor ([1976] 1991: 84–106), Christopher (1979), Hurford (1986), Scarre (1989: 104–25), Skorupksi (1989: 164–6). See Metcalfe (1988) for a defence of Henry L. Mansel. For criticisms of Husserl's and Frege's arguments, see Baker and Hacker (1989), Currie (1987), Føllesdal (1958), Gethmann (1989), Katz (1981: 162, 166), Massey (1991), Meiland (1976, 1977), Naess (1977), Nunn (1978), Philipse (1989), Pivcevic (1970: 38–41), Sukale (1976).

For more recent discussions of Protagorean relativism, see Burnyeat (1976), Jordan (1971), Kusch (1991a: 200–6), Matthen (1985), Meiland (1979, 1980), Siegel (1987), Smith (1985), Waterlow (1977). For further discussion on Nunn (1978), see Mackenzie (1984) and Mohanty (1982: 31). Obviously, modern discussions over whether or not human mind is 'cognitively closed' are also relevant here. See e.g. Fodor (1983: 119–25), McGinn (1989), Nagel (1986: 90–109). Cf. Unwin (1987).

5 VARIETIES OF 'PSYCHOLOGISM', 1866–1930

1 In addition to the texts cited in the last chapter, the corpus of texts I have analysed includes the following: Adickes (1923), Adler ([1925] 1982), Anschütz (1912a, 1915), Baeumker (1916), Bauch (1918, 1926, 1929), Bergmann (1909), E. Blumenthal (1904), Brentano ([1911] 1959), C. Bühler (1921), Bullaty (1906), Buzello (1911), Cassirer (1923, 1927), Clauberg and Dubislav (1923), Cohen (1902), Cohn (1902, 1904, 1908, 1913), Cornelius (1916, 1923), Dessoir (1911),

NOTES

Drews (1924), Driesch (1911, 1912), Dubs (1911), Dürr (1906), Eisler (1899, 1902, 1904, 1907, 1908, 1910), Eisler and Müller-Freienfels (1922), Eisler and Roretz (1929) Elsenhans (1897, 1898), Endriß (1921), Enoch (1893), Erdmann ([1866] 1964), Eucken (1901), Ewald (1906, 1907, 1908, 1909, 1920), Fogarasi (1916), Frischeisen-Köhler (1912, 1917–18, 1919–20), Geyser (1909a, 1916), Gomperz (1908), Groos (1912), Gutberlet (1898, 1901, 1908, 1911), Güttler (1896), Hartmann (1928), Heidegger ([1912] 1978a, [1913] 1978b), Heim (1902), Hessen (1910), Heyelmann (1921), Heymans (1922), Höfler (1905), Hofmann (1921), Honecker (1921), Hönigswald (1908, 1914b), Husserl ([1903] 1979, [1925] 1989, [1929] 1974), Jaspers (1919), Jerusalem (1905, 1914), Kern (1910), Koppelmann (1913–18), Kreis (1930), Kronfeld (1913), Külpe (1912b, 1923), Kynast (1923, 1930), Lanz (1912), Lask (1913), Lasswitz (1893), Liebert (1914, 1925, 1926), Linke (1924), Lipps (1893, 1903, 1905, 1906, 1908), Maier (1908, 1914), Marty (1908), Mauthner (1924), Medicus (1907), Meinong (1907, 1912, 1913, 1921), Messer (1908, 1912, 1913, 1914b), Michaltschew (1909), Moog (1913, 1917, 1918, 1919, 1922), Morgenstern (1920–21), Münsterberg (1900, 1908), Natorp (1901, 1912a, 1912b), Nelson ([1908] 1973a, [1914] 1973b), Palágyi (1902), Petersen (1913), Pos (1922b), Rehmke (1918), Renner (1902), Rickert (1902, 1904, 1909, 1911–12, 1913a, 1917, 1920, 1920–21, 1921, 1929), Salomon (1914), Scheler ([1925] 1982), Schultz (1903, 1907, 1922), Schwarz (1911, 1917), Seifert (1925), Spitzer (1914), Spranger (1905), Ssalagoff (1911), L. Stein (1903), Steinmann (1917), Stern (1903), Sternberg (1920, 1922), Stumpf (1892), Thormeÿer (1922), Troeltsch (1918–19), Ueberweg and Heinze (1897, 1906), Weinmann (1898), Windelband (1880, 1884, 1909, 1920), Wundt (1910b, 1914a, 1914b, 1915), Ziehen (1920).

2 *Avenarius*: Eisler (1907: 12; 1910: 1090), Eisler and Müller-Freienfels (1922: 511), Eisler and Roretz (1929: 551), Husserl ([1900] 1975: 196–213), Lanz (1912: 63), Michaltschew (1909: 178), Moog (1913: 93), Thormeÿer (1922: 157) – *Bain*: Dubs (1911: 119), Eisler (1904: 615), Husserl ([1900] 1975: 47), Külpe (1923: 88) – *Baldwin*: Eisler (1910: 1090), Eisler and Roretz (1929: 551), Külpe (1923: 89) – *Beneke*: Dessoir (1911: 180–7), Eisler (1904: 164; 1907: 12), Eisler and Müller-Freienfels (1922: 511), Enoch (1893: 512), Husserl ([1900] 1975: 47), Külpe (1923: 89), Moog (1913: 92; 1918: 304), Nelson ([1908] 1973a: 300), Windelband (1880: 393; 1884: 248), Ziehen (1920: 156) – *Bergson*: Eisler and Müller-Freienfels (1922: 511) – *Berkeley*: Eisler (1904: 615; 1907: 12; 1910: 1090), Eisler and Müller-Freienfels (1922: 511), Eisler and Roretz (1929: 551), Husserl ([1929] 1974: 178), Külpe (1923: 87), Michaltschew (1909: 237), Moog (1913: 100), Thormeÿer (1922: 157) – *Bolzano*: Michaltschew (1909: 57–63) – *Bouterwek*: Windelband (1880: 394) – *Brentano*: Cohn (1913: 227), Eisler (1899: 602; 1904: 615; 1907: 12), Ewald (1908: 228), Heidegger ([1913] 1978b: 121–4), Kreis (1930: 16), Moog (1918: 333), Thormeÿer (1922: 157), Ueberweg and Heinze (1897: 276; 1906: 332), Wundt (1910b: 519) – *Busse*: Geyser (1916: 223) – *Calker*: Windelband (1880: 390) – *Cohen*: Groos (1912: 272), Moog

281

NOTES

(1918: 342; 1919: 216–18) – *Cohn*: Michaltschew (1909: 54), Moog
(1919: 230) – *Cornelius*: Eisler (1904: 164; 1907: 12; 1910: 1090), Eisler
and Müller-Freienfels (1922: 511), Geyser (1909a: 266), Husserl
([1900] 1975: 196–213), Koppelmann (1913–18: 12), Michaltschew
(1909: 42), Moog (1919: 229), Ssalagoff (1911: 168), Thormeÿer (1922:
157), Weinmann (1898: 242) – *Cousin*: Eisler (1904: 164) – *Democritus*:
Michaltschew (1909: 29) – *Deneke*: Eisler (1910: 1090), Eisler and
Roretz (1929: 551) – *Dilthey*: Drews (1924: 4), Eisler (1907: 12), Moog
(1919: 266), Spranger (1905: 13) – *Dittes*: Ziehen (1920: 156) –
Dreßler: Ziehen (1920: 156) – *Dühring*: Ziehen (1911: 119) – *Ehrenfels*:
Ueberweg and Heinze (1897: 276) – *Eisenmeyer*: Moog (1917: 4; 1919:
213) – *Elsenhans*: Eisler (1904: 164), Ewald (1907: 290), Gutberlet
(1898: 147), Ziehen (1920: 156) – *Epicurus*: Michaltschew (1909: 29) –
Erdmann: Dubs (1911: 119), Frischeisen-Köhler (1912: 10), Geyser
(1909a: 259), Husserl ([1900] 1975: 67, 142–58), Moog (1918: 304),
Natorp (1901: 277), Ssalagoff (1911: 161), Wundt (1910b: 526) –
Fichte: Moog (1919: 216) – *Fouillée*: Eisler (1904: 164) – *Fowler*: Eisler
(1904: 164) – *Frege*: Moog (1919: 7) – *Fries*: Dessoir (1911: 180–7),
Eisler (1904: 164; 1907: 12), Moog (1918: 304), Thormeÿer (1922: 157),
Windelband (1880: 387; 1884: 248) – *Frischeisen-Köhler*: Moog (1919:
266) – *Gomperz*: Eisler (1907: 12; 1910: 1090), Eisler and Roretz (1929:
551), Messer (1908) – *Göring*: Eisler (1907: 12) – *Groos*: Cohn (1904:
138) – *Gruppe*: Ziehen (1920: 156) – *Hamilton*: Geyser (1909: 258) –
Hartmann: Ssalagoff (1911: 161) – *Hartley*: Külpe (1923: 88) – *Herbart*:
Enoch (1893: 512), Husserl ([1900] 1975: 221), Moog (1919: 222),
Wundt (1910b: 519) – *Herder*: Eisler (1910: 1090), Eisler and Müller-
Freienfels (1922: 511), Eisler and Roretz (1929: 551) – *Heymans*: Eisler
(1904: 164; 1907: 12), Eisler and Roretz (1929: 551), Geyser (1909:
266), Heidegger ([1912] 1978a: 22), Husserl ([1900] 1975: 97, 104,
110–17), Koppelmann (1923: 12), Külpe (1923: 89), Lanz (1912: 59),
Natorp (1901: 277), Ssalagoff (1911: 160), Thormeÿer (1922: 157),
Ziehen (1920: 156) – *Hillebrand*: Ueberweg and Heinze (1906: 334) –
Hobbes: Külpe (1923: 87), Stein (1903: 325) – *Höffding*: Eisler (1904:
164) – *Höfler*: Eisler (1904: 164), Geyser (1909a: 259), Husserl ([1900]
1975: 69, 97, 184–6), Koppelmann (1913: 12) – *Horwicz*: Eisler (1907:
12) – *Hume*: Eisler (1904: 164; 1907: 12; 1910: 1090), Eisler and Müller-
Freienfels (1922: 511), Eisler and Roretz (1929: 551), Geyser (1909a:
259), Husserl ([1900] 1975: 95; [1903] 1979: 223; [1929] 1974: 178),
Külpe (1923: 88), Michaltschew (1909: 237), Moog (1918: 302), Stein
(1903), Thormeÿer (1922: 157) – *Husserl*: see Chapter 4; Kreis (1930:
39), Ueberweg and Heinze (1897: 276) – *James*: Eisler (1910: 1090),
Eisler and Müller-Freienfels (1922: 511), Eisler and Roretz (1929: 551),
Geyser (1909a: 267), Groos (1912: 272), Moog (1913: 93) – *Jaspers*:
Rickert (1920–21: 34) – *Jerusalem*: Eisler (1907: 12; 1910: 1090), Eisler
and Müller-Freienfels (1922: 511), Eisler and Roretz (1929: 551),
Geyser (1909a: 259), Husserl ([1903] 1979: 223), Thormeÿer (1922:
157) – *Jevons*: Dubs (1911: 119) – *Jodl*: Eisler (1904: 164; 1907: 12; 1910:
1090), Eisler and Roretz (1929: 551), Thormeÿer (1922: 157) – *Jouffroy*:
Eisler (1904: 164; 1907: 12) – *Kant*: Dubs (1911: 119), Geyser (1909a:

282

257), Gutberlet (1911: 147), Höfler (1905: 326), Husserl ([1900] 1975: 102), Moog (1919: 216), Rehmke (1918: 152), Wundt (1914a: 312–15) – *Kleinpeter*: Michaltschew (1909: 42) – *Kraus*: Ueberweg and Heinze (1906: 332) – *Kreibig*: Geyser (1909a: 259), Ueberweg and Heinze (1906: 332) – *Krug*: Windelband (1880: 394) – *Külpe*: Cohn (1904: 139) – *Kuntze*: Ssalagoff (1911: 168) – *Laas*: Stein (1903: 325) – *Lachelier*: Eisler (1904: 164) – *Lamprecht*: Seifert (1925: 133) – *C. Lange*: Cohn (1904: 139) – *F.A. Lange*: Ewald (1920: 326), Husserl ([1900] 1975: 101–2), Moog (1913: 92), Ssalagoff (1911: 161) – *K. Lange*: Cohn (1904: 144) – *Lask*: Michaltschew (1909: 54) – *Lazarus*: Eisler (1904: 615), Windelband (1884: 248) – *Liebmann*: Husserl ([1900] 1975: 104), Ssalagoff (1911: 161) – *Lipps*: Cohn (1904: 138), Dubs (1911: 119), Dürr (1906), Eisler (1904: 615; 1907: 12), Geyser (1909a: 257), Gomperz (1908: 21), Heidegger ([1913] 1978b: 148–59), Husserl ([1900] 1975: 64–8, 76), Koppelmann (1913: 12), Külpe (1923: 89), Lipps (1903: 58), Moog (1913: 92; 1917: 10; 1918: 336; 1919: 219), Natorp (1901: 277), Nelson ([1908] 1973a: 190), Renner (1902: 20), Spranger (1905: 16), Ssalagoff (1911: 161), Thormeÿer (1922: 157), Ueberweg and Heinze (1897: 276; 1906: 332), Wundt (1910b: 515) – *Locke*: Eisler (1907: 12; 1910: 1090), Eisler and Müller-Freienfels (1922: 511), Eisler and Roretz (1929: 551), Külpe (1923: 87), Michaltschew (1909: 237), Moog (1913: 99; 1918: 302), Thormeÿer (1922: 157), Windelband (1920: 211) – *Lossius*: Ssalagoff (1911: 161) – *Lotze*: Koppelmann (1913: 13), Moog (1918: 304; 1919: 214) – *Mach*: Buzello (1911: 34–53), Dubs (1911: 118), Eisler (1904: 164; 1907: 12; 1910: 1090), Eisler and Müller-Freienfels (1922: 511), Eisler and Roretz (1929: 551), Geyser (1909a: 266), Gutberlet (1908: 4), Husserl ([1900] 1975: 196–213; [1929] 1974: 175), Messer (1914c: 373), Michaltschew (1909: 178), Moog (1913: 93; 1919: 213), Stein (1903: 325), Thormeÿer (1922: 157), Wundt (1910b: 515) – *H. Maier*: Heidegger ([1913] 1978b: 103–13) – *Marty*: Adickes (1898), Eisler (1904: 164), Heidegger ([1913] 1978b: 121–4), Ueberweg and Heinze (1897: 276; 1906: 334) – *Meinong*: Eisler (1904: 164; 1907: 12), Gomperz (1908: 30), Koppelmann (1913: 12), Lipps (1903: 69, 77), Michaltschew (1909: 79), Moog (1918: 333), Thormeÿer (1922: 157), Ueberweg and Heinze (1897: 276), Wundt (1910b: 519) – *Miklosisch*: Ueberweg and Heinze (1906: 334) – *J.S. Mill*: Dubs (1911: 119), Eisler (1899: 602; 1904: 164; 1907: 12; 1910: 1090), Eisler and Roretz (1929: 551), Geyser (1909a: 266), Gomperz (1908: 21), Husserl ([1900] 1975: 47, 64, 88–91, 97, 183–4), Koppelmann (1913: 12), Külpe (1923: 88), Moog (1918: 304), Natorp (1901: 277), Ssalagoff (1911: 161), Stein (1903: 325), Thormeÿer (1922: 157), Wundt (1910b: 523) – *Müller-Freienfels*: Eisler and Roretz (1929: 551) – *Münsterberg*: Spranger (1905: 13) – *Natorp*: Bauch (1929: 29), Moog (1917: 12; 1918: 345; 1919: 216) – *Nelson*: Moog (1918: 356) – *Nietzsche*: Moog (1919: 190) – *Ostwald*: Stein (1903: 325) – *R. Otto*: Troeltsch (1918–19: 76) – *Palágyi*: Moog (1919: 266) – *Petzoldt*: Michaltschew (1909: 178) – *Protagoras*: Eisler (1910: 1090), Stein (1903: 325) – *Reid*: Geyser (1909a: 258) – *Richter*: Geyser (1909a: 259) (1909),

NOTES

Moog (1913: 90; 1918: 353; 1919: 90, 112, 116, 122, 128, 219, 222), Nelson ([1908] 1973a: 180–1) – *Riehl*: Natorp (1901: 277) – *Rosmini*: Eisler (1899: 602; 1910: 1090) – *F.C.S. Schiller*: Eisler (1910: 1090), Eisler and Müller-Freienfels (1922: 511), Eisler and Roretz (1929: 551), Groos (1912: 272), Moog (1913: 93; 1919: 225) – *Schlick*: Eisler and Roretz (1929: 551) – *Schneider*: Enoch (1893: 512) – *Schopenhauer*: Michaltschew (1909: 40) – *Schrader*: Ziehen (1920: 156) – *Schultz*: Eisler (1910: 1090), Eisler and Müller-Freienfels (1922: 511), Eisler and Roretz (1929: 551), Spranger (1905: 14), Ziehen (1920: 156) – *Schuppe*: Eisler (1904: 164), Michaltschew (1909: 43), Natorp (1901: 277), Wundt (1910b: 529) – *Schwarz*: Eisler (1904: 615), Ueberweg and Heinze (1897: 276; 1906: 332) – *Siegel*: Eisler (1907: 12; 1910: 1090) – *Sigwart*: Dubs (1911: 119), Geyser (1909a: 258), Husserl ([1900] 1975: 69, 80, 97, 101, 105–9, 131–42, 184), Lanz (1912: 60), Moog (1918: 331), Natorp (1901: 277), Spranger (1905: 13), Ssalagoff (1911: 168), Wundt (1910b: 526) – *Simmel*: Spranger (1905: 16) – 3*Spencer*: Geyser (1909a: 266), Husserl ([1900] 1975: 90) – *Spengler*: Sternberg (1922: 107) – *Spitta*: Geyser (1909a: 268) – *Stallo*: Stein (1903: 325) – *Steinthal*: Windelband (1884: 248), Cassirer (1923: vii) – *Stöhr*: Eisler and Roretz (1929: 551), Gutberlet (1898: 139) – *Stoics*: Michaltschew (1909: 29) – *Störring*: Moog (1919: 214) – *Stumpf*: Eisler (1907: 12), Moog (1919: 230), Rehmke (1918: 158), Spranger (1905: 14), Thormeÿer (1922: 157), Ueberweg and Heinze (1906: 332), Wundt (1910b: 519) – *Suarez*: Michaltschew (1909: 29) – *Troxler*: Windelband (1880: 392) – *Uphues*: Eisler (1899: 602; 1904: 615), Ueberweg and Heinze (1897: 276; 1906: 332) – *Vaihinger*: Eisler and Müller-Freienfels (1922: 511), Husserl ([1929] 1974: 175), Liebert (1914: 63), Moog (1919: 190) – *Verworn*: Eisler (1910: 1090), Eisler and Roretz (1929: 551) – *Volkelt*: Geyser (1909a: 259) – *Wahle*: Eisler (1910: 1090), Eisler and Roretz (1929: 551) – *Weisse*: Eisler (1904: 164), Windelband (1880: 390) – *Wenzig*: Eisler and Roretz (1929: 551) – *Windelband*: Michaltschew (1909: 54), Moog (1919: 130, 222) – *Witasek*: Cassirer (1923: vi), Cohn (1904: 139), Geyser (1909a: 259) – *Wundt*: Dubs (1911: 119), Eisler (1899: 602), Geyser (1909a: 259), Heidegger ([1913] 1978b: 79–90), Husserl ([1900] 1975: 69, 80, 184), Moog (1918: 360; 1919: 101; 1922: 110–129), Natorp (1901: 277), Spranger (1905: 14), Ssalagoff (1911: 161), Windelband (1884: 248) – *Zeller*: Ssalagoff (1911: 168) – *Ziehen*: Cassirer (1927: 36), Eisler (1907: 12; 1910: 1090), Eisler and Roretz (1929: 551), Eisler and Müller-Freienfels (1922: 511), Messer (1913: 268), Michaltschew (1909: 42), Petersen (1913: 194), Thormeÿer (1922: 157).

3 Adickes, Bauch, Blumenthal, Busse, Buzello, Cassirer, Cohn, Cornelius, Dessoir, Drews, Dubs, Dürr, Eisler, Enoch, Ewald, Geyser, Gomperz, Groos, Gutberlet, Heidegger, Heim, Heinze, Höfler, Husserl, Jerusalem, Kleinpeter, Koppelmann, Kreis, Kroner, Külpe, Lanz, Lapp, Liebert, Lipps, Maier, Meinong, Messer, Michaltschew, Moog, Müller-Freienfels, Natorp, Nelson, Palágyi, Petersen, Rehmke, Renner, Rickert, Roretz, Seifert, Sigwart, Spranger, Ssalagoff, Stein, Sternberg, Stumpf, Thormeÿer, Troeltsch, Weinmann, Windelband, Wundt, Ziehen.

284

4 I have excluded Eisler's philosophical dictionaries from the data used for this figure.

5 Heim (1902), Palágyi (1902), Renner (1902), Stern (1903), Michaltschew (1909), Heidegger ([1913] 1978b), Moog (1919), Heyelmann (1921).

6 ROLE HYBRIDISATION: THE RISE OF THE NEW PSYCHOLOGY

1 For a brief summary, see Appendix 3. See also Leary (1978, 1980), Murray (1988), Verwey (1985), Boring (1950).

2 The translation is Mischel's (1970: 5), whose important paper I am here following.

3 Tr. Mischel (1970: 6).

4 Tr. Mischel (1970: 8).

5 Tr. Mischel (1970: 8).

6 In 1908 Wundt mentions art as a fourth topic (1908b: 232).

7 ROLE PURIFICATION: THE REACTION OF 'PURE PHILOSOPHY' AGAINST THE NEW PSYCHOLOGY

1 I have greatly profited from Ash (1980a, 1980b). The petition was signed by Prof. v. Aster (Munich), Dr Baensch (Strasburg), Prof. Barth (Leipzig), Prof. Bauch (Jena), Dr Bergmann (Leipzig), Dr Braun (Münster), Prof. v. Brockhoff (Kiel), Dr Brunstäd (Erlangen), Dr Brunswig (Munich), Dr von Bubnoff (Heidelberg), Dr Cassirer (Berlin), Prof. Cohen (Marburg), Prof. J. Cohn (Freiburg i. B.), Prof. Cornelius (Frankfurt a. M.), Prof. Deussen (Kiel), Prof. Dinger (Jena), Prof. Drews (Karlsruhe), Prof. Driesch (Heidelberg), Dr Eleutheropulos (Zurich), Prof. Erhardt (Rostock), Dr Ehrenberg (Heidelberg), Prof. Eucken (Jena), Dr Ewald (Vienna), Prof. Falckenberg (Erlangen), Dr A. Fischer (Munich), Dr Focke (Poznań), Prof. Freytag (Zurich), Dr Frischeisen-Köhler (Berlin), Dr Geiger (Munich), Prof. Geyser (Münster), Prof. Goedeckemeyer (Königsberg), Prof. Goldstein (Darmstadt), Dr Gomperz (Vienna), Dr Görland (Hamburg), Dr Groethuysen (Berlin), Prof. Güttler (Munich), Dr Guttmann (Wrocław), Dr Häberlin (Basle), Dr Hammacher (Bonn), Dr Hartmann (Marburg), Prof. Heman (Basle), Dr Henning (Braunschweig), Prof. Hensel (Erlangen), Dr Heyfelder (Tübingen), Prof. Hönigswald (Wrocław), Prof. Husserl (Göttingen), Dr Jacoby (Greifswald), Prof. Jerusalem (Vienna), Prof. Jodl (Vienna), Prof. Joël (Basle), Dr Kabitz (Wrocław), Prof. Kinkel (Giessen), Dr Klemm (Leipzig), Dr Köster (Munich), Dr Kroner (Freiburg i. B.), Dr Kuntze (Berlin), Prof. Lask (Heidelberg), Prof. Lasson (Berlin), Prof. Lehmann (Poznań), Prof. Leser (Erlangen), Dr Lessing (Hanover), Dr Linke (Jena), Prof. G.F. Lipps (Zurich), Prof. Medicus (Zurich), Dr Mehlis (Freiburg i. B.), Dr Menzel (Kiel), Prof.

Messer (Giessen), Dr Metzger (Leipzig), Dr Meyer (Munich), Prof. Misch (Marburg), Prof. Natorp (Marburg), Dr Nelson (Göttingen), Dr Nohl (Jena), Prof. Pfänder (Munich), Prof. v. d. Pfordten (Strasburg), Prof. Rehmke (Greifswald), Dr Reinach (Göttingen), Dr Reininger (Vienna), Prof. Rickert (Freiburg i. B.), Prof. Riehl (Berlin), Prof. Ritter (Tübingen), Dr Ruge (Heidelberg), Dr Schlick (Rostock), Prof. Schmeckel (Greifswald), Prof. F. A. Schmid (Heidelberg), Prof. H. Schneider (Leipzig), Dr Schrempf (Stuttgart), Prof. Schwarz (Greifswald), Dr Seidel (Zurich), Dr Siegel (Vienna), Prof. Simmel (Berlin), Prof. Spitta (Tübingen), Prof. Spitzer (Graz), Prof. Spranger (Leipzig), Prof. Tönnies (Kiel), Prof. Uphues (Halle), Dr Utitz (Rostock), Prof. Vaihinger (Halle), Dr Verweyen (Bonn), Prof. Wahle (Chernovtsy), Prof. Wallaschek (Vienna), Dr Weidenbach (Giessen), Prof. Wentscher (Bonn), Prof. Wernicke (Braunschweig), Prof. Willmann (Prague), Prof. Windelband (Heidelberg).

2 In passing we might note that Hensel's claim concerning an alliance between Thomists and experimental psychologists would seem to be justified by the fact that the leading neo-Thomist philosophical journal did follow the developments in psychology quite closely (Gutberlet 1891, 1892, 1896, 1898, 1901, 1904, 1907, 1908, 1910, 1911, 1913, 1917), and that the leading neo-Thomist philosopher of the day called Fechner, Lotze and Wundt 'the most important representatives of non-ecclesiastical philosophy in our time' (Gutberlet 1898: 127). Hensel's attempt to link experimental psychology to the neo-Thomists does not, however, take into account the fact that neo-Thomists were highly critical not just of the 'technomania' of experimental research (Anonymous 1903), but also opposed to the project of a 'psychology without a soul': 'What philosophical or objective value can one possibly attribute to a 'psychology without a soul'? That recently one is even proud of it . . . is a sign of the deep decay of philosophical knowledge' (Gutberlet 1898: 128).

3 In his rejoinder, Lamprecht granted that the philosopher Simmel must have a better view of philosophy's present than the cultural historian; however, he reserved the right for the latter to predict the future of philosophy based on 'the iron reservoir of historical and psychological experiences' (1913b: 423).

4 See Appendix 4. There I summarise the contributions of Fischer (1913), Frischeisen-Köhler (1913), Hillebrand (1913) and Eisenmeyer (1914).

8 WINNER TAKES ALL: *LEBENSPHILOSOPHIE* AND THE TRIUMPH OF PHENOMENOLOGY

1 For a more detailed summary and analysis of German philosophers' wartime writings, see Lübbe (1974).

2 Husserl himself did not publish any war speeches, although in public lectures he too advocated the view that a German victory would be a victory for 'the whole of humankind' ([1917] 1987: 293).

3 Wundt's one-time student and father of experimental pedagogy, Ernst Meumann, too sought to make a contribution to the war effort from perspectives provided by *Völkerpsychologie*. Meumann's paper 'Wesen und Bedeutung des Nationalgefühls' (1915) distinguished national feeling from other social phenomena like language and *Zeitgeist*, and described its different forms and ingredients. National feeling was 'the product of the total spirit of communities' rather than the product of individuals. It differed from other products of the total spirit, e.g. language, in that it had no 'objective existence' (1915: 87). National feeling existed only in and through its effects: it influenced all individuals of a given community in roughly the same way. Moreover, national feeling had two aspects, a 'content of ideas' and characteristic emotions and volitions. The upshot of Meumann's subsequent discussion of these two aspects was that German national feeling was superior to the degenerate national feelings of Germany's enemies. Two examples may suffice to illustrate Meumann's style of reasoning.

Meumann informed his readers that each national feeling comes with an understanding of the value of one's nation. He was quick to add, however, that a nation could be mistaken about its own value:

> It is not the case that *every* trait of a nation is valuable. The following list consists of items that all are specific traits of the respective nations, *although none of them is valuable*, none of them is valuable for all of mankind: the Russian people are dependent on liquor, accept their fate passively, are superstitious and practise embezzlement and misappropriation on a large scale; the French display an almost pathological vanity; and the English regard all other nations as *barbarians* and cannot bear the thought that anyone else could be their equal ... Every nation has an instinctive awareness of that which is valuable about its traits, of what is valuable for all of mankind. And such values can be found in every nation that is not degenerated or in the process of dissolving. No one can deny the German people the right to regard the following spiritual and moral values as crucial for the progress of all mankind: the German consciousness of duty, the German depth of feeling, the moral seriousness of our religiousness, the objective spirit of our science, and the power and intelligence of our organisations in the social and military domain.
>
> (1915: 91–2)

Meumann also claimed that nations differed in the extent to which their national feeling allows them to understand other nations. He suspected that no member of one nation can ever come to fully understand the national consciousness and feeling of another nation. Nevertheless, according to Meumann there was ample evidence to support the claim that Germans were unique in the world for their readiness and ability to understand other nations:

> If there is any nation in the world which has developed such 'international' understanding ... then it is us Germans. We Germans are the only nation that has a world literature, and no other nation

in the world has equally opened its national life to the arts of alien nations . . . In similar ways our science uses international research more than do the sciences in any other nation . . . I would even say this: our ability to confront other nations in an objective and open manner is immediate proof that we have a *national consciousness* which ranks *higher* than that of some other nations.

(1915: 105)

4 Scheler's strictures on 'sociologism' would be faithfully repeated and rehearsed from the 1920s onwards (Grünwald [1934] 1982; Mannheim 1931; Spranger 1930).

5 Psychotechnics was defined by Münsterberg as 'the practical application of psychology in the service of tasks set by culture' (1914: 10). In 1910 Münsterberg was the first lecturer in Germany who delivered a lecture series on applied psychology (Münsterberg 1912).

6 For a more detailed account, see Kusch (forthcoming).

BIBLIOGRAPHY

Adickes, E. (1898), Review of Marty (1897), *Berliner Literatur-Zeitung*: 155–6.

Adickes, E. (1923), 'Erich Adickes', in R. Schmidt (ed.), *Philosophie der Gegenwart in Selbstdarstellungen*, vol. 2, 2nd ed., Meiner, Leipzig (pages are not numbered consecutively.)

Adler, M. ([1925] 1982), 'Soziologie und Erkenntniskritik', in V. Meja and N. Stehr (eds.), *Der Streit um die Wissenschaftssoziologie*, vol. 1, Suhrkamp, Frankfurt am Main, 158–91.

Amsterdamska, O. (1985), 'Institutions and schools of thought: the neogrammarians', *American Journal of Sociology* 91: 332–58.

Anonymous (1903), 'Ein Experimentator über die experimentelle Psychologie', *Philosophisches Jahrbuch* 16: 267.

Anschütz, G. (1912a), 'Tendenzen im psychologischen Empirismus der Gegenwart: Eine Erwiderung auf O. Külpes Ausführungen "Psychologie und Medizin" und "Über die Bedeutung der modernen Denkpsychologie"', *Archiv für die gesamte Psychologie* 26: 189–207.

Anschütz, G. (1912b), 'Spekulative, exakte und angewandte Psychologie: Eine Untersuchung über die Prinzipien der psychologischen Erkenntnis II', *Archiv für die gesamte Psychologie*: 24: 1–30.

Anschütz, G. (1915), 'Theodor Lipps', *Archiv für die gesamte Psychologie* 34: 1–13.

Apel, M. and P. Ludz (1958), *Philosophisches Wörterbuch*, 5th ed., revised by P. Ludz, de Gruyter, Berlin.

Aschkenasy, H. (1909), 'Zur Kritik des Relativismus in der Erkenntnistheorie', *Archiv für systematische Philosophie* 15: 392–405.

Ash, M. (1980a), 'Academic politics in the history of science: experimental psychology in Germany, 1879–1941', *Central European History* 13: 255–86.

Ash, M. (1980b), 'Wilhelm Wundt and Oswald Külpe on the institutional status of psychology: an academic controversy in historical context', in W.G. Bringmann and R.D. Tweney (eds.), *Wundt Studies: A Centennial Collection*, Hogrefe, Toronto, 396–421.

Ash, M. (1985), 'Gestalt psychology: origins in Germany and reception in the United States', in C. Buxton (ed.), *Points of View in the Modern History of Psychology*, Academic Press, New York, London, 295–344.

Aster, E. v. (1908), 'Die psychologische Beobachtung und experimentelle Untersuchung von Denkvorgängen', *Zeitschrift für Psychologie und Physiologie der Sinnesorgane, I: Zeitschrift für Psychologie* 49: 56–107.

Avenarius, R. (1877), 'Über die Stellung der Psychologie zur Philosophie: Eine Antrittsvorlesung', *Vierteljahrsschrift für wissenschaftliche Philosophie* 1: 471–88.

Baeumker, C. (1916), 'Nachruf auf Oswald Külpe', *Jahrbuch der königlich bayerischen Akademie der Wissenschaften*, Franz, Munich, 73–107.

Baker, G.P. and P.M.S. Hacker (1989), 'Frege's anti-psychologism', in M.A. Notturno (ed.), *Perspectives on Psychologism*, Brill, Leiden, 74–127.

Barnes, B. (1974), *Scientific Knowledge and Sociological Theory*, Routledge & Kegan Paul, London.

Bauch, B. (1915), *Review* of Wundt (1915), *Kantstudien* 20: 305–10.

Bauch, B. (1916–17), 'Vom Begriff der Nation', *Kantstudien* 21: 138–62.

Bauch, B. (1918), 'Wahrheit und Richtigkeit (Ein Beitrag zur Erkenntnislehre)', in P. Barth et al., *Festschrift Johannes Volkelt zum 70. Geburtstag dargebracht*, Beck, Munich, 40–57.

Bauch, B. (1926), 'Logos und Psyche: Ein synthetischer Versuch', *Logos: Internationale Zeitschrift für Philosophie der Kultur* 15: 173–93.

Bauch, B. (1929), 'Bruno Bauch', in R. Schmidt (ed.), *Philosophie der Gegenwart in Selbstdarstellungen*, vol. 7, Meiner, Leipzig (pages are not numbered consecutively).

Beauchamp, T. (1987), 'Ethical theory and the problem of closure', in H. Engelhardt and A. Caplan (eds.), *Scientific Controversies: Case Studies in the Resolution and Closure of Dispute in Science and Technology*, Cambridge University Press, Cambridge, 27–48.

Bell, D. (1990), *Husserl*, Routledge, London.

Ben-David, J. and R. Collins (1966), 'Social factors in the origins of a new science: the case of psychology', *American Sociological Review* 31: 451–65.

Beneke, F.E. (1833), *Die Philosophie in ihrem Verhältnis zur Erfahrung, zur Spekulation und zum Leben dargestellt*, Mittler, Berlin.

Beneke, F.E. (1842), *System der Logik als Kunstlehre des Denkens*, Dümmler, Berlin.

Bergmann, H. (1909), *Das philosophische Werk Bernard Bolzanos*, Niemeyer, Halle.

Block, N. (1981), 'Psychologism and behaviorism', *Philosophical Review* 90: 5–43.

Bloor, D. (1973), 'Wittgenstein and Mannheim on the sociology of mathematics', *Studies in the History and Philosophy of Science* 4: 173–91.

Bloor, D. (1983), *Wittgenstein: A Social Theory of Knowledge*, Columbia University Press, New York.

Bloor, D. ([1976] 1991), *Knowledge and Social Imagery*, 2nd ed., Chicago University Press, Chicago.

Blumenthal, A. (1985a), 'Shaping a tradition: experimentalism begins', in C. Buxton (ed.), *Points of View in the Modern History of Psychology*, Academic Press, New York, 51–83.

Blumenthal, A. (1985b), 'Wilhelm Wundt: psychology as the propaedeutic science', in C. Buxton (ed.), *Points of View in the Modern History of Psychology*, Academic Press, New York, 19–49.

Blumenthal, E. (1904), 'Über den Gegenstand der Erkenntnis: Gegen Heinrich Rickert', *Abhandlungen der Fries'schen Schule. Neue Folge* 1: 343–72.

BIBLIOGRAPHY

Boehm, M. (1914), *Review* of Natorp (1913), *Archiv für die gesamte Psychologie* 31: 47–8.

Boring, E.G. (1950), *A History of Experimental Psychology*, Appleton-Century-Crofts, New York.

Brante T. and A. Elzinga (1990), 'Towards a theory of scientific controversies', *Science Studies* 2: 33–46.

Braunshausen, N. (1911), 'Eine Krisis der experimentellen Psychologie?', *Archiv für die gesamte Psychologie* 21: 1–10.

Brentano, F. ([1866] 1968), 'Die 25 Habilitationsthesen', in F. Brentano, *Über die Zukunft der Philosophie*, ed. by O. Kraus, Meiner, Hamburg, 133–42.

Brentano, F. ([1874] 1924), *Psychologie vom empirischen Standpunkt*, vol. 1, ed. by O. Kraus, Meiner, Hamburg.

Brentano, F. ([1893] 1968), 'Über die Zukunft der Philosophie', in F. Brentano, *Über die Zukunft der Philosophie*, ed. by O. Kraus, Meiner, Hamburg, 1–82.

Brentano, F. (1895), *Meine letzten Wünsche für Österreich*, Cotta, Stuttgart.

Brentano, F. ([1911] 1959), *Psychologie vom empirischen Standpunkt*, vol. 2, 2nd ed., edited by O. Kraus, Meiner, Hamburg.

Bringmann, W.G. and G. Ungerer (1980a), 'Experimental vs. educational psychology: Wilhelm Wundt's letters to Ernst Meumann', *Psychological Research* 42: 57–73.

Bringmann, W.G. and G. Ungerer (1980b), 'The foundation of the Institute for Experimental Psychology at Leipzig University', *Psychological Research* 42: 5–18.

Brockhaus, R. (1991), 'Realism and psychologism in 19th century logic', *Philosophy and Phenomenological Research* 51: 493–523.

Brugger, W. (ed.) (1988), *Philosophisches Wörterbuch*, 19th ed., Herder, Freiburg.

Bühl, G. (1966), 'Die algebraische Logik im Urteil der deutschen Philosophie des 19. Jahrhunderts', *Kantstudien* 57: 360–72.

Bühler, C. (1921), 'Die Aufgaben der Ästhetik', *Kantstudien* 26: 403–15.

Bühler, K. (1907), 'Tatsachen und Probleme zu einer Psychologie der Denkvorgänge: I. Über Gedanken', *Archiv für die gesamte Psychologie* 9: 297–365.

Bühler, K. (1908a), 'Nachtrag: Antwort auf die von W. Wundt erhobenen Einwände gegen die Methode der Selbstbeobachtung an experimentell erzeugten Erlebnissen', *Archiv für die gesamte Psychologie* 12: 93–123.

Bühler, K. (1908b), 'Tatsachen und Probleme zu einer Psychologie der Denkvorgänge: II. Über Gedankenzusammenhänge', *Archiv für die gesamte Psychologie*, 12: 1–23.

Bühler, K. (1908c), 'Tatsachen und Probleme zu einer Psychologie der Denkvorgänge: III. Über Gedankenerinnerungen', *Archiv für die gesamte Psychologie* 12: 24–92.

Bühler, K. (1909), 'Zur Kritik der Denkexperimente', *Zeitschrift für Psychologie und Physiologie der Sinnesorgane, I. Abteilung. Zeitschrift für Psychologie* 51: 108–18.

Bühler, K. (1926), 'Die Krise der Psychologie', *Kantstudien* 31: 455–526.

Bullaty, E. (1906), 'Erkenntnistheorie und Psychologie', *Archiv für systematische Philosophie* 12: 169–208, 285–335.

Burgert, H. (1925), 'Zur Kritik der Phänomenologie', *Philosophisches Jahrbuch* 38: 226–30.

Burnyeat, M.F. (1976), 'Protagoras and self-refutation in Plato's Theaetetus', *Philosophical Review* 85: 172–95.

Busse, L. (1894), *Philosophie und Erkenntnistheorie*, vol. 1, Hirzel, Leipzig.

Busse, L. (1903), Review of Husserl ([1900, 1901] 1975, 1984), *Zeitschrift für Psychologie und Physiologie der Sinnesorgane* 33: 153–7.

Buzello, H. (1911), 'Kritische Untersuchung von Ernst Mach's Erkenntnistheorie', *Kantstudien*, supp. vol. 23, Reuther & Reichardt, Berlin.

Bynum, T.W. (1972), 'On the life and work of Gottlob Frege', in Frege (1972), 1–54.

Callon, M. and J. Law (1982), 'On interests and their transformation: enrolment and counter-enrolment', *Social Studies of Science* 12: 615–25.

Callon, M., J. Law and A. Rip (1986), 'Glossary', in M. Callon, J. Law and A. Rip (eds.), *Mapping the Dynamics of Science and Technology*, Macmillan, London, xvi–xvii.

Carnap, R. (1950), *Logical Foundations of Probability*, Routledge & Kegan Paul, London.

Cassirer, E. (1918), *Kants Leben und Lehre*, Cassirer, Berlin.

Cassirer, E. (1920), *Das Erkenntnisproblem in der Philosophie und Wissenschaft der neueren Zeit*, vol. 3, Cassirer, Berlin.

Cassirer, E. (1921), *Zur Einsteinschen Relativitätstheorie*, Cassirer, Berlin.

Cassirer, E. (1923), *Philosophie der symbolischen Formen*, vol. 1: *Die Sprache*, Cassirer, Berlin.

Cassirer, E. (1925a), 'Paul Natorp', *Kantstudien* 30: 273–98.

Cassirer, E. (1925b), *Philosophie der symbolischen Formen*, vol. 2: *Das mythische Denken*, Cassirer, Berlin.

Cassirer, E. (1927), 'Erkenntnistheorie nebst den Grenzfragen der Logik und Denkpsychologie', in W. Moog (ed.), *Jahrbücher der Philosophie: Eine kritische Übersicht der Philosophie der Gegenwart*, vol. 3, Liebing, Würzburg, 31–92, 333–4.

Cassirer, E. (1929), *Philosophie der symbolischen Formen*, vol. 3: *Phänomenologie der Erkenntnis*, Cassirer, Berlin.

Cassirer, E. (1932), *Die Philosophie der Aufklärung*, Mohr, Tübingen.

Chisholm, R. (1966), *Theory of Knowledge*, Prentice-Hall, Englewood Cliffs, N.J.

Christopher, D. (1979), 'Husserl and Mill: a rejoinder', *Mill News Letter* 14: 12–17.

Churchland, P. (1987), 'Epistemology in the age of neuroscience', *Journal of Philosophy* 84: 544–53.

Clauberg, K.W. and W. Dubislav (1923), *Systematisches Wörterbuch der Philosophie*, Meiner, Leipzig.

Cohen, H. (1866), 'Die platonische Ideenlehre psychologisch entwickelt', *Zeitschrift für Völkerpsychologie und Sprachwissenschaft* 4: 403–64.

Cohen, H. (1868), 'Mythologische Vorstellungen von Gott und Seele, psychologisch entwickelt', *Zeitschrift für Völkerpsychologie und Sprachwissenschaft* 5: 396–434.

Cohen, H. (1902), *Logik der reinen Erkenntnis*, Cassirer, Berlin.

BIBLIOGRAPHY

Cohn, J. (1902), 'Der psychische Zusammenhang bei Münsterberg', *Vierteljahrsschrift für wissenschaftliche Philosophie und Soziologie* 26: 1–20.
Cohn, J. (1904), 'Psychologische oder kritische Begründung der Ästhetik', *Archiv für Philosophie. Neue Folge* 10: 131–59.
Cohn, J. (1908), *Voraussetzungen und Ziele des Erkennens*, Engelmann, Leipzig.
Cohn, J. (1913), 'Grundfragen der Psychologie', in M. Frischeisen-Köhler (ed.), *Jahrbücher der Philosophie: Eine kritische Übersicht der Philosophie der Gegenwart*, vol. 1, Mittler, Berlin, 200–35, 374–5.
Cohn, J. (1914–15), 'Widersinn und Bedeutung des Krieges', *Logos. Internationale Zeitschrift für Philosophie der Kultur* 5: 125–44.
Cohn, J. (1923–24), 'Über einige Grundfragen der Psychologie', *Logos. Internationale Zeitschrift für Philosophie der Kultur* 12: 50–87.
Collins, H.M. (1981a), 'Stages in the empirical programme of relativism', *Social Studies of Science* 11: 3–10.
Collins, H.M. (1981b), 'What is TRASP? The radical programme as a methodological imperative', *Philosophy of the Social Sciences* 11: 215–24.
Collins, H.M. (1983), 'An empirical relativist programme in the sociology of scientific knowledge', in K. Knorr-Cetina and M. Mulkay (eds.), *Science Observed: Perspectives on the Social Study of Science*, Sage, London, 85–113.
Collins, H.M. (1985), *Changing Order: Replication and Induction in Scientific Practice*, Sage, London.
Collins, R. (1987), 'A micro-macro theory of intellectual creativity: the case of German idealist philosophy', *Sociological Theory* 5: 47–69.
Collins, R. (1989), 'Towards a theory of intellectual change: the social causes of philosophies', *Science, Technology, and Human Values* 14: 107–40.
Collins, R. and S. Restivo (1983), 'Robber barons and politicians in mathematics: a conflict model of science', *The Canadian Journal of Sociology* 8: 199–227.
Cornelius, H. (1906), 'Psychologische Prinzipienfragen: I. Psychologie und Erkenntnistheorie', *Zeitschrift für Psychologie und Physiologie der Sinnesorgane, I. Abteilung. Zeitschrift für Psychologie* 42: 401–13.
Cornelius, H. (1916), *Transcendentale Systematik: Untersuchungen zur Begründung der Erkenntnistheorie*, Reinhard, Munich.
Cornelius, H. (1923), 'Hans Cornelius', in R. Schmidt (ed.), *Philosophie der Gegenwart in Selbstdarstellungen*, vol. 2, 2nd ed., Meiner, Leipzig (pages are not numbered consecutively).
Cristaudo, W. (1991), 'Heidegger and Cassirer: being, knowing and politics', *Kantstudien* 82: 469–83.
Currie, G. (1987), 'Remarks on Frege's conception of inference', *Notre Dame Journal of Formal Logic* 28: 55–68.
Cussins, A. (1987), 'Varieties of psychologism', *Synthese* 70: 123–54.
Danziger, K. (1979), 'The positivist repudiation of Wundt', *Journal of the History of the Behavioral Sciences* 15: 205–30.
Danziger, K. (1980a), 'The history of introspection reconsidered', *Journal of the History of the Behavioral Sciences* 16: 241–62.
Danziger, K. (1980b), 'Wundt's psychological experiment in the light of his philosophy of science', *Psychological Research* 42: 109–22.

Danziger, K. (1990), *Constructing the Subject: Historical Origins of Psychological Research*, Cambridge University Press, Cambridge.

Dessoir, M. (1911), *Abriß einer Geschichte der Psychologie*, Winter, Heidelberg.

Dessoir, M. (1916), *Kriegspsychologische Betrachtungen*, Hirzel, Leipzig.

Dilthey, W. ([1894] 1974), 'Ideen über eine beschreibende und zergliedernde Psychologie', in W. Dilthey, *Gesammelte Schriften V*, ed. by G. Misch, Teubner, Stuttgart, 136–240.

Dilthey, W. (1911), 'Die Typen der Weltanschauung und ihre Ausbildung in den metaphysischen Systemen', in W. Dilthey et al., *Weltanschauung*, Reichl & Co., Berlin, 1–51.

Dilthey, W. and P. Yorck von Wartenburg (1923), *Briefwechsel zwischen Wilhelm Dilthey und dem Grafen Paul Yorck v. Wartenburg 1877–1897*, Niemeyer, Halle a. S.

Dippe, A. (1895), *Sozialismus und Philosophie auf den deutschen Universitäten*, Hirzel, Leipzig.

Dorsch, F. (1963), *Geschichte und Probleme der angewandten Psychologie*, Huber, Berne.

Drews, A. (1924), 'Arthur Drews', in R. Schmidt (ed.), *Philosophie der Gegenwart in Selbstdarstellungen*, vol. 5, Meiner, Leipzig (pages are not numbered consecutively).

Driesch, H. (1911), 'Über die Bedeutung einer Philosophie der Natur für die Ethik', in W. Dilthey et al., *Weltanschauung*, Reichl & Co., Berlin, 189–216.

Driesch, H. (1912), *Ordnungslehre*, Diederichs, Jena.

Drüe, H. (1963), *Edmund Husserls System der phänomenologischen Psychologie*, Walter de Gruyter, Berlin.

Du Troit, A. (1983), 'The critique of psychologism in its historical and philosophical setting', *South African Journal of Philosophy* 2: 72–84.

Dubs, A. (1911), *Das Wesen des Begriffs und des Begreifens: Ein Beitrag zur Orientierung in der wissenschaftlichen Weltanschauung*, Niemeyer, Halle.

Dummett, M. (1973), *Frege: Philosophy of Language*, Duckworth, London.

Dummett, M. (1978), *Truth and Other Enigmas*, Duckworth, London.

Dummett, M. (1981), *The Interpretation of Frege's Philosophy*, Duckworth, London.

Dummett, M. (1991), *Frege and Other Philosophers*, Clarendon Press, Oxford.

Dürr, E. (1903), 'Über die Frage des Abhängigkeitsverhältnisses der Logik von der Psychologie', *Archiv für die gesamte Psychologie* 1: 527–44.

Dürr, E. (1906), *Review* of Lipps (1905), *Archiv für die gesamte Psychologie* 7: 265–78.

Ebbinghaus, H. (1885), *Über das Gedächtnis*, Duncker & Humblot, Leipzig.

Ebbinghaus, H. (1896), 'Über erklärende und beschreibende Psychologie', *Zeitschrift für Psychologie und Physiologie der Sinnesorgane* 9: 161–205.

Ebbinghaus, H. (1907), 'Psychologie', in W. Dilthey et al., *Systematische Philosophie*, Teubner, Berlin and Leipzig, 173–246.

Eisenmeyer, J. (1914), *Die Psychologie und ihre zentrale Stellung in der Philosophie*, Niemeyer, Halle a. S.

Eisler, R. (1899), *Wörterbuch der philosophischen Begriffe und Ausdrücke*, Mittler & Sohn, Berlin.

Eisler, R. (1902), *Wundts Philosophie und Psychologie in ihren Grundlehren dargestellt*, Barth, Leipzig.

Eisler, R. (1904), *Wörterbuch der philosophischen Begriffe und Ausdrücke*, 2nd ed., Mittler & Sohn, Berlin.

Eisler, R. (1907), *Einführung in die Erkenntnistheorie*, Barth, Leipzig.

Eisler, R. (1908), *Grundlagen der Philosophie des Geisteslebens*, Barth, Leipzig.

Eisler, R. (1910), *Wörterbuch der philosophischen Begriffe und Ausdrücke*, 3rd ed., Mittler & Sohn, Berlin.

Eisler, R. and R. Müller-Freienfels (1922), *Handwörterbuch der Philosophie*, 2nd ed., revised by R. Müller-Freienfels, Mittler & Sohn, Berlin.

Eisler, R. and K. Roretz (1929), *Wörterbuch der philosophischen Begriffe historisch-quellenmässig bearbeitet*, vol. 2, 4th ed., revised by K. Roretz, Mittler & Sohn, Berlin.

Elias, N. (1978), *Über den Prozeß der Zivilisation: Soziogenetische und psychogenetische Untersuchungen*, Suhrkamp, Frankfurt am Main.

Ellis, B. (1979), *Rational Belief Systems*, Rowman & Littlefield, Totowa, N.J.

Ellis, B. (1990), *Truth and Objectivity*, Blackwell, Oxford.

Elsenhans, T. (1897), 'Das Verhältnis der Logik zur Psychologie', *Zeitschrift für Philosophie und philosophische Kritik* 109: 195–212.

Elsenhans, T. (1898), Review of Krüger (1896), *Zeitschrift für Philosophie und philosophische Kritik* 111: 164–6.

Elsenhans, T. (1906), *Fries und Kant. Ein Beitrag zur Geschichte und zur systematischen Grundlegung der Erkenntnistheorie: II. Kritisch-systematischer Teil*, Töpelmann, Giessen.

Elsenhans, T. (1915), 'Phänomenologie, Psychologie, Erkenntnistheorie', *Kantstudien* 20: 224–75.

Elsenhans, T. (1917–18), 'Phänomenologie und Empirie', *Kantstudien* 22: 243–61.

Endriß, K.F. (1921), Review of Moog (1919), *Kantstudien* 26: 193–4.

Engel, P. (1991), *The Norm of Truth*, Toronto University Press, Toronto.

Engelhardt, H. and A. Caplan (1987), 'Patterns of controversy and closure: the interplay of knowledge, values, and political forces', in H. Engelhardt and A. Caplan (eds.), *Scientific Controversies: Case Studies in the Resolution and Closure of Dispute in Science and Technology*, Cambridge University Press, Cambridge, 1–23.

Enoch, W. (1893), Review of Schwarz (1892), *Philosophische Monatshefte* 29: 322–30.

Enoch, W. (1894). 'Transzendentalpsychologie: Eine kritische Studie', *Philosophische Monatshefte* 30: 506–34.

Erdmann, B. (1892), *Logische Elementarlehre*, Niemeyer, Halle.

Erdmann, B. (1907), *Logische Elementarlehre*, 2nd, revised edition, Niemeyer, Halle.

Erdmann, J.E. (1866), *Grundriß der Geschichte der Philosophie*, Hertz, Berlin.

Erismann, T. (1924), *Die Eigenart des Geistigen: Induktive und einsichtige Psychologie*, Quelle & Meyer, Leipzig.

Erismann, T. (1926), 'Erklären und Verstehen in der Psychologie', *Archiv für die gesamte Psychologie*, 55: 111–136.

Erklärung (1931), 'Erklärung des Deutschen Lehrervereins zur Stellung der Psychologie an den deutschen Hochschulen', *Archiv für die gesamte Psychologie* 79: 575–6.

Eucken, R. (1896), *Der Kampf um einen geistigen Lebensinhalt: Neue Grundlagen einer Weltanschauung*, Veit & Co., Leipzig.

Eucken, R. (1901), 'Thomas von Aquino und Kant: Ein Kampf zweier Welten', *Kantstudien* 6: 1–18.

Ewald, O. (1906), *Kants Methodologie in ihren Grundzügen: Eine erkenntnistheoretische Untersuchung*, Hofmann, Berlin.

Ewald, O. (1907), 'Die deutsche Philosophie im Jahre 1906', *Kantstudien* 12: 273–302.

Ewald, O. (1908), 'Die deutsche Philosophie im Jahre 1907', *Kantstudien* 13: 197–237.

Ewald, O. (1909), 'Die deutsche Philosophie im Jahre 1908', *Kantstudien* 14: 353–91.

Ewald, O. (1920), 'Welche wirklichen Fortschritte hat die Metaphysik seit Hegels und Herbarts Zeiten in Deutschland gemacht?', *Kantstudien* supp. vol. 53, Reuther & Reichardt, Berlin.

Farias, V. (1987), *Heidegger und der Nationalsozialismus*, Fischer, Frankfurt am Main.

Faust, A. (1927), *Heinrich Rickert und seine Stellung innerhalb der deutschen Philosophie der Gegenwart*, Mohr, Tübingen.

Fechner, G.T. (1860), *Elemente der Psychophysik*, 2 vols., Breitkopf und Härtel, Leipzig.

Fischer, A. (1913), 'Philosophie und Psychologie: Eine prinzipielle Betrachtung zu einer aktuellen Frage der Fortbildung der Hochschule', *Die deutsche Schule* 17: 338–47.

Fodor, J. (1983), *The Modularity of Mind*, MIT Press, Cambridge, Mass.

Fogarasi, A. (1916), 'Das Prinzip der Ergänzung in der Geschichtslogik', *Kantstudien* 21: 270–93.

Føllesdal, D. (1958), *Husserl und Frege: Ein Beitrag zur Beleuchtung der Entstehung der phänomenologischen Philosophie*, Aschehoug, Oslo.

Føllesdal, D. (1982), 'Husserl's notion of noema', in H. Dreyfus (ed.), *Husserl. Intentionality and Cognitive Science*, MIT Press, Cambridge, Mass., 73–80.

Forman, P. (1971) 'Weimar culture, causality, and quantum theory, 1918–1927: adaptation by German physicists and mathematicians to a hostile intellectual environment', *Historical Studies in the Physical Sciences* 3: 1–115.

Foucault, M. (1984), *The Archaeology of Knowledge*, tr. by A.M. Sheridan Smith, Tavistock, London.

Frede, M. (1987), *Essays in Ancient Philosophy*, University of Minnesota Press, Duluth.

Frede, M. (1988), 'The history of philosophy as a discipline', *Journal of Philosophy* 85: 666–72.

Frege, G. (1879), *Begriffsschrift, eine der arithmetischen nachgebildete Formelsprache des reinen Denkens*, Nebert, Halle.

Frege, G. ([1884] 1934), *Grundlagen der Arithmetik*, Marcus, Wrocław.

Frege, G. (1893), *Grundgesetze der Arithmetik, begriffsschriftlich abgeleitet*, vol. 1, Pohle, Jena.

BIBLIOGRAPHY

Frege, G. (1894), Review of Husserl (1891b), *Zeitschrift für Philosophie und philosophische Kritik* 103: 313–32.

Frege, G. (1969), *Nachgelassene Schriften*, ed. by G. Gabriel et al., Meiner, Hamburg.

Frege, G. (1972), *Conceptual Notation and Related Articles*, tr. and ed. by T.W. Bynum, Clarendon Press, Oxford.

Frege, G. (1983), *Nachgelassene Schriften*, ed. by H. Hermes, F. Kambartel and F. Kaulbach, 2nd ed., Meiner, Hamburg.

Friedell, E. (1931), *Kulturgeschichte der Neuzeit*, vol. 2, DTV, Munich, 1976.

Frischeisen-Köhler, M. (1912), *Wissenschaft und Wirklichkeit*, Teubner, Leipzig.

Frischeisen-Köhler, M. (1913), 'Philosophie und Psychologie', *Die Geisteswissenschaften* 1: 371–3, 400–3.

Frischeisen-Köhler, M. (1917–18), 'Philosophie und Pädagogik', *Kantstudien* 22: 27–80.

Frischeisen-Köhler, M. (1919–20), 'Georg Simmel', *Kantstudien* 24: 1–51.

Frischeisen-Köhler, M. (1921), 'Philosophie des Lebens', *Kantstudien* 26: 112–38.

Fuller, S. (1988), *Social Epistemology*, Indiana University Press, Bloomington.

Gabriel, G. (1986), 'Frege als Neukantianer', *Kantstudien* 77: 84–101.

Gadamer, H.-G. (1975), *Wahrheit und Methode*, 4th ed., Mohr, Tübingen.

Gadamer, H.-G. (1977), *Philosophische Lehrjahre*, Klostermann, Frankfurt am Main.

Gassen, K. and M. Landmann (eds.) (1956), *Buch des Dankes an Georg Simmel: Briefe, Erinnerungen, Bibliographie*, Duncker & Humblot, Berlin.

Geiger, M. (1913), 'Philosophie und Psychologie an den deutschen Universitäten', *Süddeutsche Monatshefte* 10,2: 752–5.

Gethmann, C.F. (1989), 'Phänomenologische Logikfundierung', in C. Jamme and O. Pöggeler (eds.), *Phänomenologie im Widerstreit: Zum 50. Todestag Edmund Husserls*, Suhrkamp, Frankfurt am Main, 192–212.

Geuter, Ulfried (ed.) (1986), *Daten zur Geschichte der deutschen Psychologie*, Hogrefe, Göttingen.

Geyser, J. (1909a), *Grundlagen der Logik und Erkenntnistheorie*, Schöningh, Münster.

Geyser, J. (1909b), 'Logistik und Relationslogik', *Philosophisches Jahrbuch* 22: 123–43.

Geyser, J. (1916), *Neue und alte Wege der Philosophie*, Schöningh, Münster.

Giere, R. (1987), 'Controversies involving science and technology: a theoretical perspective', in H. Engelhardt and A. Caplan (eds.), *Scientific Controversies: Case Studies in the Resolution and Closure of Dispute in Science and Technology*, Cambridge University Press, Cambridge, 125–50.

Gjertsen, D. (1989), *Science and Philosophy: Past and Present*, Penguin, London.

Goldschmidt, R.H. (1912), 'Bericht über den V. Kongress für experimentelle Psychologie, Berlin vom 16.–19 April 1912', *Archiv für die gesamte Psychologie* 24: 71–97.

Gomperz, H. (1908), *Weltanschauungslehre: Ein Versuch die Hauptprobleme der allgemeinen theoretischen Philosophie geschichtlich zu entwickeln und sachlich zu bearbeiten*, vol. 2: *Noologie, Erste Hälfte: Einleitung und Semasiologie*, Eugen Diederichs, Jena.

Gracia, J. (1992), *Philosophy and its History: Issues in Philosophical Historiography*, State University of New York Press, Albany, N.Y.

Green, K. (1986), 'Psychologism and anti-realism', *Australasian Journal of Philosophy* 64: 488–500.

Groos, K. (1912), 'Untersuchungen über den Aufbau der Systeme: IV. Die Behandlung kantischer Dualismen durch die unmittelbaren Nachfolger Kants', *Zeitschrift für Psychologie und Physiologie der Sinnesorgane, I. Abteilung. Zeitschrift für Psychologie* 60: 1–25.

Grünwald, E. ([1934] 1982), 'Wissenssoziologie und Erkenntniskritik', in V. Meja and N. Stehr (eds.), *Der Streit um die Wissenssoziologie*, vol. 2: *Rezeption und Kritik der Wissenssoziologie*, Suhrkamp, Frankfurt am Main, 748–55.

Gutberlet, C. (1891), 'W. Wundt's System der Philosophie', *Philosophisches Jahrbuch* 4: 281–96, 341–59.

Gutberlet, C. (1892), 'Die Willensfreiheit und die physiologische Psychologie', *Philosophisches Jahrbuch* 5: 172–87.

Gutberlet, C. (1896), 'Ist die Seele Tätigkeit oder Substanz?' *Philosophisches Jahrbuch* 9: 1–17, 133–70.

Gutberlet, C. (1898), 'Die "Krisis in der Psychologie"', *Philosophisches Jahrbuch* 11: 1–19, 121–46.

Gutberlet, C. (1901), 'Eine neue aktualistische Seelentheorie', *Philosophisches Jahrbuch* 14: 353–65.

Gutberlet, C. (1904), Review of Wundt (1903), *Philosophisches Jahrbuch* 17: 324–31.

Gutberlet, C. (1907), Review of Möbius (1907), *Philosophisches Jahrbuch* 20: 93–6.

Gutberlet, C. (1908), 'Der gegenwärtige Stand der psychologischen Forschung', *Philosophisches Jahrbuch* 21: 1–32.

Gutberlet, C. (1910), 'Experimentelle Pädagogik', *Philosophisches Jahrbuch* 23: 3–22.

Gutberlet, C. (1911), 'Religionspsychologie', *Philosophisches Jahrbuch* 24: 147–76.

Gutberlet, C. (1913), 'Differenzielle Psychologie', *Philosophisches Jahrbuch* 26: 1–21.

Gutberlet, C. (1917), 'Die experimentelle Psychologie im Dienste des Lebens', *Philosophisches Jahrbuch* 30: 131–71.

Güttler, K. (1896), *Psychologie und Philosophie*, Piloty & Löhle, Munich.

Haack, S. (1978), *Philosophy of Logics*, Cambridge University Press, Cambridge.

Habermas, J. (1973), *Erkenntnis und Interesse*, 2nd ed., Suhrkamp, Frankfurt am Main.

Hamburg, C.H. (1964), 'A Cassirer-Heidegger Seminar', *Philosophy and Phenomenological Research* 25: 208–22.

Hamilton, P. (1974), *Knowledge and Social Structure: An Introduction to the Classical Argument in the Sociology of Knowledge*, Routledge & Kegan Paul, London.

BIBLIOGRAPHY

Hannay, A. (1979), 'The "what" and the "how"', in D.F. Gustafson and B. Tapscott (eds.), *Body, Mind, and Method*, Reidel, Dordrecht, 17–36.

Harman, G. (1973), *Thought*, Princeton University Press, Princeton.

Hartmann, N. (1928), 'Max Scheler', *Kantstudien* 33: ix–xvi.

Heidegger, M. ([1912] 1978a), 'Neue Forschungen über Logik', in M. Heidegger, *Frühe Schriften*, ed. by F.-W. von Herrmann, *Gesamtausgabe*, vol. 1, Klostermann, Frankfurt am Main, 17–43.

Heidegger, M. ([1913] 1978b) 'Die Lehre vom Urteil im Psychologismus: Ein kritisch-positiver Beitrag zur Logik,' in M. Heidegger, *Frühe Schriften*, ed. by F.-W. von Herrmann, *Gesamtausgabe*, vol. 1, Klostermann, Frankfurt am Main, 59–188.

Heidegger, M. (1914–15), 'Die Lehre vom Urteil im Psychologismus', *Zeitschrift für Philosophie und philosophische Kritik* 155 (1914): 148–72; 156 (1915): 41–78.

Heidegger, M. ([1916] 1978c), 'Die Kategorien- und Bedeutungslehre des Duns Scotus', in M. Heidegger, *Frühe Schriften*, ed. by F.-W. von Herrmann, *Gesamtausgabe*, vol. 1, Klostermann, Frankfurt am Main, 189–411.

Heidegger, M. (1927), *Sein und Zeit*, Niemeyer, Tübingen.

Heidegger, M. (1981), *Aristoteles, Metaphysik Q 1–3. Von Wesen und Wirklichkeit der Kraft: Vorlesungen 1931*, ed. by H. Hüni, *Gesamtausgabe*, vol. 33, Klostermann, Frankfurt am Main.

Heidegger, M. (1991), *Kant und das Problem der Metaphysik*, ed. by F.-W. von Herrmann, *Gesamtausgabe*, vol. 3, Klostermann, Frankfurt am Main.

Heim, K. (1902), *Psychologismus oder Antipsychologismus? Entwurf einer erkenntnistheoretischen Fundamentierung der modernen Energetik*, Schwetschke, Berlin.

Hellpach, W. (1906), 'Universität und Psychologie', *Die Zukunft* 57: 103–8.

Hensel, P. (1909), 'Die Aussichten der Privatdozenten für Philosophie', *Frankfurter Zeitung*, 29 July 1909: 1–2.

Hensel, P. (1913), 'In Sachen der Psychophysik und in eigener Sache', *Frankfurter Zeitung*, 24 July 1913: 1–2.

Hepp, C. (1987), *Avantgarde: Moderne Kunst, Kulturkritik und Reformbewegungen nach der Jahrhundertwende*, DTV, Munich.

Hessen, S. (1910), Review of Michaltschew (1909), *Kantstudien* 15: 326–31.

Heyelmann, G. (1921), *Über das Problem des Psychologismus in der modernen Logik*, Fieseler, Bonn.

Heymans, G. (1905), *Die Gesetze und Elemente des wissenschaftlichen Denkens: Ein Lehrbuch der Erkenntnistheorie in Grundzügen*, vol. 1, 2nd, revised edition, Barth, Leipzig.

Heymans, G. (1911), *Das künftige Jahrhundert der Psychologie*, Barth, Leipzig.

Heymans, G. (1922), 'G. Heymans', in R. Schmidt (ed.), *Philosophie der Gegenwart in Selbstdarstellungen*, vol. 3, Barth, Leipzig (pages are not numbered consecutively).

Hillebrand, F. (1913), 'Die Aussperrung der Psychologie', *Zeitschrift für Psychologie und Physiologie der Sinnesorgane, I. Abteilung. Zeitschrift für Psychologie* 67: 1–21.

Hintikka, J. (1981), 'Semantics: a revolt against Frege', in G. Fløistad and

BIBLIOGRAPHY

G.H. von Wright (eds.), *Contemporary Philosophy: A New Survey*, vol. 1: *Philosophy of Language/Philosophy of Logic*, Nijhoff, The Hague, 57–82.

Hoffmeister, J. (ed.) (1955), *Wörterbuch der philosophischen Begriffe*, 2nd ed., Meiner, Hamburg.

Höfler, A. (1905), 'Sind wir Psychologisten?', *Atti del V Congresso Internazionale di Psicologia*, Forzani, Rome, 322–8.

Hofmann, P. (1921), *Die Antinomie im Problem der Gültigkeit*, de Gruyter, Berlin.

Holzhey, H. (1986), *Der Marburger Neukantianismus in Quellen*, 2 vols., Schwabe, Basle.

Honecker, M. (1921), *Gegenstandslogik und Denklogik*, Dümmler, Berlin.

Hönigswald, R. (1908), 'Zum Begriff der kritischen Erkenntnistheorie', *Kantstudien* 13: 409–56.

Hönigswald, R. (1914a), *Die Skepsis in Philosophie und Wissenschaft*, Vandenhoeck & Ruprecht, Göttingen.

Hönigswald, R. (1914b), 'Über Thomas Hobbes' systematische Stellung', *Kantstudien* 19: 19–35.

Hönigswald, R. (1931), *Grundfragen der Erkenntnistheorie: Kritisches und Systematisches*, Mohr, Tübingen.

Hoorn, W. van and T. Verhave (1980), 'Wundt's changing conceptions of a general and theoretical psychology', in W. G. Bringmann and R. D. Tweney (eds.), *Wundt Studies: A Centennial Collection*, Hogrefe, Toronto, 71–113.

Horwicz, A. (1882), *Review* of *Philosophische Studien* I, *Philosophische Monatshefte* 18: 497–502.

Hull, D.L. (1988), *Science as a Process: An Evolutionary Account of the Social and Conceptual Development of Science*, Chicago University Press, Chicago.

Hurford, J.R. (1986), *Language and Number*, Blackwell, Oxford.

Husserl, E. ([1891a] 1979), Review of Schröder (1890), in E. Husserl, *Aufsätze und Rezensionen (1890–1910), mit ergänzenden Texten*, ed. by B. Rang, Husserliana XXII, Nijhoff, The Hague, 3–43.

Husserl, E. ([1891b] 1970), 'Philosophie der Arithmetik: Logische und psychologische Untersuchungen', in E. Husserl, *Philosophie der Arithmetik*, ed. by L. Eley, Husserliana XII, Nijhoff, The Hague, 5–283.

Husserl, E. ([1900] 1975), *Logische Untersuchungen*, vol. 1: *Prolegomena zur reinen Logik*, ed. by E. Holenstein, Husserliana XVIII, Nijhoff, The Hague.

Husserl, E. ([1901] 1984), *Logische Untersuchungen*, vol. 2: *Untersuchungen zur Phänomenologie und Theorie der Erkenntnis*, ed. by U. Panzer, Husserliana XIX, Nijhoff, The Hague.

Husserl, E. ([1903] 1979), 'Bericht über deutsche Schriften zur Logik in den Jahren 1895–99', in E. Husserl, *Aufsätze und Rezensionen (1890–1910)*, ed. by B. Rang, Husserliana XXII, Nijhoff, The Hague, 162–258.

Husserl, E. ([1911] 1987), 'Philosophie als strenge Wissenschaft', in E. Husserl, *Aufsätze und Vorträge (1911–1921)*, Husserliana XXV, ed. by T. Nenon and H.R. Sepp, Kluwer, Dordrecht, 3–62.

Husserl, E. ([1913] 1950), *Ideen zu einer reinen Phänomenologie und phänomenologischen Philosophie. Erstes Buch: Allgemeine Einführung in die reine Phänomenologie*, Husserliana III, ed. by W. Biemel, Nijhoff, The Hague.

BIBLIOGRAPHY

Husserl, E. ([1917] 1987), 'Fichtes Menschheitsideal', in E. Husserl, *Aufsätze und Vorträge (1911–1921)*, Husserliana XXV, ed. by T. Nenon and H. R. Sepp, Kluwer, Dordrecht, 267–93.

Husserl, E. ([1925] 1989), 'Über die Reden Gotamo Buddhos', in E. Husserl, *Aufsätze und Vorträge (1922–37)*, Husserliana XXVII, ed. by T. Nenon and H. R. Sepp, Kluwer, Dordrecht, 125–81.

Husserl, E. ([1929] 1974), *Formale und transzendentale Logik*, ed. by P. Janssen, Husserliana XVII, Nijhoff, The Hague.

Husserl, E. ([1931] 1989), 'Phänomenologie und Anthropologie', in E. Husserl, *Aufsätze und Vorträge (1922–37)*, Husserliana XXVII, ed. by T. Nenon and H. R. Sepp, Kluwer, Dordrecht, 164–181.

Husserl, E. (1939), 'Entwurf einer "Vorrede" zu den "Logischen Untersuchungen" (1913)', *Tijdschrift voor Philosophie* 1: 106–33, 319–39.

Illemann, W. (1932), *Husserls vor-phänomenologische Philosophie*, Hirzel, Leipzig.

Jaensch, E. (1927), 'Die Psychologie in Deutschland und die inneren Richtlinien ihrer Forschungsarbeit', in W. Moog (ed.), *Jahrbücher der Philosophie: Eine kritische Übersicht der Philosophie der Gegenwart*, vol. 3, Liebing, Würzburg, 93–168, 334–40.

James, W. (1890), *The Principles of Psychology*, vol. 1, Dover, New York, 1950.

Janssen, F. (1917), 'Psychologie und Militär', *Zeitschrift für Pädagogische Psychologie und experimentelle Pädagogik* 18: 97–109.

Janssen, P. (1989), 'Psychologismus', in J. Ritter and K. Gründer (eds.), *Historisches Wörterbuch der Philosophie*, vol. 7, Wissenschaftliche Buchgesellschaft Darmstadt, Schwabe, Basle, 1675–8.

Jaspers, K. (1912), 'Die phänomenologische Forschungsrichtung in der Psychopathologie', *Zeitschrift für die gesamte Neurologie und Psychiatrie* 9, 391–408.

Jaspers, K. (1919), *Psychologie der Weltanschauungen*, Springer, Berlin.

Jaspers, K. (1957), 'Philosophical autobiography', in P.A. Schilpp (ed.), *The Philosophy of Karl Jaspers*, Open Court, La Salle, Ill., 5–94.

Jeffrey, R. (1989), *Formal Logic: Its Scope and Limits*, McGraw-Hill, New York.

Jerusalem, W. (1905), *Der kritische Idealismus und die reine Logik: Ein Ruf im Streite*, Braumüller, Vienna.

Jerusalem, W. (1914), 'Psychologen und Philosophen', *Die Zukunft* 88: 85–97.

Jordan, J.N. (1971), 'Protagoras and relativism: criticisms good and bad', *Southwestern Journal of Philosophy*: 7–29.

Kant, I. ([1783] 1979), *Prolegomena zu einer jeden künftigen Metaphysik*, ed. by S. Dietzsch, Reclam, Leipzig.

Katz, J.J. (1981), *Language and Other Abstract Objects*, Rowman & Littlewood, Totawa, N.J.

Kerferd, G.B. (1981), *The Sophistic Movement*, Cambridge University Press, Cambridge.

Kern, B. (1910), *Das Erkenntnisproblem und seine kritische Lösung*, Hirschwald, Berlin.

Kern, I. (1964), *Husserl und Kant: Eine Untersuchung über Husserls Verhältnis zu Kant und zum Neukantianismus*, Phänomenologica 16, Nijhoff, The Hague.

BIBLIOGRAPHY

Kitcher, Pa. (1990), *Kant's Transcendental Psychology*, Oxford University Press, Oxford.

Kitcher, Ph. (1979), 'Frege's epistemology', *Philosophical Review* 86: 235–62.

Klages, L. (1920), *Prinzipien der Charakterologie*, 2nd ed., Barth, Leipzig.

Kleinpeter, H. (1913), *Der Phänomenalismus*, Barth, Leipzig.

Kockelmans, J. J. (1967), *Edmund Husserl's Phenomenological Psychology: A Historico-Critical Study*, Duquesne University Press, Pittsburgh, Pa.

Köhnke, K. (1986), *Entstehung und Aufstieg des Neukantianismus: Die deutsche Universitätsphilosophie zwischen Idealismus und Positivismus*, Suhrkamp, Frankfurt am Main.

Koppelmann, W. (1913–18), *Untersuchungen zur Logik der Gegenwart*, 2 vols., Reuther & Reichard, Berlin.

Kraft, W. (1973), *Spiegelung der Jugend*, Suhrkamp, Frankfurt am Main.

Kreis, F. (1930), *Phänomenologie und Kritizismus*, Heidelberger Abhandlungen zur Philosophie und ihrer Geschichte 21, Mohr, Tübingen.

Kreiser, L. and G. Grosche (1983), 'Einleitung zur Nachschrift einer Vorlesung und Protokolle mathematischer Vorträge Freges', in Frege (1983), 326–42.

Kroner, R. (1909), 'Über logische und ästhetische Allgemeingültigkeit', *Zeitschrift für Philosophie und philosophische Kritik* 134: 231–66; 135: 10–36, 216–57.

Kronfeld, A. (1913), 'Über Windelbands Kritik am Phänomenalismus', *Archiv für die gesamte Psychologie* 26: 382–413.

Krüger, F. (1896), *Ist Philosophie ohne Psychologie möglich?*, Ackermann, Munich.

Krüger, F. (1915), *Über Entwicklungspsychologie: Ihre sachliche und geschichtliche Notwendigkeit*, Engelmann, Leipzig.

Krüger, F. (1924), 'Der Strukturbegriff in der Psychologie', in K. Bühler (ed.), *Bericht über den VIII. Kongreß für experimentelle Psychologie in Leipzig vom 18.–21. April 1923*, Fischer, Jena, 31–56.

Külpe, O. (1893), *Grundriss der Psychologie auf experimenteller Grundlage dargestellt*, Engelmann, Leipzig.

Külpe, O. (1894), 'Aussichten der experimentellen Psychologie', *Philosophische Monatshefte* 30: 281–94.

Külpe, O. (1912a), 'Psychologie und Medizin', *Zeitschrift für Psychopathologie* 1: 187–267.

Külpe, O. (1912b), 'Über die moderne Psychologie des Denkens', *Internationale Monatsschrift für Wissenschaft, Kultur und Technik* 6: 1069–110.

Külpe, O. (1915), *Die Ethik und der Krieg*, Hirzel, Leipzig.

Külpe, O. (1920), *Die Philosophie der Gegenwart in Deutschland*, 6th ed., Teubner, Leipzig.

Külpe, O. (1923), *Vorlesungen über Logik*, ed. by O. Selz, Hirzel, Leipzig.

Kusch, M. (1989), *Language as Calculus vs. Language as Universal Medium: A Study in Husserl, Heidegger and Gadamer*, Synthese Library, Kluwer, Dordrecht.

Kusch, M. (1991a), *Foucault's Strata and Fields: An Investigation into Archaeological and Genealogical Science Studies*, Synthese Library, Kluwer, Dordrecht.

BIBLIOGRAPHY

Kusch, M. (1991b), 'The sociological deconstruction of philosophical facts: the case of "psychologism"', *Science Studies* 4: 45–60.

Kusch, M. (1994), 'The criticism of Husserl's arguments against psychologism in German philosophy 1901–1920', in L. Haaparanta (ed.), *Mind, Meaning and Mathematics: Essays on the Philosophical Views of Husserl and Frege*, Kluwer, Dordrecht, 51–84.

Kusch, M. (forthcoming), 'Recluse, interlocutor, interrogator: the imageless thought controversy revisited'.

Kynast, R. (1923), 'Zum Gedankengang der Kritik der reinen Vernunft', *Kantstudien* 28: 1–15.

Kynast, R. (1930), *Logik und Erkenntnistheorie der Gegenwart*, Junker & Dünnhaupt, Berlin.

Lakatos, I. (1978), *Philosophical Papers*, vol. 1: *The Methodology of Scientific Research Programmes*, Cambridge University Press, Cambridge.

Lamont, M. (1987), 'How to become a dominant French philosopher: the case of Jacques Derrida', *American Journal of Sociology* 93: 584–622.

Lamprecht, K. (1896), *Alte und neue Richtungen in der Geschichtswissenschaft*, Gaertner, Berlin.

Lamprecht, K. ([1904] 1971), *Moderne Geschichtswissenschaft*, Weidmann, Zurich.

Lamprecht, K. (1913a), 'Eine Gefahr für die Geisteswissenschaften', *Die Zukunft* 83: 16–24.

Lamprecht, K. (1913b), 'Eine Gefahr für die Geisteswissenschaften: Antwort an Herrn Prof. Dr. Georg Simmel', *Die Zukunft* 83: 421–9.

Lange, F.A. (1866), *Geschichte des Materialismus und Kritik seiner Bedeutung in der Gegenwart*, Baedecker, Iserlohn.

Lanz, H. (1912), 'Das Problem der Gegenständlichkeit in der modernen Logik', *Kantstudien*, supp. vol. 26, Reuther & Reichardt, Berlin.

Lapp, A. (1913), *Die Wahrheit: Ein erkenntnistheoretischer Versuch orientiert an Rickert, Husserl und an Vaihinger's 'Philosophie des Als-Ob'*, Spemann, Stuttgart.

Lask, E. (1913), Review of Michaltschew (1909), *Zeitschrift für Philosophie und philosophische Kritik* 150: 190–4.

Lasswitz, K. (1893), Review of Stumpf (1892), *Philosophische Monatshefte* 29: 466–73.

Latour, B. (1983), 'Give me a laboratory and I will raise the world', in K. Knorr-Cetina and M. Mulkay (eds.), *Science Observed: Perspectives on the Social Study of Science*, Sage, London, 141–70.

Latour, B. (1987), *Science in Action*, Harvard University Press, Cambridge, Mass.

Latour, B. and S. Woolgar (1986), *Laboratory Life: The Construction of Scientific Facts*, 2nd ed., Princeton University Press, Princeton, N.J.

Lazarus, M. and H. Steinthal (1860), 'Einleitende Gedanken über Völkerpsychologie, als Einladung zu einer Zeitschrift für Völkerpsychologie und Sprachwissenschaft', *Zeitschrift für Völkerpsychologie und Sprachwissenschaft* 1: 1–73.

Leary, D.E. (1978), 'Philosophical development of the conception of psychology in Germany, 1780–1850', *Journal of the History of Behavioral Sciences* 14: 113–21.

Leary, D.E. (1980), 'German Idealism and the development of psychology in the 19th century', *Journal of the History of Philosophy* 18: 299–317.

Lehmann, R. (1906), 'Der Rückgang der Universitätsphilosophie', *Die Zukunft* 54: 483–7.

Leichtman, M. (1979), 'Gestalt theory and the revolt against positivism', in *Psychology in Social Context*, ed. by Allan R. Buss, Irvington, New York, 47–75.

Lessing, H.-U. (1985), 'Briefe an Dilthey anläßlich der Veröffentlichung seiner 'Ideen über eine beschreibende und zergliedernde Psychologie', *Dilthey-Jahrbuch für Philosophie und Geschichte der Geisteswissenschaften* 3: 193–232.

Levi, I. (1980), *The Enterprise of Knowledge*, The MIT Press, Cambridge, Mass.

Lewalter, E. ([1930] 1982), 'Wissenssoziologie und Marxismus', in V. Meja and N. Stehr (eds.), *Der Streit um die Wissenssoziologie*, vol. 2: *Rezeption und Kritik der Wissenssoziologie*, Suhrkamp, Frankfurt am Main, 551–83.

Lewin, K. ([1927] 1992), 'Law and experiment in psychology', *Science in Context* 5: 385–416.

Liebert, A. (1914), 'Das Problem der Geltung', *Kantstudien*, supp. vol. 32, Reuther & Reichardt, Berlin.

Liebert, A. (1924), *Die geistige Krisis der Gegenwart*, Heise, Berlin.

Liebert, A. (1925), 'Zu Wilhelm Diltheys Gesammelten Schriften und Briefen', *Kantstudien* 30: 471–83.

Liebert, A. (1926), 'Zur Logik der Gegenwart', *Kantstudien* 31: 297–310.

Linke, P. (1924), 'Die Existentialtheorie der Wahrheit und der Psychologismus der Geltungslogik', *Kantstudien* 29: 395–415.

Lipps, T. (1880), 'Die Aufgabe der Erkenntnistheorie und die Wundt'sche Logik I', *Philosophische Monatshefte* 16: 529–39.

Lipps, T. (1893), *Grundzüge der Logik*, Leopold Voss, Hamburg.

Lipps, T. (1901), *Psychologie, Wissenschaft und Leben*, Franz, Munich.

Lipps, T. (1903), 'Fortsetzung der "Psychologischen Streitpunkte"', *Zeitschrift für Psychologie und Physiologie der Sinnesorgane* 31: 47–78.

Lipps, T. (1905), 'Inhalt und Gegenstand, Psychologie und Logik', *Sitzungsberichte der philosophisch-philologischen und der historischen Klasse der Königlich Bayerischen Akademie der Wissenschaften* 4: 511–669.

Lipps, T. (1906), 'Die Wege der Psychologie', *Archiv für die gesamte Psychologie* 6: 1–21.

Lipps, T. (1908), *Philosophie und Wirklichkeit*, Winter, Heidelberg.

Lübbe, H. (1974), *Politische Philosophie in Deutschland*, DTV, Munich.

Löwith, K. (1986), *Mein Leben in Deutschland vor und nach 1933: Ein Bericht*, Metzler, Stuttgart.

McCarthy, M. (1990), *The Crisis of Philosophy*, SUNY Press, Albany, N.Y.

McDowell, J. (1977), 'On the sense and reference of a proper name', *Mind* 86: 159–85.

McGinn, C. (1989), 'Can we solve the mind–body problem?', *Mind* 98: 349–66.

Mach, E. ([1904] 1988), *Die Mechanik in ihrer Entwicklung*, Akademie Verlag, Berlin.

BIBLIOGRAPHY

MacKenzie, D. (1981), *Statistics in Britain, 1865–1930: The Social Construction of Scientific Knowledge*, Edinburgh University Press, Edinburgh.

Mackenzie, J.D. (1984), 'Functionalism and Psychologism', *Dialogue* XXIII: 239–48.

McKinsey, M. (1983), 'Psychologism in semantics', *Canadian Journal of Philosophy* 13: 1–26.

McMullin, E. (1987), 'Scientific controversy and its termination', in H. Engelhardt and A. Caplan (eds.), *Scientific Controversies: Case Studies in the Resolution and Closure of Dispute in Science and Technology*, Cambridge University Press, Cambridge, 49–91.

Macnamara, J. (1986), *A Border Dispute: The Place of Logic in Psychology*, The MIT Press, Cambridge, Mass.

Maier, H. (1908), *Psychologie des emotionalen Denkens*, Mohr, Tübingen.

Maier, H. (1914), 'Logik und Psychologie', in *Festschrift für Alois Riehl, von Freunden und Schülern zu seinem siebzigsten Geburtstage dargebracht*, Niemeyer, Halle, 311–78.

Mannheim, K. (1925), *Konservatismus: Ein Beitrag zur Soziologie des Wissens*, edited by D. Kettler, V. Meja and N. Stehr, Suhrkamp, Frankfurt am Main, 1984.

Mannheim, K. ([1931] 1960), 'Sociology of knowledge', in K. Mannheim, *Ideology and Utopia: An Introduction to the Sociology of Knowledge*, Routledge & Kegan Paul, London, 237–80.

Marbe, K. (1898), Review of Rickert (1896), *Zeitschrift für Philosophie und philosophische Kritik* 111: 266–79.

Marbe, K. (1901), *Experimentell-psychologische Untersuchungen über das Urteil: Eine Einleitung in die Logik*, Engelmann, Leipzig.

Marbe, K. (1912), 'Die Bedeutung der Psychologie für die übrigen Wissenschaften und die Praxis', *Fortschritte der Psychologie und ihrer Anwendungen* 1: 5–82.

Marbe, K. (1913), *Die Aktion gegen die Psychologie: Eine Abwehr*, Teubner, Leipzig.

Marbe, K. (1922), 'Die Stellung und Behandlung der Psychologie an den Universitäten', in K. Bühler (ed.), *Bericht über den VII. Kongreß für experimentelle Psychologie in Marburg vom 20.–23. April 1921*, Fischer, Jena, 150–1.

Marbe, K. (1961), 'Autobiography', in C. Murchison (ed.), *A History of Psychology in Autobiography*, vol. 3, Russell & Russell, New York, 181–213.

Markle, G. and J. Petersen (1981), 'Controversies in science and technology: a protocol for comparative research', *Science, Technology, and Human Values* 6: 25–30.

Marty, A. (1896), 'Was ist Philosophie?', in A. Marty, *Gesammelte Schriften*, vol. 1, Niemeyer, Halle a.S., 69–93.

Marty, A. (1897), *Was ist Philosophie?*, Calve, Prague.

Marty, A. (1908), *Untersuchungen zur Grundlegung der allgemeinen Grammatik und Sprachphilosophie*, Niemeyer, Halle.

Massey, G.J. (1991), 'Some reflections on psychologism', in T. Seebohm, D. Føllesdal and J. Mohanty (eds.), *Phenomenology and the Formal Sciences*, Kluwer, Dordrecht, 183–94.

BIBLIOGRAPHY

Matthen, M. (1985), 'Perception, relativism, and truth: reflections on Plato's Theaetetus 152–160', *Dialogue* 24: 33–58.

Mauthner, F. (1924), *Wörterbuch der Philosophie: Neue Beiträge zu einer Kritik der Sprache*, 3 vols., 2nd ed., Meiner, Leipzig.

Medicus, F. (1907), 'Kant und die gegenwärtige Aufgabe der Logik', *Kantstudien* 12: 50–74.

Mehlis, G. (1914–15), 'Der Sinn des Krieges', *Logos. Internationale Zeitschrift für Philosophie der Kultur* 5: 252–66.

Meiland, J. (1976), 'Psychologism in logic: Husserl's critique', *Inquiry* 19: 325–39.

Meiland, J. (1977), 'Concepts of relative truth', *The Monist* 60: 568–82.

Meiland, J. (1979), 'Is Protagorean relativism self-refuting?', *Grazer Philosophische Studien* 9: 51–68.

Meiland, J. (1980), 'On the paradox of cognitive relativism', *Metaphilosophy* 11: 115–26.

Meinong, A. (1902), 'Über Annahmen', *Zeitschrift für Psychologie und Physiologie der Sinnesorgane, I. Abteilung. Zeitschrift für Psychologie*, supp. vol. 2, Barth, Leipzig.

Meinong, A. ([1904] 1913), 'Über Gegenstandstheorie', in A. Meinong, *Abhandlungen zur Erkenntnistheorie und Gegenstandstheorie*, Barth, Leipzig, 483–530.

Meinong, A. (1907), *Über die Stellung der Gegenstandstheorie im System der Wissenschaften*, Voigtländer, Leipzig.

Meinong, A. (1912), 'Für die Psychologie und gegen den Psychologismus in der allgemeinen Werttheorie', *Logos. Internationale Zeitschrift für Philosophie der Kultur* 3: 1–14.

Meinong, A. (1913), *Abhandlungen zur Erkenntnistheorie und Gegenstandstheorie*, Barth, Leipzig.

Meinong, A. (1965), *Philosophenbriefe*, ed. by R. Kindinger, Akademische Druck- und Verlagsanstalt, Graz.

Messer, A. (1906), 'Experimentell-psychologische Untersuchungen über das Denken', *Archiv für die gesamte Psychologie* 8: 1–224.

Messer, A. (1907), 'Bemerkungen zu meinen 'Experimentell-psychologischen Untersuchungen über das Denken', *Archiv für die gesamte Psychologie* 10: 409–28.

Messer, A. (1908), 'Heinrich Gomperz' Weltanschauungslehre', *Kantstudien* 13: 275–304.

Messer, A. (1912), 'Husserls Phänomenologie in ihrem Verhältnis zur Psychologie', *Archiv für die gesamte Psychologie* 22: 117–29.

Messer, A. (1913), 'Die experimentelle Psychologie im Jahre 1911', in M. Frischeisen-Köhler (ed.), *Jahrbücher der Philosophie: Eine kritische Übersicht der Philosophie der Gegenwart*, vol. 1, Mittler, Berlin, 236–69, 375–7.

Messer, A. (1914a), 'Der Krieg und die Schule', *Zeitschrift für Pädagogische Psychologie und experimentelle Pädagogik* 15: 529–40.

Messer, A. (1914b), 'Die Bedeutung der Psychologie für Pädagogik, Medizin, Jurisprudenz und Nationalökonomie', in M. Frischeisen-Köhler (ed.), *Jahrbücher der Philosophie: Eine kritische Übersicht der Philosophie der Gegenwart*, vol. 2, Mittler, Berlin, 183–218, 232–7.

Messer, A. (1914c), *Psychologie*, Deutsche Verlags-Anstalt, Stuttgart.

BIBLIOGRAPHY

Messer, A. (1914d), 'Husserls Phänomenologie in ihrem Verhältnis zur Psychologie. (Zweiter Aufsatz)', *Archiv für die gesamte Philosophie* 32: 52–67.

Messer, A. (1922), in R. Schmidt (ed.), *Philosophie der Gegenwart in Selbstdarstellungen*, vol. 3, Barth, Leipzig (pages are not numbered consecutively).

Metcalfe, J.F. (1988), 'Husserl and early Victorian philosophical logic', *Eidos* 7: 15–33.

Metzke, E. (1949), *Handlexikon der Philosophie*, Kerle, Heidelberg.

Meumann, E. (1915), 'Das Nationalgefühl', *Zeitschrift für Pädagogische Psychologie und experimentelle Pädagogik* 16: 84–106.

Meyer (1911), 'Experimentelle Analyse psychischer Vorgänge beim Schießen mit der Handfeuerwaffe', *Archiv für die gesamte Psychologie* 20: 397–413.

Meyer (1912a), 'Psychologische und militärische Ausbildung', *Zeitschrift für Pädagogische Psychologie und experimentelle Pädagogik* 13: 81–5.

Meyer (1912b), 'Vorschläge zu Versuchen im Anschluss an meinen Aufsatz "Experimentelle Analyse psychischer Vorgänge beim Schießen mit der Handfeuerwaffe"', *Archiv für die gesamte Psychologie* 22: 47–9.

Meyering, T. C. (1989), *Historical Roots of Cognitive Science*, Kluwer, Dordrecht.

Michaltschew, D. (1909), *Philosophische Studien: Beiträge zur Kritik des modernen Psychologismus*, Engelmann, Leipzig.

Mill, J.S. (1979), *An Examination of Sir William Hamilton's Philosophy*, in *The Collected Works of John Stuart Mill*, vol. 9, edited by J.M. Robson, Routledge and University of Toronto Press, London and Toronto.

Misch, G. (1931), *Lebensphilosophie und Phänomenologie*, Teubner, Leipzig.

Mischel, T. (1970), 'Wundt and the conceptual foundations of psychology', *Philosophy and Phenomenological Research* 31: 1–26.

Möbius, P. J. (1907), *Die Hoffnungslosigkeit aller Psychologie*, Marhold, Halle.

Mohanty, J.J. (1964), *Edmund Husserl's Theory of Meaning*, Nijhoff, The Hague.

Mohanty, J.J. (1982), *Husserl and Frege*, Indiana University Press, Bloomington.

Moog, W. (1913), 'Zur Kritik der Erkenntnistheorie', *Zeitschrift für Philosophie und philosophische Kritik* 149: 86–106.

Moog, W. (1917), 'Die Stellung der Psychologie in der Philosophie', *Zeitschrift für Philosophie und philosophische Kritik* 163: 1–16.

Moog, W. (1918), 'Die Kritik des Psychologismus durch die moderne Logik und Erkenntnistheorie', *Archiv für die gesamte Psychologie* 37: 301–62.

Moog, W. (1919), *Logik, Psychologie und Psychologismus*, Niemeyer, Halle.

Moog, W. (1922), *Die deutsche Philosophie des 20. Jahrhunderts in ihren Hauptrichtungen*, Enke, Stuttgart.

Morgenstern, G. (1920–21), Review of Moog (1919), *Annalen der Philosophie und philosophischen Kritik* 2: 539–42.

Mortan, G. (1961), 'Einige Bemerkungen zur Überwindung des Psychologismus durch Gottlob Frege und Edmund Husserl', *Atti del XII Congresso Internazionale di Filosofia*, vol. 12, Sansoni, Florence, 327–34.

Müller, M. and A. Halder (eds.) (1988), *Philosophisches Wörterbuch*, revised by H. Brockard et al., Herder, Freiburg.

Müller-Freienfels, R. (1923), *Die Philosophie des Zwanzigsten Jahrhunderts in ihren Hauptzügen*, Mittler, Berlin.

Münsterberg, H. (1889), 'Einleitung', in H. Münsterberg, *Beiträge zur Experimentellen Psychologie*, vol. 1, Mohr, Freiburg i. Br., 1–63.

Münsterberg, H. (1900), *Grundzüge der Psychologie*, Barth, Leizpig.

Münsterberg, H. (1908), *Philosophie der Werte*, Barth, Leipzig.

Münsterberg, H. (1912), *Psychologie und Wirtschaftsleben: Ein Beitrag zur angewandten Experimental-Psychologie*, Barth, Leipzig.

Münsterberg, H. (1914), *Grundzüge der Psychotechnik*, Barth, Leipzig.

Murray, D.J. (1988), *A History of Western Psychology*, 2nd ed., Prentice Hall, Englewood Cliffs, N.J.

Musgrave, A. (1972), 'George Boole and psychologism', *Scientia* 107: 593–608.

Naess, A. (1977), 'Husserl on the apodictic evidence of ideal laws', in J. N. Mohanty (ed.), *Readings on Edmund Husserl's 'Logical Investigations'*, Nijhoff, The Hague, 57–75.

Nagel, T. (1986), *The View from Nowhere*, Oxford University Press, Oxford.

Natorp, P. (1887), 'Über objektive und subjektive Begründung der Erkenntnis I', *Philosophische Monatshefte* 23: 257–86.

Natorp, P. (1888), *Einleitung in die Psychologie nach kritischer Methode*, Mohr, Freiburg.

Natorp, P. (1901), 'Zur Frage der logischen Methode: Mit Beziehung auf Edm. Husserls "Prolegomena zur reinen Logik"', *Kantstudien* 6: 270–83.

Natorp, P. (1910), *Die logischen Grundlagen der exakten Wissenschaften*, Teubner, Leipzig.

Natorp, P. (1912a), *Allgemeine Psychologie nach kritischer Methode*, Mohr, Tübingen.

Natorp, P. (1912b), 'Das akademische Erbe Hermann Cohens', *Frankfurter Zeitung*, 12 October 1912: 1–2.

Natorp, P. (1912c), 'Kant und die Marburger Schule', *Kantstudien* 17: 193–222.

Natorp, P. (1913), 'Philosophie und Psychologie', *Logos* 4: 176–202.

Natorp, P. (1915), *Der Tag des Deutschen*, Rippel, Hagen.

Natorp, P. (1918a), *Die Seele des Deutschen*, Diederichs, Jena.

Natorp, P. (1918b), *Deutscher Weltberuf*, Diederichs, Jena.

Nelson, L. ([1908] 1973a), 'Über das sogenannte Erkenntnisprobem', in L. Nelson, *Geschichte und Kritik der Erkenntnistheorie: Gesammelte Schriften in neun Bänden*, vol. 2, edited by P. Bernays et al., Meiner, Hamburg, 59–394.

Nelson, L. ([1914] 1973b), 'Die sogenannte neukantische Schule in der gegenwärtigen Philosophie', in L. Nelson, *Die Schule der kritischen Philosophie und ihre Methode, Gesammelte Schriften in neun Bänden*, vol. 1, edited by P. Bernays et al., Meiner, Hamburg, 207–17.

Neurath, O. ([1921] 1973), 'Anti-Spengler', in O. Neurath, *Empiricism and Sociology*, ed. by M. Neurath and R.S. Cohen, Reidel, Dordrecht, 158–213.

Neurath, O., R. Carnap, and O. Hahn ([1929] 1973), 'Wissenschaftliche Weltauffassung: Der Wiener Kreis', in O. Neurath, *Empiricism and Sociology*, ed. by M. Neurath and R.S. Cohen, Reidel, Dordrecht, 299–318.

Nordquest, D. A. (1979), 'Husserl and Mill's "psychologism"', *Mill News Letter* 14: 2–9.

BIBLIOGRAPHY

Normore, C. (1990), 'Doxology and the history of philosophy', *Canadian Journal of Philosophy*, supp. vol. 16: 203–26.

Notturno, M.A. (1985), *Objectivity, Rationality and the Third Realm: Justification and the Grounds of Psychologism. A Study of Frege and Popper*, Nijhoff, Dordrecht.

Nunn, R.T. (1978), 'Psychologism, functionalism, and the modal status of logical laws', *Inquiry* 22: 343–57.

Nyíri, J.C. (1974), 'Beim Sternenlicht der Nichtexistierenden: Zur ideologiekritischen Interpretation des platonisierenden Antipsychologismus', *Inquiry* 17: 399–443.

Osier, D.V. and R.H. Wozniak (1984), *A Century of Serial Publications in Psychology 1850–1950: An International Bibliography*, Kraus International Publications, Millwood, N.Y.

Palágyi, M. (1902), *Der Streit der Psychologisten und Formalisten in der modernen Logik*, Engelmann, Leipzig.

Pandit, G.L. (1971), 'Two concepts of psychologism', *Philosophical Studies* 22: 85–91.

Peckhaus, V. (1988), 'Historiographie wissenschaftlicher Disziplinen als Kombination von Problem- und Sozialgeschichtsschreibung: Formale Logik im Deutschland des ausgehenden 19. Jahrhunderts', in H. Poser and C. Burrichter (eds.), *Die geschichtliche Perspektive in den Disziplinen der Wissenschaftsforschung*, TUB-Dokumentation 39, Berlin, 177–215.

Petersen, P. (1913), 'Referat über psychologische Literatur: Das Jahr 1912', *Zeitschrift für Philosophie und philosophische Kritik* 149: 193–221.

Philipse, H. (1989), 'Psychologism and the prescriptive function of logic', in M.A. Notturno (ed.), *Perspectives on Psychologism*, Brill, Leiden, 58–74.

Pietersma, H. (1967), 'Husserl and Frege', *Archiv für Geschichte der Philosophie* 49: 298–323.

Pinch, T.J. and W.E. Bijker (1984), 'The social construction of facts and artefacts', *Social Studies of Science* 14: 399–441.

Pivcevic, E. (1970), *Husserl and Phenomenology*, Hutchinson, London.

Popper, K. (1968), *The Logic of Scientific Discovery*, Harper & Row, New York.

Pos, H.J. (1922a), Review of Pos (1922b), *Kantstudien* 27: 232–3.

Pos, H.J. (1922b), *Zur Logik der Sprachwissenschaft*, Winter, Heidelberg.

Pos, H.J. (1949), 'Recollections of Ernst Cassirer', in P.A. Schilpp (ed.), *The Philosophy of Ernst Cassirer*, The Library of Living Philosophers, Inc., Evanston, Ill., 61–72.

Pulkkinen, J. (1994), *The Threat of Logical Mathematism: A Study on the Critique of Mathematical Logic in Germany at the Turn of the 20th Century*, Lang, Frankfurt am Main.

Quine, W. ([1951] 1961), 'Two dogmas of empiricism', in W. Quine, *From a Logical Point of View*, Harvard University Press, Cambridge, Mass., 20–46.

Quine, W. ([1969] 1985), 'Epistemology naturalized', in H. Kornblith, *Naturalizing Epistemology*, Bradford Books, Cambridge, Mass., 15–29.

Rehmke, J. (1918), *Logik oder Philosophie als Wissenslehre*, Quelle & Meyer, Leipzig.

Renner, H. (1902), *Beneke's Erkenntnistheorie: Ein Beitrag zur Kritik des Psychologismus*, Fock, Leipzig.

BIBLIOGRAPHY

Renner, H. (1905), 'Absolute, kritische und relative Philosophie', *Vierteljahrsschrift für wissenschaftliche Philosophie und Soziologie* 29: 131–64.

Richards, J. (1980), 'Boole and Mill: differing perspectives on logical psychologism', *History and Philosophy of Logic* 1: 19–36.

Rickert, H. (1892), *Der Gegenstand der Erkenntnis: Ein Beitrag zum Problem der philosophischen Transzendenz*, Mohr, Freiburg.

Rickert, H. (1896), *Die Grenzen der naturwissenschaftlichen Begriffsbildung: 1. Hälfte*, Mohr, Freiburg.

Rickert, H. (1899), *Kulturwissenschaft und Naturwissenschaft*, Mohr, Freiburg.

Rickert, H. (1902), *Die Grenzen der naturwissenschaftlichen Begriffsbildung: 2. Hälfte*, Mohr, Tübingen.

Rickert, H. (1904), *Der Gegenstand der Erkenntnis: Ein Beitrag zum Problem der philosophischen Transzendenz*, 2nd, revised edition, Mohr, Tübingen.

Rickert, H. (1909), 'Zwei Wege der Erkenntnistheorie: Transzendentalpsychologie und Transzendentallogik', *Kantstudien* 14: 169–228.

Rickert, H. (1911–12), 'Das Eine, die Einheit und die Eins: Bemerkungen zur Logik des Zahlbegriffs', *Logos. Internationale Zeitschrift für Philosophie der Kultur* 2: 26–78.

Rickert, H. (1913a), *Die Grenzen der naturwissenschaftlichen Begriffsbildung*, 2nd, revised edition, Mohr, Tübingen.

Rickert, H. (1913b), 'Zur Besetzung der philosophischen Professuren mit Vertretern der experimentellen Psychologie', *Frankfurter Zeitung* and *Handelsblatt* 4, 4 March 1913: 1–2.

Rickert, H. (1917), 'Hugo Münsterberg', *Frankfurter Zeitung*, 3/4 January 1917.

Rickert, H. (1920), *Philosophie des Lebens*, Mohr, Tübingen.

Rickert, H. (1920–21), 'Psychologie der Weltanschauungen und Philosophie der Werte', *Logos. Internationale Zeitschrift für Philosophie der Kultur* 9: 1–42.

Rickert, H. (1921), *System der Philosophie*, part 1: *Allgemeine Grundlegung der Philosophie*, Mohr, Tübingen.

Rickert, H. (1923–24a), 'Das Leben der Wissenschaft und die griechische Philosophie', *Logos. Internationale Zeitschrift für Philosophie der Kultur* 12: 303–39.

Rickert, H. (1923–24b), 'Die Methode der Philosophie und das Unmittelbare: Eine Problemstellung', *Logos. Internationale Zeitschrift für Philosophie der Kultur* 12: 235–280.

Rickert, H. (1929), 'Die Erkenntnis der intelligiblen Welt und das Problem der Metaphysik', *Logos* 18: 36–82.

Ricoeur, P. (1970), *Freud and Philosophy: An Essay on Interpretation*, tr. D. Savage, Yale University Press, New Haven.

Rieffert, J.B. (1922), 'Psychotechnik im Heer', in K. Bühler (ed.), *Bericht über den VII. Kongreß für experimentelle Psychologie in Marburg vom 20.–23. April 1921*, Fischer, Jena, 79–96.

Riehl, A. ([1915] 1925), 'Die geistige Kultur und der Krieg', in A. Riehl, *Philosophische Studien aus vier Jahrzehnten*, Quelle & Meyer, Leipzig, 313–25.

Ringer, F.K. (1969), *The Decline of the German Mandarins 1890–1933*, Harvard University Press, Cambridge, Mass.

Rorty, R., J.B. Schneewind and Q. Skinner (eds.) (1984), *Philosophy in*

BIBLIOGRAPHY

History: Essays on the Historiography of Philosophy, Cambridge, Cambridge University Press.

Ross, D. (1967), 'On the origins of psychology', *American Sociological Review* 32: 466–9.

Russell, A. (1966), 'A note on Lotze's teaching of psychology, 1842–1881', *Journal of the History of the Behavioral Sciences* 2: 74–5.

Salomon, M. (1914), Review of Wielikowski (1914), *Kantstudien* 19: 412–13.

Scarre, G. (1989), *Logic and Reality in the Philosophy of John Stuart Mill*, Kluwer, Synthese Historical Library, Dordrecht.

Scheler, M. ([1901] 1971), 'Die transzendentale und die psychologische Methode: Eine grundsätzliche Erörterung zur philosophischen Methodik', in M. Scheler, *Frühe Schriften*, ed. by M. Scheler and M. S. Frings, Francke, Berne: 197–336.

Scheler, M. (1913), *Zur Phänomenologie und Theorie der Sympathiegefühle und von Liebe und Hass*, Niemeyer, Halle.

Scheler, M. ([1913–16] 1980), *Der Formalismus in der Ethik und die materiale Wertethik: Neuer Versuch einer Grundlegung eines ethischen Personalismus*, in *Gesammelte Werke*, vol. 2, Francke, Berne.

Scheler, M. (1915a), *Der Genius des Krieges und der deutsche Krieg*, Der Neue Geist Verlag, Leipzig.

Scheler, M. ([1915b] 1972), 'Versuche einer Philosophie des Lebens: Nietzsche – Dilthey – Bergson', in M. Scheler, *Gesammelte Werke*, vol. 3, Francke, Berne.

Scheler, M. (1916), *Krieg und Aufbau*, Der Neue Geist Verlag, Leipzig.

Scheler, M. (1919), *Die Ursachen des Deutschenhasses*, Der Neue Geist Verlag, Leipzig.

Scheler, M. ([1922] 1973), 'Die deutsche Philosophie der Gegenwart', in M. Scheler, *Gesammelte Werke*, vol. 7, ed. by M.S. Frings, Francke, Berne, 259–326.

Scheler, M. ([1924] 1980), 'Probleme einer Soziologie des Wissens', in M. Scheler, *Gesammelte Werke*, vol. 6, Francke, Berne, 15–190.

Scheler, M. ([1925] 1982), 'Wissenschaft und soziale Struktur', in V. Meja and N. Stehr (eds.), *Der Streit um die Wissenschaftssoziologie*, vol. 1, Suhrkamp, Frankfurt am Main, 68–127.

Schilpp, P.A. (ed.) (1957), *The Philosophy of Karl Jaspers*, Open Court, La Salle, Ill.

Schingnitz, W. (1932), 'Geleitwort des Herausgebers', in W. Illemann, *Husserls vor-phänomenologische Philosophie*, Hirzel, Leipzig.

Schlick, M. (1910a), 'Das Wesen der Wahrheit nach der modernen Logik', *Vierteljahrsschrift für wissenschaftliche Philosophie und Soziologie* 34: 386–477.

Schlick, M. (1910b), 'Die Grenze der naturwissenschaftlichen und philosophischen Begriffsbildung', *Vierteljahrsschrift für wissenschaftliche Philosophie und Soziologie* 34: 121–42.

Schlick, M. (1918), *Allgemeine Erkenntnislehre*, Springer, Berlin.

Schlick, M. (1927), 'On the meaning of life', in M. Schlick, *Philosophical Papers, vol. II (1925–1936)*, ed. by H.L. Mulder and B.F.B. Van de Velde-Schlick, Reidel, Dordrecht, 1979, 112–29.

Schmidt, H. (1969), *Philosophisches Wörterbuch*, 18th ed., revised by G. Schischkoff, Kröner, Stuttgart.

BIBLIOGRAPHY

Schmidt, W. de (1976), *Psychologie und Transzendentalphilosophie: Zur Psychologie-Rezeption bei Hermann Cohen und Paul Natorp*, Bouvier, Bonn.

Schneider, C. M. (1990), *Wilhelm Wundts Völkerpsychologie: Entstehung und Entwicklung eines in Vergessenheit geratenen, wissenschaftshistorisch relevanten Fachgebietes*, Bouvier, Bonn.

Schnädelbach, H. (1984), *Philosophy in Germany 1831–1933*, tr. E. Matthews, Cambridge University Press, Cambridge.

Scholem, G. (1977), *Von Berlin nach Jerusalem: Jugenderinnerungen*, Suhrkamp, Frankfurt am Main.

Scholem, G. (1981), *Walter Benjamin: The Story of a Friendship*, The Jewish Publication Society of America, Philadelphia.

Scholz, H. (1931), *Geschichte der Logik*, Junker & Dünnhaupt, Berlin.

Schröder, E. (1880), Review of Frege (1879), *Zeitschrift für Mathematik und Physik* 25: 81–94.

Schröder, E. (1890), *Vorlesungen über die Algebra der Logik*, vol. 1, Teubner, Leipzig.

Schuhmann, K. (1973), *Die Dialektik der Phänomenologie*, Nijhoff, The Hague.

Schuhmann, K. (1977), *Husserl-Chronik*, Nijhoff, The Hague.

Schultz, J. (1903), 'Über die Fundamente der formalen Logik', *Vierteljahresschrift für wissenschaftliche Philosophie und Soziologie* 27: 1–37.

Schultz, J. (1907), *Die drei Welten der Erkenntnistheorie*, Vandenhoeck & Ruprecht, Göttingen.

Schultz, J. (1922), 'Julius Schultz', in R. Schmidt (ed.), *Philosophie der Gegenwart in Selbstdarstellungen*, vol. 3, Barth, Leipzig (pages are not numbered consecutively).

Schuppe, W. (1878), *Erkenntnistheoretische Logik*, Weber, Bonn.

Schuppe, W. (1894), *Grundriß der Erkenntnistheorie und Logik*, Gaertner, Berlin.

Schuppe, W. (1901), 'Zum Psychologismus und zum Normcharakter der Logik: Eine Ergänzung zu Husserl's "Logischen Untersuchungen"', *Archiv für Philosophie* 7: 1–22.

Schwarz, H. (1892), *Das Wahrnehmungsproblem vom Standpunkte des Physikers, des Physiologen und des Philosophen*, Duncker, Leipzig.

Schwarz, H. (1911), 'Die Seelenfrage', in W. Dilthey et al., *Weltanschauung*, Reichl & Co., Berlin, 253–82.

Schwarz, H. (1917), *Fichte und wir*, Zickfeldt, Osterwick a. Harz.

Seifert, F. (1925), *Der Streit um Karl Lamprechts Geschichtsphilosophie*, Filser, Augsburg.

Sellars, W. (1949), 'Realism and the new way of words', in H. Feigle and W. Sellars (eds.), *Philosophical Analysis*, Appleton, New York, 424–546.

Shapin, S. and S. Schaffer (1985), *Leviathan and the Air-Pump*, Princeton University Press, Princeton.

Siegel, H. (1987), *Relativism Refuted*, Reidel, Dordrecht.

Sigwart, C. ([1904] 1921), *Logik*, 4th, revised edition, edited by H. Maier, Mohr, Tübingen (Sigwart's reply to Husserl can already be found in the 1904 edition).

Simmel, G. (1913), 'An Herrn Prof. Karl Lamprecht', *Die Zukunft* 83: 230–4.

Simon, M. (1913), 'Die Besetzung der philosophischen Lehrstühle und die Lehrer der Mathematik', *Frankfurter Zeitung* 21 January 1913: 1–2.

BIBLIOGRAPHY

Skinner, Q. (1969), 'Meaning and understanding in the history of ideas', *History and Theory* 8: 3–53.

Skorupksi, J. (1989), *John Stuart Mill*, Routledge, London.

Slezak, P. (1989), 'How not to naturalize the theory of action', in P. Slezak and W.R. Albury (eds.), *Computers, Brains and Minds*, Kluwer, Dordrecht, 137–66.

Sluga, H. (1976), 'Frege as a rationalist', in M. Schirn (ed.), *Studies on Frege*, Problemata, Stuttgart, 27–47.

Sluga, H. (1980), *Gottlob Frege*, Routledge & Kegan Paul, London.

Sluga, H. (1984), 'Frege: the early years', in Rorty et al. (1984), 329–56.

Smith, B. (ed.) (1988), *Foundations of Gestalt Theory*, Philosophia, Munich.

Smith, D.W. and R. McIntyre (1982), *Husserl and Intentionality*, Kluwer, Dordrecht.

Smith, J.W. (1985), 'Meiland and the self-refutation of protagorean relativism', *Grazer Philosophische Studien* 23: 119–28.

Sober, E. (1978), 'Psychologism', *Journal for the Theory of Social Behaviour* 8: 165–92.

Spengler, O. (1918), *Der Untergang des Abendlandes: Umrisse einer Morphologie der Weltgeschichte*, vol. 1: *Gestalt und Wirklichkeit*, Beck, Munich.

Spengler, O. (1966), *Spengler Letters*, tr. and ed. by A. Helps, Allen & Unwin, London.

Spiegelberg, H. (1960), *The Phenomenological Movement*, Nijhoff, The Hague.

Spitta, H. (1889), *Die psychologische Forschung und ihre Aufgabe in der Gegenwart*, Mohr, Freiburg.

Spitzer, H. (1914), 'Der unausgesprochene Kanon der Kantischen Erkenntnistheorie', *Kantstudien* 19: 36–145.

Spranger, E. (1905), *Die Grundlagen der Geschichtswissenschaft*, Reuther & Reichardt, Berlin.

Spranger, E. (1913), 'Zum Streit um die Psychologie', *Deutsche Literaturzeitung* 34,12: 709–15.

Spranger, E. (1923–24), 'Rickerts System', *Logos. Internationale Zeitschrift für Philosophie der Kultur* 12: 183–98.

Spranger, E. (1926), 'Die Frage nach der Einheit der Psychologie', *Sitzungsberichte der Preussischen Akademie der Wissenschaften. Jahrgang 1926. Philosophisch-historische Klasse*, Verlag der Akademie der Wissenschaften, Berlin: 172–99.

Spranger, E. ([1930] 1982), 'Ideologie und Wissenschaft', in V. Meja and N. Stehr (eds.), *Der Streit um die Wissenssoziologie*, vol. 2, Suhrkamp, Frankfurt am Main, 634–6.

Ssalagoff, L. (1911), 'Vom Begriff des Geltens in der modernen Logik', *Zeitschrift für Philosophie und philosophische Kritik* 143: 145–90.

Stein, A. (1920–21), Review of Jaspers (1919), *Logos. Internationale Zeitschrift für Philosophie der Kultur* 9: 122–31.

Stein, L. (1903), 'Der Neo-Idealismus unserer Tage', *Archiv für systematische Philosophie* 9: 265–330.

Steinmann, H. G. (1917), 'Zur systematischen Stellung der Phänomenologie', *Archiv für die gesamte Psychologie* 36: 391–422.

BIBLIOGRAPHY

Stern, P. (1903), *Grundprobleme der Philosophie: I. Das Problem der Gegebenheit, zugleich eine Kritik des Psychologismus in der heutigen Philosophie*, Cassirer, Berlin.

Stern, W. (1903), Review of Rickert (1902), *Zeitschrift für Psychologie und Physiologie der Sinnesorgane* 33: 207–13.

Sternberg, K. (1920), 'Der Neukantianismus und die Forderungen der Gegenwart', *Kantstudien* 25: 396–410.

Sternberg, K. (1922), 'Die philosophischen Grundlagen in Spenglers "Untergang des Abendlandes"', *Kantstudien* 27: 101–38.

Stumpf, C. (1883–90), *Tonpsychologie*, 2 vols., Hirzel, Leipzig.

Stumpf, C. (1892), 'Psychologie und Erkenntnistheorie', *Abhandlungen der philosophischen Klasse der königlich bayerischen Akademie der Wissenschaften* 19, G. Franz, Munich, 466–516.

Stumpf, C. ([1907a] 1910), 'Die Wiedergeburt der Philosophie', in C. Stumpf, *Philosophische Reden und Vorträge*, Barth, Leipzig, 161–96.

Stumpf, C. (1907b), 'Erscheinungen und psychische Funktionen', *Aus den Abhandlungen der königlichen Preussischen Akademie der Wissenschaften vom Jahre 1906*, Verlag der königlichen Akademie der Wissenschaften, Berlin.

Stumpf, C. (1907c), 'Zur Einteilung der Wissenschaften', *Aus den Abhandlungen der königlichen Preussischen Akademie der Wissenschaften vom Jahre 1906*, Verlag der königlichen Akademie der Wissenschaften, Berlin.

Stumpf, C. (1918), 'Über den Entwicklungsgang der neueren Psychologie und ihre militärtechnische Verwendung', *Deutsche militärärztliche Zeitschrift* 5/6: 273–82.

Sukale, M. (1976), *Comparative Studies in Phenomenology*, Nijhoff, The Hague.

Thormeÿer, P. (1922), *Philosophisches Wörterbuch*, Teubner, Leipzig.

Titchener, E.B. (1909), *Lectures on the Experimental Psychology of the Thought Processes*, Macmillan, New York.

Titchener, E.B. (1921), 'Brentano and Wundt: empirical and experimental psychology', *American Journal of Psychology* 32: 108–20.

Troeltsch, E. (1918–19), 'Zur Religionsphilosophie', *Kantstudien* 23: 65–76.

Ueberweg, F. and M. Heinze (1897), *Grundriß der Geschichte der Philosophie*, vol. 3, 8th ed., revised by M. Heinze, Mittler & Sohn, Berlin.

Ueberweg, F. and M. Heinze (1902), *Grundriß der Geschichte der Philosophie*, vol. 4, 9th ed., revised by M. Heinze, Mittler & Sohn, Berlin.

Ueberweg, F. and M. Heinze (1906), *Grundriß der Geschichte der Philosophie*, vol. 4, 10th ed., revised by M. Heinze, Mittler & Sohn, Berlin.

Ueberweg, F. and T.K. Oesterreich (1951), *Grundriß der Geschichte der Philosophie*, vol. 4, 13th ed., revised by T.K. Oesterreich, Schwabe, Basle.

Unger, P. (1984), *Philosophical Relativity*, Blackwell, Oxford.

Unwin, N. (1987), 'Beyond truth', *Mind* 96: 299–317.

Uphues, G. (1903), *Zur Krisis der Logik: Eine Auseinandersetzung mit Dr. Melchior Palágyi*, Schwetschke & Sohn, Berlin.

Verwey, G. (1985), *Psychiatry in an Anthropological and Biomedical Context*, Reidel, Dordrecht.

Verworn, M. (1915), *Die biologischen Grundlagen der Kulturpolitk: Eine Betrachtung zum Weltkriege*, Fischer, Jena.

BIBLIOGRAPHY

Volkelt, J. (1918), *Gewissheit und Wahrheit: Untersuchung der Geltungsfragen als Grundlegung der Erkenntnistheorie*, Beck, Munich.

Waterlow, S. (1977), 'Protagoras and inconsistency', *Archiv für Geschichte der Philosophie* 59: 19–36.

Weinmann, R. (1898), 'Die erkenntnistheoretische Stellung des Psychologen', *Zeitschrift für Psychologie und Physiologie der Sinnesorgane* 17: 215–52.

Wielikowski, I.A. (1914), *Die Neukantianer in der Rechtsphilosophie*, Beck, Munich.

Wild, J. (1940), 'Husserl's Critique of Psychologism', in M. Farber (ed.), *Philosophical Essays in Memory of Edmund Husserl*, Harvard University Press, Cambridge, Mass., 19–43.

Willard, D. (1984), *Logic and the Objectivity of Knowledge: A Study in Husserl's Early Philosophy*, Ohio State University Press, Athens, Ohio.

Willy, R. (1897), 'Die Krisis in der Psychologie', *Vierteljahrsschrift für wissenschaftliche Philosophie* 21: 79–96, 227–49, 332–53.

Windelband, W. (1875), 'Die Erkenntnistheorie unter dem völkerpsychologischen Gesichtspunkte', *Zeitschrift für Völkerpsychologie und Sprachwissenschaft* 8: 166–78.

Windelband, W. (1876), *Über den gegenwärtigen Stand der psychologischen Forschung*, Breitkopf & Härtel, Leipzig.

Windelband, W. (1880), *Die Geschichte der neueren Philosophie in ihrem Zusammenhange mit der allgemeinen Kultur und den besonderen Wissenschaften*, vol. 2: *Von Kant bis Hegel und Herbart*, Breitkopf & Härtel, Leipzig.

Windelband, W. (1884), 'Kritische oder genetische Methode?', in *Präludien*, Mohr, Freiburg i. Br., 247–79.

Windelband, W. (1894), *Geschichte und Naturwissenschaft*, Heitz, Strassburg.

Windelband, W. (1909), *Die Philosophie im deutschen Geistesleben des XIX. Jahrhunderts: Fünf Vorlesungen*, Mohr, Tübingen.

Windelband, W. (1920), *Einleitung in die Philosophie*, Mohr, Tübingen.

Wittgenstein, L. (1961), *Notebooks, 1914–1916*, ed. by G.H. von Wright, tr. G.E.M. Anscombe, Oxford University Press, Oxford.

Woolgar, S. (1981), 'Interests and explanation in the social study of science', *Social Studies of Science* 11: 365–94.

Wundt, W. (1863), *Vorlesungen über die Menschen- und Tierseele*, Voß, Leipzig.

Wundt, W. (1873–74), *Grundzüge der physiologischen Psychologie*, 2 vols., Engelmann, Leipzig, Engelmann.

Wundt, W. (1880–83), *Logik: Eine Untersuchung der Prinzipien der Erkenntnis und der Methoden wissenschaftlicher Forschung*, 2 vols., Enke, Stuttgart.

Wundt, W. (1882), 'Logische Streitfragen', *Vierteljahrsschrift für wissenschaftliche Philosophie* 6: 340–55.

Wundt, W. (1883), 'Schlußwort zum ersten Bande', *Philosophische Studien* 1: 615–17.

Wundt, W. (1888a), 'Selbstbeobachtung und innere Wahrnehmung', *Philosophische Studien* 4: 292–310.

Wundt, W. (1888b), 'Über Ziele und Wege der Völkerpsychologie', *Philosophische Studien* 4: 1–27.

Wundt, W. (1889a), *System der Philosophie*, Engelmann, Leipzig.

Wundt, W. (1889b), 'Über die Einteilung der Wissenschaften', *Philosophische Studien* 5: 1–55.

Wundt, W. (1894), 'Über psychische Kausalität und das Prinzip des psychophysischen Parallelismus', *Philosophische Studien* 10: 1–124.

Wundt, W. (1896), 'Über die Definition der Psychologie', *Philosophische Studien*, 12: 1–66.

Wundt, W. (1903a), *Ethik*, 3rd ed., 2 vols., Enke, Stuttgart.

Wundt, W. (1903b), *Grundzüge der physiologischen Psychologie*, vol. 3, 5th ed., Engelmann, Leipzig.

Wundt, W. (1903c), 'Schlusswort des Herausgebers', *Philosophische Studien*, 18: 793–5.

Wundt, W. (1904), 'Über empirische und metaphysische Psychologie: Eine kritische Betrachtung', *Archiv für die gesamte Psychologie* 2: 333–61.

Wundt, W. (1906), *Logik: Eine Untersuchung der Prinzipien der Erkenntnis und der Methoden wissenschaftlicher Forschung*, vol. 1, 3rd ed., Enke, Stuttgart.

Wundt, W. ([1907a] 1910), 'Psychologie', in W. Windelband (ed.), *Die Philosophie im Beginn des zwanzigsten Jahrhunderts*, Winter, Heidelberg, 1–55.

Wundt, W. (1907b), 'Über Ausfrageexperimente und über die Methoden zur Psychologie des Denkens', *Psychologische Studien* 3: 301–60.

Wundt, W. (1908a), 'Kritische Nachlese zur Ausfragemethode', *Archiv für die gesamte Psychologie*, 9: 445–59.

Wundt, W. (1908b), *Logik: Eine Untersuchung der Prinzipien der Erkenntnis und der Methoden wissenschaftlicher Forschung*, vol. 3, 3rd ed., Enke, Stuttgart.

Wundt, W. (1910a), 'Das Institut für experimentelle Psychologie zu Leipzig', *Psychologische Studien* 5: 279–93.

Wundt, W. (1910b), 'Psychologismus und Logizismus', in W. Wundt, *Kleine Schriften*, vol. 1, Engelmann, Leipzig, 511–634.

Wundt, W. (1910c), 'Über reine und angewandte Psychologie', *Psychologische Studien* 5: 1–47.

Wundt, W. (1913), *Die Psychologie im Kampf ums Dasein*, Engelmann, Leipzig.

Wundt, W. (1914a), *Sinnliche und übersinnliche Welt*, Kröner, Leipzig.

Wundt, W. (1914b), *Über den wahrhaften Krieg*, Kröner, Leipzig.

Wundt, W. (1915), *Die Nationen und ihre Philosophie: Ein Kapitel zum Weltkrieg*, Kröner, Stuttgart.

Wundt, W. (1917), 'Schlusswort des Herausgebers', *Psychologische Studien* 10: 571–2.

Wundt, W. (1920), *Erlebtes und Erkanntes*, Kröner, Leipzig.

Yearley, S. (1982), 'The relationship between epistemological and sociological cognitive interests: some ambiguities underlying the use of interest theory in the study of scientific knowledge', *Studies in History and Philosophy of Science* 13: 353–88.

Zechlin, E. (1969), *Die deutsche Politik und die Juden im Ersten Weltkrieg*, Vandenhoeck, Göttingen.

Ziehen, T. (1916), *Die Psychologie großer Heerführer: Der Krieg und die Gedanken der Philosophen und Dichter vom ewigen Frieden*, Barth, Leipzig.

Ziehen, T. (1920), *Lehrbuch der Logik auf positivistischer Grundlage mit Berücksichtigung der Geschichte der Logik*, A. Marcus & E. Webers, Bonn.

INDEX

a priori/a posteriori 2, 12, 31–2,
    41, 45, 48, 68–71, 85, 87, 102,
    113, 120, 140
absurdity (*Widersinn*) 49–50, 75,
    93, 181, 183, 187, 207–8
Ach, N. 126–7, 148
act–content distinction 46, 56, 71,
    79–80, 87, 141–2
Adickes, E. 280, 283–4
Adler, M. 112, 118, 280
Adorno, T. W. 20, 22–3
Amsterdamska, O. 280
analytic/synthetic 31–2
Anschütz, G. 184–5, 280
anthropologism 49, 53, 108, 253
Apel, M. 279
Aquinas, St Thomas 110, 112, 254
Aristotle 7, 106, 115, 137, 155,
    199, 234
Armstrong, D. M. 7
Aschkenasy, H. 75–7, 89, 93
Ash, M. 127–9, 142–4, 191, 260,
    270–1, 285
Aster, E. von 264, 285
Avenarius, R. 57, 97, 99, 146–7,
    156–7, 261, 281
Ayer, A. J. 7

Baensch, O. 285
Baeumker, C. 116, 280
Bain, A. 50, 97, 281
Baker, G. P. 7, 280
Baldwin, J. M. 97, 281
Barnes, B. 15, 27
Barth, P. 285

Bauch, B. 98, 119, 215–16, 280,
    283–5
Beauchamp, T. 280
Beethoven, L. van 271
Bekhterev, V. 128
Bell, D. 141
Ben-David, J. 127, 137, 279
Beneke, F. E. 97, 101–2, 281
Benjamin, W. 20
Benussi, V. 126, 266
Bergmann, H. 280, 285
Bergson, H. 7, 97, 188, 228–31,
    244–5, 254, 281
Berkeley, G. 7, 97, 221, 253, 281
Betti, E. 7
Bijker, W. 25–6, 280
Binswanger, L. 217
biologism 108, 111, 242, 244–5,
    277
Block, N. 5
Bloor, D. 5, 7, 15, 24–5, 27, 274,
    279–80
Blumenthal, A. 129, 134–5, 144–6
Blumenthal, E. 99, 280, 283–4
Bolzano, B. 58, 80, 89, 96–9, 209
Boole, G. 7, 203
Boring, E. G. 138, 142, 144–6, 148,
    285
Bouterwek, R. 97, 281
Boyle, R. 276
Brante, T. 280
Braun, O. 285
Braunshausen, N. 156
Brentano, F. 77, 83, 89, 91, 97–8,
    107, 113, 117, 121, 125–7,

317

137–43, 148, 151–2, 157–9, 180, 182, 185, 206–7, 266, 280–1
Bringmann, W. G. 128, 261
Brockhaus, R. 3, 279
Brockhoff, A. 285
Brown, T. 168
Brugger, W. 7, 279
Brunstäd, F. 285
Brunswig, E. 285
Bubnoff, N. von 285
Büchner, L. 175
Buddha, Gautama 253
Bühl, G. 203
Bühler, K. 126, 148, 262, 264–6, 280
Bullaty, E. 280
Burgert, H. 258
Burnyeat, M. F. 280
Busse, L. 88, 90, 93, 97–8, 180, 281, 284
Buzello, H. 280, 283, 284
Bynum, T. W. 206–7

Calker, F. von 97, 281
Calkins, M. W. 145
Callon, M. 26–7
Caplan, A. 280
Carnap, R. 3, 5, 7, 11, 250–1
Cassirer, E. 99, 121, 190, 243–4, 248, 255, 257, 280, 284–5
Cattell, J. McKeen 128, 145
causality 133–4, 147, 168, 226
Chomsky, N. 7, 9
Christopher, D. 279–80
Churchland, P. 11–12
civilisation 214, 225, 231, 236
Clauberg, K. W. 119, 280
Cohen, H. 97–9, 103, 116, 119, 165, 169, 190, 212, 243, 248–9, 280–1, 285
Cohn, J. 97, 219, 262, 280–5
Collins, H. M. 24–6, 280
Collins, R. 127, 137, 279–80
Copernicus, N. 79
Cornelius, H. 57, 70–1, 89–91, 93, 97–8, 114, 126, 180, 185, 280, 282, 284–5
Cousin, V. 97, 282
Cristaudo, W. 244

Currie, G. 7, 280
Cussins, A. 5

Danziger, K. 135, 146–8
Darwin, C. 110
Darwinism 108, 110
Deleuze, G. 20
Democritos 97, 282
Deneke, H. 97, 282
Derrida, J. 20, 22
Descartes, R. 218, 220, 230
Dessoir, M. 223, 280–4
Deussen, J. 285
Dilthey, W. 7, 97, 99, 143, 161–9, 174, 188–9, 212, 228–30, 241–2, 244–5, 254, 266–70, 282
Dinger, H. 285
Dippe, A. 192
Dittes, F. 97, 282
Dorsch, F. 260
Dreßler, M. 97, 282
Drews, A. 281–2, 284–5
Driesch, H. 117, 281, 285
Drobisch, M. 144, 207
Drüe, H. 178
Du Bois-Reymond, E. 129
Du Toit, A. 279
Dubislav, W. 119, 280
Dubs, A. 89, 110, 281–4
Dührung, E. 89, 97, 282
Dummett, M. 5–8, 61–2, 279–80
Durkheim, E. 15, 257
Dürr, E. 70–1, 93, 118, 126, 281, 283–4

Ebbinghaus, H. 125–7, 143–5, 149, 155, 162, 167–9, 267
Ehrenberg, H. 285
Ehrenfels, C. von 97, 107, 126, 266, 282
Eisenmeyer, J. 97, 158, 203, 282, 286
Eisler, R. 74, 90, 93, 105–7, 114, 116, 119, 129–30, 132, 281–5
Eleutheropulos, K. 285
Elias, N. 214
Ellis, B. 10, 11, 275
Elsenhans, T. 86, 93, 97, 105–6, 188, 281–2

INDEX

Elzinga, A. 280
empiricism 2, 19, 45, 48, 62, 108, 204
Endriß, K. F. 281
Engel, P. 279
Engelhardt, H. 280
Engels, F. 2, 175
Enoch, W. 105, 281–2, 284
Epicurus 97, 282
epistemology 5, 11, 14, 57, 75–6, 81, 84, 102–8, 114, 116, 118–20, 130, 157–9, 164–5, 170, 179, 195, 208, 249, 258
Erdmann, B. 3, 35–9, 49–53, 80–1, 89, 93, 97, 207, 224–5, 282
Erdmann, J. E. 101–3, 281
Erhardt, F. 285
Erismann, T. 269
Eucken, R. 106, 161, 166, 191, 212–13, 216, 253–4, 281, 285
Ewald, O. 119, 121, 281–4, 285

Falckenberg, R. 285
Falkenfeld, H. 219
fallacy 74, 93, 208; of *hysteron-proteron* 58, 87, 208; of *petitio principii* 67, 68, 75
Farias, V. 243–4
Faust, A. 247, 257
Fechner, G. T. 145, 175–6, 201, 286
Feuerbach, L. 2, 175
Fichte, J. G. 97, 101, 112, 206, 219, 220
Fink, E. 181
Fischer, A. 285–6
Focke, R. 285
Fodor, J. 280
Fogarasi, A. 281
Føllesdal, D. 60–1, 279–80
formalism 91, 93, 108, 203
Forman, P. 225–8, 240–1, 261
Foucault, M. 20, 23
Fouillée, A. 96–7, 282
Fowler, C. 97, 282
Frede, M. 17–23
Frege, G. 3–4, 6–13, 22, 30–41, 55, 60–3, 89, 95, 97, 105–6, 123, 161, 203–9, 259, 272–3, 275,

278–80, 282
Freud, S. 22
Freytag, G. 285
Friedell, E. 249–50
Fries, J. F. 97, 102, 282
Frischeisen-Köhler, M. 82, 97, 120, 126, 242, 247, 281–2, 285–6
Fuller, S. 5, 7, 15

Gadamer, H.-G. 7, 13, 243, 254
Galileo, G. 199
Gassen, K. 200
Geach, P. 7
Geiger, M. 199, 285
George, S. 212
Gethmann, C. F. 280
Gettier, E. 11
Geuter, U. 125, 259–60
Geyser, J. 72, 93, 99, 203–4, 281–5
Giere, R. 280
Goedeckemeyer, A. 285
Goethe, J. W. von 232–4, 241–2
Goldschmidt, R. H. 260
Goldstein, J. 285
Gomperz, H. 77, 93, 97–8, 281–5
Goodman, N. 7
Göring, C. 97, 282
Görland, A. 285
Gracia, J. 17–23
Green, K. 7
Groethuysen, B. 285
Groos, K. 97–8, 118, 281–2, 284
Grosche, G. 206
Grünwald, E. 16, 288
Gruppe, O. 97, 282
Gutberlet, C. 99, 105–6, 110, 119, 261, 281–4, 286
Güttler, K. 105, 107, 192, 201, 281, 285
Guttmann, J. 285

Haack, S. 10–11, 279
Häberlin, P. 285
Habermas, J. 7, 13
Hacker, P. M. S. 7, 280
Hahn, O. 250–1
Halder, A. 279
Hall, G. S. 128
Hamburg, C. H. 244

319

Hamilton, P. 97, 280, 282
Hammacher, E. 285
Hannay, A. 280
Harman, G. 9
Hartley, E. F. 97, 282
Hartmann, E. von 97, 282
Hartmann, N. 121, 216, 243, 281, 285
Hauptmann, G. 212
Hegel, G. W. F. 2, 62, 101, 112, 155, 175–6, 206, 219, 238, 241
Heidegger, M. 12, 20, 88, 121, 204–5, 227–8, 243–4, 248–9, 252–4, 259, 281–5
Heim, K. 67, 84, 88–90, 93, 281, 284–5
Heinze, M. 89, 98, 105–7, 113–14, 281–4
Hellpach, W. 149
Helmholtz, H. von 2, 129, 169, 279
Heman, F. 285
Henning, H. 285
Hensel, P. 193, 199–200, 285–6
Hepp, C. 212–3
Herbart, J. F. 58, 97, 139, 144, 155, 168, 209, 218, 282
Herder, J. G. 97, 282
Hering, E. 145
Hessen, S. 281
Heyelmann, G. 281, 285
Heyfelder, E. 285
Heymans, G. 47–8, 67–9, 74, 93, 97, 114, 151–2, 207, 281–2
Hillebrand, F. 97, 282, 286
Hintikka, J. 279
historicism 108–9
Hobbes, T. 97, 221, 276, 282
Höffding, H. 97, 282
Höffmeister, J. 279
Höfler, A. 47, 89, 93, 97–9, 113, 119, 126, 281–4
Hofmann, P. 225, 281
Hölderlin, F. 219
Holzhey, H. 88, 190
Honecker, M. 225, 281
Hönigswald, R. 82, 116, 121, 281, 285
Horwicz, A. 97, 192, 282
Hull, D. L. 280

Humboldt, W. von 135
Hume, D. 2, 7, 19, 48, 96–7, 134, 221, 282
Hurford, J. R. 10, 280
Husserl, E. 3–8, 12–15, 22, 30, 38–101, 105, 107–8, 112–14, 116, 118, 121–3, 137, 148, 155, 157, 161, 172, 178–89, 191, 199, 203, 205–10, 212, 224–5, 228, 230, 232, 241, 244–5, 247–9, 252–5, 257–9, 263–6, 272–3, 275–86

idealism 2, 23, 32, 36–8, 62, 111, 130, 154, 176, 193, 200, 219
ideas (Vorstellungen) 31, 36–7, 39–40, 55–6, 61, 79
Illemann, W. 258
induction 32, 45, 68, 70–1, 140
inference 42, 55, 59, 67, 145
introspection 135, 140, 148, 183, 263
intuition 231–3
intuitionism 244–5
is–ought distinction 34, 54

Jacoby, G. 285
Jaensch, E. 190, 243, 262, 266, 271
James, W. 96–7, 272, 282
Janssen, F. 223
Janssen, P. 7, 279
Jaspers, K. 97, 120, 228, 236–40, 242, 246, 248, 257, 265, 267, 281–2
Jerusalem, W. 15, 69–70, 79–80, 85, 87–91, 93, 97–8, 114–15, 180, 187–8, 275, 278, 281–2, 184–5
Jevons, S. 89, 97, 203, 282
Jodl, F. 97, 282, 285
Joël, K. 285
Jordan, J. N. 280
Jouffroy, T. 97, 282
Judd, C. H. 128
judgement (Urteil) 31, 37, 42, 44, 48–51, 53, 55–7, 67, 71, 78–9, 85–6, 119, 121, 178, 205, 263

Kabitz, W. 285

Kant, I. 2, 7, 23, 31–2, 42, 58–9, 89, 96–7, 102–5, 110, 112, 115–18, 169, 176, 209, 218, 230–1, 234, 238, 240, 243–4, 253–4, 279, 282
Katz, J. J. 7, 280
Kerferd, G. B. 280
Kern, B. 281
Kern, I. 14
Kierkegaard, S. 236, 238
Kiesow, J. 126
Kinkel, W. 285
Kirschmann, A. 126
Kitcher, Pa. 279
Kitcher, Ph. 7, 280
Klages, L. 269
Kleinpeter, H. 75, 84, 87, 90, 93, 97–8, 283–4
Kleist, H. von 219
Klemm, O. 285
Kockelmans, J. J. 178
Koffka, K. 266
Köhler, W. 266, 270–1
Köhnke, K. C. 170, 274, 279
Koppelmann, W. 82, 281–3
Köster, R. 285
Kraft, W. 241
Kraus, O. 97, 283
Kreibig, J. 97, 283
Kreis, F. 281, 284
Kreiser, L. 206
Kroner, R. 64–6, 90, 93, 120, 284–5
Kronfeld, A. 281
Krug, W. 97, 283
Krüger, F. 127, 157–9, 261–2, 266–8, 271
Kuhn, T. S. 23
Külpe, O. 97–9, 125–7, 129–30, 133, 144–9, 155–6, 184, 192, 194–7, 203, 209, 220, 260, 263, 265, 281–4
Kuntze, F. 97, 283, 285
Kynast, R. 281

Laas, E. 97, 283
Lachelier, J. E. N. 97, 283
Lakatos, I. 5
Lamont, M. 279
Lamprecht, K. 96–7, 153, 172, 200–1, 213, 283, 286
Landmann, M. 200
Lange, C. 97, 283
Lange, F. A. 47, 58, 97, 169, 176, 207, 209, 283
Lange, K. 97, 126, 283
language game 25, 202, 273
Lanz, H. 88, 118, 281–2, 284
Lapp, A. 67, 80, 86, 90–1, 93, 99, 284
Lask, E. 97, 243, 281, 283, 285
Lasson, E. 285
Lasswitz, K. 105, 281
Latour, B. 24, 26–8, 272, 280
Laue, M. von der 226
Law, J. 26–7
law: descriptive 33–6, 60; ideal 55, 67–73, 90, 92–3; logical 3, 33–6, 44–7, 51–5, 57–8, 60–1, 64–5, 67–74, 81–2, 87, 90, 93, 102, 113, 119, 131, 158; mathematical 69; of nature 51, 55, 68–70, 78, 104, 118; of non-contradiction 35, 47, 49–50, 66, 69, 73; prescriptive 33–5, 60; psychological 30, 32–5, 45–7, 55, 67–8, 132, 158; real 67–73, 92–3; of syllogistics 45, 48, 74; of thought 33–4, 52, 130–1
Lazarus, M. 97, 102, 135, 283
Leary, D. 285
Lebensphilosophie 211–71, 278
Lehmann, R. 126, 192, 285
Leibniz, G. W. 58, 155, 285
Leichtman, M. 270
Leser, H. 285
Lessing, H.-U. 167
Lessing, T. 285
Levi, I. 8
Lewalter, E. 15
Lewin, K. 266
Liebert, A. 247, 281, 284
Liebmann, O. 97, 283
Linke, P. 114, 120, 281, 285
Lipps, G. F. 190, 285
Lipps, T. 3, 10, 50, 89, 93, 97–8, 106–7, 114, 119–21, 131, 153, 157, 168, 182, 184–5, 224, 263, 275, 281, 283–4

Locke, J. 2, 7, 97, 221, 283
logic 30–94, 101–2, 105, 106,
    118–19, 130–2, 146, 178, 180,
    187, 249, 258; different
    (alternative) 35, 51–3, 75–6; as
    Kunstlehre 41, 43–4, 54, 56, 64,
    116; mathematical (*Logistik*)
    113, 203–5; as normative,
    prescriptive discipline 10, 42,
    67, 131; as physics of thought 3,
    10, 131; psychological 37, 39,
    61; pure 41, 44, 54–5, 58–60,
    66–7, 85, 87–8, 90, 93, 112, 178,
    186, 208–9, 225; as science of
    values 64–5, 112; as theory of
    science (*Wissenschaftslehre*) 41–2
logicism 84, 91, 108, 180, 240
Lossius, R. 283
Lotze, H. 55, 58, 97, 126, 141, 144,
    162, 167, 175–6, 209, 258, 283,
    286
Löwith, K. 241
Lübbe, H. 286
Ludz, P. 279
Lyotard, F. 20

McCarthy, M. 3, 279
McDowell, J. 6–7
McGinn, C. 280
Mach, E. 57, 87, 89, 93, 97, 99,
    133, 146–7, 261, 283
McIntyre, R. 279
MacKenzie, D. 15, 27
Mackenzie, J. D. 280
McKinsey, M. 7
McMullin, E. 280
Macnamara, J. 8–9
McTaggart, J. E. 7
Maier, H. 66, 78–9, 90–1, 93, 97–8,
    117, 121, 180, 281, 283–4
Mann, T. 212, 272
Mannheim, K. 15–16, 288
Mansel, H. L. 280
Marbe, K. 126–7, 148, 152, 155,
    176, 197–200, 260
Markle, G. 280
Martius, G. 126–7
Marty, A. 89, 93, 97, 99, 107, 113,
    117–19, 137, 159, 281, 283

Marx, K. 2, 22–3, 175, 257, 280
Massey, G. 280
materialism 108–9, 169, 175, 202,
    220, 24
mathematics 3, 30–1, 39, 48, 51,
    55–6, 59–60, 67, 69–70, 91, 165,
    186–7, 203–6, 209
mathematism 203, 277
Matthen, M. 280
Mauthner, F. 115, 117, 281
Mayer, R. 126
Medicus, F. 112, 118, 281, 285
Mehlis, G. 219, 285
Meiland, J. 280
Meinong, A. 47, 89–91, 93, 97–9,
    107, 112–14, 118, 120, 126, 133,
    137, 180, 266, 281, 283–4
Menzel, A. 285
Messer, A. 126–7, 148, 152, 155,
    184–7, 221–2, 242, 263–5,
    281–4, 286
metaphysics 83, 102, 120, 130,
    132–3, 138, 146, 155–6, 158–9,
    163, 170, 185, 188, 195–6, 201,
    234, 244, 249–52
Metcalfe, J. F. 280
Metzger, A. 286
Metzke, E. 279
Meumann, E. 126–7, 261, 287
Meyer (Captain) 152, 222
Meyering, T. C. 279
Michaltschew, D. 67, 80, 90, 93,
    99, 118, 281–5
Miklosisch, F. 97, 283
militarism 215, 218, 220
Mill, J. 168, 279
Mill, J. S. 2, 7, 10, 30, 32–3, 47, 50,
    96–7, 164, 207, 280, 283
Misch, G. 241–2, 286
Mischel, T. 134, 285
Mises, R. von 227
Mohanty, J. J. 279, 280
Moog, W. 68–9, 84, 88–91, 93, 99,
    111, 118–20, 224, 281–5
Moore, G. E. 3
Morgenstern, G. 281
Mortan, G. 60
Müller, G. E. 125–7, 144–6, 206
Müller, J. 129

Müller, M. 279
Müller-Freienfels, R. 97–8, 242, 247, 281–4
Münsterberg, H. 97, 105, 107, 109, 126, 145, 149, 152, 155, 192, 281, 283, 288
Murray, D. J. 129, 285
Musgrave, A. 3, 7, 279
Musil, R. 212
mysticism 91, 93, 108

Naess, A. 280
Nagel, T. 280
Natorp, P. 55, 67, 75, 83, 88–91, 93, 97–9, 119, 121, 165–6, 189–92, 204, 206, 209, 213–14, 220, 243, 248, 253, 257, 281–4, 286
naturalism 1–3, 11, 16, 62, 108–9, 181, 212, 247, 254, 273, 278
Nelson, L. 70, 90–1, 93, 97–9, 118, 120, 180, 281–4, 286
Neoscholasticism 98–9, 106, 110, 112, 258
Neurath, O. 7, 250–1
Newton, I. 78
Nietzsche, F. 7, 22–3, 97, 202, 228–30, 238, 245, 254, 283
Nohl, H. 286
Nordquest, D. A. 7, 279
normative antipsychologism 44–5, 54–5, 60–1, 64–7
Normore, C. 17–24
Notturno, M. A. 4, 13
number 3, 31–3, 36, 38, 40, 56, 59, 189, 204
Nunn, R. T. 280
Nyíri, J.C. 279

object: abstract/ideal 3, 9–10, 31, 36, 64, 90; transcendent 37–8, 76
Oesterreich, T. K. 13
Orth, W. 126, 148
Osier, D. V. 124
Ostwald, W. 97, 283
Otto, R. 96–7, 283

Palágyi, M. 72, 80, 88–91, 93, 97–8,

119, 281, 283–5
Pandit, G. L. 7
Peckhaus, V. 279
Peirce, C. S. 10
perception of essences (Wesensschau) 183, 187–8, 231, 244–5, 258
Petersen, J. 280
Petersen, P. 281, 284
Petzoldt, W. 97, 99, 283
Pfänder, A. 286
Pfordten, O. von 286
phenomenology 1, 12–14, 90, 98–9, 112, 119, 143, 148, 178–9, 199, 216–17, 224–5, 227, 230–1, 244, 249, 252–9, 263–4, 266, 271, 273, 275–6
Philipse, H. 280
philosophy: analytical 6, 20, 278; as applied psychology 119, 157–9; continental 12–13, 20, 278; inductive 129, 137; Neokantian 14, 88, 90, 98–9, 103–4, 111–12, 115–16, 161, 166, 169–78, 190, 206, 212–16, 231, 242–9, 252–7; pure 16, 122, 160–211, 213, 219, 262–3, 273; scientific 208, 249–52; transcendental 2, 14, 100–2, 111, 253
physiology 2, 91, 127, 133, 137, 139, 143, 145, 147–8, 156, 169, 171–2, 183, 192
Pietersma, H. 280
Pilzecker, A. 126
Pinch, T. 25–6, 280
Pivcevic, E. 280
Planck, M. 227
Plato 7, 152, 234
Platonism 9, 62, 90, 120
Plenge, J. 213
Poincaré, R. 257
Popper, K. 3–7
Pos, H. J. 244, 281
positivism 2, 109, 146–7
principle of non-contradiction, see law of non-contradiction
Protagoras 49, 96–7, 283
Protestantism 106, 108–10, 200

psychologism 1–16, 22, 27–8,
30–121, 171, 178–80, 186, 202,
207–11, 221, 224–5, 228, 230,
237, 240, 246, 248, 253, 256–7,
273, 275, 277–8; aesthetic 108;
aprioristic 108; critical-
teleological 108; delicate 108;
emotional 108; empiricistic 108,
190; epistemological 108;
ethical 108; evolutionary 108;
extreme 108; false 108; hidden
108; historical 108; immanent
108; intellectual 108; inverse
108; justified (wohlverstanden)
108, 113; linguistic 108; logical
108, 259; loose 108;
mathematical 108; metaphysical
108; moderate 108, 113;
nativistic 91; new 108; objective
(intersubjective) 108; obvious
108; old 108; one-sided/
tendentious 108; ontological
108; open 108; pedagogical
108; pragmatist 108; rationalist
108, 189, 190; religious 108;
sensualist 108; sociological 108;
strict 108; strong 10;
transcendent 108;
transcendental 108; true 108,
113; universal 108; weak 10
psychology: applied 102, 123–5,
157, 200, 212, 259, 261; common-
sense 189; descriptive 90,
162–9, 174, 178–80, 183–4,
188–9; eidetic 184, 186;
educational 260–1, 268; of
elements 268–9; empirical 102,
107, 138–9, 157, 173–4, 177,
179–80, 185, 189, 196;
experimental 16, 98, 119,
122–61, 166, 175, 181–6,
189–94, 196–200, 202, 209,
211–12, 219, 224, 234–6, 255,
259–72; explanatory 162–9, 180,
209, 230, 262, 268;
geisteswissenschaftliche 268–9;
general (or pure) 123–5, 157,
186, 260; genetic 139–40; Gestalt
257, 265–6, 268, 270–1;

historical 174, 200;
interpretative 237, 262, 267–8;
of logic 9; of mathematics 10;
military 152, 222–3; modern
198–200, 235–6, 269; new 101,
122–59, 187–8, 190;
philosophical 123, 130, 149–50,
194, 212; physiological 129,
147; rational 81–2; scientific
153, 158, 160, 172, 174, 177,
230; social 174, 223; of
structures 268–9;
transcendental 90, 279;
Völkerpsychologie 102, 135–6, 143,
147, 154, 194, 220, 287;
voluntaristic 136, 138; of
Weltanschauungen 236–40, 244,
267
psychophysical parallelism 135,
164, 235
psychophysics 144–5
psychotechnics 222, 260, 288
Pulkkinen, J. 203

Quine, W. V. O. 7, 11

realism 37, 116, 119, 188
reduction (in Husserl) 14, 115,
186, 266
Rehmke, J. 98–9, 120, 161, 166,
281, 283–4, 286
Reid, T. 97, 283
Reinach, A. 286
Reininger, R. 286
relativism 16, 49, 50, 53, 62, 72,
75–7, 90, 93, 108, 119, 171, 235,
243, 248, 275, 277, 280;
Protagorean 49; of species
49–50, 79, 81
Renner, H. 75, 93, 281, 283–5
Restivo, S. 279–80
Richards, J. 4, 279
Richter, R. 97, 283
Rickert, H. 64, 66, 75, 90–1, 93,
98–9, 109, 112, 117–19, 161,
165, 170, 172–7, 180, 188–91,
196–8, 200, 203–4, 206, 212,
215, 219, 239–40, 243–9, 252,
255, 257–8, 281–4, 286

Ricoeur, P. 22
Rieffert, J. B. 222
Riehl, A. 55, 89, 97, 103, 161,
    166–7, 191, 209, 214–15, 242,
    284, 286
Ringer, F. K. 212–14, 225–8, 240,
    271
Rip, A. 26
Ritter, J. 286
role hybridisation 122–59, 160, 190
role purification 160–210
Roretz, K. 281–4
Rosmini, A. 97, 284
Ross, D. 127
Ruge, A. 286
Russell, B. 3, 7

Sachphilosophie 254–6
Salomon, M. 281
Scarre, G. 4, 279–80
scepticism 16, 48, 53, 62, 75, 77,
    84, 90, 93, 108, 164, 232, 277
Schaffer, S. 275–6, 280
Scheler, M. 120, 212, 216–20,
    228–32, 238, 242, 244–6,
    248–50, 252–9, 267, 281, 288
Schelling, F. W. J. 101, 110, 201,
    206, 271
Schiller, F. 206
Schiller, F. C. S. 97, 284
Schingnitz, W. 258
Schlick, M. 67–8, 71–3, 77, 79, 86,
    93, 97, 177, 203, 251–2, 275, 286
Schmeckel, R. 286
Schmid, F. A. 286
Schmidt, H. 279
Schmidt, W. de 170
Schnädelbach, H. 95, 259
Schneider, C. M. 135
Schneider, O. 97, 284, 286
scholasticism 77, 91, 108, 182
Scholem, G. 242
Scholz, H. 112–13
Schopenhauer, A. 97, 155, 284
Schrader, E. 97, 284
Schrempf, C. 286
Schröder, E. 205–6
Schuhmann, K. 14, 206
Schultz, J. 66–7, 70, 74–5, 77, 79,

84–5, 91, 93, 97, 114–15, 278,
    281, 284
Schuppe, W. 66, 70–1, 88, 93, 97,
    284
Schwarz, H. 97, 107, 110, 118, 281,
    284, 286
sciences: historical, human and
    social (Geisteswissenschaften,
    Kulturwissenschaften,
    idiographische) 1, 118, 132, 134,
    153–4, 164–5, 168, 171–5, 177,
    185, 196, 200–1, 219, 243, 255,
    269; natural
    (Naturwissenschaften,
    nomothetische) 2, 11, 22, 101,
    116, 118, 123, 133–5, 137, 141,
    147, 155, 165, 171–5, 177, 182,
    186, 194, 201, 209, 219, 223,
    245, 255, 268, 277
Scripture, E. W. 128
Seidel, F. 286
Seifert, F. 281, 284
self-evidence 44–5, 56–7, 82–7,
    90–3, 105, 116, 118–19, 131–2,
    140; apodictic 45, 47, 51, 53, 85,
    165
self-refutation 16, 52, 248
Sellars, W. 3–4, 6–7
Shapin, S. 15, 275–6, 280
Siegel, F. 97, 284, 286
Siegel, H. 280
Sigwart, C. 3, 47, 49, 50–1, 70,
    77–8, 80–1, 90–1, 93, 97–8, 207,
    224, 284
Simmel, G. 89, 97, 200–2, 241,
    284, 286
Simon, M. 201
Skinner, Q. 279
Skorupski, J. 4, 279–80
Slezak, P. 11
Sluga, H. 62, 203, 206
Smith, B. 266
Smith, D. W. 279
Smith, J. W. 280
Sober, E. 7–8
social democracy 192, 202
social interest 13, 22, 24, 27, 29, 273
sociologism 14–16, 242, 257, 277,
    288

sociology of knowledge 15, 112, 257, 274; of philosophical knowledge (SPK) 4, 14–15, 17, 19, 23–9, 92, 94, 272, 274, 278; of scientific knowledge (SSK) 2, 14–16, 23–9, 275
solipsism 36–8, 62
Sommerfeld, A. 227
Spearman, C. E. 128
Spencer, H. 47–8, 73, 97, 164, 221, 284
Spengler, O. 7, 97, 226–8, 232–6, 238, 240–4, 246, 248, 250, 252–3, 257, 267, 271, 284
Spiegelberg, H. 242
Spitta, H. 97, 284, 286
Spitzer, H. 119, 281, 286
Spranger, E. 15, 99, 119, 247, 257, 262, 267–9, 271, 281–4, 286, 288
Ssalagoff, L. 88, 281–4
Stallo, J. B. 97, 284
Stein, A. 238
Stein, L. 166, 281–4
Steinmann, H. G. 116, 188, 281
Steinthal, H. 96–7, 102, 135, 167, 284
Stern, W. 109, 126, 177, 281, 285
Sternberg, K. 242, 247, 281, 284
Stirner, M. 175
Stöhr, A. 97, 284
Störring, G. 97, 126, 284
Stratton, G. M. 128
Stumpf, C. 89–91, 93, 97–9, 103–7, 117, 125–7, 137, 141, 145, 150, 157, 159, 162, 165, 167, 175, 180, 182, 206–7, 222, 242, 266, 278, 281, 284
Suarez, F. 96–7, 284
subjectivism, 108–10, 119
Sukale, M. 280
symmetry 24, 274–5

Taine, H.-A. 164
taking-to-be-true (*Fürwahrhalten*) 33–6, 242
Thormeÿer, P. 281–4
thought economy (Mach, Avenarius) 57–8, 87–8, 93
Titchener, E. B. 128, 138

Tönnies, F. 286
Troeltsch, E. 226, 281, 283–4
Troxler, J. P. V. 97, 284
truth 5, 21, 31, 34–6, 42, 47, 50–4, 57–8, 62, 71–2, 78–80, 86–7, 90, 105, 119, 187; as-such 77, 80–1, 83, 85; consensus theory 53, 80; correspondence theory 116; eternal 50; independence theory of 77–82, 92–3; mathematical 31–2; relative 35, 76–7

Ueberweg, F. 13, 89, 98, 105–6, 113–14, 281–4
Ungerer, G. 128, 261
Unwin, N. 280
Uphues, G. 91, 93, 97, 107, 284, 286
Utitz, E. 286

Vaihinger, H. 97, 99, 107, 284, 286
validity 45, 67, 85
value (in Windelband and Rickert) 64–5, 116, 119–20, 189, 200–1, 239–40, 243, 246–9
Verwey, G. 285
Verweyen, J. M. 286
Verworn, M. 97, 223–4, 284
Vesalius, A. 11
Vienna Circle 250–2
Vogt, J. G. 175
Volkelt, J. 66, 86, 93, 97, 284
Voltaire, F. M. A. 19

Wahle, R. 97, 284, 286
Wallaschek, R. 286
Waterlow, S. 280
Watt, H. J. 148
Weber, M. 238
Weidenbach, O. 286
Weierstrass, K. 206
Weimar mentality 24, 225–7, 240–1, 248, 273–4
Weinmann, R. 105, 281–2, 284
Weisse, C. 97, 284
Wentscher, E. 286
Wenzig, C. 97, 284
Wernicke, A. 286

Wertheimer, M. 266, 270, 271
Wild, J. 4, 7
Willard, D. 7, 11
Willmann, O. 286
Willy, R. 261
Windelband, W. 64, 89, 97, 99,
    102–3, 109, 161, 165–6, 169–73,
    175–7, 188–9, 191, 194, 198,
    209, 213, 243, 248, 255, 281–4,
    286
Wirth, W. 126
Witasek, S. 97, 126
Witmer, L. 128
Wittgenstein, L. 3, 7, 20
Wolfe, W. B. 128
Woolgar, S. 27–8, 272, 280
World War I 100, 123, 202,
    211–24, 273

Wozniak, R. H. 124
Wundt, W. 2, 50, 83, 88–91, 93,
    97–99, 102, 107, 114, 118, 121,
    125–38, 142–50, 153–5, 161,
    166, 169–70, 172, 180–1, 184–6,
    192–8, 206, 213, 216, 220–1,
    224, 149–50, 260–1, 263–5, 267,
    278, 282–6
Würzburg School 148, 187, 196,
    257, 263–5

Yearley, S. 27
Yorck von Wartenburg, P. 162, 167

Zechlin, E. 212, 216
Zeller, E. 97, 284
Ziehen, T. 83, 91, 93, 97–8, 222–4,
    281–2, 284